Family Life Education

Third Edition

Family Life Education

Working with Families across the Lifespan

Third Edition

Carol A. Darling, PhD, CFLE
Florida State University
University of Helsinki

Dawn Cassidy, MEd, CFLE
National Council on Family Relations

with Lane Powell, PhD, CFLE
Texas Tech University

WAVELAND

PRESS, INC.

Long Grove, Illinois

For information about this book, contact:
Waveland Press, Inc.
4180 IL Route 83, Suite 101
Long Grove, IL 60047-9580
(847) 634-0081
info@waveland.com
www.waveland.com

10-digit ISBN 1-4786-1143-X
13-digit ISBN 978-1-4786-1143-1

Printed in the United States of America

7   6   5   4

Contents

PART II
Practice of Family Life Education   57

PART III
Content of Family Life Education   171

Preface

"The ruin of a nation begins in the homes of its people."
—Ghanaian proverb

In the eyes of a family life educator, the above Ghanaian proverb may be looking at the issue in the wrong way. A version that is more representative of family life education would be "The *success* of a nation begins in the homes of its people." The foundation of family life education includes a positive, proactive approach to individual and family functioning. We believe that most family life educators are "glass half full" people. They believe in the key role that strong, healthy families play in supporting and strengthening society and the good that can come from providing individuals and families with the knowledge and skills needed to be happy, contributing members of their communities. It is our hope that this book will contribute to this effort.

This third edition welcomes a new author. Dr. Lane Powell, CFLE, who coauthored the first and second editions of this book with Dawn Cassidy, has turned over the reins to Dr. Carol Darling, CFLE, Distinguished Teaching Professor and Professor Emerita at Florida State University. Carol and Dawn have worked closely to bring forth this revised, updated, and expanded edition. We are indebted to Lane for originally perceiving the need for this book and providing the vision, creativity, and commitment to see the first two editions come to light.

Although this book is written primarily with undergraduate majors in human development and family studies in mind, it can be useful to persons in related fields of study who are preparing for careers in community education and outreach. Such careers will require the preparation, presentation, and evaluation of educational programs and workshops for persons at all stages of the lifespan. It is imperative that practitioners have a working knowledge of how to accomplish these tasks effectively. The text is a realistic blend of theory and praxis (action with reflection) designed to encourage the type of hands-on experience needed to interact comfortably with diverse groups and a variety of topics.

In this third edition, we retain our focus on presenting family life education (FLE) as a profession with a history and an exciting future. Persons seeking certification as family life educators through the certification program of the National

Council on Family Relations will find this book a great assist in understanding and developing competency in the area of family life education. The chapters have been reorganized to include current demographics, issues, program options, and practice in planning, implementation, and evaluation of FLE programs. There is greater attention to the diversity of our audience and settings with the inclusion of personal reflections of current practice from family life educators in various settings. Additionally, the content and context of FLE have been expanded within Chapters 8 to 12, including Relating Theory to Practice and Approaches to Sexuality Education, Relationship and Marriage Education, Parent Education, and International Family Life Education. These chapters have not only been updated and revised, but also contain various conceptual models and interactive classroom activities. Additionally, the chapter on International Family Life Education includes the results of an international qualitative study with responses from six continents and 29 countries.

As in the first two editions, each chapter includes a series of questions and issues for class discussion, as well as research problems and activities for independent or auxiliary study. Class activities and case studies are included as they pertain to the content of the chapter. The activity suggestions are indicative of a problem-based learning focus, which many educational specialists now recommend as preferable to a lecture course based on a body of content. Certainly it is more desirable for a class that emphasizes praxis. When students are challenged to figure things out for themselves, they tend to retain information and strengthen their personal skills.

Writing this book has been a tremendous learning experience and one that has left us better informed and further committed to family life education. We want to acknowledge and thank our friends and colleagues who have helped us with this third edition by reviewing chapters, contributing teaching activities, and providing guidance and moral support.

Sharon Ballard, PhD, CFLE, East Carolina University

Julie Baumgardner, MS, CFLE, First Things First

Maureen Bourgeois, BA, National Council on Family Relations

Jean Illsley Clarke, MA, LD (hc), CFLE, J.I. Consults

Catherine Coccia, PhD, Florida International University

Betty Cooke, PhD, CFLE, University of Minnesota, *retired*

Jodi Dworkin, PhD, University of Minnesota

Nancy Gonzalez, MEd, CFLE

Kathy Harding, PhD, Morning Star School

Stephanie Jones, MS, Possibility Parenting

Dana McDermott, PhD, CFLE, DePaul University

Judy Nordstrom, MA, T.E.P.E. Training Institute

Ann Possis, MBA, Best friend and proofreader extraordinaire

Marsha Rehm, PhD, Florida State University

Jason Samuels, BA, National Council on Family Relations

Ethan Schwab, PhD, Florida State University

Natalie Senatore, PhD, Judson University

Bethanne Shriner, PhD, CFLE, University of Wisconsin—Stout

Mary Kay Stranik, MS, MELD Executive Director, *retired*

Ellen Taner, MPH, Taner Associates

Susan Walker, PhD, University of Minnesota

Cynthia Wilson, PhD, CFLE, University of Montevallo

Steven Wages, PhD, CFLE, Abilene Christian University

Thank you to the twelve colleagues who contributed their personal insights about the joys and challenges of providing family life education in a variety of settings. Their names, affiliations, and statements are included in Chapter 4, Settings in Family Life Education.

We truly appreciate the 48 family professionals from six continents and 29 countries who responded to the survey on the status of family life education in their countries. Responses were received from colleagues in Australia, Brazil, Canada, China/Hong Kong, Germany, Ghana, Guatemala, Ireland, Israel, Italy, Jamaica, Japan, Malaysia, Netherlands, Nigeria, Pakistan, Portugal, Republic of South Korea, Saudi Arabia, Scotland, Serbia, Singapore, Sweden, Switzerland, Taiwan, Trinidad Tobago, Turkey, United Arab Emirates, and United Kingdom/England.

We are deeply indebted to the many family life educators, too numerous to mention, that have contributed to the evolution of the field and profession of family life education, as well as to our own personal development. Additionally, we would especially like to thank our Waveland Press editors, Don Rosso and Dakota West, for their support, guidance, and editorial assistance. We want to acknowledge our professors, teachers, and mentors who have shared so much of their time, energy, and wisdom. We greatly appreciate our colleagues, friends, and students who have accompanied us on this adventure. Most importantly, we would like to acknowledge and thank our encouraging and supporting spouses, Paul Anderson and Tom Cassidy, who kept themselves occupied over many evenings and weekends while we worked on this book. They, and all our family members, including Dawn's children, Hamil and Elaina, are evidence of the value of family.

About the Authors

Carol A. Darling, a Certified Family Life Educator, is the Florida State University's Margaret Sandels Professor of Human Sciences and Distinguished Teaching Professor, as well as Professor Emerita in the Department of Family of Child Sciences. She is also on the faculty in the College of Behavioural Sciences at the University of Helsinki in Helsinki, Finland, as a Docent in Family and Consumer Sciences and has twice been a Fulbright Scholar in teaching and research at the University of Helsinki. She is the recipient of three national teaching awards and several teaching awards at Florida State University. Her PhD is in Family Ecology from Michigan State University with emphases in family relations and child development.

Dr. Darling has a long history of commitment to the National Council on Family Relations having served as president of NCFR from 2001–2003. One of her ongoing contributions nationally and internationally has been to NCFR's Certified Family Life Educator (CFLE) program. She was a member of the committee to develop and implement this program and has been involved in the CFLE Academic Program Review Committee, Subject Matter Committee to define the profession of family life education, the CFLE Examination Item-Writing Committee, and the CFLE Advisory Board.

Dr. Darling's research activities have been in the areas of family life education; human sexuality and sexuality education; family stress and crises; women's health issues; and multicultural education and cultural diversity in relation to individuals, families, and educational programs. She has had a life-long commitment to family life education both *locally* at Florida State University, other universities, and the public schools; *nationally* through the National Council on Family Relations and various state affiliates; and *internationally* through her research, presentations, and courses taught in various countries such as Australia, Costa Rica, Finland, South Korea, Switzerland, and Taiwan.

Dawn Cassidy, a Certified Family Life Educator, is the Director of Education for the National Council on Family Relations (NCFR). She has an MEd in Work, Family, and Community Education from the University of Minnesota and was a co-author of the first two editions of this book. She served as a parent facilitator for the MELD program for two years and as a member of the Southwest Family Room Collaborative Council, a United Way community resource program for families with young children. As a member of the Ethics Committee of the Minnesota Council on Family Relations, she was involved in developing guidelines for ethical thinking and practice for parent and family educators.

As administrator of NCFR's Certified Family Life Educator credentialing program, Dawn was involved in the development of the CFLE exam, which included an extensive job analysis for the field of family life education. She recently traveled to Singapore to assist the Singapore Ministry of Social and Family Development in the development of a certificate program for family life educators.

PART I

Field of
Family Life Education

What Is Family Life Education?

Understanding Family Life Education

As a student in a family life education class you may have been asked: "What exactly *is* family life education?" The following parable might help provide some clarification.

> There was once a village built upon the edge of a river where the water churned roughly over the rocks. There were signs at the river's edge warning of the danger, but people often ignored the signs and fell into the river. They often drowned or flowed downstream to a waterfall and were never seen again. The villagers came up with a plan. A net was put downstream to catch those who had fallen in the river. A full-time crew was hired to watch for villagers floating downstream, pull them from the river, dry them off, and get them to ambulances. A new hospital was built closer to the river's edge. All these efforts increased the survival rate but many were still injured or drowned.
>
> A couple who moved to the village watched what was happening and asked if something more could be done to save people (*collaboration*). The villagers were resistant, explaining that they had developed a good system and while they weren't able to save everyone, they felt that things had improved. The couple wasn't satisfied and decided to take matters into their own hands by helping to build a large fence along the rough part of the river (*prevention*), offering swimming lessons, teaching people how to maneuver their boats around the rocks (*prevention and education*), and speaking to villagers about the dangers of going into the river without a life jacket (*prevention and education*). Soon fewer and fewer people were falling into the river and those that did fall in were better equipped to save themselves. (NCFR, n.d.a)

Family life education is about working upstream. Rather than waiting to act until problems develop and individuals and families are suffering and struggling, family life education incorporates a *preventive, educational,* and *collaborative* approach to individual and family issues. This proactive approach can prevent problems and enhance potentials. It can take place in a variety of settings aimed at a varied audience dealing with a myriad of issues, interests, concerns, and situations. The following situations describe some of the family life education activities taking place in communities near you.

> The Liberty High School young mothers' class, composed of 10 pregnant teenagers, watch their teacher bathe and change a real baby. Questions underscore their nervousness and fear about their impending role as young mothers. In the next period they will be discussing infant development. In the afternoons they work in the nursery with the young children of other teen mothers, under the close attention of the nursery director or lab teacher, who will model, instruct, and guide their participation.

> At a local community center, parents of 9th and 10th grade students gather together for another in a series of talks on *Parenting Your Teen*. They are there to learn more about adolescent development and behavior. Last week's discussion on adolescent brain development was especially enlightening. Having the opportunity to hear from other parents who are facing the same issues was reassuring; it's helpful to know that they are not the only parents whose child's personality seems to have changed overnight!

In a neighborhood apartment, a young college graduate completes an online financial literacy program offered by the local Extension Service. He's learning about insurance, retirement plans and investments, and how to create a household budget. One of the modules is on goal-setting, another on making informed decisions. He's hoping to avoid the bankruptcy and foreclosure faced by his parents.

A nearby church is holding a marriage education class for engaged couples. The facilitator is "walking them through" an exercise aimed at helping participants identify their expectations for the marriage. Later they'll learn about active listening and practice some new communication skills.

At a senior housing complex, a group of older adults are attending the first of a four-part series on *Planning for Retirement*. They are looking forward to learning more about how to budget their income, stay healthy and active, maintain social relationships, and adjust to a life without a regular job.

Family . . . life . . . education is a concept that encompasses a multitude of images and expectations. These scenarios describe only a few of the many topics and audiences addressed through family life education. All call for a combination of skills and expectations of the leader-educator and of the "student" group. How do we define family life education in a way that encompasses its multifaceted contexts? How do we even define "family"? And what value does family life education have in supporting and educating individuals for family living? How do you, as a professional or future professional who will be working with families, develop the skills to respond effectively to so many demands?

This book was written to address the many issues involved in the educational preparation of family life educators, using an approach that promotes the interactive teaching style that is typical of the family life education model. Chapter 1 provides an overview of the definitions, history, and future directions of family life education, setting the context and developing an understanding and appreciation for the profession. Chapter 2 discusses the evolution of the profession of family life education, including current challenges and strategies for growth, the personal skills and qualities of the family life educator, and the importance of ethical guidelines. Chapters 3 through 7 address the practice of family life education, from understanding the audience and settings of family life education to designing, implementing, and evaluating family life education programs. Chapters 8 through 11 become more specific and address four content areas of family life education that are the most developed and the most often presented within the profession: family theory, sexuality education, marriage and relationship education, and parent education. Chapter 12 discusses international perspectives of family life education including its need, status, and methods. This is truly designed to be a practitioner's handbook; so when you get the call "Will you help us start a group for . . . ?" you'll be ready!

The Definition Debate

A definition for "family life education" has been the focus of numerous articles and conversations over the past 50 years. There have been differences in opinion regarding the content, purpose, audience, focus, timing, etc. of the practice. The problem of coming to general agreement on a definition of family life education is fully examined in the *Handbook of Family Life Education, Volume 1* (Arcus, Schvaneveldt, & Moss, 1993). Box 1.1 summarizes the attempts at further definition. As you can see, there are a number of common conceptions and characteristics, but there is no one universally adopted definition.

Box 1.1 Emerging Definitions of Family Life Education, 1962–2011

Date	Definition and Author
1962 1963 and 1964	"Family life education involves any and all school experiences deliberately and consciously used by teachers in helping to develop the personalities of students to their fullest capacities as present and future family members—those capacities which equip the individual to solve most constructively the problems unique to his family role" (Avery, 1962, p. 28; Avery & Lee, 1964, p. 27; Lee, 1963, p. 106).
1964	"Family life education included facts, attitudes, and skills related to dating, marriage, and parenthood. . . . Throughout the concept of family life education is woven the idea of relationships—parent-child, husband-wife, boy-girl, and so on" (Kerckhoff, 1964, p. 883).
1967	"Family life education is the study of the behavior of people as family members . . . to broaden the student's understanding of the alternatives from which he can choose in his functioning as a family member in a changing society which brings new responsibilities and opportunities in spousal, parental, filial, sibling, and grandparental roles" (Somerville, 1967, p. 375).
1968	"It is a program of learning experiences planned and guided to develop the potentials of individuals in their present and future roles as family members. Its central concept is that of relationships through which personality develops, about which individuals make decisions, to which they are committed, and in which they gain convictions of self worth" (Smith, 1968, p. 55).
1968	"To help individuals and families learn what is known about human growth, development, and behavior throughout the life cycle is the main purpose of family life education. Learning experiences are provided to develop the potentials of individuals in their present and future family roles. The central concept is that of relationships through which personality develops, about which individuals make decisions, to which they are committed, and in which they develop self-esteem" (National Commission on Family Life Education, 1968, p. 211).
1969	"Family life education . . . deals with people in groups primarily on a cognitive and information exchange level, around issues and problems of family life . . . [and] the cognitive components of behavioral and emotional functioning. Its techniques involve discussions and didactic teaching around ideas, values, and behavioral patterns of the family as a social system and the consequences of these on individual functioning, as well as more behavioristic material concerning interpersonal functioning within the family unit" (Stern, 1969, p. 40).
1971	". . . any activity by any group aimed at imparting information concerning family relationships and providing the opportunity for people to approach their present and future family relationships with greater understanding" (The Vanier Institute of the Family, 1971, p. i).
1973	"Programs of family-life education that will help individuals to prove [sic] their understanding of and capacity for forming and maintaining effective human interrelationships . . . [it] has come to center about the many interactions between individuals and within the family, and the characteristics in individuals that influence the quality of interpersonal relationships" (Kirkendall, 1973, p. 696).

Date	Definition and Author
1973	"... human education in the broadest sense, the essence being human relations ... concerned with one's total being: physical, mental, and emotional" (Whatley, 1973, p. 193).
1974	"Family life education is the study of individual roles and interpersonal relationships, family patterns and alternative life styles, emotional needs of individuals at all ages, and the physiological, psychological and sociological aspects of sexuality" (Herold, Kopf, & deCarlo, 1974, p. 365).
1975	"... an educational program geared to enrich family life and help the individual better understand himself in relation to others" (Levin, 1975, p. 344).
1976	"Family life education promotes the development, coordination and integration of family development resources to individual family units in order to improve family life" (Cromwell & Thomas, 1976, p. 15).
1984	"... instruction to develop an understanding of physical, mental, emotional, social, economic, and psychological aspects of interpersonal relationships ... between persons of varying ages" (Sheek, 1984, p. 1).
1985	"Family life education ... builds on the strengths of individuals to extend their knowledge of personality development, interpersonal relations, and the influence of environmental factors on behaviors" (Barozzi & Engel, 1985, p. 6).
1985	"... as the professional process by which information is offered to individuals of all ages, about various life issues, through the use of the small group setting" (Gross, 1985, p. 6).
1987	"... concerned with preserving and improving the quality of human life by the study of individuals and families as they interact with the resources in their multi-faceted environments" (Darling, 1987, p. 818).
1989	"Family life education ... is devoted to enabling adults to increase the effectiveness of their skills in daily living, that is, in relating to others, in coping with life events, and in realizing personal potential" (Tennant, 1989, p. 127).
1995	"the goal of family life education has been to assist families and family members with their family roles and tasks through formalized educational programs as a means of improving family living and reducing family-related social problems (Arcus, 1995, p. 336).
2001	"Family life education incorporates a preventative and educational approach to individual and family issues. Family life education includes areas such as communication skills, conflict resolution, relationship skills, parenting education, marriage education, decision-making and other skills and knowledge that help families cope with the stress of everyday life" (Boyd, Hibbard, & Knapp, 2001).
2005	"Outreach FLE is any educational activity occurring outside a traditional school classroom setting, usually involving adults, that is designed to strengthen relationships in the home and foster positive individual, couple and family development" (Duncan & Goddard, 2005)
2011	"using information about healthy family development within a preventive, family systems perspective in order to teach knowledge and build skills so that individuals and families may function at their optimal levels (NCFR, n.d.b)

Adapted from Arcus, M. E., Schvaneveldt, J. D., & Moss, J. J. (1993). The nature of family life education. In M. E. Arcus, J. D. Schvaneveldt, & J. J. Moss (Eds.), *Handbook of family life education* (Vol. 1, pp. 5–6). Newbury Park, CA: Sage.

More success at consensus has been achieved by moving beyond a concise definition to a descriptive discussion of the aims and concepts (e.g., "analytical inquiry") that comprise family life education. Arcus et al. (1993) reduced the aims, or rationale, for family life education to three primary ones: (1) dealing with problems that impinge upon families, (2) preventing problems, and (3) developing potentials for individuals and families. In other words, family life education is a process designed to "strengthen and enrich individual and family well-being" (p. 12).

To develop an operational definition of family life education, Thomas and Arcus (1992) posed the question, "What features must something have in order to be called family life education?" After extensive review of the literature and of program designs, Arcus et al. (1993) concluded that family life education generally:

- Is relevant to individuals and families across the lifespan
- Is based on the needs of individuals and families
- Is a multidisciplinary area of study and multiprofessional in its practice
- Is offered in many different settings
- Is an educational rather than a therapeutic approach
- Presents and respects differing family values
- Requires qualified educators who are cognizant of the goals of family life education

Additionally, Arcus and Thomas identified a variety of goals and objectives relevant to the practice of family life education. The most common are (1) gaining insight into self and others, (2) learning about human development and behavior in the family setting over the life cycle, (3) learning about marriage and family patterns and processes, (4) acquiring skills essential for family living, (5) developing the individuals' potentials in their current and future roles, and (6) building strengths in families. "One of the assumptions in family life education appears to be that, if these and other similar objectives are met through family life education programs, then families will be better able to deal with problems, to prevent problems, and/or to develop their potentials" (Arcus & Thomas, 1993, p. 5). Family life education can in turn help to strengthen society because the development of more stable and functioning families results in a more stable and functioning society.

A continued effort to define family life education and gain consensus regarding its approach and content has helped to bring more clarity to the field. While not a definition per se, the description of family life education on the National Council on Family Relations' (NCFR) website provides a helpful overview regarding the purpose, content, and goals of family life education:

> Family life education focuses on healthy family functioning within a family systems perspective and provides a primarily preventive approach. The skills and knowledge needed for healthy functioning are widely known: strong communication skills, knowledge of typical human development, good decision-making skills, positive self-esteem, and healthy interpersonal relationships. The goal of family life education is to teach and foster this knowledge and these skills to enable individuals and families to function optimally.

Family life education professionals consider societal issues including economics, education, work-family issues, parenting, sexuality, gender and more within the context of the family. They believe that societal problems such as substance abuse, domestic violence, unemployment, debt, and child abuse can be more effectively addressed from a perspective that considers the individual and family as part of larger systems. Knowledge about healthy family functioning can be applied to prevent or minimize many of these problems. Family life education provides this information through an educational approach, often in a classroom-type setting or through educational materials. (NCFR, n.d.a)

NCFR is an international multidisciplinary, nonpartisan professional membership organization focused on family research, practice, and education. It provides an educational forum for family researchers, educators, and practitioners to share in the development and dissemination of knowledge about families and family relationships, establish professional standards, and work to promote family well-being. It is the primary professional organization for the field of family life education for many reasons including its involvement in the development of a number of relevant resources including the Certified Family Life Educator (CFLE) certification program, discussed later in this chapter.

The Framework for Life Span Family Life Education, first developed by the National Council on Family Relations in 1984 and revised in 1997 and 2011 (Bredehoft & Walcheski, 2011) provides a context for the many topics that can be addressed within the practice of family life education. It has gone through a number of revisions since 1984 (the 2011 revision was retitled *The Family Life Education Framework*) but the general concept remains. The *Framework* is organized around three major dimensions of family life education: age (broadly defined as childhood, adolescence, adulthood, and later adulthood), topic area (families and individuals in societal contexts, internal dynamics of families, human growth and development across the lifespan, human sexuality, interpersonal relationships, family resource management, parent education and guidance, family law and public policy, and professional ethics and practice), and content (the areas of individual and family development to be addressed at each life stage through education). Also illustrated in the *Framework* is the inclusive perspective of the educator, which considers justice, value, and diverse cultures, communities, and individuals. The 2011 revision of the *Framework* included the addition of a wheel graphic which demonstrates the process involved in program planning, implementation, and evaluation and reflects the application of the educational process to the *Framework* (Clarke, 1984). Revisions to the 2011 *Framework* were the results of focus group meetings and outreach to family professionals. The changes over the years reflect the increasing clarification and evolution of the content and context of family life education. Appendix A presents the entire framework by age category. The National Council on Family Relations has produced the *Framework* in a poster format with an accompanying PowerPoint presentation for use in the classroom.

Models of Family Life Education

Over the years there have been various attempts to further conceptualize and clarify family life education through the use of models. Two of the more recent models are the Levels of Family Involvement Model (LFI) and Domains of Family Practice Model (DFP).

The Levels of Family Involvement Model

This model considers the practice of family life education (FLE) in relation to family therapy (FT) and identifies a five-level approach to clarify the professional boundaries between them (Doherty, 1995). These levels include (1) minimal emphasis on families, (2) information and advice, (3) feelings and support, (4) brief-focused intervention, and (5) family therapy. See Figure 1.1 for a depiction of these levels. The goal of the LFI model is to help family life educators avoid "crossing the boundary into family therapy" (p. 353).

Some of the concerns with this model include its conceptualization of FT and FLE in a hierarchical relationship, implying that only the first three levels are appropriate for FLE. While some advanced FLE professionals may occasionally function professionally in Level 4, if they are assisted by therapists to use Level 4 effectively, they should not enter the domain of family therapists. Although not specifically stated, this model implies that family therapists are able to professionally practice at all five levels. While educators do not possess the knowledge and skills of a therapist, it is also true that therapists do not necessarily have the knowledge and skills to provide educational experiences. Another concern with the LFI model is that it is unclear regarding the content of FLE and FT. For example, within the LFI model anger management is appropriate for family life educators in Level 4, but anger management with spouses or in-laws is not. There are also times that couples may benefit from both family life education courses and family therapy, although the methods would be different.

Figure 1.1   Levels of Family Involvement

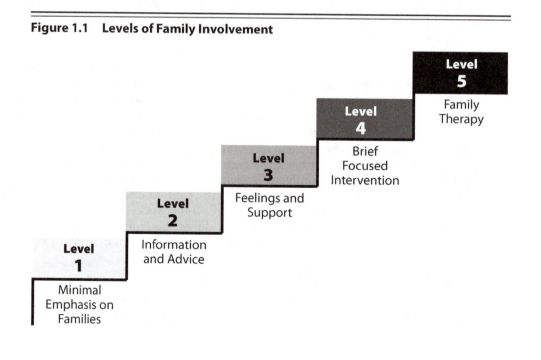

Domains of Family Practice Model (DFP)

In order to facilitate understanding the domains and boundaries of family life education, the DFP model incorporates a collaborative paradigm of family life education (FLE), family therapy (FT), and family case management (FCM), although FCM is only one kind of case management within social services (Myers-Walls, Ballard, Darling, & Myers-Bowman, 2011). In order to differentiate the domains and boundaries of these three professions, we will use the following journalistic questions: *Why? What? When? For whom?* and *How?*

The "Why" of family life education focuses on the purpose of each of these professions and why each profession works with families. While all three professions want to promote strong healthy families, FLE tries to help families build knowledge and skills, FT helps families repair families and functioning, and FCS helps families comply with legal and policy systems and locate resources (see Figure 1.2).

The "What" element of the model refers to the content or research base that family professionals use for working with families. When examining the websites for NCFR, AAMFT, and other organizations such as the American Academy of Health Care Professionals and Center for Case Management, family life education incorporated the 10 family life education content areas, family therapy had six core competencies, and family case management had various components found in multiple sources (DePanfilis, 2003; National Adult Protective Services, 2005). The specific components that comprise "what" can be seen in Figure 1.3 (on p. 12) whereas the overlap of content from FLE, FT, and FCM can be seen in Figure 1.4 (on p. 13). Certain elements can be found in all three professions such as family systems theory and an ecosystems context, sensitivity to diversity, research-based practice, and values and ethics. However, the methodology of each varies.

Figure 1.2   Why

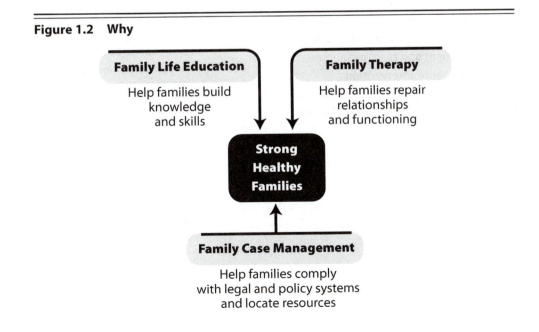

Figure 1.3   What—Content

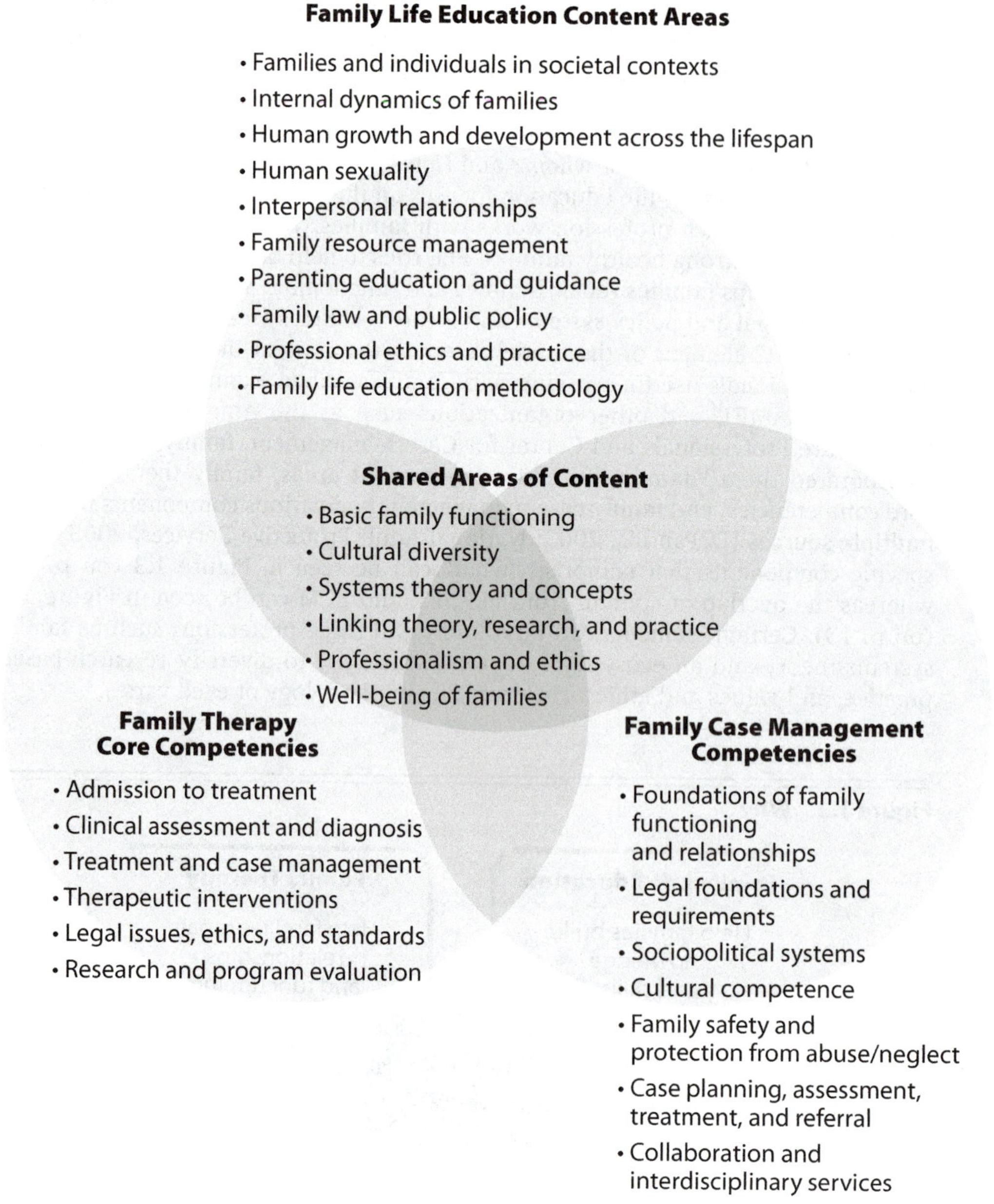

Family Life Education Content Areas

- Families and individuals in societal contexts
- Internal dynamics of families
- Human growth and development across the lifespan
- Human sexuality
- Interpersonal relationships
- Family resource management
- Parenting education and guidance
- Family law and public policy
- Professional ethics and practice
- Family life education methodology

Shared Areas of Content

- Basic family functioning
- Cultural diversity
- Systems theory and concepts
- Linking theory, research, and practice
- Professionalism and ethics
- Well-being of families

Family Therapy Core Competencies

- Admission to treatment
- Clinical assessment and diagnosis
- Treatment and case management
- Therapeutic interventions
- Legal issues, ethics, and standards
- Research and program evaluation

Family Case Management Competencies

- Foundations of family functioning and relationships
- Legal foundations and requirements
- Sociopolitical systems
- Cultural competence
- Family safety and protection from abuse/neglect
- Case planning, assessment, treatment, and referral
- Collaboration and interdisciplinary services

Figure 1.4   What—Overlap

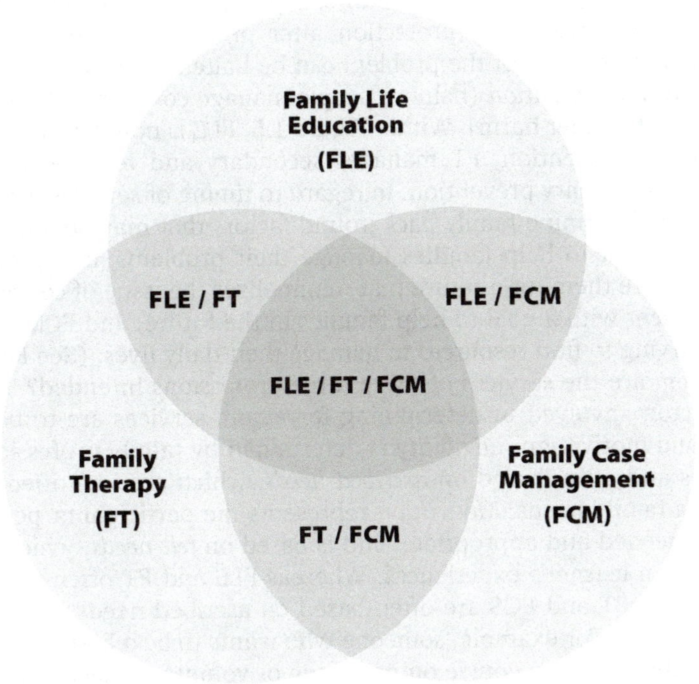

FT
- Therapeutic intervention
- Assessment and diagnosis
- Psychotherapy

FLE
- Family life education methodology
- Normal, healthy functioning
- Broad, inclusive knowledge base
- Education/ prevention focus

FCM
- Coordination of services
- Family advocacy
- Focus on meeting family needs

FLE / FT
- Interpersonal relationship skills
- Healthy sexual functioning
- Life course perspective

FT / FCM
- Focus on family problems
- Intervention techniques
- Treatment goals / methods
- Managment of client records
- Closure of cases

FLE / FCM
- Family resource management
- Family policy

FLE / FT / FCM
- Family systems theory
- Sensitivity to diversity
- Research-based practice
- Ecological context
- Values and ethics

The "When" dimension focuses on when family practitioners in each role deliver services and the timing of those services. The timing of services is based on *primary prevention* (protection of healthy people from harm before something happens), *secondary prevention* (protection after problems, conflicts, or risks have occurred so the progress of the problem can be halted or slowed as early as possible), and *tertiary prevention* (helping people manage complicated, long-term problems to prevent further harm). Within Figure 1.5, FLE is noted as including primary and secondary prevention, FT manages secondary and tertiary prevention, and FCM focuses on tertiary prevention. In regard to timing of services, FT often focuses on the past to determine family background factors that may be affecting the family, on the present to help families manage their problems, and projects into the future to prepare them for a future that minimalizes the issue of concern. FLE deals with the present with a goal to help families in the future, and FCM deals with the present by trying to find resources to manage their daily lives. (See Figure 1.6.)

For whom are the services of these three professions intended? There are two primary factors involved in determining for whom services are to be delivered— eligibility and motivation. *Eligibility* is determined by family professionals delivering services and often based on *ascribed needs*, which are identified by others as something a family needs. *Motivation* represents the participants' perceptions that a service is needed and appropriate, and is based on *felt needs*, which are personal and based on a learner's experiences. Whereas FLE and FT often deal with felt or ascribed needs, FT and FCS are often based on ascribed needs, referrals, or mandated attendance. For example, someone who wants to be a better parent might go to a family life education course on parenting or voluntarily seek a therapist, while a parent whose child is in the juvenile justice system may be mandated to go FT or see a FCM to help with their parenting issues. (See Figure 1.7.)

The *How*, or techniques and strategies of these three professions, is highly variable and dependent on the responses to the questions of *Why, What, For whom* and *When*. In other words, one has to examine the participant's needs, as well as the best delivery system. Are the needs felt or ascribed? What needs assessment techniques can be used? How are services to be delivered and what methods will be

Figure 1.5   Timing of Services

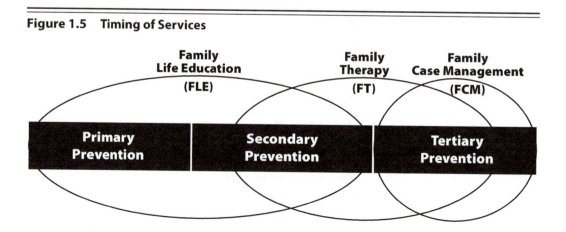

used to best meet the family's needs? Do you use lesson plans, treatment plans, or case planning? What is the best setting (community, schools, institutions, or private offices) or mode (mass, distance learning, group, or individual)? Moreover, how are families involved in the services? Are learners active partners, therapeutic alliances, or involved in case planning?

Hopefully the diagrams have led to an understanding of Table 1.1 (on the following page), which contains the responses to the questions for these three family professions. There is not one profession that is better than the others, as all three are interrelated and collaborative (see Figure 1.8 on p. 17). All have different purposes, methods, timing of services, and individuals and families that can benefit

Figure 1.6   Orientation of Services

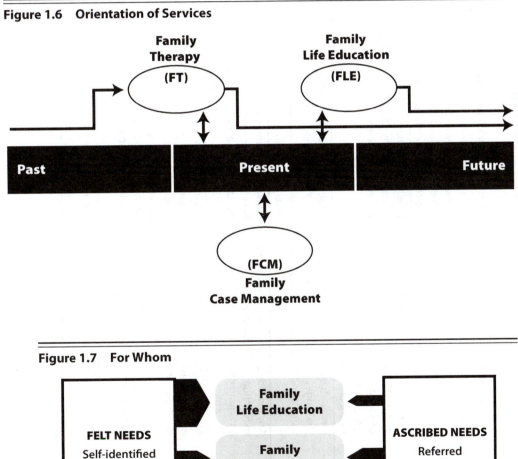

Figure 1.7   For Whom

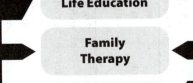

Table 1.1   Domains of Family Practice Model

Question	Family Life Education's Responses	Family Therapy's Responses	Family Case Management's Responses
Why? Purpose and goals of work with families	To increase knowledge and develop skills so families may build on their strengths to function at their optimal levels	To ameliorate relationship problems and mental or emotional disorders to achieve stable, long-term, emotionally enriching family relationships	To help families negotiate systems, understand and comply with legal and regulatory requirements to increase family safety, permanence and well-being
What? Content base and foundation	Family and lifespan theory and research in the 10 FLE content areas; learning, pedagogical or andragogical and educational philosophies and methodologies	Family and relationship theory and research; therapy-focused philosophies and methodologies	Case management theories and methodologies; research and information about social systems, resources, and policies; information about family dysfunction
When? The timing of work with families	Deal with current family needs and challenges to prepare for and improve current and future family functioning	Cope with past and current family problems focusing on past causes and patterns to improve current and future family functioning	Deal with current problems and immediate crises
For whom? Target population for services	Any individual or family willing and able to function in an educational environment and committed to learning	Individuals, couples, and families who have been diagnosed with functional difficulties who are willing to participate in a therapeutic environment	Families identified as being at risk or who demonstrate a need for assistance in meeting legal and societal regulations
How? Techniques and methods used	Assess family-related educational needs; set goals on the basis of family needs and strengths; can occur in a variety of settings; teach about knowledge, attitudes, and skills; families—individually or in groups—are active in the learning process	Diagnose family problems; identify a treatment plan guided by particular theories or philosophies; occurs in private settings; establish a therapeutic alliance with one family at a time; families have input but little or no interaction with other families	Assess family functioning; set goals to fill gaps in family functioning; occurs in the field; coordinate community services while monitoring compliance, difficulties, and successes; families (may include extended family) participate in services but rarely interact with other families

Source: Myers-Walls, J., Ballard, S., Darling, C., & Myers-Bowman, K. (2011). Reconceptualizing the domain and boundaries of family life education. *Family Relations, 60,* 357–372.

Figure 1.8   Professional Collaboration

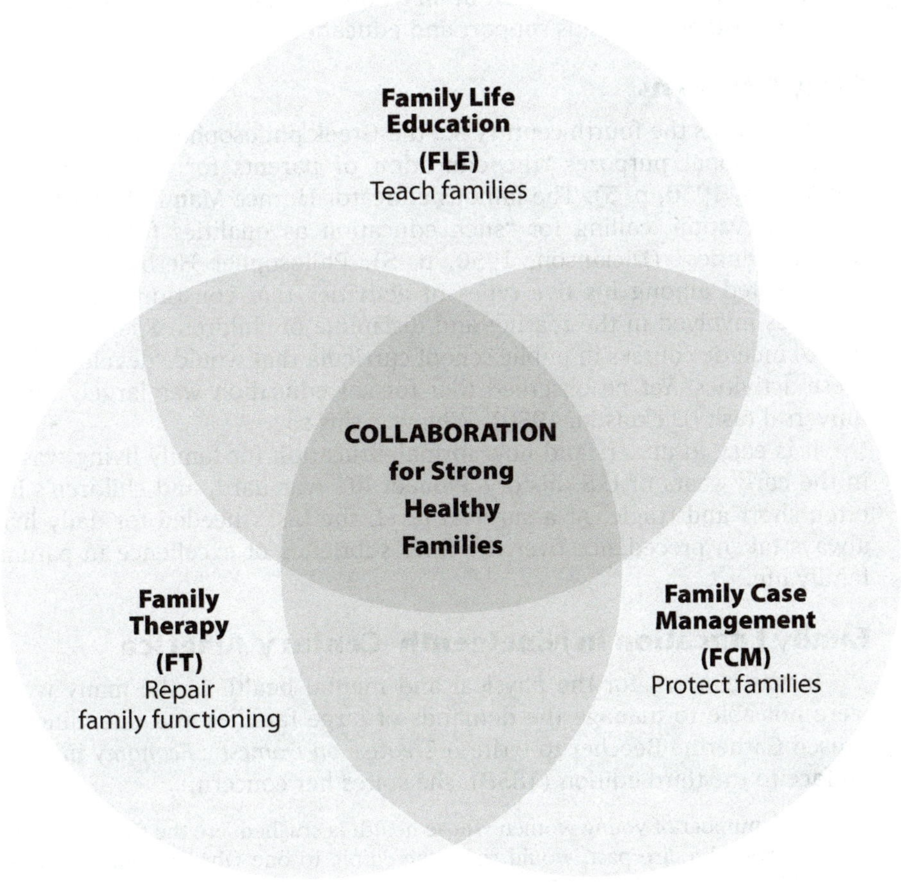

Family Life
Education

(FLE)
Teach families

**COLLABORATION
for Strong
Healthy
Families**

**Family
Therapy**

(FT)
Repair
family functioning

**Family Case
Management**

(FCM)
Protect families

from the services provided. However, at times a family may benefit from being involved with one, two, or all three of these family professionals. Understanding the domains and boundaries of these professions can be helpful when advising students and planning curricula, as well as when seeking and advertising positions for family professionals. Oftentimes family agencies have various persons who serve families in different ways. Understanding the DFP model may help both the employer and employee better define the roles and expectations of a professional position within that setting. Further, it can give service providers the flexibility needed to meet individual, family, and community needs.

The History of Family Life Education

The task of passing on knowledge in family living to the next generation has been part of the human experience since life began; but how and by whom it is done has varied among family groups, tribes, and cultures. It has also changed drastically over time and is, in fact, still evolving. However, at the beginning of the 21st century, one thing is agreed upon by all: The family—in all its different forms and circumstances—needs support and education.

Early Concerns

As early as the fourth century BC, the Greek philosopher Aristotle listed among his educational purposes "the education of parents for raising their children" (Dickinson, 1950, p. 5). The famous educator Horace Mann (1796–1859) echoed that observation, calling for "such education as qualifies for the fulfillment of parental duties" (Dickinson, 1950, p. 5). Philosopher Herbert Spencer (1820–1903) listed among his five types of activities that constitute human life those activities involved in the rearing and discipline of children. Spencer urged educators to include courses in public school curricula that would "develop efficiency" in these activities. Yet he observed that formal education was largely ignoring this universal task (Dickinson, 1950). Why was this so?

It is easy to understand how formal education for family living was bypassed in the early years of U.S. history. Pioneer life was hard, and children's lives were often short and tragic. At a survival level, the tasks needed for daily living have always taken precedence over the finer subtleties of excellence in parenting and family life.

Family Education in Nineteenth-Century America

It was concern for the physical and mental health of the many women who were not able to manage the demands of large families and unending tasks that caused Catherine Beecher to write *A Treatise on Domestic Economy* in 1842. In the preface to the third edition (1858), she states her concern:

> The number of young women whose health is crushed, ere the first few years of married life are past, would seem incredible to one who has not investigated this subject, and it would be vain to attempt to depict the sorrow, discouragement, and distress experienced in most families where the wife and mother is a perpetual invalid. (p. 5)

While the poor struggled with basic survival for their families, middle- and upper-class families lived an existence in stark contrast. The new and popular ladies' magazines pictured the ideal home as a refuge for the family. Here the tired husband relaxed from the struggles of the wage-earning day and happy children played under the benevolent eye of a loving mother. Home was no longer the center of work for the whole family, as it had been in colonial days, and motherhood was considered the purpose of life for women. "Of course, some women were beginning to question their confinement to a golden cage and to stand up for women's rights. A small number entered the professions and were economically independent" (Youcha, 1995, p. 123).

Jane Addams (1860–1935) was such a young woman. Born to affluence, she struggled with physical and emotional distress until she discovered a valuable purpose for her life: bettering the lives of poor families by living among them and offering parent education and childcare services. Centered around what was to be known as the settlement house model, Addams' Hull House in Chicago, developed a model of family intervention and education that was—and is—one of the most successful to be found:

> Addams envisioned the settlement as serving two purposes: It would help the poor "Germans and Bohemians and Italians and Poles and Russians and Greeks in Chicago, vainly trying to adjust their peasant habits to the life of a large city," while at the same time giving privileged young women a purpose and a place. (Youcha, p. 138)

As the women of Hull House cared for the children of desperate mothers who were widowed or abandoned by their husbands and had to work 10- to 12-hour days for pennies, they did parent education as well. Using the child as the "bridge" for education, they introduced new habits of hygiene and medical care, new foods, and activities. The children then demonstrated to their parents the advisability of the education by their improved health and spirits. The parents asked for recipes and explanations of what the teachers did. The teachers asked for daily reports on each child's activities at home, including diet, bedtime, and bowel movements. This interchange called attention to the importance of such factors and routines in children's lives, and the parents made adjustments to carry them out. Weekly mothers' meetings that included instruction on making children's clothes and preparing American foods were also held. Often the meetings were the mothers' only social outlet in a life of burdened toil. They were eagerly attended. Addams noted, "Through this medicine, the faces of the mothers have been noticeably softened . . ." (Youcha, p. 145).

Addams' highly successful model of family life education, which included home visits, interactive learning, and individualized group learning goals, developed concurrently with the charity organization movement. The settlement's focus was not on charity, however, but rather centered on reform through social justice. It was based on the idea that social and economic conditions, rather than personal weakness, were the root causes of poverty. The heart of the movement was community building and the belief that "healthy communities could be built by first fostering healthy relationships among all of its members, not simply by dispensing charity. Rich and poor lived side by side in fellowship. Rather than asking residents, 'What can we do for you?' settlement workers asked. 'What can we do together?'" (Alliance for Children and Families, n.d.). This perspective is at the heart of family life education.

Formalizing the Study of Families

Another issue that has been addressed, then ignored, then addressed again for more than 150 years, is whether family life education is worthy or appropriate for academic study. Quoting a well-known educator of the day, George B. Emerson, Catherine Beecher (1858) wrote in her 19th-century text:

> It may be objected that such things cannot be taught by books. Why not? Why may not the structure of the human body and the laws of health deduced therefrom, be as well taught as the laws of natural philosophy? Why are not the

application of these laws to the management of infants and young children as important . . . as the application of the rules of arithmetic to the extraction of the cube root? (p. 7)

The Morrill Land Grant Act of 1862 was the first federal legislation supporting an educational delivery system for training in work related to the family (USDA NIFA, n.d.). In 1872, the Massachusetts legislature became the first state to recognize and support family life education in a public school setting by passing a statute to legalize domestic science for educating young women (Quigley, 1974). Other states soon followed suit, and between 1875 and 1890, domestic science and industrial education courses in public schools proliferated nationwide. In 1884, the first college program to meld subject matter and teaching methodology was offered at Columbia University. By 1895, 16 colleges were offering courses in home economics (East, 1980). Their subject matter and focus varied widely, but recognition of the importance of training for family living skills was certainly increasing. Male, as well as female, scholars promoted the concern for home and family education as the home economics movement gained credibility. When the New York Board of Regents decided to include household science on college entrance exams, Ellen Richards was invited to construct the questions (Quigley, 1974). Richards, who held degrees in chemistry from Vassar and the Massachusetts Institute of Technology, was interested in household management and the quality of family life. In 1898, she was invited to speak at a conference in Lake Placid, New York, on the topic of applying scientific principles to management of the home.

Nine annual conferences at Lake Placid were instrumental in making the last years of the 19th century a time of clarification on expanded views of education for family, home, and household management orientations. "Home economics" was given formal recognition as the name for education for home and family life in the public school system (Lake Placid Conference Proceedings, 1901).

Another outgrowth of the conferences was the official formation of the American Home Economics Association (AHEA) on January 1, 1909, with 830 charter members: 765 women and 65 men. Its stated purpose was "the improvement of life conditions in the home, the institutional household, and the community" (Baldwin, 1949, p. 2). In addition, AHEA started a journal publication during the same year (Parker, 1980). The first White House Conference on Child Welfare was also held in 1909 and resulted in a 1914 publication on infant care for parents (Bridgeman, 1930). The two decades that followed (1910–1930) were a time of great support and study of the American family. In 1914, the Cooperative Extension Service was established at land-grant universities in each state. Included in their responsibilities was the charge to "aid in diffusing . . . useful and practical information in subjects relating to . . . home" (Rasmussen, 1989, p. 153). In the first year, it was reported that home economists visited 5,500 homes and trained 6,000 women to lead in educating others (Rasmussen, 1989).

Research on child development and family organization became a strong interest of sociologists and social psychologists. The first Child Welfare Research Center was established at the University of Iowa in 1917, and other centers, including the Merrill Palmer Institute, rapidly followed at several major universities (Frank, 1962). Parent education became a national interest during the 1920s. The National

Congress of Parents and Teachers, organized during this decade, boasted more than 500 study groups by 1929, comprised of both fathers and mothers. In total, more than 75 major organizations were conducting parent education programs at this time. Many were supported with government grants, which were then seriously curtailed in the 1930s. The cause was that the increasing instability of marriages made some professionals question if money spent on parent education was worth the effort when families appeared to be crumbling (Brim, 1959). This was a curious logic, but perhaps understandable in the years of a depressed economy and the resulting stress on families. Ernest Burgess, who developed the first documented course on the family at the University of Chicago in 1917, described the crisis in contemporary families in a 1926 journal article:

> In a stable, homogeneous society, ideas of family life and the roles of its different members are relatively fixed and constant. In a changing society composed of heterogeneous elements, familiar attitudes are almost inevitably in a state of flux. Instead of a common pattern of family life entrenched in tradition and crushing out all impulse to variation by the sheer weight of universal conformity, our American society presents what at first sight seems to be a chaotic conglomeration of every conceivable pattern of family organization and disorganization, from the patriarchal kinship groups of our Southern Mountain highlands to the free unions of our Greenwich Villages. Hardly a day passes but the public is shocked and outraged by some new form of wild and reckless behavior, particularly of youth in revolt no longer regulated by customary controls. (Burgess, 1926, p. 5)

Burgess was not a pessimist, however, and he challenged the gloomy prediction that the family was disintegrating into chaotic ruin:

> But these random and aimless variations away from the basic pattern of family life are not, as some believe, an indication of the future of family life and sexual relationships. They are only the symptoms in the present, as in similar times in the past, that society is undergoing change. When equilibrium is re-established a new pattern of family life will emerge, better adapted to the new situation, but only a different variety of the old familiar pattern of personal relationships in the family. (p. 6)

One professional response to the growing family crisis brought together representatives from the American Home Economics Association, the American Social Hygiene Association, the Teachers College of Columbia, and other professionals from fields of sociology and psychology for the Conference on Education for Marriage and Family Social Relations in 1934. Their concern for collaboration among professionals who study the family resulted in the organization of the National Conference on Family Relations in 1938, which was renamed the National Council on Family Relations in 1947 (Walters & Jewson, 1988).

Ninety percent of all research and publication about family sociology and related issues has been written since 1940 (Mogey, as cited in Howard, 1981, pp. viii–ix). The first textbook for use in high school and college family living courses was written in 1945 by Evelyn Mills Duvall, executive secretary of NCFR, and Reuben Hill, a family sociologist at the University of Minnesota. Entitled *When You*

Marry, the book had a very readable style, with many examples and cartoon illustrations. Because it was written at the end of World War II, it particularly addressed the problems of war brides' adjustment to couple living after the war (Duvall & Hill, 1945). The book was expanded in 1950 to respond to some 25,000 questions asked by student readers of the first text and was published as *Family Living* (Duvall, 1950).

> Because of home economics' ties to public education delivery systems, Duvall's book helped set the stage for home economics to replace sociology as the preponderant discipline in family life education. Home economics' position of dominance was enhanced nationally through the publication of specific materials related to family life education and enhanced internationally as home economists, supported by such government programs as the Marshall Plan, established family life education programs nationwide. (Lewis-Rowley, Brasher, Moss, Duncan, & Stiles, p. 39)

The National Council on Family Relations continued to contribute to the evolution of the academic study of families. A combined interest in theory, research, and practice allowed NCFR to develop a membership base among academicians and practitioners in several disciplines related to family studies—primarily human development, marriage and family therapy, family sociology, and developmental psychology. In the late 1960s, NCFR spearheaded the development of standards and certification for family life educators Certified Family Life Educator (CFLE). The CFLE Standards and Criteria provide the following accounting of NCFR's involvement in defining the content and context of the practice of family life education.

> The desirability of defining the necessary knowledge, skills and abilities of family life educators resulted in the appointment of a task force on family life education in 1968. The National Commission on Family Life Education published its report, "Family Life Education Programs, Principles, Plans, Procedures: A Framework for Family Life Education," in 1968. The Committee on Educational Standards and Certification for Family Life Educators proposed criteria for the education of family and sex education teachers in 1970. In 1978, a Committee on Standards for Family Life Educators reported recommendations to the National Council on Family Relations' membership. Based on this continued concern, and the added impetus from the 1980 White House Conference on Families, the Committee on Standards and Criteria for Certification of Family Life Educators received unanimous approval from the Board of Directors in 1981 to establish a certification program for professional family life educators. "The College/University Curriculum Guidelines," received final approval in October 1982. "Standards and Criteria for the Certification of Family Life Educators" received final Board approval in October 1982, as did "An Overview of the Content in Family Life Education: A Framework for Planning Programs over the Life Span. The Board of Directors recommended "immediate implementation" of the Certification Program. The National Council on Family Relations began certifying family life educators through a portfolio review process in 1985. (NCFR, 2013)

Canada has also seen considerable activity in the area of family life education in the last 40 years. In 1964, the first Canadian Conference on the Family brought together leaders in the family area (Gross, 1993). Out of the conference was born a permanent organization, the Vanier Institute of the Family, in order to "encourage research and study in family life as well as serve as a clearing house for information" (Gross, p. 10). The Vanier Institute also recognized the importance of high qualifications and standards for family educators. In 1970, they issued a statement regarding qualifications of family life educators, emphasizing that more than academic training is needed. The "quality of mind and spirit" was seen as equally important. This concept was further defined as depth of perception, personal integrity, flexibility in teaching methods, sensitive awareness to the human condition, and commitment to growth, both intellectually and emotionally, as a person and a professional (Gross). Canada has incorporated family studies in a number of Canadian colleges and universities. In 1993, the Canadian Certified Family Educator (CCFE) was initiated by Family Service Canada, and is currently supported by the Canadian Association of Family Resource Programs (FRP Canada).

The American Home Economics Association remained a strong force in public school education for family life skills. However, as family roles and responsibilities have changed drastically during the last half of the 20th century, public concern and undergraduate student interest shifted away from a generalist approach that taught traditional homemaking skills (e.g., clothing construction, food preparation), as well as family living (Schultz, 1994). In 1994, members of the national organization voted to change their name to the American Association of Family and Consumer Sciences (AAFCS) in order to more accurately reflect the new emphases. Many public schools, under state legislature mandates to add more "academic" course requirements for their graduates, have phased out vocational education programs, which often included the home economics curriculum. Many college and university home economics programs have also been phased out because of low enrollment of majors in the traditional home economics education area. At the same time, interest in the area of human development and family studies (HDFS) has expanded rapidly. Students see the HDFS major as a good foundation from which to launch careers in marriage and family counseling, family ministry, social work, and child life and early childhood education. All of these careers could carry an expectation of expertise in conducting family life education classes in a variety of community settings and for diverse audiences.

The availability of family studies degree programs is demonstrated through a comprehensive list of approximately 300 undergraduate and graduate programs in the United States and Canada accessible through the *Degree Programs in Family Science* section of the NCFR website (www.ncfr.org/degree-programs). In addition to sponsoring the Certified Family Life Educator credential, NCFR also provides recognition to universities and colleges that have incorporated content into their academic coursework for each of the 10 family life content areas needed for certification. Graduates of these programs, who have successfully completed all of the CFLE-approved courses at their school, can apply for the CFLE designation through an abbreviated application process. (A national exam is available to all other CFLE candidates). Currently 127 universities and colleges in the U.S. and Canada are identified as NCFR CFLE-approved programs. Availability of this national recognition has helped bring consistency to the academic content of family degrees.

Future Directions of Family Life Education

In predicting future directions for the field, Lewis-Rowley et al. (1993) foresaw four major trends:

1. Collaborative approaches to family life education will increase between generalists and specialists who value each other's contributions and realize that issues are too complex to be solved by one single organization or professional group.

2. More refinement of theory and research will strengthen understanding and practice of educational intervention and support. The research is expanding and becoming more discriminating as it is driven by the full force of computer-age technology. A challenge continues to be the communication of findings to practitioners, legislators, and the general public.

3. Intervention in private and public spheres will focus more on prevention and education, appreciating the involvement of the total family as part of the teaching/learning team.

4. Global information-gathering and policy-making will increase, as technology allows information to flow across oceans and continents and as cross-cultural studies and diversity in families is recognized and appreciated.

SUMMARY

We continue to ask the same questions regarding the value of family life education. Why wait until children and families have suffered great emotional anguish when we know education could prevent many tragedies from occurring? Why do we invest so much time and energy into fixing people, families, and situations, rather than investing in prevention and providing education about the skills and knowledge to enhance individual and family life? Such solutions have always been the emphasis of visionary educators and social reformers. Unfortunately, society and the government are still more likely to respond to crises than preventive measures.

But there is reason for hope. In the recent past (the last 50 years) more attention has been focused on collaboration, definition, academic research and theory, and leader training and certification for the family field. Family life education is moving to a new level of appreciation among behavioral scientists and program developers. Issues of abuse, exploitation, and violence, long hidden from public view, have seen the light of celebrity confession and intense media coverage. Divorce and single parenthood are no longer squelched by social stigma. The sexual revolution has "outed" us all. Courts are mandating anger control and parent education programs. Technology is taking us to new levels of involvement with one another, offering new opportunities for distance education and resources. Around the world, we are interacting with diverse cultures and discovering new ways of being family. And families, struggling to survive and to thrive, are becoming more willing to ask for help. It is time to bring knowledge and families together, and it can be done face-to-face and online with person-centered, trained professionals and effective programs. Chapter 2 addresses the growing field of family life education and the issue of professionalism.

QUESTIONS AND ISSUES FOR DISCUSSION

1. How do the demands and stresses of family life today differ from those in the past? Consider particularly the dual-career family, single-parent low income family, and immigrant family.

2. What makes prevention and education programs hard to document in terms of effectiveness?

3. Should public school curricula include parenting courses? Why or why not?

4. What is the value of prevention/education programs in comparison to crisis intervention and remediation programs?

ACTIVITIES

1. From the list of definitions in Box 1.1, choose the definition that best describes the range of tasks and settings for family life education described by Thomas and Arcus (1992) and explain why you chose this particular one. In reviewing all the definitions, what do you see that has endured over time? What elements have expanded or contracted?

2. Explain how the major trend predicted by Lewis-Rowley is or is not supported by the development of the "Domains of Family Practice Model": *Collaborative approaches to family life education will increase between generalists and specialists who value each other's contributions and realize that issues are too complex to be solved by one single organization or professional group.*

2

Family Life Education as a Profession

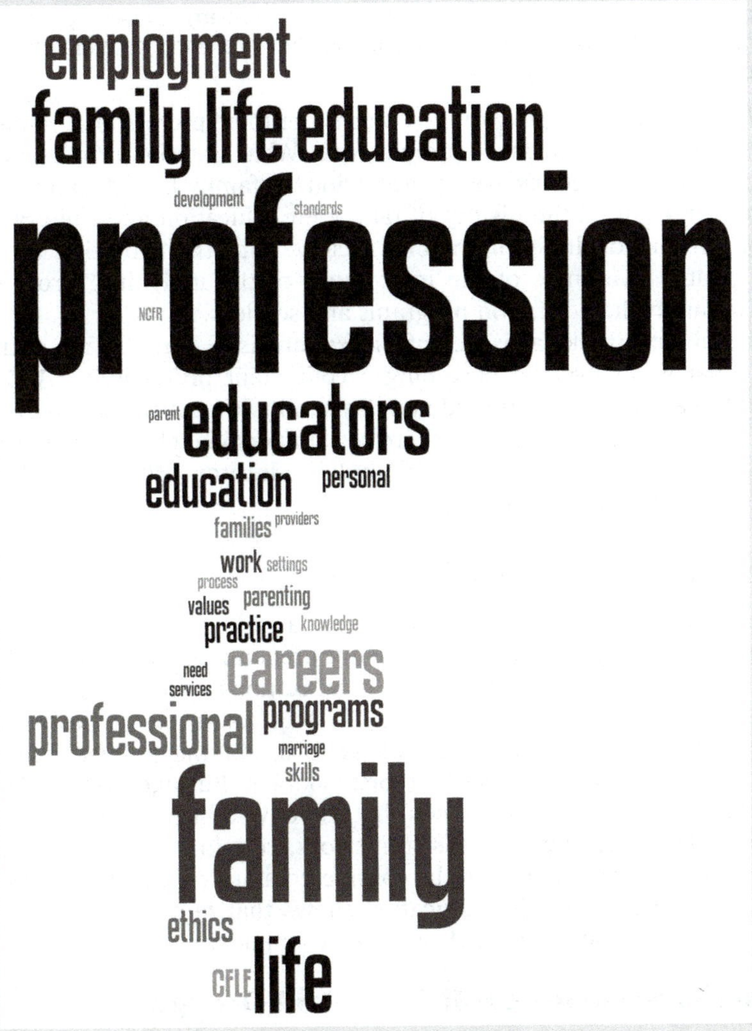

Carl has a baccalaureate degree in art history. He has worked for the past nine years as a youth coordinator for the YMCA and organizes activities and classes for neighborhood youth identified as high risk. He is a member of the National AfterSchool Association (NAA) and has served on their board of directors.

Juanita has a degree in child development. She organizes a parent group in her neighborhood for other stay-at-home moms and dads with children under 2 years old. The group meets regularly and discusses a predetermined topic each time. Members rotate responsibility for researching the topic and presenting information. Much of the meeting is spent in casual conversation and support.

Kathleen is the executive director of a neighborhood family resource center. She has a degree in human development and family studies and is a Certified Family Life Educator (CFLE). Her responsibilities include overseeing the development and implementation of family activities, well-baby classes, parent-support groups, and a home-visiting program. She has worked in the field of family life education for more than 12 years.

Which of these people would you consider to be professional family life educators? What makes someone a professional? What criteria are needed in order for an occupation to be considered a profession? Is family life education a profession? Chapter 1 recounted the history of family life education and the gradual recognition of its function in strengthening society. With the evolution of the field has come greater awareness of the importance of the individual's role in providing effective family life education programs and services.

This chapter looks at issues of professionalism. How do we define a profession? What is involved in becoming a competent professional? What skills and knowledge are needed to provide quality family life education experiences and to develop effective materials? Are there certain personal characteristics or traits that make someone a more effective family life educator? What ethical practices are necessary underpinnings of the profession?

Defining the Profession

The word *profession* can be defined as "a calling requiring specialized knowledge and often long and intensive academic preparation" (Merriam-Webster Dictionary, n.d.). Numerous individuals and organizations have studied professionalism. Some identify certain attributes commonly acquired in the process of professionalization (Weigley, 1976), whereas others focus on the political and sociological aspects of identifying professions (Torstendahl & Burrage, 1990). One approach developed by East (1980) contends that the development of a profession involves eight criteria. According to East's framework, certain criteria must be in place in order for a field or occupation to be considered a profession. Applying East's criteria to the practice of family life education shows that family life education has progressed as a profession. Table 2.1 provides a summary of the findings.

1. Activity Becomes a Full-Time Paid Occupation

Although the title "family life educator" is not always used specifically, family life education is practiced by professionals in various settings throughout the

Table 2.1   Family Life Education: Defining the Profession

East's Criteria (East 1980)	Progress Made	Room to Grow	Criterion 1= No Progress 5= Criterion Has Been Fully Met
1. Activity becomes a full-time paid occupation	Though rarely called family life education, many professionals practice family life education on a full-time basis under such descriptions as parent education, sex education, marriage enrichment.	Family life education is often only part of a family life educator's job responsibilities as employment specifically in family life education may only be available on a part-time basis	4
2. Training schools and curricula are established	Family-related degrees have been offered since the 1960s. NCFR began recognizing academic programs that met the criteria needed for the CFLE designation, beginning in 1996. Currently there are 127 approved programs.	Few degrees are called Family Life Education, but rather Child and Family Studies, Human Development and Family Studies, Human Services, Family Studies, Family and Child Studies. The lack of consensus results in fragmented identity for the field.	4
3. Those who are trained establish professional associations	Numerous family-related associations have been in existence since the early 1900s including NCFR and AAFCS. Associations focused specifically on parenting (NPEN) and marriage education (NARME) have also been formed.	There are numerous family-related associations and organizations, which can cause a fragmented identity.	4
4. Name, standards of admission, core body of knowledge, and competencies for practice are developed	NCFR developed University and College Curriculum Guidelines and Standards and Criteria for the Certification of Family Life Educators in 1984.		5

(continued)

East's Criteria (East 1980)	Progress Made	Room to Grow	Criterion 1= No Progress 5= Criterion Has Been Fully Met
5. Internal conflict within the group and external conflict from other professions lead to a unique role definition	Numerous organizations and credentials exist with some overlapping content, but development of NCFR Curriculum Guidelines and CFLE Criteria defines family life content areas. Domains of Family Practice Model helps clarify unique role of the FLE.	Employers and public are still unclear on what family life education is and how family life educators differ from social workers, therapists, counselors.	4
6. Public served expresses some acceptance of the expertise of those practicing the occupation	Increased popularity of parenting, marriage, and sexuality education programs throughout the US reflects public's increased acceptance of education related to family issues.	Public is often unaware that specific credentials exist for family life educators.	3
7. Certification and licensure are legal signs that a group is sanctioned for particular service to society and is self-regulated	CFLE designation was developed to regulate qualifications of family life education providers. CFLEs must meet continuing education requirements to maintain designation.		5
8. A code of ethics is developed to eliminate unethical practice and protect the public	The Family Science Section of NCFR established Ethical Principles and Guidelines in 1995. In 2009 NCFR formally adopted principles from the Minnesota Council on Family Relations' ethical guidelines process as the official CFLE Code of Ethics.		5

Adapted from Bredehoft, D., & Walcheski, M. (2009). *Family life education: Integrating theory and practice.* Minneapolis, MN: National Council on Family Relations.

world, including junior and senior high schools, Extension programs, the military, community education, health care, human services, faith communities, and higher education. Family life education is carried out under such titles as parent education, sex education, health education, life coaching, marriage enrichment and education, life skills, youth advocacy, and more.

In many cases, family life education is a full-time position, but it is also common for it to represent a percentage of the work carried out in settings with more focus on intervention. Many family life educators work in settings to help families that have been identified as at-risk or who have demonstrated difficulty with parenting, money-management, or relationship skills. Much of the professional's time might be spent in activities considered to be intervention, but there are opportunities for providing family life support within those settings through education. In another example, preschool directors might focus most of their time on administration of a preschool program, but they could also be responsible for identifying and implementing parenting education workshops. The time spent developing and/or offering parenting workshops would be considered family life education.

2. Training Schools and Curricula Are Established

The first documented course on family was offered in 1917 by Ernest Burgess at the University of Chicago, but it was not until the 1960s that degrees focused on the family were more commonplace. The desirability of defining the necessary knowledge, skills, and abilities of family life educators resulted in the development of "Family Life Education Programs, Principles, Plans, Procedures: A Framework for Family Life Education" by the National Council on Family Relations (NCFR, 1968). In 1982, NCFR developed the *College/University Curriculum Guidelines*, and in 1984, the *Standards and Criteria for the Certification of Family Life Educators* and *An Overview of the Content in Family Life Education: A Framework for Planning Programs over the Life Span* (NCFR, 1984). NCFR approved the first Certified Family Life Educators (hereafter referred to as CFLE) in 1985.

In 1996, NCFR introduced the *Academic Program Review* and began to review university and college family degree programs for adherence to the standards and criteria needed for CFLE-approved programs. Numerous programs have sought this "industry" approval, which recognizes a defined and accepted curriculum content for the field. A list of the *Degree Programs in Family Science* (Hans, 2013), which is available on the NCFR website, includes information on over 300 family specific degree programs, of which over 127 meet CFLE standards.

3. Those Who are Trained Establish Professional Associations

Professional associations can have significant influence on the public's perception of a profession by establishing standards of practice and advocating for the profession. Additionally, they provide opportunities for members to enhance their practice through networking and the sharing of information. A number of related professional organizations relevant to families exist, including the American Association of Family and Consumer Sciences (formerly the American Home Economics Association), and the National Council on Family Relations. NCFR is widely recognized as the professional association for family life educators because of its involvement in the development of standards related to the content of family life education and its sponsorship of the Certified Family Life Educator (CFLE) program.

Development of a professional association recognizes a shared body of knowledge and common interests among a select group of professionals. Professional family associations offer membership at several levels of involvement and provide opportunities for continuing education and networking with others practicing in the family field.

4. Name, Standards of Admission, Core Body of Knowledge, and Competencies for Practice Are Developed

As mentioned previously, NCFR identified standards of admission, the core body of knowledge, and competencies for practice through the work of a number of task forces and committees working from the late 1960s to the early 1980s, and resulting in the establishment of the CFLE credential.

The CFLE Standards and Criteria originally included nine family life content areas considered to represent the core of family life education. They are: families in society, internal dynamics of families, human growth and development, human sexuality, interpersonal relationships, family resource management, parent education and guidance, family law and public policy, and ethics. Family life education methodology was added as a 10th content area in 1991. From 1984 to 2007, professionals seeking certification provided documentation of academic preparation, professional development, and work experience in each of the 10 content areas via a portfolio application process. With the development of the Academic Program Review in 1996, NCFR began approving university and college family degree programs for adherence to the criteria needed for the CFLE designation. The NCFR academic program review process recognizes the 10 content areas as a defined and accepted curriculum content for the field. Graduates of "CFLE-approved" academic programs were able to forego the portfolio application process and instead apply through an Abbreviated Application Process, as long as they had completed specific pre-approved courses at their schools.

In 2007, NCFR replaced the portfolio application process with a national standardized multiple-choice exam. Development of the exam involved an extensive practice analysis that further identified and confirmed the knowledge, skills and abilities needed for the effective practice of family life education (Darling, Fleming, & Cassidy, 2009). Appendix B includes the NCFR Family Life Education Content Areas: Content and Practice Guidelines, which reflect the theory, research, and practice within the field of family life education.

5. Internal Conflict within the Group and External Conflict from Other Professions Lead to a Unique Role Definition

There are a number of professional organizations relevant to families. As we have discussed, the National Council on Family Relations has been active in defining and developing family life education curriculum and certification criteria since the early 1960s. Additionally, the American Home Economics Association (AHEA) identified competencies and criteria for home economics in 1974 and established the Certified Home Economist (CHE) designation in 1987. When AHEA changed its name to the American Association of Family and Consumer Sciences (AAFCS) in 1995 they subsequently changed the name of the certification credential to Certified in Family and Consumer Sciences (CFCS).

There are similarities and differences between the NCFR and AAFCS certification programs. Both require a minimum level of education and knowledge in the areas of human growth and development, family systems and dynamics, and family resource management. The redesign and expansion of the AAFCS credentialing program in 2004 resulted in three separate credentials with a competency-based qualifying exam for each. AAFCS maintained the original broad CFCS credential, but also created separate credentials focused on Human Development and Family Studies (CFCS-HDFS) and Hospitality, Nutrition, and Food Science (CFCS-HNFS), and, more recently, the Certified Personal and Family Finance Educator (CPFFE). The Human Development and Family Studies credential more closely resembles the CFLE credential than did the original composite CFCS credential because of the separation of topics related to nutrition and design. However, the overall focus of the HDFS credential is broader than that of the CFLE and focuses more specifically on topics within the context of human development. The CFLE credential also considers issues relevant to human development but approaches them from a lifespan and family systems perspective within the context of relationships. Additionally, the CFLE standards include greater emphasis on knowledge and skills relevant to human sexuality, parenting, and educational methods and techniques relevant to family life education.

While both CFLE and CFCS-HDFS designates work in government and human services settings, professionals carrying the CFCS-HDFS credential tend to work more in settings involving early childhood and secondary and post-secondary programs, whereas CFLEs work in a broader range of settings including faith communities, the military, health care, work-life programs, and in the private sector as consultants providing a range of family life education services relevant to parenting, relationships skills, money management, and more.

Numerous other organizations exist with interests relevant to family life education. For example, professionals involved directly in sex education might join the American Association of Sexuality Educators, Counselors, and Therapists (AASECT) or the Society for the Scientific Study of Sexuality (SSSS), and parent educators might be members of the National Parenting Education Network (NPEN). Couples or educators active in couples and marriage education may wish to join Better Marriages (formerly the Association for Couples in Marriage Enrichment, ACME) or the National Association for Relationship and Marriage Education (NARME) or become involved with the Coalition for Marriage, Family, and Couples Education (CMFCE). These organizations have formed to provide a professional forum for discussion of the many issues inherent in family life education. This abundance of related organizations reflects the multidisciplinary nature of family life education.

The recent proliferation of life and parent "coaches" has provided an opportunity to clarify the knowledge and skills needed to be a family life educator and has contributed to a unique role definition. While there is an increasing number of training programs, certifications, and organizations focused on coaching, it is still a relatively undefined and emerging field. A search on the Internet for the term *life coach* results in a plethora of companies and organizations offering certification and training. However, there does not appear to be an identified national standard for the practice. The lack of consensus regarding the criteria needed to be a coach creates opportunities for those without sufficient education, training, or oversight to offer coaching services. The popularity of coaching addresses the apparent need of individuals to seek guidance in dealing with daily life issues from a strengths-based perspective. Family life educators can benefit from this interest by promoting their unique qualifications to coach by offering the guidance sought with the benefit of knowledge and skills supported by research.

The Domains of Family Practice Model, discussed in Chapter 1, represents advancement in the field of family life education by helping to identify the overlaps and contrasts among the fields of family life education, family therapy, and family case management (Myers-Walls et al., 2011). The development of the model has contributed to a unique role definition for family life educators that may help encourage collaboration among the fields. Ultimately the debate over role definition may subside as more widespread agreement evolves over the content and practice of family life education and its place in the continuum of services provided to families.

6. Public Served Expresses Some Acceptance of the Expertise of Those Practicing the Occupation

As society faces increasing crises and challenges related to families (e.g., divorce, single parenting, blended families, economic recession, delinquency, substance abuse, and youth violence), there has been greater recognition of the value of prevention and education. Even health maintenance organizations are more frequently offering classes dealing with parenting, stress management, and balancing work and family, because they recognize the relationship between stress and health (CDC, 2013). Additionally more businesses are recognizing that personal and family problems account for decreased productivity and attendance (Bond, Galinsky, & Hill, 2004) and are offering lunchtime "brown-bag" seminars and other educational opportunities to increase employee well-being and productivity.

When groups or organizations offer family life education programs, they often seek someone to lead the experience who has expertise in an academic discipline or profession related to families. Family-specific degrees, as well as certification and experience, can enhance one's credibility as an expert in the area of family relationships. However, individuals and families seeking guidance related to relationships and parenting skills can find themselves choosing from a wide range of providers with varying training and expertise.

For more than 40 years, the marriage enrichment movement has offered opportunities for enhancing couple-relationship skills and intentional-growth activities (Mace, 1982). The value of trained leadership has always been emphasized by such international marriage enrichment organizations as ACME, founded by David and Vera Mace in 1973, and Marriage Encounter, founded by Father

Gabriel Calvo in 1962. Both groups offer rigorous and well-developed leader-training programs that require leader-couples to have experience, as well as academic preparation. Leaders in training must also work under the supervision of an experienced leader-couple and receive positive evaluations of their skills by participants before receiving full certification.

The increased interest in marriage education over the past years has led to a proliferation of "scripted" marriage education programs that can be taught "out of the box." These programs are designed to be presented by lay leaders who do not have specific academic training in marriage and family or educational methodology. Similar issues exist related to parenting education as seen by the explosion of "mommy and daddy" blogs and websites devoted to parenting. As with the marriage education field, there are a variety of parenting programs promoted to meet the needs of struggling parents. These approaches have created some tension between those who have specific education and training in family education and those who do not. While some feel it is possible to be an effective marriage or parenting educator by following prescribed guidelines provided through specific curricula or approaches, others feel the most effective educators are those with formal training in family systems and dynamics, sexuality, interpersonal relationships, human development, and parenting, in addition to proven skills in program development and implementation.

Some would argue that formally trained family life educators are better able to draw from a variety of approaches and techniques that are more specifically adapted to the audience and situation, rather than applying a "one size fits all" approach. Persons trained in a specific approach or curriculum may, in fact, be very effective, but they would not be considered "professionals" in that their expertise is limited to just one curriculum or setting. As long as they stay with the script, all is well, but questions can arise for which a certain level of expertise is needed.

Family life education professionals, as well as program participants, recognize that it takes more than being a "good parent" or a "happy couple" to facilitate effective learning experiences and the skill building that enhances interpersonal relationships. Adequate training and experience are imperative. However, the availability of such a variety of programs, learning opportunities, and the varying qualifications and training levels of the providers continue to challenge the solid establishment of family life education as a recognized profession.

7. Certification and Licensure Are Legal Signs That a Group Is Sanctioned for Particular Service to Society and Is Self-Regulated

At times there is some confusion regarding the terms *accreditation* and *licensure* and the difference between a *certification* and a *certificate*. Therefore some clarification may be helpful when noting the use of certain terms below, such as voluntary versus mandatory, professional organization versus government or licensing bureau, and program versus individual.

- *Accreditation* is a voluntary process by which a professional agency or association recognizes that a program meets certain requirements. Most universities and colleges are regionally accredited.

- *Certification* is a voluntary process by which a professional agency or association grants recognition to an individual who has met certain predetermined qualifications or standards specified by that agency (e.g., CFLE, CFCS). Certification is an ongoing credential that requires demonstration of continuing education in order to be maintained.

- *Licensure* is a mandatory process by which a government or licensing bureau permits individuals to practice in a designated profession (e.g., teachers, social workers, therapists). It gives qualified people the right to engage in a particular occupation or profession in that state, to use a specific title, or to perform a specific function. Licensure typically represents the minimum standard for practice (e.g., teachers, therapists).

- *Certificates* are offered by a professional agency, association, commercial enterprise, or university in response to the completion of a defined training program (e.g., gerontology, parent education). It is a terminal award, meaning that there is no ongoing requirement for continuing education or additional learning.

As has been discussed, the National Council on Family Relations offers a certification program for individuals, as does the American Association of Family and Consumer Sciences. AAFCS also accredits university degree programs in Family and Consumer Science. NCFR offers approval of degree programs for adherence to the CFLE standards, but does not provide accreditation as that also involves review of program facilities and faculty.

The CFLE program was developed by NCFR for the purpose of regulating the qualifications of family life education providers and, indirectly, the quality of the materials presented. There is currently no state licensure requirement for family life educators, but since 1989 Minnesota has required early childhood and parent educators to be licensed in order to provide family education through the Early Childhood Family Education (ECFE) program. More recently, a number of educational institutions including North Carolina State University, Wheelock College, Plymouth State University, River College, University of Minnesota, and University of North Texas at Denton have begun offering graduate certificate programs in parenting education (NPEN, 2013). The National Parenting Education Network (NPEN) is continuing to pursue the option of a national parenting education credential. Likewise, there are specific certifications for focused areas of family life education including sexuality education (through AASECT), and personal and family finance (through AAFCS). These efforts reflect recognition of the importance of establishing some form of formal recognition of minimum standards for effective practice.

8. A Code of Ethics Is Developed to Eliminate Unethical Practice and Protect the Public

In 1995 the Family Science Section of the National Council on Family Relations approved *Ethical Principles and Guidelines* for use by family scientists. These guidelines dealt primarily with ethical issues inherent in teaching and research in academic settings. Two years later the Minnesota Council on Family Relations published *Ethical Thinking and Practice for Parent and Family Educators* (MCFR,

1997) for family life education practitioners. In 2009, NCFR formally adopted the principles identified in the MCFR ethical guidelines process as the official Code of Ethics for the Certified Family Life Educator designation (NCFR, 2009a). The fact that a need was perceived for these ethical guidelines and codes provides further evidence of the recognition of family life education as a unique profession.

This step-by-step discussion of East's (1980) criteria for defining a profession shows that family life education is indeed an evolving profession that is moving toward maturity. Through the efforts of family life education pioneers and those currently working in the field, the profession continues to make progress toward the goal of recognition and participation on the same level as marriage and family therapy, counseling, and social work. Ultimately family life education will be the norm.

Challenges in the Field of Family Life Education

What needs to happen in order for family life education to be a recognized and valued approach to family issues and well-being? How can we get the CFLE credential and/or a degree in family science included as an employment requirement? Also, how do we get more people to participate in family life education? What if all expectant parents took parenting classes as part of childbirth preparation? Imagine the impact on the divorce rate if all engaged couples participated in marriage education or if married couples regularly invested in their relationships by attending marriage enrichment programs? Imagine the personal and societal problems avoided if all high school students were required to complete a course in communication skills, money management, and conflict resolution? How many adolescent high-risk behaviors could be avoided with family life education at that critical developmental time?

Family life education is making tremendous progress in advancing as a profession and an approach to daily life; but before family life education can become the norm a number of challenges need to be addressed. Some of the most readily identified challenges to the advancement of family life education include the lack of identity as an academic discipline and profession, the diversity of settings in which family life education takes place, and the unstable funding of family life education programs and services.

Lack of Identity as a Discipline

Perhaps the biggest struggle faced by family life educators is the lack of public awareness and understanding of who they are and what they do. As demonstrated, substantial progress has been made in establishing consensus on the content of family life education and the standards needed for effective practice. However, there is less agreement on what to call an academic degree meeting these standards. Very few degree programs are specifically titled "family life education." Rather, family-related degree programs carry a myriad of titles including family sciences; family studies; individual and family studies; family and consumer sciences; family and child development; human ecology; human development and family studies, family, youth and community sciences; family and child sciences; child, adolescent, and family studies; family relations; and more. The overall field of family studies has struggled with the issue of identity for many years, as noted by having approximately 300 academic programs and over 100 different titles for family-related majors (Hans, 2013). The establishment of a core body of knowledge and standards of practice has helped to establish a clearer identity for family life education, but a more consistent name for the academic degree awarded to family professionals is needed. This would enable employers to more easily identify professionals qualified to apply a preventive, family-centered, lifespan approach to family well-being. Additionally, a consistent name for the academic degree would make it easier for family life educators to be recognized providers of mandated parent education or to have their services covered by insurance providers.

Diversity of Settings in Which Family Life Education Takes Place

There are probably numerous instances of family life education occurring in your community on any given day. There are family life educators working in health care settings, community education, faith communities, junior and senior high schools, colleges and universities, social service agencies, corporate settings, government agencies, corrections, retirement communities, and the military. The multidisciplinary nature of family life education and the variety of settings in which it takes place can be both an asset and a liability. On the positive side, numerous opportunities fit the "generalist" training that is family life education. Negatively, the variety of settings makes it difficult to target efforts when seeking jobs. Do you apply with hospitals or through community education programs? Which job titles do you look for when searching the classified ads or the Internet? The diversity of settings in which family life education occurs requires family life educators to be their own advocates. They must be able to articulate what family life educators do and what they have to offer. Appendix C includes a list of settings in which family life education can occur.

The *2012–13 Occupational Outlook Handbook* (OOH) of the United States Department of Labor, Bureau of Labor Statistics (www.bls.gov/ooh) does not include "family life education" as an occupation. In fact, the only occupations listed with "family" in the title include family and consumer science professors, family and general practitioners, family child care providers, family services social workers, and family therapists. The occupation of family services social worker only includes information on social work with no reference to any other family-related positions. As those involved in family life education know, the social work field has done an excellent job of branding itself and incorporating social work training (and in many cases social work licensure) into state and federal legislation. While this works well for jobs focusing on intervention and case management, it excludes a great many well-qualified family professionals who possess the skills and knowledge needed to help families through a preventive approach. A new licensure requirement for non-social work family professionals is not likely in the near future. Generally, most legislators are interested in creating new licensure requirements only in fields that involve significant health or welfare risks to the public.

The National Council on Family Relations is working with the U.S. Department of Labor (DOL) to include the occupation of *family life educator* in their official coding system. The first step for professional identification within the DOL is to get the term connected with an existing Standard Occupational Classification (SOC) system code that will at least alert DOL employees who gather occupational information to the existence of this profession. The more they see the title *family life educator* being used, the more likely the DOL will cite it within the SOC system and, eventually, within the Occupational Outlook Handbook.

The long-term goal is for employers, college students, and job-seekers to be able to go to the Occupational Outlook Handbook, enter the term *family life educator*, and pull up a page with information on the profession of family life educator similar to what would appear if the terms *social worker* or *counselor* were entered. This would include information on the nature of the work, working conditions, training, other qualifications, advancement, employment, job outlook, earnings, related occupations, and sources of additional information. Unfortunately, it could be a number of years before the title *family life educator* receives its own specific listing within the SOC system. A profession is added to the system when the title or position appears with a certain level of frequency. *Family life educator* does not yet appear often enough in the labor environment and will only do so when people identify themselves by this specific title or when employers identify their employees as such.

Family life educators should be encouraged to start this process by using the title *family life educator* on websites, business cards, and publications, and by encouraging employers to use the term in job postings when appropriate. Hopefully, with a collective and focused effort, the term *family life educator* will one day be recognized specifically by the Department of Labor, as well as others, which in turn will enhance family life education as a profession.

Unstable Funding of Family Life Education Programs

Many family life education programs are funded through federal and private grants. In most cases this funding is available for a specified period. Therefore, grantees often find themselves focusing much of their efforts on maintaining existing grants and obtaining new funding rather than carrying out the programs. Often, effective and proven family life education programs are discontinued due to the cessation of the funding period and a failure of funders to require inclusion of sustainability strategies into the original grant.

Additionally, the funding of family life education programs through grants typically involves administration of these programs through government and non-profit agencies. This can result in a stigma for those attending these programs by sending a message that family life education is only for people and families that are having difficulties. No one questions the value of pregnant women taking classes to learn about the birthing process, but we have not yet reached the point where all parents attend parenting classes throughout their children's development. Funding of family life education by insurance providers and administration of programs through a variety of providers including employers, schools, faith communities, hospitals, private companies, and employee wellness programs could result in increased and consistent availability of opportunities and recognition of family life education as the norm.

≡ Strategies for Growth

A number of strategies can be implemented to increase the visibility and value of educational and preventive efforts focused on the family that in turn will advance the profession. This includes the promotion and support of standards of practice, education of employers and the public, incorporation of family life education into intervention settings, recognition of family life educators as qualified providers in legislation, improved and stable funding, creation of niche markets, and promotion and normalization of family life education through the media.

Promote and Support Standards of Practice

CFLE and CFCS certifications are perhaps the most relevant and appropriate credentials for those working in family life education. Family professionals can support the field of family life education by recognizing the need for established standards of practice. This might involve pursuing certification themselves or hiring or promoting those who carry the CFLE or CFCS designation. Increasing the number of people who identify themselves as family life educators and are actively promoting this identification through the use of CFLE and CFCS initials after their names in their promotional materials, on their resumes and vitae, and in job titles will help increase awareness of family life education as a profession. Likewise, increasing the number of qualified Certified Family Life Educators and professionals Certified in Family and Consumer Sciences is an important strategy in recognizing the value of family life education. The CFLE and CFCS initials after a designee's name bring attention to family life education as a practice with identified standards and requirements.

Educate Employers and the Public

Family life educators may find that they need to do a fair amount of educating about family life education and its value. They often need to be creative and proactive in finding employment settings and willing to market themselves to potential employers. Employers may not really understand what a family degree or certification represents. They need to be educated on the fact that these credentials denote a solid understanding of families, a lifespan perspective, and the skills and knowledge needed to develop and present educational programs. Most family life educators trained specifically in family will work from a systems perspective, i.e., individual couple and family systems, as well as social service, business, and government systems. Graduates of family degree programs need to see themselves working as family life educators at *any* system level in *any* organization. They need to see themselves very broadly in terms of training and skills and encourage employers to do the same. Employers that benefit from hiring an employee with such skills and knowledge will be more likely to hire similar candidates in the future and to encourage others to do so as well.

Incorporate Family Life Education into Intervention Settings

Family life educators working in settings that focus primarily on intervention or counseling can often identify opportunities for offering family life education within that same setting. For example, an agency that works primarily with families struggling with financial issues might want to offer money-management workshops to the community. Those offering home visits to parents identified as at-risk might also sponsor evidence-based family education programs that provide opportunities for all families to gather together to share information, support, and friendship. While there will always be families needing the assistance of social workers or counselors, most family professionals recognize that preventing problems is best for families and society. The Domains of Family Practice Model discussed in Chapter 1 does an excellent job of identifying how family life educators can work in collaboration with family case managers and therapists to assist and strengthen families.

Increase Recognition of Family Life Educators as Providers in Legislation

The growing fields of marriage education and parenting education should expand opportunities to increase the legal recognition of family life educators as providers of services. A number of states have established or are considering legislation that mandates or offers incentives for people completing marriage education or parent education classes. Typically this legislation includes a listing of recommended providers of these services. Unfortunately, legislators tend to favor bills that include a finite list of qualified providers. These providers are usually people who possess credentials, such as licensure, that are already sanctioned and recognized by state or federal bodies. It simplifies the passage of the bill, but may not provide the best measure of who is qualified to provide these services. For example, mandated parent education programs, required in some states for divorcing couples with children, often identify licensed social workers, counselors, therapists, or clergy as the only approved providers. While many of these providers may be well qualified to provide education regarding parenting, being licensed as a social worker, counselor, or therapist, or serving as a pastor, does not guarantee any specific knowledge in parenting or the ability to develop and implement educational workshops or work individually with parents in an educational capacity. Someone trained specifically in family life education is at least as qualified, and most likely more qualified, to provide marriage or parenting education than social workers, therapists, or pastors who are identified as providers simply by virtue of their professional titles in that particular state. Additionally, family life educators can provide a more comprehensive, family-centered, strengths-based perspective compared to a singular focus on crisis management.

Fortunately, legislators, lawyers, and judges are beginning to recognize that professionals with family degrees and/or certification have the skills and knowledge to work with families, whereas in the past they automatically enlisted the services of therapists or social workers. For example, in the state of Texas, Certified Family Life Educators and professionals with degrees in family are recognized as qualified providers for some parenting education programs mandated by judges. Parenting Coordinators that work with divorcing parents must also complete training in mediation, but their family degree and/or CFLE designation helps them to meet the minimum requirements.

Those interested in promoting family life education need to monitor applicable legislation and take the opportunity to educate those who introduce relevant bills to include family life educators among the list of approved or recommended providers. Inclusion of family life educators as "approved providers" in federal legislation would open the door for recognition by states and local entities in the public and private sectors.

Increase and Stabilize Funding for Evidence-Based Prevention Programs

There is a wealth of data supporting the effectiveness of evidence-based family education programs. These reports consistently show a positive return on investment for funds provided to support preventive programs addressing early childhood education (Karoly, Kilburn, Cannon, Bigelow, & Christina, 2005), parenting, (McGroder & Hyra, 2009), teen pregnancy (Alford, 2008; Kirby, 2007), and juvenile delinquency and substance abuse (Miller & Hendrie, 2008; Spoth, Guyll, & Day, 2002).

While the emotional cost of family dysfunction can be difficult to measure, the financial costs are clear. Substance abuse alone was shown to cost the nation $510.8 billion in 1999, the most recent year for which data are available (Miller & Hendrie, 2008). A 2003 study by the Centers for Disease Control estimated the annual costs of domestic violence in the United States to be as high as $5.8 billion (CDC, 2013). The estimated annual cost of child abuse and neglect is over $80 billion (Gelles & Pearlman, 2012).

The Adverse Childhood Experiences (ACE) Study (Felitti, Anda, Nordenberg, & Williamson, 1998) found a strong relationship between a traumatic experience in a person's life occurring before age 18, and the lifelong health and well-being of that person as an adult. Those occurrences, defined as an Adverse Childhood Experiences, include physical, sexual, and/or verbal abuse; mental illness of a household member; problematic drinking or alcoholism of oneself or a household member; illegal street or prescription drug use by a household member; loss of a parent through divorce or separation; domestic violence toward a parent; and incarceration of a household member. Problems stemming from divorce, substance abuse, teen pregnancy, child abuse and neglect, violence, bankruptcy, and many other individual and societal problems are all areas in which education and prevention programs could avert or ameliorate social ills, but as discussed previously, funding for such programs is often grant-based, and therefore unstable.

A more consistent funding stream is needed to ensure that family life education becomes the norm. One opportunity for growth in this area centers on efforts to incorporate family life education into the Affordable Care Act (Taner, 2013a). The Affordable Care Act mandates substance use disorders and mental health prevention initiatives. The availability of health insurance funding for evidence-based family life education programs focused on parenting and relationship skills and substance abuse prevention could result in increased access and participation by making such programs more available and affordable and removing the stigma related to seeking help.

Carve a Niche

As noted, family life education takes place in a myriad of settings. Its multidisciplinary nature means that family life educators might find themselves competing for jobs or working alongside those trained in social work, psychology, child development, sexuality, or therapy. One approach to increasing the visibility of family life education is to establish or identify a setting in which family life educators are uniquely qualified to provide services. Health care providers are increasingly offering workshops on parenting and stress management. Community education catalogs list numerous classes related to family life. Youth programs and faith communities are some of the most common settings for family life education.

The area of *work life* holds tremendous potential for family life educators. More corporations and businesses recognize the interconnectedness of work and family life. They understand that the personal lives of employees can have a detrimental effect on their work life, especially if their personal lives are riddled with substance abuse, domestic violence, or serious financial difficulties. Much of the estimated cost of substance abuse results from lost work productivity and increased health-care spending (Harwood, Fountain, & Livermore, 1998). However, less serious or problematic issues can affect work life as well and can include issues related to normative family stressors, such as couple relationships, parenting, and elder care. Investment in "brown-bag lunch" workshops or webinars on "communicating with your adolescent" or "time management" can result in increased productivity and/or decreased employee absence. Family life educators are uniquely qualified to provide these types of learning opportunities.

In many situations family life education can be incorporated into existing settings and provided as one of many services. For example, workshops focused on planning for retirement, estate planning, and caregiving issues can be offered in a retirement community or nursing home. Parenting education might be provided at a preschool or day care through a published newsletter or a series of evening workshops. A doctor's office might find value in hiring a full or part-time parent educator to address parenting concerns often raised during medical appointments. These more specific efforts can be a way to introduce organizations to the value of family life education that could ultimately lead to more full-time services.

Few can argue with the merits of providing individuals and families with the knowledge and skills needed to lead satisfying and productive lives; but general acceptance of, or the lack of argument against, such efforts are not enough to ensure the advancement of the field. The challenge before advocates of family life education lies in increasing awareness of the research supporting the return on investment for evidence-based programs focused on primary, secondary, and tertiary prevention. We need societal awareness of parent education, marriage enrichment, and life skills training, along with recognition of the value of participating in these activities on a regular basis. When professionals in related fields recognize and value the knowledge and skills possessed by family life educators and understand the role that family life education can hold in a variety of settings and situations, we can work effectively as a team to assist families. Family life education does not compete with social work, therapy, counseling, or ministry.

Rather, it is a complement and part of a collaborative collection of resources and services available to help families function as effectively as possible (Myers-Walls et al., 2011).

Promote and Normalize Family Life Education through Media

Another strategy for advancing family life education lies within the intentional use of media. *Cultivation theory* proposes that conceptions of the social world are shaped in part by exposure to images portrayed in the media (Gerbner, 2009). Television and movies have substantial influence in portraying and normalizing various family forms including single parents, same-sex couples, cohabitation, and divorce. Television shows like *Will and Grace* and *Modern Family* helped introduce and normalize gay characters. Media provides unlimited opportunities to incorporate family life education into story lines that can help educate the public about relationships, parenting, and sexuality. *Parenthood* is a great example of a television show that incorporates topics including autism, teen pregnancy, cancer, substance abuse, single parenthood, dating, adoption, and aging, and the influence these issues have on the family. The way in which the characters deal with their circumstances provides educational insights into both positive and negative strategies. The characters portrayed in television and movies can model the best practices for healthy parenting and relationships. Family life education advocates can help advance and normalize family life education by influencing the producers of television and movies to incorporate family life education into their programming. Imagine the impact of having a character seek help from a parent educator when dealing with a troublesome teen, or if a couple struggling with communication problems attended a marriage education class rather than immediately consulting with a therapist. Like all worthy goals, the elevation of family life education to a recognized and valued profession will require the targeted, sustained efforts of all family education professionals and the organizations, businesses, schools and governmental agencies whose missions and services stand to be enhanced by the profession.

The Professional Family Life Educator

Another important piece in elevating the field of family life education is to ensure the professionalism of those who practice. The heart of professionalism lies in the skills and qualities of those who practice and/or deliver services to the public. By its nature, family life education often deals with personal and sensitive issues. A major component of family life education involves helping participants analyze, clarify, and determine their own values and value systems. Unlike an educator providing instruction in a hard science such as math or chemistry, the family life educator deals in matters of personal values, decision-making, and behavior, along with sensitive issues such as sexuality, communication skills, parenting, and money. Participants may respond with more emotion or defensiveness due to the personal nature of the topics discussed. In family life education, the feelings, motives, attitudes, and values of the learners are central to the learning process (Darling, 1987).

Personal Attitudes and Biases

Because of the personal nature of the content and process of family life education, it is imperative that educators have a solid understanding of their own values, attitudes, and biases. Professional family life educators need to be comfortable with other people's feelings and accepting of various points of view. Many family degree programs require students to examine and study their own family of origin and family roles, rules, and values to increase awareness of the influence of their own family experiences (Bahr, 1990). This helps to identify conflicts that may influence their ability to effectively practice family life education. Without critical self-reflection, educators could be unaware of what values, philosophies, or paradigms guide their personal and professional lives (Hennon, Radina, & Wilson, 2013).

In our increasingly diverse society it is important for family life education professionals to work toward cultural competence. "Beyond simply knowing about diversity, family life educators must also be cognizant of the unique challenges and opportunities that arise from developing and implementing programs specifically for diverse populations." (Ballard & Taylor, 2012b). Awareness of one's biases toward such things as culture, race, physical ability, gender, sexual orientation, and socioeconomic status is necessary in order to practice effectively.

Family life educators must have the ability to function ethically and effectively in a variety of diverse settings (Allen & Blaisure, 2009). In order to do so, they must consider the following questions: How do I view differences among people? Are differences something to value, celebrate, ignore, or fear? Do I see my role as a helper, leader, advocate, or partner? How comfortable am I working with someone different from myself?

Asay, Younes, and Moore (2006) developed a cultural transformation model which illustrates the changes in cultural perspectives that a person might experience as they progress toward becoming culturally competent. The model includes five phases: cultural smugness, cognitive overload and emerging insecurity, realization and surrender, self and cultural examination, and adaptations. Recognition and appreciation of the differences and similarities between cultures will enhance both the practice and personal life of the family life educator.

Additionally, family life educators need to take time to seriously consider their perceptions and attitudes about such things as individual and societal responsibility. For example, are poor people poor because of the choices they have made or because of circumstances beyond their control? A *Typology of Helping Models* provides a meaningful framework to consider the locus of a problem and of responsibility including a Moral Enlightenment, Medical, and Compensatory/Empowerment Model (Brickman, Rabinowitz, Karuza, Coates, & Kidder, 1982). The educators' perspectives on these issues can influence the ways in which they practice and interact with an audience.

Often perceptions and attitudes are so ingrained that we do not even know we have them. It takes conscious effort and thought to examine the way in which we see the world. This can be uncomfortable and challenging, but if educators fail to face these issues they run the risk of compromising their ability to practice as effectively as possible, and cheat themselves out of a wealth of opportunities to grow and learn from those around them.

Personal Skills and Qualities

The National Council on Family Relations, as part of the Certified Family Life Educator program criteria, identified certain characteristics as crucial to the success of a family life educator (NCFR, 1984). They include general intellectual skills, self-awareness, emotional stability, maturity, awareness of one's own personal attitudes and cultural values, empathy, effective social skills, self-confidence, flexibility, understanding and appreciation of diversity, verbal and written communication skills, and the ability to relate well with all ages on a one-to-one basis, as well as in groups.

Clearly, personal traits and characteristics play an important role in the success of a family life educator. A self-assessment (Box 2.1) gives the reader an opportunity to evaluate personal attributes and identify areas that need improvement. Working with a mentor or supervisor, participating in peer evaluations, and observing experienced educators are some of the ways to enhance personal characteristics relevant to professional practice.

Developing a Personal Philosophy

Although certain personal qualities can enhance a family life educator's effectiveness, it is also important to develop a philosophical basis for teaching about families. Educators must thoroughly consider their beliefs in order to be effective. How do they define a family? What is the purpose of family life education? They must be clear about the benefits of family life education and how it can be accomplished most effectively. A philosophy of family life education is important because it provides a sense of direction and purpose; allows the educators to be in touch with themselves; enables assessment of educational problems; clarifies the relationship of family life education to the needs and activities of the larger society; and provides a basis for understanding the reality of the family, its value in society, the nature of family membership for the individual, and the role of family life education (Dail, 1984). Having a personal philosophy provides a deeper meaning to the educator's life.

Four beliefs that need to be addressed when constructing a philosophy of family life education include (Dail, 1984):

- Beliefs about the family and the quality and nature of family life
- Beliefs about the purpose of family life education
- Beliefs about the content of family life education
- Beliefs about the process of learning for families

Beliefs about the family and the quality and nature of family life

Family life educators must look at their own beliefs about how they define family. Is a family defined by bloodlines, function, proximity, intention and/or legal recognition? Family life educators who do not consider a gay or lesbian couple to be a family, for example, need to be aware of this bias, as it could influence their ability to effectively work with such a couple.

See Box 2.2 (on p. 48) for an exercise to consider the criteria used in defining family. Each example describes a different group formation. Students should inde-

Box 2.1   Assessing Your Personal Qualities as a Family Life Educator

Listed below are qualities considered as critical for effectiveness as a family life educator. Rate yourself on the following scale:

1   Needs much improvement

2   Needs some improvement

3   Average, but not well developed

4   Above average, moving toward competency

5   Competent in this area

- *General intellectual skills.* Ability to gather, read, and process information and to apply it to a topic and to group needs; to articulate concepts and ideas; to organize materials and stay on track when presenting them; to hear and incorporate ideas of others.

- *Self-awareness.* Ability to recognize and articulate one's own personal opinions, attitudes, and cultural values and not to assume that they are everyone's opinions, attitudes, and values; to understand personal tendencies to assume certain roles in a group, such as caretaker, controller, placater, dominant authority; to acknowledge one's own strengths and limitations.

- *Emotional stability.* Ability to recognize one's own level of emotional comfort or discomfort in a given situation; to express emotions in appropriate ways and at appropriate times; to maintain calmness in the face of crisis or confrontation and to refrain from personal attack on another person, either verbally or physically.

- *Maturity.* Ability to handle success, disappointment, frustration, or confrontation with dignity and understanding; to acknowledge one's own mistakes and weaknesses and not blame others; to move past grievances and continue to see each person as someone with value and potential.

- *Empathy.* Ability to put oneself in another person's place; to reflect the feeling to the other person; to understand her or his dilemma.

- *Effective social skills.* Ability to feel comfortable and enjoy the company of others; to share in group activities; to engage in conversation and to actively listen to others.

- *Self-confidence.* Ability to speak and act decisively in personal conversation or in front of a group; to accept the challenge of one's ideas without defensiveness and to state one's position with enthusiasm and documentation, not personal criticism or attack; to acknowledge personal strengths and accept words of appreciation graciously.

- *Flexibility.* Ability to adapt plans to suit a changing situation; to recognize when change is needed and be willing to try a new approach.

- *Understanding and appreciation of diversity.* Ability to acknowledge differences in others' values, attitudes, and lifestyles; to respect and appreciate cultural and ethnic differences in dress, customs, and language; to understand socioeconomic differences in income, education, and status and how these differences affect lifestyles and decision making; to actively resist gender, racial, and socioeconomic biases or stereotypes.

- *Verbal and written communication skills.* Ability to speak articulately, convincingly, and concisely; to write clearly in language that is not "over the head" of one's audience; to use illustrations and examples that support one's points; to know when an audience has been "overloaded" with information.

- *Ability to relate well with all ages and groups and on a one-to-one basis.* Ability to talk with and not down to any group or person; to resist judgment; to appreciate humor and sharing; to practice patience in listening and interacting.

pendently determine if they would consider each grouping to be a family. Class discussion often reveals varying opinions about what does and does not constitute a family, often with fairly soft criteria.

In addition to how students define a family, educators need to have an understanding of how they think a family *should* be. What role does the family play in an individual's life? Where does the family fit within society? What needs to be in place for a family to function optimally? Understanding their beliefs about the role of a family and the characteristics needed for healthy functioning provides educators with a goal to strive for and a foundation on which to base their programs and other services.

Box 2.2   What Makes a Family?

Which of the following groups is a family?

1. A newly married couple moves into their first apartment together. They have both agreed that they do not want to have any children.

2. A man and a woman have shared an apartment for the past two years. They contribute equally in the maintenance and cost of the household. They have made a personal commitment to each other and plan to stay together for the rest of their lives, although they have no plans to marry.

3. A man and a woman have shared an apartment for the past two years. They contribute equally in the maintenance and cost of the household. They are good friends, but are dating other people.

4. A group of 10 people (5 men, 3 women, and 2 children) live together on a farm. They share responsibility for the maintenance of the household, including growing their own food. All household members take part in the care of the two children. The group is committed to living together harmoniously.

5. Two gay men live together in a house. They have made a personal commitment to each other.

6. Two gay women live together in a house. They have made a personal commitment to each other and were legally married in the state of Hawaii.

7. A divorced woman lives with her son from her marriage and her daughter from a relationship with another man whom she no longer sees.

8. A man and a woman share an apartment. They have a personal relationship and are committed to staying together as long as the relationship is beneficial to them both.

9. Two divorced heterosexual men live together in a house with their children and share the expense and maintenance of the household. Each man sometimes cares for the other's children while the other is working.

10. A woman lives alone, but speaks daily with her sister and brother who live in another state.

11. A brother and sister live with their grandparents while their divorced mother attends school in another city. The mother stays with the children and her parents on the weekends.

12. A widower moves in with his son and his wife.

Beliefs about the purpose of family life education

The family life educator must understand the purpose of family life education in order to develop appropriate goals and objectives. Is the goal of family life education to change behavior? Is it to provide insight, skills, and knowledge? Is it proactive or reactive? Is it to provide support? Is it to promote a particular ideology or belief system? Family life educators must be clear about what they want to accomplish and why because assumptions regarding the purpose of family life education can influence program design.

There are various perspectives through which family life education programs can be viewed (Miller and Seller, 1990). Each perspective has implications for the purpose of family life education and type of curriculum developed. The *transmission* perspective equates accumulation of facts with mastery of subject matter and skills. Learners are expected to be attentive to the teacher and basically passive consumers. (They may ask or respond to a question, but no further involvement is expected.) The purpose of family life education from this perspective is the transmission of knowledge, attitudes, and skill development, along with information about values that prepares one to fit into society.

The *transaction* perspective implies more involvement between the teacher and the learner. Learners are viewed as autonomous beings capable of rational thought and active involvement in their own learning experience. Therefore, the purpose of family life education from the transaction perspective would focus on developing cognitive skills and critical thinking abilities in order to use them in individual problem-solving situations.

The *transformation* perspective recognizes the personal element of knowledge and the strong influence of social interaction and cultural context in determining personal behavior and values. Although learners are seen as diverse and unique, they also share many basic human needs and concerns. The purpose of family life education from this perspective is to facilitate social interaction that results in personal and social change.

Beliefs about the content of family life education

When developing a philosophy of practice, the family life educator should consider a variety of issues relevant to the content of family life education programs including the appropriateness of certain content, the need to have program content that is free of bias or stereotypes, and the importance of supporting content with up-to-date research and sources.

For example, although issues of personal sexual or physical abuse may arise in family life education settings, continued discussion is not appropriate. In this case, a participant should be referred for counseling, therapy, or possibly to law enforcement. Professional family life educators should be familiar with appropriate sources of information and services so they can make referrals and research topics when necessary. A family life educator who attempts to deal with such issues directly or allows lengthy discussion in a group setting would not be acting professionally. The *Domains of Family Practice Model* provides a helpful framework for considering which professionals are best qualified to address particular issues in varying contexts.

In addition to being clear about what content and level of disclosure is appropriate for a family life education setting, effective family life educators want to be sure that their program content is culturally appropriate in order to be effective. Course content should consider family members of all ages; portray nonsexist roles for family members; include information about families of different racial, ethnic, and cultural groups; recognize the uniqueness of individuals and families regardless of age, sex, race, ethnicity, sexual orientation, and cultural and socioeconomic backgrounds; recognize that composition of families varies; and be based on current research (Ballard & Taylor, 2012b). The book *International Family Studies: Developing Curricula and Teaching Tools* (Hamon, 2006) includes discussion of numerous aspects of developing and teaching family content with cultural sensitivity and respect. Attention to program content needs to extend beyond program design and take into account the ways in which participants learn, barriers to participation, and environmental considerations that will vary depending on the population (Ballard & Taylor, 2012b).

Beliefs about the process of learning for families

Family life educators need to be concerned with how families learn and function as a group, as well as how the group affects the learning and thinking of individual members within it (Clarke, 1998). Do groups learn differently than individuals? How can small groups be used most effectively? Are the developmental, social, and emotional needs of the group important? What is the role of learning goals and evaluation? How does the education of one family member affect others in the family?

An understanding of human development and the learning process enables the educator to use the most effective techniques for each audience and each individual. In addition, an educator who understands families as a system can recognize the value of including all family members in the learning process. When that is not possible, they consider the implications of introducing new information, such as parenting methods, into the family and are prepared to help other family members to adjust to new ways of thinking or acting. Chapter 6 discusses various teaching methods and learning experiences in more detail. The important methodology concept to consider in this chapter is awareness of one's own personal beliefs about how individuals and families best learn.

Constructing a personal philosophy can be a difficult process. It involves questioning, evaluating, and accepting and rejecting ideas. It is just that—a process—and it is continually evolving as the educator grows and learns. The time and effort spent in developing a personal philosophy of family life education will be well worth the effort. Family life educators who have a solid understanding of their personal philosophies of family life education will be better equipped to assist individuals and families to lead more satisfying and productive lives.

Ethical Guidelines for Practice

Let's revisit two of the family life educators introduced earlier in this chapter in order to examine the issue of professional ethics.

Carl has a baccalaureate degree in art history. He has worked for the past nine years as a youth coordinator for the YMCA and organizes activities and classes for neighborhood youth identified as high risk. Carl learns that Chris, a child with whom he has a close relationship, has become involved in gang activity. The child's parents have told Carl that they want him to keep close tabs on their son. They don't know about their son's involvement with the gang. Should Carl talk to the parents?

Juanita has a degree in child development. She organizes a parent group in her neighborhood for other stay-at-home moms and dads with children under 2 years old. The group meets regularly and discusses a predetermined topic each time. Members rotate responsibility for researching the topic and presenting information. Much of the meeting is spent in casual conversation and support. Lately, one parent named Gretchen has been monopolizing the discussion and has disclosed information about her relationship with her husband. Some of the other group members appear to be uncomfortable with this level of disclosure, but Gretchen seems to be in need of the group's attention and input. What should Juanita do?

We often see ethical issues in the news, whether it relates to politicians, corporate executives, or Wall Street officials. While many professions have specific codes of ethics, there are some general rules of thumb to also consider. These include the *Golden Rule* (act in the way you expect others to act toward you); *Professional Rule* (take only actions that would be viewed as appropriate by an *impartial* panel of professional colleagues); and the *TV Rule* (a person should always ask, "Would I feel comfortable explaining to a national TV audience why I took this action?").

Professionals in fields ranging from medicine to law to auto mechanics are faced with ethical issues at one time or another. Family life education is no exception and may, in fact, be more susceptible to ethical dilemmas due to the sensitive and personal nature of some of the issues faced in practice. Because family life education often deals with values and belief systems, it is imperative that professional family life educators have an understanding of the role of ethics in their professional lives.

Codes of ethics are designed to prevent harm to consumers and professionals and to the professions themselves. For the helping professions, these codes commonly address five principles of ethical practice that are based on the teachings of Hippocrates (Brock, 1993). These are:

- Practice with competence
- Do not exploit
- Treat people with respect
- Protect confidentiality
- Do no harm

Additionally, the values for family life education might consist of the following provisions (Brock, 1993):

- *Responsibility to Consumers.* Family life educators should respect the rights of their students, supervisees, and employees and promote the well-being of families.

- *Professional Competence.* Family life educators should maintain high standards of practice, stay abreast of new developments through continuing education, and keep within the boundaries of their profession.
- *Confidentiality.* Family life educators should protect the confidences shared by clients and students and not disclose them, except if required by law.
- *Discrimination.* Family life educators do not discriminate against or deny services to anyone based on race, gender, religion, national origin, or sexual orientation. If unable to provide services, they are to make referrals to other qualified professionals.
- *Dual Relationships.* Family life educators do not exploit the trust of clients or students with dual relationships.
- *Sexual Intimacy.* Family life educators should not be sexually intimate with their students or clients.
- *Harassment.* Family life educators should not engage in sexual or other harassment.
- *Personal Help.* Family life educators should seek assistance for their personal problems.
- *Responsibility to the Profession.* Family life educators should advance the goals of their profession (e.g., promote the incorporation of family life educators as providers of family knowledge in state legislation)

Developing a code of ethics, which is an important indicator of the evolution of a profession, can identify expectations for professional behavior and reflect important values (East, 1980; Palm, 2012). As professionals, family life educators need access to ethical guidelines for practice, as well as the capability to consider and act upon these guidelines. "Ethical codes guide our professional interactions with each other, as well as with our constituents. A code lets the public know what it can expect from those who call themselves professionals and helps us as practitioners face with confidence some of the difficult decisions that come with our work" (Freeman, 1997, p. 64).

The diversity and complexity of today's families require family life educators to increase and modify their roles. With this increased complexity, the potential for doing harm also grows (Palm, 1998). Awareness of this complexity inspired the Parent/Family Education section of the Minnesota Council on Family Relations (MCFR) to develop ethical guidelines specifically for use by practitioners in parent and family education. They recognized that family life education was an emerging field and that many practitioners faced ethical dilemmas in relative isolation and with limited guidance (MCFR, 1997).

A multi-perspective approach to ethics was developed that integrated the *relational ethics approach, principles approach to ethics,* and *virtues ethics* (MCFR, 2009). Relational ethics focuses on understanding relationships as a basis for making ethical decisions and developing caring and respectful relationships with family members. It asks, "Who are the stakeholders?" and considers the role of each person in relation to the other. The principles approach to ethics considers agreed-upon principles for professional practice along with such standards as "we will do no harm to children and insist on the same from others" and "we will define our role as family educators and practice within our level of competence." Previously, the way of defining professional behavior focused on technical competence and recognized the importance of considering the "greater good" for families and society, as opposed to only considering the aspirations of a single individual. However, now various organizations have codes of ethics and expectations of professional behavior. For example, marriage and family therapists use a medical model, and while family life educators may duplicate therapists in some ways, the relationship is not as intense. There are two approaches within the principles approach—*Mandatory* (compliance with lay and specific codes of moral conduct for a profession) and *Aspirational* (motivation to follow a set of ideal standards within one's practice.)

The introduction of *Virtues Ethics* involves a more individualized lens that fills the gap of defining professional behavior and focuses more on technical competence than on moral character. In other words, do the right thing for the right reasons. There are three virtues noted for family life educators: *Caring*, which enhances the welfare of family members as agents in their own lives; *Prudence and Practical Wisdom*, which is the ability to understand competing needs and make decisions based on reflection and consultation; and *Hope/Optimism*, which is a disposition to look at the strengths of family members and other individuals to see positive potential in situations. "Good practice in family life education should be tied to internal standards of excellence" (MCFR, 1997, p. 2).

When examining an ethical dilemma there are five steps (NCFR, 2012).

- Step 1   Identify Important Relationships
- Step 2   Identify Relevant Ethical Principles
- Step 3   Identify Contradictions/Tensions between Principles
- Step 4   Identify Possible Solutions
- Step 5   Select an Action(s)

The *Tools for Ethical Thinking and Practice in Family Life Education* (NCFR, 2012) publication provides a more detailed description of the principles, as well as a step-by-step process for their use when dealing with ethical dilemmas. NCFR adopted the principles identified in the MCFR guidelines for ethical thinking and practice as the official *Code of Ethics* for the Certified Family Life Educator program. All CFLE applicants must read and sign the CFLE Code of Ethics as part of the application process.

Personal morals are not sufficient when dealing with ethical dilemmas in a work setting. Practitioners need to understand and internalize their profession's core values. Because of the nature of their work, family life educators are expected to balance the needs of a variety of clients. They have an ethical responsibility to children, parents, colleagues, employers, and society. Often ethical dilemmas arise out of the conflicting needs or interests of those involved (Freeman, 1997). Consideration of ethical principles and the implementation of an ethical-guideline process can provide family life educators with guidance to help make a decision that is right for them and for the situation.

▬▬ Importance of Professional Development

As you walk up to the stage to accept your degree and prepare to throw your mortarboard in the air, it is tempting to think that your time as a student is over. You have completed the course work needed for your degree, taken your last test, and submitted your last paper. Now it is time to get to work and put all the knowledge to good use! Newly graduated professionals often give little thought to any need to continue their education beyond graduation (Darling & Cassidy, 1998), but it is an integral part of professionalism. Qualified professionals must stay current on research and developments within their field along with technology and best practices.

Continuing education and professional development can be accomplished through a number of avenues. Some examples include attending workshops, seminars, and professional conferences; completing online learning opportunities including webinars and self-paced learning modules; reviewing current research through professional publications, such as newsletters and journals; presenting research at professional meetings; and networking with others in the field through membership in professional organizations and associations.

Most certification and licensing programs require professionals to earn a minimum amount of continuing education credits (CEUs), sometimes called PDUs (professional development units), in order to maintain the designation or license (Knapp & Reynolds, 1996). Therefore, professionals need to actively seek continuing education opportunities and to maintain records that document attendance at meetings and professional activities. Membership in one or more professional organizations can provide numerous opportunities for continued growth.

SUMMARY

This chapter has looked closely at the field of family life education and issues of professionalism. We have determined that the field of family life education meets many of the criteria set forth by experts in defining a profession. Challenges in getting the profession recognized and strategies for growth were considered. We have looked at the importance of developing a personal philosophy including personal insights, values, and beliefs about families and family life education. Additionally, we explored the personal qualities and traits needed for effective practice. Finally, we discussed the importance of ethical guidelines in assuring best practices. These considerations provide the foundation for further discussion about the practice of family life education.

QUESTIONS AND ISSUES FOR DISCUSSION

1. Which people described on the first page of this chapter would you consider to be a "professional" family life educator? Why?
2. How do *you* define "family"?
3. What is the goal of family life education?
4. Can a person have a different set of values in their personal life than in their professional life? Why or why not?

5. How would you search for a position as a family life educator in your community?

6. What are some ways for family life educators to promote their services?

ACTIVITIES

1. Trace the development of another social science profession (e.g., social work, marriage and family therapy) and apply East's criteria.

2. Interview a representative sample of family majors in your department and a sample of family life educators in your area. Compare their responses to the ethical dilemmas presented in the case studies in this chapter. On what bases do they make their judgments?

3. Using the *Case Study Process* in the NCFR publication *Tools for Ethical Thinking and Practice in Family Life Education*, determine the appropriate course of action for a family life educator when a parent in a parent education group reveals having been physically abused by his or her spouse.

4. Read through the two ethical dilemmas described on page 51. What should Carl do? What should Juanita do?

PART II

Practice of
Family Life Education

PART II

Practices of
Quality Time Education

3

Understanding Your Audience

Addressing the Needs of Your Audience

Family life education is relevant across the lifespan. Whether involving parents learning about their new babies, sex education with adolescents, college students making decisions about career options, newlyweds practicing communication and conflict resolution skills, or senior citizens preparing for retirement, family life educators need to be cognizant of the participants involved in their programs. This may include knowledge of the demographic data for your community, as well as learner backgrounds, needs, interests, and goals. Have they had any previous experiences with the subject matter and what do they want to accomplish by attending your class? In other words, what kinds of needs do they have?

Recognizing Types of Needs—Needs Assessment

Since family life education should be based on individual and family needs, a *needs assessment* can help to determine what those needs are. A needs assessment is a tool for making better decisions that can be used *proactively* to help you plan, *continuously* as an ongoing process of improving one's program, and *reactively* in response to some undesirable results (Watkins, Meirs, & Visson, 2012). By incorporating needs assessment strategies, you can plan your program priorities, curriculum, and modes of instruction to be more effective and better target your participants' needs, interests, and goals (Chamberlain & Cummings, 2003).

The Domains of Family Practice (DFP) Model examines *for whom* family life education is designed and includes two primary factors—*motivation* and *eligibility* (Myers-Walls et al., 2011). *Motivation* represents the perceptions by participants that a service is necessary and appropriate according to their *felt needs* (Arcus et al, 1993). Felt needs are self-identified; evolve from their own experiences; and encompass the wants, desires, and wishes of the learner. Much of family life education is based on felt needs, which are usually normative and related to age or events, such as becoming a parent, being a parent of an adolescent, getting married, or retiring. In other words, new parents or parents of adolescents, along with engaged couples or newly retired persons, may desire some knowledge to help them in the role changes they are, or will be, experiencing. There are also some instances of family life education related to non-normative issues that result from job loss, financial difficulties, or health issues (Arcus & Thomas, 1993). In comparison, *eligibility* is determined by the professionals delivering services and is often based on *ascribed needs,* which others identify as a need. Some parents may be mandated to attend family life education classes because of issues that arise from juvenile legal problems, abuse or neglect, or divorce. As an example, when someone says, "I'd like to be a better parent" they are expressing a felt need, but if someone was told that they "should" be a better parent, this would be an example of an ascribed need. Family life educators also consider *future needs*, as they often teach from a preventative paradigm regarding issues learners may have to face in the future. As a result, learners often enroll in family relations courses while in school to prepare them for future life changes or take courses prior to becoming new parents, having their last child leave home, or retirement.

Conducting an Assessment

The "how" question of the DFP model employs needs assessment techniques to determine the characteristics and needs of the target participants (Myers-Walls et al., 2011). It is a systematic process to determine the needs or "gaps" between current conditions and desired outcomes or "wants," and plan for improvements in individuals, education, or communities (Kizlik, 2012). Knowledge of these needs can result from (1) examining the *demographic characteristics* of the target population and (2) pertinent *research findings* related to your audience, along with (3) participation of the learners in the planning process through a *needs assessment*.

To exemplify the process of determining the needs of your participants, consider offering a course on relationships for singles. *Demographic data* can tell you that there are increasing numbers of singles 18 years of age and older with about 102 million (41.1%) single Americans (53% of females and 47% of males). The number of people who lived alone in 2012 was 27%, which was up from 17% in 1970 (Vespa, Lewis, & Kreider, 2013). The percentage of unmarried U.S. citizens who had never been married was 62% with another 24% divorced and 14% widowed. The number of unmarried men 18 and older was 89 for every 100 unmarried women (U.S. Census Bureau, 2012b). However, what about the lifestyles of singles? Singles can control how they use their time and what they eat; can spend time and money in bars, restaurants, cafes, gyms, and book clubs; and can attend events, such as book readings, art classes, and public activities. Singles tend to be more in contact with friends, neighbors, siblings, and parents and proudly consider themselves to be more generous and civic-minded than marrieds (DePaulo, 2006). (To help students better understand the general demographics of potential participants see the activity in Box 3.1 on the following page.)

Examining research related to your target population (e.g., singles) is another critical step in the assessment process. For example, research has indicated that there is a widespread form of bias towards singles that has evolved in our culture in that singles are targets of *singlism*—negative stereotypes and discrimination (DePaulo & Morris, 2013). Married persons are typically described positively, whereas singles are at times presumed to be immature, maladjusted, and self-centered. While the "perceived" differences between married and single persons are large, the "actual" differences are not. Nevertheless, when singlism is acknowledged, it is often accepted as legitimate. Interpersonal discrimination in relationships with others in one's environment may account, in part, for lower levels of self-esteem and higher levels of depression in singles (Simon, 2002; Waite & Gallagher, 2000). One suggestion is to transition from a simple contrast of married versus single persons to thinking of singles as diverse and distinct groups that are unpartnered, cohabiting, widowed, or divorced. Some are single by choice and others may choose to have a partner one day, whereas some may face physical or psychological challenges that affect their ability to develop lasting relationships (Byrne & Carr, 2005). Young adult singles (36% of young adults ages 18 to 31) are increasingly living at home with their parents, especially males (40%) compared to females (32%). This is due in part to increased numbers of singles attaining college degrees, lack of employment prospects, and delays in marriage (Fry, 2013).

Box 3.1   Knowing Your Audience

This activity can be helpful for demonstrating the importance of recognizing that there may be many things about the participants in a class that you have no way of knowing just by looking at them.

Have ten volunteers from the class stand at the front of the room. The volunteers do not need to do or say anything other than stand there. Clarify that the following scenarios are completely hypothetical and not directly specific to any of the people standing at the front of the room. Ask the class to consider the following questions. No response is needed. These questions are just for consideration.

How many of the people before you are/have been:

- Impacted by alcoholism or substance abuse?
- Adopted or have family members that are adopted?
- Victims of sexual abuse?
- Victims of physical or psychological abuse?
- Affected by dyslexia or ADHD?
- Gay, lesbian or transgender?
- Divorced or impacted by divorce?
- Politically conservative?
- Politically liberal?
- Devoutly religious?
- Impacted by Alzheimer's or dementia?
- Of mixed race?
- Impacted by depression?
- Caring for a loved one?
- A veteran?
- Raising one or more grandchildren?
- Involved in foster care?

Another option is to obtain statistics for the relevancy of these situations within a local or national population. Data can be collected from a variety of sources, such as the U.S. Census Bureau, professional organizations, and newspaper articles. Using these data the questions can be modified to represent the actual percentage of a given population that might meet the criteria. For a group of 10, each person can represent 10% of the population. For example, if you know that 3 in 10 people in your state are affected by Alzheimer's disease you can ask, "Which three people are affected by Alzheimer's disease?" This approach helps to add focus to the relevancy of certain situations or issues. However the main focus of the exercise is to increase the awareness and sensitivity of educators to the varying situations and issues that participants might encounter.

Appreciation to Jean Ilsley Clarke, CFLE, for demonstrating this activity in a Group Leadership workshop.

Research has also indicated that as singles age they were willing to date different people. Males who were in midlife, never-married, and sexually permissive were more willing to date heterogeneous partners (partners of a different race, religion, and lower economic status), which could cause friction in relationships with other friends and family members (Fitzpatrick, Sharp, & Reifman, 2009). These relationship decisions may mean that generic programs for singles may not meet their needs. Searching research literature can provide insight into issues that singles are facing and provide recommendations for practice that can facilitate understanding the needs of your target audience and designing a needs assessment measure.

While you can examine *demographic data* and *research* findings about your target audience (e.g., singles), it is also essential to make contact with potential participants and conduct a *needs assessment*. A needs assessment is a systematic approach to studying the state of knowledge, ability, interests, or attitudes of a target audience in order to design an effective educational program. What does your audience know and think and what can you do to make your program more accessible, acceptable, and useful to potential learners (McCawley, 2009)? For example, what issues would singles want covered about relationships? What is their age and single status (never married and alone, divorced, separated, or partnered)? Are they seeking intimate relationships, close friendships, connections in the community, or assistance with family members who may be exerting pressure for a lasting relationship or seeking their services as a caregiver? Are they happy or unhappy with their single life? What are their issues of concern?

Whereas some needs assessments can be *indirect* through discussions with interested persons, such as an advisory committee, *direct needs assessments* are accomplished by gathering qualitative or quantitative data from potential participants. However, it will involve greater resources to design, implement, and analyze the resulting data. In general, you want the best data possible within the constraints of your available resources (e.g., time and money). Whether or not you have conducted an in-depth needs assessment, during the first class session it is always good to ask participants their reasons for taking the class, what experiences they have with the topic, and what would they like to accomplish. It is important to share your plan for the class session(s) and determine if your strategy for the course will meet their needs. If not, ask them what changes they would recommend. You may not be able to accommodate all their suggestions, but at least you will have a chance to make some possible adjustments, if time and resources permit.

Steps in Conducting a Needs Assessment

Planning a needs assessment

Before actually beginning a needs assessment, it is best to create your objectives. In other words, what type of information would you like to gain? Do you want to know the learners' ages and interests in the topic; issues of concern; or best time, location, and format for the class? Who is your audience and how will you select your sample? Will you go to various singles groups affiliated with churches, schools, senior centers, or exercise facilities? What methodology or instruments will you use and how will you collect your data? Will you use online surveys or focus groups? How will you analyze the data and use it in your decision making? (For specific details on conducting different types of needs assessment see McCawley, 2009.)

Obtaining approval

Depending on your approach to needs assessment, you may need institutional approval, especially if the educational program or research project is funded through a university or grant. This might occur through a university human subjects review, Institutional Review Board (IRB), and/or additional permissions from schools, churches, institutions, or parents that are involved. Make sure to allow time in your planning to get these approvals. If, however, you use secondary data that already exist, or a more informal method, such as discussions with advisory boards or other interested persons, you may not need to obtain IRB approval.

Collection of data

There are several methods to collect data, including surveys, interviews, focus groups, and other creative approaches. Below is a brief overview of needs assessment techniques, along with some advantages and disadvantages of each method. Further examination of the procedures involved in each method is highly recommended. After you have designed the assessment method questions, it is good to pilot test your instrument and procedures with some selected potential participants (Dillman, Smyth, & Christian, 2009; McCawley, 2009).

- *Surveys.* Written surveys can be conducted by mail, e-mail, online, phone, or in-person. While some methods of quantitative data collection are cost-effective (e.g., online or in-person groups), others are not, due to printing and postage charges. Data are anonymous and easy to summarize, but unless you ask the right questions, you may not gain the additional insights and details that you desire (Dillman et al., 2009). During phone surveys you can get supplementary information without having to depend on the literacy skills of the participants, however, many people do not answer phone calls from an unknown number. E-mail and online surveys work well if you anticipate the learners will have computers, are Internet savvy, and will respond to an e-mail message from an unknown person prior to deleting it. At times you may be attending a group that has some potential participants in your target audience. If you have some surveys with you, it would be easy to get responses if the context of the environment facilitates this process. In other words, you might ask participants at a PTA meeting for their suggestions, but you will need to get prior permission to make this request of parents.

- *Interviews.* Interviews involve conversations between two or more people to collect needs assessment data. They can be conducted face-to-face or through the use of technology, such as phones, video conferencing, or online. Interviews are inexpensive to conduct and work well with open-ended questions. In addition, the interviewer can look for nonverbal cues and ask clarifying questions, as needed. The interviews can be taped with permission of the participants and then transcribed and coded, but this can be time intensive. One should develop statements to facilitate rapport and clarity about the intent and data needed by the interviewer (Dillman et al., 2009; McCawley, 2009). Again, as with surveys, some people do not respond to unknown callers unless they have some previous communication about an upcoming phone call to gather needs assessment data. This, however, may not be time and cost effective.

- *Focus Groups.* Focus groups involve a social experience of 6 to 8 persons who not only express their own opinions, perceptions, beliefs, and attitudes, but also listen to the opinions of others, which they may or may not incorporate into their comments. This format adds a "group dynamic" element that may produce more information than structured individual interviews (Polson & Piercy, 1993). Focus group methodology is not only a means to plan a needs assessment process, but also has the unique ability to facilitate understanding "reality" from the point of view of those involved in the group. Within the qualitative paradigm, focus group methods probe the attitudes and opinions of small groups, are stimulating to the respondents, and provide rich data through cumulative and elaborative responses often not obtained in individual interview settings (Denzin & Lincoln, 2008). Whereas focus groups are easy to establish, the data collection process can be intense with many different opinions and suggestions being offered in a rapid-fire sequence. With permission, recording the responses for later transcription is most helpful. Having a competent moderator, who is able to facilitate questioning and pursue major issues, is critical.

- *Other Creative Techniques.* Your constant challenge as an educator is to design creative ways to do the assessment tasks of asking, studying, and observing. You may be visiting a home, office, or classroom; calling by phone; handing out questionnaires; or polling participants. If you are doing a webinar, you may want to send out a brief survey to participants as they register to determine their background, interests, and needs regarding the topic. You may also do something more innovative, such as posing a "three wishes" question to children about their family life or asking a group of pregnant teens to draw their greatest fears about becoming a mother. It may be asking a group of new parents to take a pretest about infant development at the beginning of class. This is an effective method because it gives the leader a chance to note knowledge gaps and provide accurate information while involving the group in a "kinetic" activity. The point is to form warm, caring connections with the participants so that you become an informed friend instead of the "sage on the stage."

- *Interpretation of Data.* Once you have collected and analyzed your needs assessment data, it is time to interpret them. This goes beyond simple tabulation by using various decision-making tools and techniques, such as prioritizing issues, engaging in consensus planning, using multiple criteria to make comparisons across options, and employing facilitator-led discussions to identify gaps (see Watkins et al., [2012] for further details). Now you have to decide the meaning of the results, determine if there are any patterns, and identify what actions will be most helpful to your target learners. Share and discuss your results with others, as interpretations can vary.

≡ Role of Culture

In addition to assessing the needs of our participants, we should examine the concept of culture and how it can be applied. *Culture* is the total way of life of people—the customs, beliefs, values, attitudes, and communication patterns that characterize a group and provide a common sense of identity. Taken together, these components form a way of interpreting reality that is shared among members of a group. In past years, the *cultural deficit* or *compensatory model*, which emphasized the need to intervene and improve families, was used to design programs for children and families from different cultural groups (Hildreth & Sugawara, 1993). This model undermined strengths and diminished self-worth. However, more recently the *cultural difference paradigm*, which makes no value judgment about needed assistance for a cultural group, has become more common. Thus, all cultural groups are valued for their unique qualities and dignity. Family life education programs will be more successful if they are sensitive to the strengths of cultural groups (Hildreth & Sugawara, 1993). While we often think of culture in terms of race-ethnicity, culture extends beyond this paradigm to include age, gender, socioeconomic status, generational cohorts, family structure (single parent, extended), sexual orientation, special circumstances (health issues, crises, military roles, incarceration), or combinations of various cultural lenses, such as a gay single parent or mother serving in the military.

We often do not perceive the influence of culture, so one way to introduce a discussion of the multifaceted aspects of culture is by asking students if they wear sunglasses. If they are readily available, have students put them on and ask others to identify differences in their sunglasses. Students will often note the varying shapes and sizes of the frames and lenses, including colors and types. When looking through sunglasses, you see things differently. Similarly, ask students what kinds of filters people have that affect how they see individuals and families. Responses vary and may include race, ethnicity, sexual orientation, gender, religion, education, social class, political affiliation, geographical location, age, marital status, professional role, and living in a home or being homeless.

While we want to avoid *stereotypes* about people, we also need to understand how they differ from *generalizations*. Generalizations give insights into the tendencies of a particular group of people and often come from synthesizing available information from research and/or informed cultural experts and professionals. In comparison, stereotypes are oversimplified representations of a group of persons (e.g., race, nationality, sexual orientation, religion, age, family type) that can be inaccurate in terms of how they exaggerate real differences and the perceptions of these differences. Although stereotypes are often negative, they can also be positive (Peterson, 2004). For example, you might say that a particular cultural group is good at math. The problem is that this is only a partial picture and an individual from this culture who is not good in math may feel undue pressure to perform. *Generalizations* may seem similar to stereotypes, but stereotypes are often taken to the extreme and become exaggerated beliefs that are applied to every member of a particular group. Which of the following examples are generalizations or stereotypes? (See p. 91 for the answers.)

1. Many people in the U.S. attend football games.
2. Everyone in the U.S. likes football.
3. Lots of Americans like fast food.
4. All Americans eat fast food every day.
5. Johan is going to be stubborn because he is from Country X.
6. Johan might be really stubborn because he is from Country X.
7. Many people from Country Z keep their feelings to themselves.
8. People from Country Z never share anything about themselves.
9. Maria will be late because women are never on time.
10. Maria might be late because some women are more likely not to be punctual.

We all deal with other cultures whether we are in our home country, abroad, at work, or in our neighborhoods. Therefore, it is important to become more culturally aware. If we gain some knowledge about cultures (facts and traits) along with an awareness of others (their skills and behaviors), and ourselves, we can become more culturally sensitive and intelligent about other persons in our environmental context (Peterson, 2004). When we learn about different cultural groups within and beyond our own culture, we can see different points of view and better understand and deal with cultural differences.

There are various analogies to incorporate when considering culture. Historically we have often heard of the United States as being a *melting pot* of various cultures all blended together into one conglomeration, but this paradigm no longer works because some of our cultural groups have remained distinctive. Another view is to think about culture as a *salad bowl* in which there are crisp vegetables with distinct flavors, colors, and textures, and some dressing that helps pull all the ingredients together. A more recent analogy is that of *vegetable soup*. The soup has the essence of the vegetables and seasonings that make up the soup, but there is a broth that is flavored by all the ingredients and combines everything into one tasty dish. It should be noted that within the cultural composition of Americans, some refer to various groups as "hyphenated-Americans." In other words, we may use terms such as Italian-Americans, Polish-Americans, or Asian-Americans. While at times that is acceptable, when something happens such as 9/11 or the terrorist attack at the Boston Marathon, we are all "Americans." In other words, the vegetables can have some distinct flavor, but the American broth is what unites the cultural soup.

An *iceberg* has also been used as an analogy for culture. There is the part that is above the waterline or the *visible* part of culture, such as the customs and language, but the vast majority is below the waterline and constitutes the *invisible* part of culture including values, cultural assumptions, nonverbal communications, thought patterns, and cognitive perceptions. Similarly we talk of the *Big C* of culture, which is what you see, and the *little c* of culture, which you do not see. (See Figure 3.1 on the following page.)

We rarely get to know the essence of other cultural groups, so I (C. Darling) will use my own cultural heritage as an example as I am more familiar with it than other cultures. All four of my grandparents were born in Finland and came to the U.S. as young adults, so I lived within a culture of individuals in the U.S. who had

Figure 3.1   Role of Culture in Understanding Participants

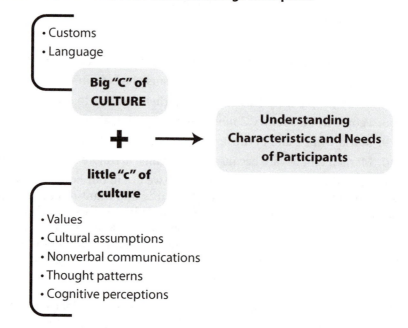

emigrated from Finland. Thus, I was immersed into the culture of Finnish-Americans. The *Big C* of culture contained the following:

- *Customs*—Traditions and holidays (e.g., I have participated in celebrating Finnish Midsummer, Independence Day, foods, clothing, arts, literature, politics, architecture and design, crafts, folk dances, and music. Having attended a camp for Finnish youth as a child, I was able to learn about and participate in many examples of Finnish culture and appreciate the music of Jean Sibelius, the poetry of Johan Runeberg, and the architecture and design of Alvar Aalto and Eero Saarinen.)

- *Language*—Verbal and nonverbal (e.g., I learned some of the language from my parents and took courses both in the U.S. and Finland to facilitate learning the Finnish language. I was also exposed to periods of silence, which spoke volumes, along with minimal facial expression and eye contact. Silence means privacy, personal thinking, or respectful listening. Finns may be quiet, but they are always thinking. Finland is more of a monologue culture compared to some other countries, such as the U.S., which is a dialogue culture.)

In addition, I also assimilated elements of the *little c* (Tamminen, 2003) of Finnish-American culture, including:

- *Values*—Basis of how we act and what is right and wrong (e.g., Many Finns have a strong sense of fairness, honesty, and trust. They have an ethic of hard work based on the need to survive. They also value promptness, the appreciation of women in politics, respect of nature, and the role of "sisu," which is a Finnish term for fortitude and perseverance.)

- *Cultural Assumptions*—Things taken for granted about a culture, which are not necessarily always true (possible stereotypes), (e.g., I learned that Finnish people are perceived to be hardworking, creative, and reliable, but they also can be introverts, direct, and impatient. Additionally, because they have so many saunas in Finland, they are often perceived to be clean.)

- *Non-verbal Communications*—Touch, eye contact, finger symbols (e.g., I found that generally Finnish people tend to be somewhat shy, quiet, and use the phrase, "It goes without saying." There is minimal touching—in business, only handshakes are acceptable, although between good friends there might be some hugging, more often with women. Finns also keep their distance and are concerned about invading another person's private space. Houses and clothing should be modest.)

- *Thought Patterns*—Ways we think and process information (e.g., I learned that many Finns will often be direct, logical, and to the point, but extolling one's own virtues would be considered inappropriate. Finns should not boast about their education, money, status, or family background, and generally do not talk about it.)

- *Cognitive Perceptions*—Ways we understand knowledge (e.g., I was aware that Finland was a poor nation until the late 1950s and Finns worked hard for the collective good. They took pride in being the only country to pay back their war debt to the U.S. after WW2. Prior hardships of family members in previous generations affected perceptions of one's country of heritage. Thus, my parent's generation in the U.S. was taught that we had it better than our family members in Finland, so we should try to assist them in any way we could.)

When I taught in Finland, although I had been steeped in the Finnish culture through my U.S. family, friends, and community, I still did not know all there was to know about the *little c* of the Finnish culture. However, because of my background, which is both American and Finnish, I am able to ask questions and get insightful answers. I am still learning and need to continue doing so, because culture both stays the same and changes. The *Big C* characteristics tend to remain the same, but the *little c* themes can change over months or years (Peterson, 2004). This example shows that there is no way we can know all the *Big C* and *little c* characteristics of our own culture and especially multiple cultures. However, by trying to learn as much as we can about other cultures, especially those represented in our classrooms, we will begin to understand how to design a class and implement it to best meet the needs of a specific culture or multi-cultural groups. The *Big C* and *little c* of culture not only pertain to race and ethnicity, but can also apply to varying family structures, sexual orientations, and age-generations.

Characteristics and Needs of Various Groups

As family life educators we are dedicated to advancing the well-being and learning of our students. Thus, we personalize our instruction as much as possible by trying to do our best for students. We often identify groups by age, gender, or ethnicity; however, there are multiple diversities resulting in a combination of characteristics, such as gay adolescent Latinos, single Asian mothers, black parents of a disabled child, or white incarcerated females. While one cannot know the characteristics of all cultural groups, it is important to examine demographics, research, and theory relating to various cultural groups, while incorporating an ecosystems context (O-E Relationship). (See Chapter 8.) When studying individuals or families, how would you characterize the environments within which they interact, including the legal, political, economic, religious, educational, and medical systems? If we can take existing data and think critically about any cultural grouping from an ecosystems perspective, we can create a better understanding to assist us in our teaching.

Developmental Stages and Generations

The developmental stages of your students need to be understood as they relate to their individual and family needs. Moreover, people born at different times in varying generational cohorts will also have different personal needs, attitudes, and values that can influence their learning styles.

Developmental stages

While there are various stage-based theories of development, a commonly used one is that of Erik Erikson (1950, 1963), who proposed eight stages to clarify the developmental challenges faced at various times in people's lives. These stages and the approximate ages for each stage include: *Basic Trust vs. Mistrust* (0–1); *Autonomy vs. Shame and Doubt* (1–3); *Initiative vs. Guilt* (3–6); *Industry vs. Inferiority* (6–11); *Identity vs. Role Confusion* (adolescence); *Intimacy vs. Isolation* (early adulthood); *Generativity vs. Stagnation* (middle adulthood); and *Ego Identity vs. Despair* (late adulthood). While each stage builds on the successful completion of earlier stages, mastery of a stage is not required to advance to the next stage. Each stage has various components to negotiate, such as one's biological changes, sociocultural forces, and psychological crises (for further information see Harwood, Miller, & Vasta, 2008). Although we could be teaching all ages of the population, we more commonly work with adolescent and adult learners, whether they are young adults or seniors.

Adolescence is a time of profound changes in physical, cognitive, socio-emotional, and moral development during which teens are making critical life choices (Tippett, 2003). This period is marked by tremendous growth, physical variability, and hormone changes, along with a focus on appearance, physical changes, and seeking self-identity. While in early adolescence same-sex friendships are predominant, maturation results in increased comfort with friends of both genders and an increased desire for independence from parents. There are also changes in brain development and cognition, as well as a shift from concrete to formal operations, which is tied to moral development and an adolescent transitioning from the desire to do something good because there is a reward, to doing good to maintain positive relations. As they become aware of themselves, adolescents not only become egocentric, but also aware of their skills and career potential that may help them focus on a future path. In order to facilitate learning in this age group, you may want to acknowledge the varying rate of growth and development, plan activities that build self-esteem, involve families, use a variety of teaching techniques to meet different learning styles, be responsive to diversity of all kinds, and give opportunities for development of critical thinking skills and evaluation of alternatives to various actions, especially those that involve risk taking (Tippett, 2003).

Young adults are strong, in good physical condition, and have stamina. Their memory and cognitive abilities are at their highest and they have a strong ambition to succeed, select a life partner, start a family, and accept responsibilities. In *middle adulthood*, there is a loss of strength, vision, sharpness, coordination, and some memory loss. Some adults can have a mid-life crisis, causing them to reevaluate their life goals and accomplishments and make some positive changes. *Later adulthood* is marked by menopause, osteoporosis (a reduction of bone density), gray hair, less skin elasticity, and a loss of muscle mass. Memory and mobility tend to decrease as well.

Lifelong learning for adults is a function of their needs and wants based on societal changes that affect the complexity of their lives, such as increased life expectancy, shifts in caregiving to family members, concerns for health and wellness, use of technology, and expanding knowledge in all areas of life. Adult learners may have different reasons for engaging in family life education. They may have a desire to know more about a certain topic (*felt needs*) or have a mandated expectation of their need to know (*ascribed needs*). Maybe it is a way to connect with others with similar interests. An examination of the topics of high interest to adults aged 50 and older indicated that their highest-rated topics were nutrition and health, fitness and exercise, and positive aspects of aging (Ballard & Morris, 2003). Because adult learners are generally responsible for their own lives and capable of self-direction, teachers often assume a facilitator role. Adult learners not only bring rich experiences to the classroom, but may also bring some biases, such as the value of certain discipline methods. Most often adults are highly motivated to learn as they perceive the information will help them in their lives at home or work (Tippett, 2003). They want real life situations that might be incorporated into a class with case studies or role-play. (See Chapter 6.)

Of course, some adults are no longer working because they have reached *retirement age* and beyond. The fastest growing segment of the U.S. population is the group that is 65 years and older with a rapid increase in the "old-old" or those who are 85 years and older. Older women outnumber men with a ratio of three to two, but for those who are 85 and older, there are five women for every two men with 80% of those persons aged 85 being women. This means that they are most likely living on social security. The population 65 years and older is projected to double between 2012 and 2060 from 43.1 million to 92.0 million. Those 85 years and older are projected to more than triple from 5.9 million to 18.2 million, or 4.3% of the total population (U.S. Census Bureau, 2012c). The implications of living longer have some important considerations for older persons and their families (Zinn, Eitzen, & Wells, 2011). Elder learners may want to attend classes to both learn and interact with others. Health issues are important along with financial planning and family relationships within the context of their advancing age. Remember that their hearing, sight, and physical abilities may no longer be as astute as when they were younger. Thus, educators need to pay attention to their physical abilities and limitations along with their issues of concern. To facilitate understanding the limitations faced by older learners, see the activity in Box 3.2.

Generations

We frequently see terms in the news such as Greatest Generation; Baby Boomers; Millennials; and Generations X, Y, and Z, which are all used to describe groups of people of varying ages or generations of people who developed different value systems. Generational theory has become increasingly popular in recent years as a way to conceptualize individuals in a broad approach according to their birth generation. It seeks to facilitate understanding by characterizing cohorts of people according to their birth generation and how that time affected their values and views of the world. A *generation* is an average interval of time between the birth of one's parents and the birth of their offspring, typically about 20 to 22 years. Generations are not defined by a formal process, but by demographers, the media, popular

---

Box 3.2   Aging Changes

An aging simulation activity can help students increase their knowledge about the physical changes in older adults related to sensory-motor functioning and their sensitivity to the feelings of older persons. (Wood, 2003).

In small groups, have volunteer members modify one or more of their abilities to perform daily activities. These limitations could include the following:

- Put on glasses that cause blurred vision by coating the lenses with petroleum jelly (e.g., cataracts) or cover part of the outer edges of the lenses to stimulate loss of peripheral vision (e.g., glaucoma).
- Insert ear plugs or absorbent cotton balls into both ears (e.g., hearing loss).
- Divide a cotton ball and insert into one nostril (diminished sense of smell and taste).
- Place transparent tape on the thumb, index, and middle finger joints of the dominant hand (e.g., stiffness due to arthritis).
- Insert dried split peas or sunflower seeds in the sole of each shoe (e.g., foot pain, loss of balance associated with bunions and corns).
- Restrict one knee with an ace bandage (arthritis).
- Use a straw to breathe while walking upstairs (e.g., respiratory problems).

Students who are not impaired will be designated caregivers and are responsible for the safety and assistance to those with aging impairments, along with observing their responses and the reactions of others. The groups of students will experience the effect of these limitations for about 30 to 60 minutes during which time they can move around campus and be involved in activities, such as going to the library, purchasing and consuming a snack, making a phone call, and/or using a computer, vending machine, and bathroom.

A debriefing discussion can include the following questions: what difficulties and feelings did they experience; what changes did they observe in themselves and others; did the experience stimulate any thoughts about older individuals and their impairments; what changes in feelings and behaviors toward older persons might evolve from this experience.

culture, market researchers, and members of each generation (Pendergast, 2009). Generations have their own defining experiences and identifiable sets of assumptions, values, attitudes, and approaches to life, along with shared aspirations about their role in society (McGregor & Toronyi, 2009; Strauss & Howe, 1991). During these periods there are significant events that tend to shape development and values, such as wars, terrorism, major political events, and technological advances.

While some do not highly regard generational theory because "pop-psychologists" and reporters have overused the generational labels, others believe it is scientifically acceptable and grounded in good social science (Codrington, 2008). Studying generational similarities and differences is interesting, but tricky. There is no consensus about the calendar years associated with any particular generation, so most generations do not have precise beginning and end dates with some generations overlapping, thus producing a group that may have characteristics of two generations. However, generally the majority of persons born between a tentative set of dates share many similar characteristics (Rosen, 2010). Table 3.1 has been developed to give an approximation of the generations, their characteristics, and the values of those born in that generation (Codrington, 2008; Pendergast, 2006, 2009; Rosen, 2010).

Table 3.1   Generational Charcteristics

Birth Years	Generation Name(s)	Notable Occurrences, Characteristics, and Values
1901–1924	Lost G.I. Greatest Generation (born)	WW1; technical practice with social mission; civic mindedness; public health; management and family with scientific base; frugal; male and female roles defined with first wave of feminism
1925–1945	Silent Greatest Generation (served in WW2)	WW2; focus on management and thrift as result of decline of world economy from wars and "Great Depression"; hard work; law and order; self sufficient; sacrifice; conformity; modesty; patience
1946–1964	Baby Boomers (their parents were Greatest Generation)	Civil Rights Movement; 1960s social revolution; anti-Vietnam rallies; focus on personal growth and self-expression; expanding consumerism; assassination of J. F. Kennedy; drugs, sex, rock 'n' roll; moon landing
1965–1981	Generation X	Rise of media and consumerism; end of cold war; feminist movement; widespread introduction of contraceptive pill; MTV; undefined/heterogeneous identity; global awareness; grew up as "latch-key kids"
1982–2001	Generation Y Millennials Echo Boomers	Globalization; information age/birth of WWW; use of communication, media, digital technology; increased peer orientation; culturally liberal; boomerang kids; trophy generation; school violence; 9/11 marks end
2002 +	Generation Z iGeneration Homeland Net	Life-long use of communication and technology; expanded use of WWW; instant messaging, text messaging, cell phones, Facebook, Twitter; dreamers; impatient; ADD; individualistic; have helicopter parents

Three generations that comprise a majority of the learners in family life education programs are the Baby Boomers, Generation X, and Millennials, also known as Generation Y. To better understand these three generations some of their general characteristics and values are noted below: (McGregor & Toronyi, 2009; Pendergast, 2006):

- *Baby Boomers* (Born from 1946–1964) value family, education, individualism, change, quality, inspiration and motivational support, conformance to team norms, success, conflict resolution, being open, freedom and choice, personal growth and fulfillment, and a mix of spontaneity and discipline. They try to balance materialism and generosity; are workaholics; are optimistic; need hands-on involvement; like loose structures, temporariness, task forces, and holding meetings; reject authority, but value sensitive authority figures; and work to get ahead and move up the ladder.

- *Generation X* (Born 1965–1981) values independence, fun, challenges, creativity, access to lots of information, specific and focused feedback, and doing things their own way. They are resilient, independent, and economically conservative; have low perceived job security; appreciate directness and being up-front; accept diversity; are not civic minded; reject rules; are self-absorbed, aloof, isolated; perceive friends are not family; have varying interpersonal skills; and will not sacrifice life for work.

- *Millennials (Generation Y)* (Born 1982–2001) value mentoring, nurturance, and guidance; education and skill building; and work as a means to personal fulfillment. They feel special; live for and through technology; are drawn to competence; like positive reinforcement; plan and are goal directed; are civic minded and social activists; celebrate diversity; perceive friends as equal to family; are entrepreneurial and reinvent rules; are naive about how the workplace functions (not work savvy); need supervised environment and structure; are team oriented; and enjoy extreme fun.

The last 25 to 30 years have been a period of an unprecedented transition from an industrial to an information-based culture and economy. Whereas Baby Boomers in general prefer face-to-face or phone communication with many using e-mail regularly, Generation X is more ambiguous and has embraced cell phones, e-mail, and instant messaging. Thus, the alignment of Millennials with the information age has had an enormous impact creating a larger than usual generation gap between Millennials and previous generations (Pendergast, 2009). While prior generations were known as *digital immigrants*, Millennials are known as *digital natives* (Prensky, 2006). *Digital natives* are characterized as operating at "twitch speed" and not at conventional speed, as they employ random access, parallel processing, graphics, and generally get more screen time (television, computer, and phones) than fresh air. In other words they are connected, play-oriented, and graphics focused. They are comfortable with mass communication technologies and engage in online chats with others around the world (Pendergast, 2009). They use many technologies and forms of social media, such as Facebook, Myspace, Skype, instant messaging, text messaging, Instagram, and Twitter.

The *Net* or *iGeneration,* which only began in 2002 (see Table 3.1), has taken this even further and are consuming massive amounts of media on a daily basis. A majority of their waking hours is spent on media and technology, although they are even multi-tasking in their media usage. According to the Nielsen Company, the typical teenager, sends and receives 3,146 text messages per month, while only making and receiving 191 phone calls. They perceive a smart phone as a portable computer to use for social media and texting (Rosen, 2010).

Understanding participants from different generations helps you plan your classes. If the teachers are *digital immigrants*, they need to realize that their students may be *digital natives*. Whereas past generations grew up using newspapers and records albums, Millennials actively use computers and portable media players (e.g., smartphones, tablets, iPods).

For *Millennials,* learning in an ideal world involves having it adapted to their needs, at a time and place they want it, with just enough detail, and on a device they have in front of them. All knowledge is connected to data and each other. Whereas students find, filter, and focus on content, teachers are perceived as guides, facilitators, and coaches (McGee, n.d.). *Digital natives* will respond better to graphics and visuals than to text. They are not just literate, but multi-literate and commonly use reading patterns associated with digital text browsing and scanning for meaning, preferring virtual texts to physical texts (Pendergast, 2010). The use of *tag clouds* (*word clouds*) or visualizations of term frequencies might be a meaningful learning tool. A tag cloud is a visual representation for text data using single words with the importance of each word shown with a font type, weighted font size, or color. They can be used as website navigation aids to tag resources by hyperlinking the term to digital information, such as web pages, photos, or video clips. Teachers have adopted these new technologies by creating Facebook sites for their courses, but can get frustrated having to post class information in more than one location, as well as dealing with students who are multitasking in classrooms by trying to participate in social media and classroom learning simultaneously. Millennials, who have been reared on evolving technologies, may also have little tolerance for lecture-style learning (Prensky, 2001). Using active learning is critical to maximize their learning along with incorporating a "flipped" classroom model. Instructors adopting the flipped classroom, assign electronic class lectures or instructional content as homework, and utilize class time to work through problems, advance concepts, and participate in collaborative learning (Roehl, Reddy, & Shannon, 2013.)

While Millennials are at the leading edge of technology, 91% of adults own some kind of cell phone and 56% use smartphones (Pew Research Center, 2013b; Smith, 2013). Moreover, 59% of all adults use desktop computers and 52% use laptops (Zickuhr, 2011). In other words, Millennials may have had a leading role in technology, but adults of other ages are also engaged in online activities. This has implications for family life educators. An online survey of 2240 parents indicated that 75% of parents reported that the Internet has improved the way they obtain parenting information, although 19.7% reported that parenting websites are difficult to use and 13.1% indicated that they cannot find the types of parenting websites and information that they need (Connell, 2012). Both young and old use the Internet, but may have different skills, goals, needs, devices, and varying amounts of time available for online learning. Even the workforce is affected by the technology practices of Millennials who prefer telecommuting, but have an aversion to using the phone for conversations, which is important in some professions (Permenter, 2013). Not only should we address the characteristics and needs of different generations of people, but we also have to pay attention to how different generations use technology. This gives family life educators a greater opportunity to develop creative methods for reaching learners and give them access to the information that was previously difficult to obtain. To better reach our participants, we need to know them and understand their needs, as well as their technological resources.

Class, Gender, and Race/Ethnicity

Class, gender, and race/ethnicity influence family life through unequal distribution of resources and opportunities. Whatever the class, gender, or race/ethnicity group to which you belong, they all have characteristics of the *Big C* and *little c* of culture. We may perceive what it is like to be in the wealthy class or to be homeless, a cultural minority or majority group, or a person of another gender, but most of us do not know the values, cultural assumptions, nonverbal communications, thought patterns, and cognitive perceptions that comprise the *little c* of these cultural groupings. While this chapter will not go into depth on all the groups that might comprise the participants in your family life education program, a few groups will be highlighted.

Class

Whereas class focuses on the distribution of economic resources and a person or group's relative social position, there is disagreement on the meaning of *class* and how to define it. Often income, occupation, and education level are used as indicators of class, along with marital status, income of spouse and others in the home, and size of household. There are many family groupings related to class, such as families in poverty and homeless families. Poverty reduces the likelihood of marriage and makes the nuclear family difficult to sustain, but the extended network provides services, assistance, and coping support. In families of professionals, family life is often subordinate to the demands of one's profession with corporate relocation being common. Little is known about wealthy families, who often have multiple residences and are connected to a web of institutions. A majority of Americans (53%) self-identify as "middle class," and often maintain this status due to the economic contributions of both partners and the support of social networks that help care for their children (Zinn et al., 2011). Even within the middle class there are four groups (Morin, 2008):

- The Top of the Class—predominantly male, well-educated, and financially secure (35%)

- The Satisfied Middle—disproportionately women and minorities (25%)

- The Struggling Middle—disproportionately old and young; have everything, but money (17%)

- The Anxious Middle—most dissatisfied and discouraged. Enjoy some economic advantages of the Top of the Class, but have many of the bleak perceptions of the Struggling Middle (23%)

While some classes of people and their issues may appear invisible in our culture, their needs should be at the forefront of our thoughts and plans. What are their primary concerns and can family life education be made affordable and accessible to them within their financial, transportation, and time constraints?

Gender

Whereas sex is related to one's biology, gender refers to socially learned attitudes, behaviors, and expectations, as well as social and cultural meanings attached to men and women, which have links to class and race. There are two approaches to view gender. Whereas the *social roles approach* perceives gender differences as roles learned by individuals, the *gendered institutions approach* examines how gender is embedded in our society resulting in advantages and disadvantages in various parts of our social and work realms (Zinn et al., 2011). While Chapters 9, 10, and 11 examine the role of gender with regard to sexuality, marriage/relationships, and parenting content, an activity to examine perceptions of the *Big C* and *little c* of gender in our lives is provided in Box 3.3

Race and ethnicity

The U.S. Census Bureau commonly uses the terms *race* and *ethnicity* to classify the population. Whereas race is a socially defined category based on a presumed common genetic heritage resulting in distinguishing physical characteristics, ethnicity refers to a broader range of affiliation by being culturally distinct on the basis of religion, language, history, national origin, dress, food, and other values (Zinn et al., 2011). [*Note: The Federal Government treats Hispanic origin and race as separate and*

Box 3.3   Gender Diary

Imagine that you wake up one day to discover that you are a member of the other sex with new gender expectations. You could be single, married, or cohabiting.

Write about your activities for that day, how you perceive the world, and how this changes (or does not change). Some questions to get you started might include:

1. How do you feel?

2. How do you feel about your body?

3. How do you spend your day?

4. How do others perceive/interact with you (e.g., friends, family, spouse, significant other, teachers, other students, landlord, the person who serves you in a restaurant)?

Write this paper as if everyone, but you, has always known you as a member of the other sex. In other words, do not write about how "freaked out" your boyfriend/girlfriend (husband/wife) is to find out you are a woman or man.

Write a concluding discussion about the insights you gained. In addition, include what you perceive are the advantages and disadvantages of being the sex that you are and what you perceive are the advantages and disadvantages of being the other sex you became for a day. Why do these perceived advantages and disadvantages exist?

This activity could be used as a small group discussion or an assignment in which the names of the authors may or may not be identifiable.

distinct concepts. In Census surveys, separate questions are asked on Hispanic origin and race. The question on Hispanic origin asks respondents if they are of Hispanic, Latino, or Spanish origin (Lofquist, Lugaila, O'Connell, & Feitz, 2012).] The U.S. population will continue to become more ethnically diverse in the next 50 years. In fact, projections for 2012–2060 suggest that the U.S. will become a *plurality nation* in which the non-Hispanic white population will continue to be the largest single group, but no group will be in the majority (U.S. Census Bureau, 2012c). The U.S. Census Bureau (2013) also announced that Asians were the nation's fastest-growing race or ethnic group in 2012 with a population increase of 2.9%. More than 60% of this growth in the Asian population has come from international migration. By comparison, the Hispanic population grew by 2.2%, which was primarily due to a natural increase (births minus deaths). Hispanics remain our nation's second largest group (behind non-Hispanic whites), representing about 17% of the total population. The percentage of the total population by race and Hispanic origin in 2012 was as follows:

- White alone 78%
- Non-Hispanic White alone 63%
- Hispanic of any race 17%
- Black alone 13%
- Asian alone 5.1%
- Two or more races 2.4%
- American Indian and Alaska Native 1.2%
- Native Hawaiian and Other Pacific Islander .2% (U.S. Census Bureau, 2012c)

[*Note: White Americans are people of the U.S. who perceive themselves as White. Non-Hispanic Whites or White, Not Hispanic or Latino (a subset of Whites) are people in the U.S., as defined by the Census Bureau, who are of the White race and are not of Hispanic or Latino origin/ethnicity* (Lofquist et al., 2012).]

Race and ethnicity configurations within the U.S. population are in flux, which means that educators need to pay attention to the changing demographics, strengths, and needs of families. Many characteristics of racial-ethnic families are culturally unique, such as how members relate to each other, perceive family, spend leisure time, and worship, as well as their forms of entertainment, language use, and customs (Zinn et al., 2011).

Because a single chapter cannot convey all the information needed to understand the characteristics of multiple cultural groups, a few highlights have been noted below along with our recommendation to review other sources, such as Ballard and Taylor's (2012) book on *Family Life Education with Diverse Populations.* This book provides insight about how family life educators can meet the needs of eleven diverse populations.

Black and African American Families are terms that are often used interchangeably and will be used to note those persons with African and non-African black racial characteristics. The African American heritage emphasizes collectivism and importance of groups of people working together for the well-being of the family through raising children and pooling resources. Black families remain strong and resilient with extended family support networks as a major asset. Religion and spirituality are important to provide hope and resources to families similar to an extended kin network. These resources include financial and emotional support, caregiving, clothing, cleaning, and transportation, along with encouragement and advice (Barnes, 2001; Hamilton-Mason, Hall, & Everett, 2009; Jarrett, Jefferson, & Kelly, 2010). Work and educational achievement are valued highly, as education is perceived as a pathway to success. While black families face certain challenges, such as economic hardships, unemployment, violence, drug abuse, inadequate education, and broken family relationships, it is important for family life educators to focus on their strengths. Family life educators can partner with community leaders and the faith community to assist with the planning, implementation, and delivery of culturally relevant programs (Baugh & Coughlin, 2012).

Hispanic and Latino Families are both terms that are used interchangeably, but there is a difference in that *Hispanic* refers to a person with ties to Spain, whereas *Latino* refers more to persons of Latin American origin, although there is an overlap between these two groups. Hispanic/Latino Americans are racially diverse and therefore constitute an ethnic category, rather than a race. Latinos value educational attainment, which may be related to level of acculturation or the level to which persons have developed a balance between their traditional culture and the majority culture. Family strengths include *familismo* (a strong emphasis and connection to family members and willingness to help them); *simpatia* (politeness and importance of pleasant interactions); *personalismo* (personal space and closeness expressed by shaking hands, hugs, a little kiss, and touching); *machismo* (males are patriarchal figures in the family who provide for and protect family members); and *marianismo* (females are sexually conservative and focused on children and family) (Falicov, 2007; HHMI, n.d.). Religion is also important to Latinos, especially Catholicism, which may be a factor in their low divorce rate (approximately 30% lower than the general population). Challenges include immigration, language barriers, transportation, and financial support that can be used to provide opportunities for family life educators to intervene and impact Latino families. Because there is considerable diversity in the Latino culture, programming should be developed for the characteristics of the cultural groups being served. Rather than using programs developed for the majority culture, family life educators should use some of the programs that have been developed or adapted for the Hispanic/Latino culture (Schvaneveldt & Behnke, 2012).

Asian Families are quite diverse with the five largest immigrant groups coming from China, India, the Philippines, Vietnam, and Korea, respectively. Some came to the U.S. voluntarily as students and later sponsored additional family members, while others came because of political and/or unstable conditions in their countries of origin. Asian families value educational attainment and employment with 49% of Asian Americans holding professional positions (Fong, 2008). However, some who were educated in their home countries have been unable to find employment in the U.S. and had to take lower status positions due to language barriers. The resultant financial stress has impacted family interactions in which certain Asian immigrant males may display punitive behaviors toward their wives or children (Kim, Lau, & Chang, 2006; Min, 2006). Family structures are often patriarchal, involve the extended family, and emphasize harmonious interpersonal relationships. In general, the family unit is valued along with family loyalty. Due to the periodic adjustments and changes of foreign-born Asian family members, they have learned to be highly resilient. Asian families desire a stable family for their children, but tend to keep family issues private within the family system and do not want to disclose any problems that would disgrace the family. Thus, they are more likely to become involved in family life education that is focused on the parent-child relationships, rather than marriage relationships, and to participate in small groups in which they can ask questions that would not be perceived as challenging an authority figure (Adler, 2003). Since Asians commonly perceive that family-related workshops are associated with mental illness, the anonymity of online programs, which are culturally sensitive and linguistically relevant, may be a viable option for Asian participants (Hwang, 2012).

American Indian/Alaska Native (AI/AN) Families are diverse, as there are 562 federally recognized tribes in the U.S., as well as numerous other tribes that are not federally recognized (BigFoot, Willmon-Haque, & Braden, 2008). Population estimates suggest that 60% to 65% of American Indians live in urban areas, but that may be skewed because recent economic difficulties have resulted in a migration back to reservations where the tribal communities and extended families can provide support (Hildebrand, Phenice, Gray, & Hines, 2008). Population estimates may also vary because in some tribes American Indian women who marry non-American Indian men are removed of their tribal status (Krouse & Howard, 2009).

The primary strengths of AI/AN families are their extended family structures, humor, and resilience (Hildebrand et al., 2008; LaFromboise, Hoyt, Oliver, & Whitbeck, 2006; Stiffman, Brown, Freedenthal, House, Ostmann, & Yu, 2007). While tribes have their unique features, a common characteristic is their sense of humor and telling of stories. Many AI/AN youth avoid problem behaviors; engage in prosocial behaviors, such as interacting with family and helping at home; and participate in school and community events. Resiliency in youth has evolved due to positive self-esteem, maternal warmth, family structure, and a sense of direction and tenacity (LaFromboise et al., 2006).

Challenges faced by AI/AN families include trauma from many sources (cultural, historical, intergenerational) and can range from a single event to multiple victimizations resulting from various forms of trauma over the years (Bigfoot, 2008). Some current issues faced by AI/AN families include sudden infant death syndrome (SIDS) in northern states (NICHD, 2010); intimate partner violence (Weahkee, 2010); and various health issues, such as diabetes, cardiovascular disease, substance abuse, psychological distress, limited leisure-time physical activities, and unmet medical needs (Barnes, Adams, & Powell-Griner, 2010).

Family life educators need to get tribal support and build on family strengths while paying attention to barriers to participation including time, child care, transportation, and weather. Building trust is critical. Modes of learning include storytelling, shared experiences, observation, participation, discussion, and offering information either directly or indirectly with educators who are respectful, humble, and do not talk too much (Perrote & Feinman, 2012).

See the activity in Box 3.4 in order to better understand intercultural awareness. BARNGA is a simulation game depicting how cultural groups may have difficulties assimilating into other groups, especially if they have language difficulties.

Box 3.4   *BARNGA*

BARNGA is a simulation game about inter-cultural awareness, that can be used to promote the realization that various cultures perceive things differently and play by different rules, requiring family life educators to understand and reconcile these differences in order to function effectively in cross-cultural groupings (Thiagarajan & Thiagarajan, 2011).

BARNGA involves a group task of playing a card game. After each group understands the rules of the game (which vary for each group) and participates in a few rounds to understand how to play the game, the instructions are removed. After that, the only word that can be spoken is "*BARNGA*," although they are permitted to gesture or draw pictures with no written words. After each round, the winner and loser from each group move to another group and the game resumes (Pittenger & Heimann, 1998).

The success lies in the discussion after the game in which a variety of questions can be posed, such as asking them about their reactions while playing the game and before and after the rules changed, when they realized that something was different, how they dealt with it, and how not being able to speak contributed to their feelings? What are their thoughts about working with people from other groups who behaved differently and why are cross-cultural communication and understanding important?

Family Structure

There are numerous configurations of families within our culture who, because of their family structure, have special needs. Some of these living arrangements include unmarried parents, families with adopted children including transracial or transcultural adoptions, transnational families, foster care families, grandparents raising grandchildren, multigenerational families, older children (or so-called "boomerang" children) still living at home, and mixed-race families. Changes in family structure are closely related to changes in poverty (Cancian & Reed, 2009). Three family groups we will briefly highlight are single-parent families, stepfamilies, and same-sex or transgender-parent families, which are all dealing with economic issues.

Single-Parent Families constitute about a third of family households that contain children. Whereas 84% of the single-parent families are headed by mothers, 16% are headed by fathers with a 11% increase in single-mother households from 2000 to 2010 compared to a 27% increase in single-father households (Lofquist, Lugaila, O'Connell, & Feliz, 2012; U.S. Census Bureau, 2012a). A single parent does not live with a spouse or partner, but has daily responsibilities for raising a child or children and is considered the primary caregiver. Between 2005 and 2011, the percentage of children living in single-parent families increased from 32% to 35%--an increase of 3 million children (Annie E. Casey Foundation, 2013a). Single parent families can result from separation, divorce, child abuse or neglect, adoption, death of a partner, or being an unmarried parent. While some single parents have never been married, most are divorced and report more negative life events, greater social isolation, more difficulties with parenting, more daily hassles, and lower levels of psychological well-being than when they were married (Amato,

2000). Single parents have new responsibilities, such as providing for their families, building new support networks, and incorporating aspects of the other parent into their parenting endeavors (Peterson, Hennon, & Knox, 2008).

Divorce is often associated with behavioral, psychological, and academic problems among the children. It is not just the marital dissolution, but also the number of transitions (e.g., multiple divorces, relocations, cohabitations of parents, and remarriages) that have affected the child's stability (Amato, 2010). However, children's adjustment after divorce can be facilitated by harmonious family relationships by both residential and nonresidential parents who are positively involved in their children's lives. Children benefit when they have close and supportive relationships with nonresidential parents, but more important than social contact is the involvement of both parents in authoritative interactions with their children, such as talking to them about their problems, providing emotional support, assisting with homework and everyday problems, setting rules, and monitoring behavior (Amato, Kane, & James, 2011). While co-parenting can be a challenge, some parents use technology (phone, e-mail, and texting) to share information when living in separate households and needing to communicate asynchronously (messages are sent and received intermittently over periods of time). For couples in effective co-parenting relationships, communication makes it easier to plan and make joint decisions about their children. Contentious parents often use technology to reduce conflicts with co-parents, withhold information, limit the co-parent's input into child-rearing decisions, and influence the behavior of the co-parent (Ganong, Coleman, Feistman, Jamison, & Markham, 2012).

Whereas couples generally negotiate responsibilities for work, caregiving, and housekeeping, single parents are responsible for all of these tasks resulting in work-family conflict. Single mothers strive to be good mothers and good employees, but may have little education and limited work experience, resulting in a nontraditional work schedule within the 24-hour a day/seven day a week economy (Zinn et al., 2011). Many single mothers do not have the skills needed to manage the nonstandard hours that accompany the types of jobs they can find. Without reliable transportation and adequate child care, they find it difficult to maintain stable employment. Higher levels of parental education are strongly associated with better outcomes for children, however in 2011, 15% of children lived in households headed by an adult without a high school diploma (Annie E. Casey Foundation, 2013a). This work-family conflict contributes to poverty, unstable living arrangements, and family stress. In general, single parents are "time challenged" with their multifaceted roles and the lack of a "back-up" parent.

While single parents are often reported to be disadvantaged and do less well than two-parent families, there are different kinds of single-parent families, such as a teen mother or a mature professional who is a single parent by choice and design. In some families, a parent may be cohabiting with the father of the child or in a visiting relationship when parents date, but do not co-reside (Osborne, 2005). Additionally, using family structure to define single parenthood does not portray the processes that occur in parent-child relationships. When examining stable single mother-child relationships, it was found that mothers and children characterized their relationship as highly intense, exclusive, and interdependent. Because of limited resources, there were shifting dynamics of power and dependence where children adopted an ethic of care, although mothers worked to maintain boundaries (Nixon, Greene, & Hogan, 2012). Further attention is needed regarding father-child relationships because of the increasing percentage of fathers who are single-custodial parents.

While it is difficult for single parents to find the time to engage in family life or parent education classes, they can get information through pediatricians' or family physicians' offices; parents, friends and relatives; and mass media, such as TV, books, magazines, and pamphlets. In addition, parents, relatives, and friends can provide not only support, but also information. In a recent study, the top three sources of information for single parents were books (94%), Internet (84%), and family (81%) (Radley & Randolph, 2009). Single parents, who are generally younger, more vulnerable, and digitally adept, were more likely to use the Internet for parenting support and information than married couples, who may turn to their spouse instead. Thus, single parents need diverse sources of information and may benefit from online websites, programs, and webinars that they can schedule into their hectic lives.

Stepfamilies are families in which one or both adult partners bring children from a previous relationship. Terminology can be an issue for some families and professionals. The term *stepfamily* is problematic to some because of stereotypes of "wicked stepmothers" from fairy tales about Cinderella and Hansel and Gretel, along with Shakespearean plays, but it is the term of choice because it is consistent with the naming of other family types as defined by parent-child relationships. While some prefer the term *blended families*, it provides unrealistic expectations that a new family will quickly "blend" and mesh together to form a harmonious family group. Thus, this terminology may make some aspects of adjustment more difficult (NSRC, 2013). Frequently, stepfamilies do not blend, so if you use cooking phrases you may try to "combine or fold gently." Another term that is used is *reconstituted families,* but this name is perceived as synonymous with "rehydrated fruit" or the re-creation of something that previously existed (Weston, 1994). Other terms that have been used are combined, merged, remarried, extended, or expanded families. Children in stepfamilies are referred to as siblings (biologically related); *stepsiblings* (related through the marriage of their parents); *half siblings* (share one biological parent); *mutual children* (child born to the remarried couple); *residential stepchildren* (live with the remarried couple more than half the time); and *nonresidential stepchildren* (live with the remarried couple less than half the time.

Because the U.S. Census Bureau discontinued providing estimates of marriage, divorce, and remarriages, it is difficult to estimate the number of stepfamilies. However, information from the 2009 Current Population Study Report estimated that 12.3% of American children under 18 years of age and living in a two-parent household were part of a stepfamily (Kreider & Ellis, 2011). In addition, 42% of adults have at least one step relative with 30% indicating they have a step- or half sibling. When examining people under the age of 30, 52% report having a step relative and 44% report having a step- or half sibling (Pew Research Center, 2011). Most adults who have step relatives perceive a stronger sense of obligation to their biological family members than to their step relatives.

For adults, new partners are thrilling, but if there are children from a previous relationship there is minimal time to adjust and build a couple relationship because of the demands and needs of their children. One of the most difficult aspects of stepfamilies is the parenting of children who experienced loss and change with the addition of a stepparent into their lives. Forming a stepfamily with young children, who thrive on cohesive family relationships, may be easier than with adolescent children, who may be seeking to disengage from the family to form their own identity (Kemp, Segal, & Robinson, 2013).

Some challenges for stepparents include differences in parenting, discipline, and lifestyle, which can be frustrating for the children. Common differences in stepfamilies include (1) age differences in children in which step siblings may be close in age resulting in changes in roles, responsibilities, and birth order; (2) parental inexperience if a stepparent has never been a parent; (3) changes in family relationships especially if both parents remarry partners with existing families so children have different roles in each family; (4) difficulty in accepting a new parent especially if a child has spent a long time in a single-parent family; (5) coping with the demands of others when dealing with custody considerations and arrangements for family events, vacations, parties, or trips; (6) changes in family traditions as most families have different ideas about how holidays and special events should be celebrated; and (7) parenting insecurities of stepparents who may be anxious about how they compare to the biological parents (Kemp et al., 2013). Stepfamilies need clear and safe boundaries, especially when disciplining children. It is important to determine the role each parent will play in raising their respective children and dealing with household rules. Keeping all parents involved is essential among biological parents and stepparents, along with open and frequent communication. Creating new family routines and rituals helps to unite family members. While focusing on the needs of the children in a stepfamily is important, building a strong marital bond is also critical. If children see love, respect, and open communication, they will feel more secure. To better understand the complexity of stepfamilies, see the activity in Box 3.5.

With the increasing prevalence of stepfamilies and biases toward "first families," stepfamily functioning is an important topic for family life education seminars for professionals that deal with families (e.g., teachers, school and family services personnel, counselors, psychologists, and attorneys). Some topics to include in these programs are the complexities of stepfamilies and how they operate differently from "first families;" inter-household relationships; empathy in adjusting to different family histories along with negotiation of roles and rules; the role of children in initiating or exacerbating conflicts; and navigating marital partner and parenting transitions, noting that relationships evolve slowly and often dyadically rather than as a family unit (Adler-Baeder, 2002). There are few family life education classes available for stepfamilies and many leaders do not initially have training in family life education, but have had personal experience in stepfamilies (Adler-Baeder, Robertson, Schramm, 2010). In a study of programs for stepfamilies, key common topics included understanding the unique characteristics of stepfamilies, building an effective stepparent-stepchild relationship, maintaining a cooperative co-parenting relationship, and couple relationship skills. When recruit-

---

Box 3.5   Changes in Family Structure and Complexity

Create several small groups of 3 to 7 members depending on the number of students in your class. This may result in 4 to 6 family groups.

These groups will become hypothetical families (e.g., intact nuclear families, extended families, and single parent families) with various assigned family incomes. Each family group will take a brief period of time to bond by creating a family name and describing some of the characteristics of their family, such as whether or not one or both parents work and in what kind of job/position are they employed; ages of the family members; the kind of house (number of bedrooms and bathrooms); chores for family members; and a favorite family activity, meal, and holiday including their traditions.

After the family groups are established, randomly assign each of them a difficulty such as divorce, remarriage, or the formation of a stepfamily. Some of the parents and children will be repositioned to join other family groups or have a family that is reduced in size.

Ask these new family groups to decide on a family name, if changed, and determine custody and visitation of children. How will they negotiate shared use of household space; expectations about chores; and participation in activities, rituals, meals, and holidays.

After discussing some of these changes, have the students share their feelings regarding the dissolution of their original families and changes in rules, roles, incomes, available household space, rituals, and holidays. How did they negotiate the incongruent life styles between their two families? What insights did they gain about the complexity of family changes?

---

ing low-income participants for classes for stepfamilies, personal contacts were the most effective strategies along with a curriculum that addressed the unique needs of stepfamilies. Incentives such as meals, monetary support, and prizes, as well as children's participation and their enthusiasm for attending, positively affected retention (Skogrand, Reck, Higginbotham, Adler-Baeder, & Dansie, 2010).

Lesbian, Gay, Bisexual, and Transgender (LGBT) Families are often invisible in our culture. They have a member(s) whose sexual orientation is not wholly congruent with the sex that was pronounced at birth and may choose not to self-disclose. While *heterosexual* persons are attracted to people of a different sex, *gays* and *lesbians* are attracted to persons of the same sex, and *bisexual persons* are attracted to someone of both a different and the same sex (Maurer, 2012). *Transgender* is a general term that groups together people whose gender identity and/or expression is different from their birth sex. A transgender identity is not based on medical procedures and does not imply any specific form of sexual orientation, as transgender persons may identify themselves as heterosexual, gay, bisexual, or asexual (Pew Research Center, 2013a). While there is no precise determination of the size of LGBT population, U.S. Demographers estimate that 4 to 7 percent of adults are LGBT (Krane, Witeck, & Coombs, 2011). However, data are difficult to obtain because they exclude single gays and lesbians, some same sex couples who reside together, and those who do not self-identify as being transgender. Moreover, data for transgender persons are not often collected. The National Center for Transgender Equality (2009) estimates that between 780,859 and 3,123435 (.25% to 1%) people in the U.S. are transgender. Whereas approximately 37% of LGBT identified adults have had a child at some time in their lives, about 6 million children and adults have an LGBT parent (Gates, 2013). In the past decade there has been a surge in the amount of research conducted on LGBT families, however, even with the use of the umbrella term "LGBT," the majority of these studies focused on lesbian parenting to the exclusion of other family types (Biblarz & Savci, 2010). LGBT family systems are vulnerable to many negative situations, such as job discrimination, harassment, isolation, stress, suicide, violence, and homelessness, as well as estrangement from family, friends, and places of worship (D'Augelli, 2002; Garofalo, Wolf, Kessel, Palfrey, & DuRant, 1998; Pew Research Center, 2013a).

A special aspect of LGBT families is their diversity, experiences, and unique legal status regarding discrimination and economic benefits (Maurer, 2012). They also have some family challenges related to negotiating family of origin concerns and issues of estrangement, building families of choice, and navigating in a complex world of peoples' reactions and assumptions of LGBT persons. Nevertheless, the wellbeing of children of LGBT parents is unrelated to parental sexual orientation, so children of LGBT parents are just as likely to flourish as children of heterosexual parents (Paige, 2005). LGBT families are perceived as resilient because of having to negotiate stressful situations throughout their lives. Transgender parents face the critical issue of disclosing their transition to their children. It is suggested that they be open and honest, discuss it in age-appropriate ways, and have continuing conversations (rather than just one), regarding this transition (Hines, 2006).

There are few family life education programs specifically for LGBT individuals and families and they may be hard to find. Checking with support organizations, mass media magazines for LGBT parents, and LGBT community centers is recommended, as well as engaging with LGBT leaders in the community (Maurer, 2012). Contacting groups can be helpful, such as *Parents, Family, and Friends of Lesbians and Gays* (*PFLAG.org*) or *Children of Lesbians and Gays Everywhere* (*COLAGE.org*), which includes their *Kids of Trans* (KOT) program. Since confidentiality is an issue, online courses may be a viable option. Educators should know general definitions and terminology; provide accurate, useful, and nonjudgmental content; establish a safe place (e.g., supportive, confidential, and knowledgeable); and incorporate appropriate terms (e.g., partner, parents), pronouns (e.g., based on the transgender person's gender expression and preference), and non-gendered names (e.g., Chris, Pat, Leslie) into examples (Maurer, 2012). By attending to the social perceptions (e.g., stigma, discrimination, economic strain) and familial issues (e.g., boundary ambiguity, social support) of LGBT individuals and families, family life educators can provide meaningful programs for this cultural group.

Families with Special Needs

While many families have special needs, two examples are highlighted below. One deals with families of children with disabilities, although this is a broad topic because children have many different kinds of disabilities that deal with physical movement, emotional issues, and sensory inabilities, such as sight or sound. The other category highlighted is families with an incarcerated family member. There are multiple issues related to incarcerated persons, their children, and their extended families.

Families of Children with Disabilities have unique parenting challenges. There has been considerable research on the stress associated with children's emotional, developmental, and behavioral disorders, which can have a substantial impact on the lives of family members (MacInnes, 2008). In the U.S. it is reported that 17% of children under the age of 18 have developmental disabilities, with males having twice the prevalence of developmental disabilities compared to females (Boyle et al., 2011; CDC, 2009). These disabilities can range from mild (e.g., asthma) to severe (e.g., cerebral palsy with extensive neurological complications). About 6.5 million American school-age children have a disability and 4.3 million have a disability that is seriously limiting (Hogan, 2012). The U.S. depends on families to provide for their medical care along with access to education in order to maximize their potential and equip them for adult life. However, the family's financial security, the parents' relationship, and the needs of other children in the home can all be stretched to the limit. Both mothers and fathers of children with disabilities report significantly greater amounts of parental and marital stress compared to parents of children without disabilities. In fact, couples that are together when their child is born are more likely to divorce than other parents (Hogan, 2012). One-third of children with disabilities live in single-parent families, with 30% of families raising a child with a disability living in poverty.

Mothers often become the primary caregivers, whereas fathers are more likely to work longer hours, have two jobs, or continue working beyond retirement age to support their families. While we often focus on mothers because of their greater caregiving roles, fathers of disabled children also experience parenting stress, stress from family life events and changes, and a reduction in life satisfaction compared to fathers who do not have disabled children (Darling, Senatore, & Strachan, 2011). Siblings grow up in homes with fewer resources and greater expenses and while they learn to assist with personal care that results in developing more helpful attitudes and tolerance, siblings are at risk for health problems. They are three times more likely to experience poor health compared to children in homes where there is no child with a disability (Hogan, 2012).

While the birth of a child with a disability is often stressful (see Box 3.6 on the following page), the stress changes during the life cycle. As children with disabilities mature and develop over time, their families face multiplying needs, services, treatments, and costs. Additionally, their families are continually engaged with multiple systems (e.g., medical, legal, educational) and involved in Individualized Educational Program (IEP) meetings, which along with the parents may include teachers, school district personnel, and guidance counselors; psychologists or educational evaluators to explain test results; related professionals providing various types of therapy; and social workers, case managers, and others that the family wants to involve. While the IEP team has an annual review of each student, any member can call a special meeting of the team. All of this adds to the complexity of family life and the potential for feeling overwhelmed. Moreover, when children with disabilities reach important developmental milestones, parental stress is heightened because of the reminder of their children's unique needs and unmet potential (Bernier, 1990). Parents of older children with disabilities face significant challenges finding suitable training and employment for their adult children. Many

---

Box 3.6   Parenting a Handicapped Child

To better understand the culture of parents who give birth to a handicapped child, this analogy can be helpful.

There was a young woman who was going to France after she graduated from college. She took classes in French and studied about French history, geography, music, culture, and cooking. She had a Facebook friend in France, studied books about the best places to visit in France, bought clothes that would work in the French climate. She prepared and prepared and prepared. Finally the big day arrived and she boarded a plane to fly to Paris. However, en route to France there was a major transportation strike that resulted in an indefinite closing of airports, railroad stations, bus stations, and roads. So, the plane landed in Italy instead. She did not know the language, culture, or customs.

How do you think she feels?

When a child is born with a handicap, it is as if the parents plan to go to France and end up going to Italy instead. (Source unknown)

---

of these parents continue to provide support for their adult child with disabilities, but wonder who will provide that support when they are no longer able to do so (Hogan, 2012).

While there are many challenges to raising special needs children with several stressful demands, one cannot assume that this challenge is largely a negative experience. Some families perceive a positive benefit from parenting a child with disabilities. Fathers have reported learning some unique aspects of rearing their child with disabilities and that learning new information from their child's condition was rewarding. Many families report being closer; resilient; and engaged in more shared activities, such as games, television, and meals; and had a renewed outlook on life (Darling et al., 2011; Hogan, 2012).

Family life educators need to focus on the strengths of families with special needs children and understand how stress influences the entire family system and ecosystem. Each type of disability and its severity comes with its own unique challenges. At times educators may need to provide information about coping with stress, financial management, the couple relationship, and/or raising a child with special needs. Some parents, who may be isolated from the outside world and overwhelmed with childcare, may want some respite from daily tasks in order to find a balance in their lives. However, other parents may not only feel burdened by work responsibilities and competing demands to provide for the family, but also perceive personal challenges in raising a child with disabilities. Thus, family life education courses might provide what each parent needs, such as stress release for mothers and father-child sessions so fathers can interact with other fathers about their personal challenges and learn about parenting a child with disabilities, while sharing bonding experiences with their children and doing things together (Darling et al., 2011). In other words, family life educators may need to focus on mother, father, couple, and sibling needs separately or jointly in order to best provide for the family system.

Families with an Incarcerated Family Member are dealing with a complex and stressful situation. The term incarceration is used as an umbrella term related to incarceration in either a *jail* or *prison*. Whereas a *jail* is a local correctional facility used to confine persons before or after a judicial decision or a sentencing for primarily misdemeanors (usually one year or less); a *prison* sentence is mostly for felonies (usually more than one year) (Bureau of Justice Statistics, 2010). With over 1 in 100 adults currently behind bars, the U.S. rate of incarceration is one of the highest in the world (Warren, 2008). Since 60% (over 2 million) of these imprisoned men and women are parents of minor-age children and approximately 2% (1.7 million) of U.S. children have at least one parent in prison, there are major implications for their family well-being (Glaze & Maruschak, 2008; Hairston, 2002; Mumola, 2000). Most incarcerated parents report having some form of contact with their children either by telephone (71%), mail (76.5%), or personal visits (49.6%). If there is a positive relationship prior to being incarcerated, then continued contact and support is likely (Loper, Carlson, Levitt, & Scheffel, 2009). Moreover, the family of a returning prisoner acts as a buffering agent for a newly-released prisoner and has a major impact on post-release success or failure (Naser & Visher, 2006).

Family challenges include financial losses, such as the costs of maintaining a household, loss of income from the imprisoned parent, legal fees for criminal defense, maintaining contact during imprisonment, potential costs to relatives who take care of the children, and maintaining the prisoner while in prison (Hairston, 2002). Prisoners' families and children also have to deal with feelings of shame and social stigma. To help with this situation, *Sesame Street* has developed a video and toolkit to explain incarceration to younger children (*Sesame Street*, 2013). Upon re-entry into society, there are additional challenges of supporting a family member who has been recently released, such as providing financial and emotional support, which can result in financial strain and increased anxiety for family members.

A primary concern is the care of prisoners' children. When parents go to prison, children often live with relatives who may be elderly. There is a marked absence of men in their lives, along with limited financial resources. Many grandparents become caregivers, but they are elderly, may have health problems, and were not planning on new childcare responsibilities. Furthermore, the children's custodians may limit or deny communication, so incarcerated parents fear their children will be taken from them or someone else will replace them in their children's lives (Hairston, 2002). In fact, incarcerated parents who have children within state care have reasons to be concerned that the legal parent-child bond will be severed. Approximately 10% of children with incarcerated mothers and 2% of children with incarcerated fathers are in foster care with an average stay of 3.9 years (Annie E. Casey Foundation, 2008; Bouchet, 2008). Children of incarcerated parents are more likely to "age out" of foster care and less likely to reunify with their parents, get adopted, enter into subsidized guardianship, or go into independent living (Annie E. Casey Foundation, 2008).

Children of incarcerated parents are at increased risk for internalizing behaviors (e.g., depression, anxiety, withdrawal) and externalizing behaviors (e.g., delinquency, substance abuse), along with cognitive delays, school difficulties, and increased risk for insecure attachment (Eddy & Poehlmann, 2010). Incarcerated parents often had difficult childhoods, did not graduate from high school, and had a history of physical or sexual abuse, along with substance abuse and mental health issues that could interfere with their parenting abilities (Glaze & Maruschak, 2008). Thus, it is unknown whether parental incarceration is the cause of the child's problems or occurs in combination with other risk factors. There are many things to consider, such as the trauma the child experienced, the age of the child, the parent that is incarcerated, the child's living situation, the child's caregiver and the quality of that relationship, the effect of incarceration upon family income, and if the child has contact with the parent. Given the potential for long-term risks and consequences for these fragile families, evidence-informed prevention and intervention efforts are needed (Shlafer, Gerrity, Ruhland, & Wheeler, 2013).

While family life educators are professionally prepared to advocate for and develop multifaceted family programs, the term "family life education" has been rarely applied to the programs and initiatives designed for inmates and their families. Programs related to life skills, anger management, and parent education are offered with four categories of parenting programs: parenting classes for incarcerated parents, parent-child visitation programs, mentoring children of incarcerated parents, and school and community-based support groups for children (Mulroy, 2012). Some barriers include pre-prison damage to relationships; refusal to contact family members; children's unavailability due to being unaware of the incarceration; and visitation challenges, such as distance to the prison, costs of visitation, and the prison context regarding the number and type of contacts, visitor "pat downs," and conditions of meeting areas (Arditti, 2008; Naser & Visher, 2006). Promoting "family friendly" visitation programs in a less restrictive environment with staff support can have positive effects for the person incarcerated, as well as their children and caregivers. These programs can result in a higher frequency of parent-child contact, improved relationships, and higher levels of parental satisfaction and esteem. While family life educators would be professionally qualified, they also need to be strong, determined, and confident individuals in order to teach these participants (e.g., correctional staff, volunteers, inmates, and family members) about parenting from a distance, stress and coping, and developmental characteristics of children (Mulroy, 2012). However, before beginning any program related to incarcerated individuals and their families, a needs assessment is essential.

SUMMARY

Within this chapter on understanding your audience in family life education, we have outlined the steps in conducting a needs assessment, paid attention to the role of culture and the *Big C* and *little c* of cultural paradigms, and examined the characteristics and needs of various groups based on developmental stages and generations. We have also included some brief comments about a few different family groups including their strengths, challenges, and suggestions for family life educators. As you can see, there is much to consider prior to teaching a diverse group of students.

It would be impossible to know everything about multiple cultural groups, so to emphasize that point the following activity might be helpful. Blow up several balloons of different colors (with multiple balloons of each color) and have them in the classroom as students enter. Have the participants stand as you toss these balloons to them saying that a certain color designates a particular group, such as black families, Asian families, Hispanic/Latino families, American Indian/Native American families, LGBT families, families of military service persons, single-parent families, families of incarcerated persons, and families of disabled children. Although all class members are trying to keep these multiple balloons in the air, it is logical that some will drop to the floor. Leave them on the floor and later discuss how it felt to keep all the balloons in the air at once and how it felt to have some "slip through the cracks" and fall to the floor. This is indicative of simultaneously dealing with multiple cultures. As hard as you try, you will not know all of the *little c* issues of cultures and may not be able to totally meet everyone's needs as you would desire, but it is important to work toward this goal.

Answer to the question on p. 66: What items are generalizations vs. stereotypes—Numbers 2, 4, 5, 8, and 9 are stereotypes.

QUESTIONS AND ISSUES FOR DISCUSSION

1. Think of a time when you worked with someone of another culture or age group. What things did you or they do that facilitated a good working relationship?
2. What are examples of cultural groups in the U.S. and what do you know about them? (e.g., family, work, school, church, clubs, classes)
3. What is a stereotype about your race or ethnicity that displeases you and why?
4. What are some generalizations and stereotypes related to various cultural groups?
5. What are some common myths and stereotypes of stepmothers, stepfathers, and stepfamilies?
6. What stepfamily issues have you seen emerge with the people you know living in this type of family?
7. How well do you fit the characteristics listed for your generational group?
8. Would you like to switch genders? Why or why not?
9. What single parents have you known and how did they manage their roles?
10. How would you handle a situation when some balloons (people of different backgrounds) "drop to the floor" and you could not handle all the various cultural issues that you are presented?

ACTIVITIES

1. Search the Internet for popular articles on different generations (e.g., Baby Boomers, Generation X, Millennials/Generation Y, Net Generation).
2. Choose an ethnic group from your community to research in the library and on the Internet, looking particularly at marriage, family experiences, and customs.

Then interview three or four persons from that ethnic group. Using the Family Life Education Framework in Appendix A, choose one of the categories (e.g., interpersonal relationships or families in society). Formulate a set of interview questions about the category across the lifespan that will help you examine how the chosen ethnic group experiences the developmental tasks articulated under that category.

3. Discuss how would you conduct a needs assessment for a parenting class (e.g., stepfamilies, single parents, incarcerated parents) using different methods (e.g., survey, interview, focus group, or other creative ideas)? What generally can you learn about the participants (e.g., developmental needs, abilities, learning styles, and unique characteristics)?

4. Discuss the felt needs that were identified through the assessment process. What other needs (ascribed, future, developmental) should also be addressed in the program?

5. Watch a television program in a language that you do not speak. What do you think occurred in this program? What cues did you use to make your observations? How accurate do you think your observations were?

6. What do you think people from other countries perceive of American values, behaviors, and culture?

4

Settings in Family Life Education

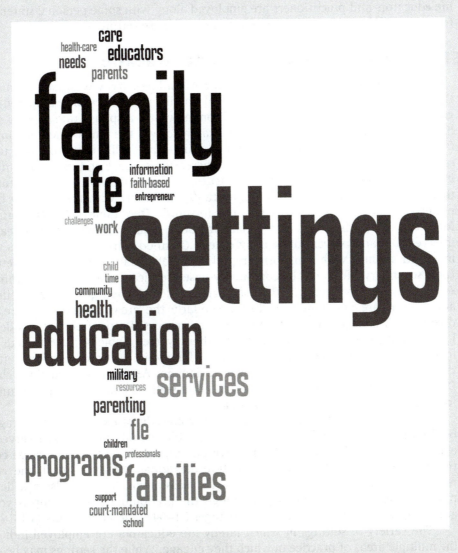

While the *Domains of Family Practice Model* sought to examine the *Why, What, When, For whom*, and *How* of family life education, one element that was not in the model was where family life education exists (Myers-Walls et al., 2011). The obvious reason is that family life education (FLE) not only occurs in numerous settings, but also the potential for family life education venues is endless. The variety of settings in which family life education is offered creates both challenges and opportunities. Family life education needs to relate to people where they live, work, and spend their time, such as schools, faith-based and medical institutions, and communities. However, each setting has its own expectations and limitations that need to be recognized. In order to understand the settings in which family life education occurs, we will give some information about the various settings in which family life educators and practitioners are employed along with some personal statements from family life educators who work in some of these settings.

Diverse Settings in Family Life Education

Where do family life educators work? An online survey was used to analyze the professional practice of 522 Certified Family Life Educators compared to a group of 396 noncertified family practitioners with a response rate of 47% (Darling et al., 2009). One of the elements examined was the employment settings of family life educators. It was important to profile family life educators due to the ongoing evolution of the profession and increasing student and academic interest in FLE. For both CFLEs and family practitioners, the organizational structure of their employers was similar (not significantly different) with the majority being nonprofit followed by government and for-profit (see Table 4.1). The primary focus of their settings was also similar for both groups and included education, intervention, and prevention, among others. Certified Family Life Educators work in varied settings with a majority reporting involvement in educational settings (post secondary), followed by community-based services, education (birth through secondary), private sector, faith-based organizations, other, government/military, and health care and family wellness. Similarly the areas of practice were also diverse with college and university education reported most frequently, followed by parenting education and counseling/therapy (see Table 4.1). Although FLE focuses on education and not therapy, many family life educators work in settings that combine more than one professional domain. As demonstrated through the *Domains of Family Practice Model*, intervention settings can provide opportunities for a preventative or educational approach.

Within their employment settings, family life educators served an average of 66.7 individuals or families per week (noncertified family practitioners served an average of 68.1 individuals or families with a range of 1 to 999). This range could result from the varied settings of family professionals who conduct home visits, teach large classes, or give presentations via mass media. There is also a wide age range of clients in these settings although the predominant age group is young adults (ages 19–30), followed by adults (ages 31–64), and adolescents (13–18).

The variety of settings in which family life educators are employed indicates the multiple areas of practice in which they engage. While the settings may be gen-

Table 4.1   Primary Practice Settings and Areas of Practice of CFLEs and Family Practitioners

Characteristic	CFLEs ($n = 522$)	Family Practitioners ($n = 369$)	Total ($n = 891$)
Organizational Structure[a]			
Non-profit	52.9%	51.6%	52.4%
Government	30.2	36.4	32.7
For-profit	16.9	12.0	14.9
Primary Focus of Organization[a]			
Education	65.5%	67.4%	66.3%
Intervention	13.7	13.5	13.6
Prevention	10.6	10.7	10.6
Other	10.2	8.4	9.5
Primary Practice Setting[a]			
Education (Post Secondary)	34.0%	38.8%	35.9%
Community-Based Services	20.3	21.9	20.9
Education (Birth through Secondary)	11.4	14.9	12.8
Private Sector	9.7	5.9	8.1
Faith-Based Organization	8.5	3.7	6.5
Other	6.6	6.5	6.5
Government/Military	5.4	4.8	5.1
Healthcare and Family Wellness	4.2	3.7	4.0
Primary Area of Practice[a]			
College/University Education	18.5%	20.4%	19.3%
Parenting Education	12.0	11.7	11.9
Counseling/Therapy	9.1	8.4	8.8
Other	6.8	7.8	7.2
Marriage/Relationship Education	8.3	5.0	7.0
Cooperative Extension/Community Ed.	4.2	5.9	4.9
Early Childhood Education	4.4	5.0	4.7
K–12 Education	3.5	5.3	4.2
Child and Family Advocacy	3.1	5.0	3.9
Aging/Gerontology	2.5	2.2	2.4
Healthcare and Wellness	1.9	2.0	1.9
Family Preservation	2.7	.6	1.8
Ministry	1.7	1.1	1.5
Community Action/Service	1.7	.8	1.4
Sexuality Education	1.5	1.1	1.4
Youth Development Programs	1.2	1.7	1.4
Work-Life Balance	1.0	2.0	1.4
Adoption/Foster Care	.8	2.0	1.3
Family Policy	.8	2.0	1.3
Child Life Specialist	1.7	.3	1.1
Daycare/Preschool	1.5	.6	1.1
Military Family Support	1.5	.6	1.1
Domestic Abuse/Violence Prevention	.8	1.7	1.1
Drug and Alcohol Prevention	.8	1.1	.9

(continued)

Characteristic	CFLEs (n = 522)	Family Practitioners (n = 369)	Total (n = 891)
Primary Area of Practice[a] (cont'd.)			
Family Financial Planning and Counseling	.8	.8	.8
Head Start Programs	1.2	.3	.8
Diversity/Cultural Awareness Education	.4	1.4	.8
Criminal Justice	1.0	.0	.6
Housing	.8	.0	.5
Crisis Hotline	.6	.0	.3
Nutrition Education and Counseling	.6	.0	.3
Peace Education	.6	.0	.3
Victim/Witness Support Services	.6	.0	.3
Family Law	.4	.3	.3
Employment Assistance	.4	.3	.3
Communication and Writing	.2	.6	.3
Program Evaluation and Assessment	.2	.6	.3
Pregnancy/Family Planning	.0	.8	.3
Residential Treatment	.0	.6	.2
Media (TV, Radio, Internet, Film)	.2	.0	.1
Recreation	.2	.0	.1
Hospice	.0	.3	.1
Age of Client [b]			
Newborns (less than 1 month)	6.7	6.6	6.6
Infants/children (1 month–12 years)	14.0	14.3	14.2
Adolescents (ages 13–18)	15.7	18.2	16.7
Young Adults (ages 19–30)	27.5	28.5	27.9
Adults (ages 31–64)	24.5	21.8	23.4
Elderly (ages 65–85)	8.2	7.8	8.0
Elderly (over age 85)	3.3	2.8	3.1

[a] Rank-ordered by total group
[b] Respondents could check all that apply
  (CFLE n = 1246)
  (Family Practitioner n = 822)
  (Total n = 2068)

Adapted from Darling, C., Fleming, M., & Cassidy, D. (2009). Professionalization of family life education: Defining the field. *Family Relations, 58*, 357–372.

erally categorized as education, faith-based organizations, health care and family wellness, or business, these settings may have employment opportunities in youth development programs, adoption agencies, teen pregnancy centers, public school or university teaching, Cooperative Extension, consumer protection agencies, family ministry, public health programs, welfare assistance programs, child or adult day care centers, Head Start programs, after-school programs, prenatal and maternity services, crisis or hotline services, disability services, senior citizen programs, hospices, or public service radio and TV programming. In fact, the nature of their work may not be defined as family life education per se, which can make it difficult to find positions. Therefore, providing student internship opportunities in a wide variety of employment settings and sharing strategies for obtaining positions can be helpful. In addition, promoting family life education within community and work settings can also advance the field. (See Appendix C for further employment settings and career opportunities for family life educators.)

Personal Perceptions of Family Life Education Settings

In order to better understand family life education in a variety of settings, family life educators were asked to share how they integrate FLE into their work setting by providing examples of the types of programs they have developed, implemented, and/or taught, or that already exist within their settings; the challenges faced; and the trends that influence FLE programming. These personal statements relate to the primary practice settings noted in Table 4.1 including education, community-based services, private sector or being entrepreneurial, government/military, and health care and family wellness.

Educational Settings

Family life education can be found in various educational settings. It is frequently taught in middle and high schools within the Family and Consumer Sciences curriculum. A variety of topics that are becoming increasingly pertinent in school environments include relationships, family violence, bullying, values education, sexual health issues, and conflict management. Some components of family life education are also taught in preschool and elementary school environments. For example, early childhood educators often teach about self-esteem, as well as family and interpersonal relationships. Thus, family life educators within a school environment have opportunities to share new knowledge and skills to help students and families. Numerous college and university programs also have courses pertaining to family life education with several undergraduate and graduate family sciences' programs providing curricula that qualify students for national certification.

■ HIGH SCHOOL SETTINGS

In the public secondary school setting, Family Life Education (FLE) is usually taught in a department with a title similar to Family and Consumer Sciences (FACS). The title and content of the courses may differ, but all must consider several key issues. First, the students live in families that come in many forms with each family's values being part of the high school student's daily life. Second, the school is part of a community and what goes on in the classroom must be acceptable in the community. In addition, the students have to find the course worth adding to their schedule since it is an elective course choice that must fit into graduation requirements. The school administration also needs to see the course as valuable and as current as other classes being offered. Many school systems are facing decreased funding that can result in the elimination of FLE courses as FACS departments are cut.

Fewer college graduates in FACS are prepared to be high school FLE teachers, leaving current secondary schools with fewer new recruits to fill vacant positions. Other challenges include teachers facing ever-changing content standards, grading requirements, assessment procedures, and licensure requirements.

Once the constraints are faced, a high school family life education class can be a highly interactive forum for the same topical content as a college class. The inclusion of community agency speakers, project-based learning, conversation dyads, current readings and video-clips, experiential learning problems, and classroom discussion in a variety of forms keeps teaching at the high school level from being a copy of the "dog-eared" notebook lecture format that may exist in a college classroom. "This is the best class I have had in high school," is a common quote on the course evaluation and makes it all worthwhile.

Marilyn Flick, MS, CFLE
Chair, Applied and Fine Arts/PE/Health
North Eugene High School
Eugene, Oregon

■ HIGHER EDUCATION/COLLEGIATE/POST-SECONDARY SETTINGS

Higher education prepares two types of graduates for FLE: Family and Consumer Sciences (FCS) teachers and Human Development and Family Studies (HDFS) family professionals. FCS graduates offer family life education to children in Kindergarten through 12th grade and are certified to teach important life management skills-based courses in public schools. Depending on the size of program, FCS instructors teach courses in child development, family life, family resource management, and foods and nutrition. The curriculum is developed to meet statewide standards and typically uses hands-on methodologies (e.g., childcare centers, foods labs). HDFS majors are likely to provide FLE in human service types of settings, offering parenting education, financial management, or other knowledge and skills in community agencies.

Family life education, as we traditionally see it implemented within schools K–12, is in real danger. In our current economic climate and with the push toward science, math, and technology skills, subjects historically taught by FCS are undervalued. Many FCS programs are being reduced or completely eliminated in some schools. This threatens the existence of FLE within the school setting and also has an impact on FCS programs in higher education. Students are anxious about entering majors for which there may not be many jobs. Of course, those of us who value family and recognize that "being" family oriented is not always easy or "commonsense" recognize the need for formal preparation for family and professional roles.

While many of the jobs are not well-paying, HDFS graduates are well equipped to offer FLE (information and skills about child development, parenting, and financial management) in community and agency settings. These positions are certainly affected by the downturn of the economy but do not seem to be as threatened. Many families really need what FLE has to offer.

One of the special challenges and opportunities in higher education is the promotion of family life education in various settings. Obtaining internship options in multiple settings provides opportunities to market family life education in the community, as well as expand the visions of students for potential future positions in FLE. Having internship students and graduates periodically return to campus or communicate electronically in discussion boards exposes them to additional settings. When involved in internships, discussions of professionalism are also pertinent, as well as having students attend professional meetings at the local, state, regional, or national levels. These professional experiences expand their knowledge, credentials, and commitment to a career in family life education.

Raeann Hamon, PhD, CFLE
Chair, Department of Human Development and Family Science
Messiah College
Mechanicsburg, Pennsylvania

Community-Based Settings

Options for family life education programs within the community are numerous. They may be offered by the Cooperative Extension Service through short programs, the Internet, or media presentations. In addition, various agencies serve multi-need families and have a team of family professionals that work with these families in order to integrate family life education, family counseling, and family case management. Other community-based family life education programs are offered within various faith-based institutions and can cover a range of topics from adolescent sexuality to marriage preparation and adjustment to aging.

■ EXTENSION SETTINGS

Cooperative Extension across the country is built around research-based programming, and this area of family development in particular is about research-based family life education (FLE). There are two key trends that have been influencing Extension's FLE programming in the past decade. First, professionals who work with families are facing fewer resources along with an increased demand for accountability. For Extension FLE programming this has resulted in a shift away from direct delivery to parents and families (typically due to staff cuts and/or a transition from a county-based delivery system to a regional system) to programming that utilizes a "train-the-trainer" or similar model. Second, there is a push toward greater use of technology for FLE in Extension. Researchers have asserted that for family life educators, the Internet provides the potential to make diverse information widely available to people who were previously unreachable with face-to-face delivery. The use of technologies can also be cost-effective, easier to maintain, update, and distribute than print resources. At the same time, families are able to access and create information on their own time, based on their own needs, beliefs, and values. However, this demands family life educators understand and keep up with rapidly changing technologies. Unfortunately research has not provided adequate information on how to best use technology for FLE; at the same time, the resources available for the development, delivery, and evaluation of family life education are becoming increasingly scarce. As a result, Extension's FLE programming is at an exciting point, one that presents opportunity for innovation as we shift programming to better align Extension's strengths and resources with family needs.

Jodi Dworkin, PhD
Associate Professor, Department of Family Social Science
University of Minnesota Extension Service
St. Paul, Minnesota

■ MULTI-NEED FAMILIES INVOLVED WITH THE FOSTER CARE SYSTEM

Child Protective Services is an agency that becomes involved with families upon allegations of child abuse and/or neglect. Once a report is made, Child Protective

Services investigates the severity of the maltreatment and makes decisions about child placement. Sometimes children are removed from the home and placed in foster care, resulting in the need for biological parents to complete a number of requirements to regain custody. Family life educators have an important role in working with such families. Although FLE often takes a preventative approach, it has many aspects that are highly relevant, and often congruent, to efforts aimed at improving the family functioning of multi-need families involved with the foster care system. FLE involves increasing a family's knowledge and skills by providing information, tools, and strategies.

There may be a number of different service providers working with a family involved with the foster care system. As such, families can benefit from the combined forces of family life educators, family therapists, and family case managers. Indeed, good practice involves drawing upon the strengths of these interdependent professions to ensure families are receiving comprehensive services. This is a good opportunity for collaboration, as noted in the *Domains of Family Practice Model* (Myers-Walls et al., 2011).

FLE aims to address a family's current needs to improve family functioning. After receiving a referral for services, family life educators collaborate with parents, caseworkers, and other service providers to gather as much information about the family as possible. In conducting a needs assessment, questions are asked, such as: what precipitated foster care involvement, what features of the family put them at risk, what are the family's strengths, and finally, what goals must parents achieve in order to successfully exit the foster care system. A contract is then made with parents to clearly define expectations of all parties. Once a solid foundation has been developed, the appropriate interventions and educational programs can proceed. If identified needs fall outside the scope of a family life educator's expertise, the family is connected with a family case manager to identify other providers who have the requisite training needed.

The foster care system is a unique societal context and, therefore, effective providers must have expertise in many of the FLE content areas. For instance, assessment involves attention to internal family dynamics including gathering an understanding of the family's strengths and weaknesses. It also is essential to assess interpersonal relationships within the family system. Upon a thorough assessment, FLEs can then focus on parent education and guidance, while keeping family law and public policy associated with the foster care system in sharp focus.

Specifically, an evidence-based parenting education program called the *Incredible Years* (IY), developed by Dr. Carolyn Webster-Stratton, has been incorporated (Webster-Stratton & Reid, 2003). The IY is a multi-faceted intervention/educational program designed to strengthen responsive and nurturing parenting and help parents promote their children's social and emotional competence. The IY includes instruction on interactive play and reinforcement strategies, nonviolent discipline, natural and logical consequences, and problem-solving strategies. This program incorporates multiple learning approaches, such as group discussion and support, hands-on practice activities, goals and self-monitoring assessments, practice activities, and video modeling through videotaped vignettes. The program is offered in a group format with meetings once a week for two hours each session.

It is important to keep context in mind when working with families involved with the foster care system. Whereas dressing professionally and communicating expertise in specific substantive areas are important in establishing our identities as "experts" in our disciplines, a different approach is often warranted when working with families. As such, we are conscious of how we dress—often wearing jeans and t-shirts when conducting parenting education programs. Rather than attempting to establish ourselves as experts by lecturing to parents about contemporary parenting research, our goal is to establish a collaborative environment, honoring the position that everyone in the group has valuable information to share. In essence, the aim is to cultivate an environment where voices are respectfully heard, and people are valued and treated with respect.

Perhaps the biggest challenge when providing services is time. Our contract with child protective services specifies that they will only pay for six parent-education sessions. While, clearly, having services paid for by child protective services provides an excellent opportunity, six sessions are often not enough time to successfully remedy the challenges that lead to child protective services involvement. To further complicate the issue, parents frequently cannot afford to pay for services once the contract with the child protective services is completed. Moreover, the parents have quite a burden. Child protective services might require, for example, a single mother to complete a parent education class, individual and family therapy, and domestic violence classes—all while maintaining employment and stable housing. Indeed, time can present a major challenge.

Fortunately, an important trend in working with the foster care system involves a push for research aimed to identify for whom and under what conditions educational programs and interventions are effective. By identifying factors associated with successful outcomes, as well as predictors of parent drop-out, services can be adapted to better meet families' needs. For multi-need families involved with the foster care system, research informed by FLE could be an important step toward achieving this goal.

Lenore M. McWey, PhD
Professor, Department of Family and Child Sciences
Florida State University
Tallahassee, Florida

■ HOMELESS POPULATION

According to the U.S. Department of Housing and Urban Development (2010), approximately a half million people are currently experiencing homelessness. With growing concerns about our economy, increasing numbers of individuals and families have experienced homelessness over the past decade. In addition to the stress experienced due to a lack of housing, families facing homelessness are confronted with multiple stressors, including employment concerns, limited social support, and parental stress, along with the environmental stressors associating with temporary or transitional housing facilities. Often times, these are families that may have once had a home, but due to loss of employment or other systemic issues, the family has been rendered homeless and is now experiencing the pileup of multiple stressors.

FLE can be extremely helpful to families experiencing homelessness who are often deemed as "at risk" given the nature of their multiple needs (Miller, 2011). The stress that these families experience can result in various concerns related to parenting, marital conflict, parent-child stress, and overall difficulties in family functioning. This setting, specifically related to transitional homeless people living in a residential facility, is another example of the use of "collaboration" as described in the *Domains of Family Practice Model* (Myers-Walls et al., 2011). More specifically, families experiencing homelessness have multiple needs, so the collaborative efforts of family life educators, family therapists, and family case managers are necessary. Families can benefit from education about the experience of homelessness, normative stressors, communication styles, parenting skills, and conflict resolution, among others. Evidence-based curricula related to parenting practices or healthy relationships can be particularly important to families experiencing multiple stressors because they have a systemic impact throughout various areas of functioning. Furthermore, these families could benefit immensely from family resource management skills that are significantly highlighted in FLE.

Working with a homeless population presents its own unique challenges. In addition to the stressors already described, the homeless population experiences multiple barriers to receiving necessary services. When specifically working with a homeless population that is in a transitional residential facility, the goal is to provide multiple supportive services to aid in the transition to sustainable housing. As a result clients experiencing homelessness may be offered or mandated, as part of their residential case plan, to participate in numerous services intended to meet their multifaceted needs. Family life educators can assist in the coordination and collaboration of these services to prevent multiple repetitive services that, in fact, become ineffective if clients are not able to participate fully in each service. An additional challenge with a population experiencing homelessness is the transient nature of their lives. Clients may not remain in one place, even in a residential community, for a significant length of time. Therefore, immediate educational and supportive services, as offered by FLEs and others, can provide the necessary tools for this specific population, even if it has to be brief. With the multiple needs and additional challenges in working with a homeless population, one can see the critical impact that FLE has in providing the necessary services to these clients.

Heather M. Farineau, PhD
Parent Educator of Homeless Families
Assistant Professor, School of Social Work
Florida Atlantic University
Boca Raton, Florida

■ FAITH-BASED SETTINGS

A parish setting, especially one with a school, offers a multitude of opportunities for FLE—covering most, if not all, of the CFLE content areas. Through the integration of ministry and FLE, a variety of classes and workshops can be offered in the areas of parenting, marriage enrichment, sex education for children and adults, financial management, and issues that affect older adults, such as living with loss, being actively retired, living arrangements, and family and friend relationships. Some congregations have also been able to implement Parish Nurse and Health Ministry programs to address health education and prevention for all ages. Excellent curriculum and resource materials developed by others are readily available, rather than having to self-create programs. This is very beneficial because of the time demands required of being a professional church worker. One example is a class for parents on how to use the *Learning About Sex* series (Concordia Publishing House) in the home. The age-appropriate books in the series assist parents in talking to their children about sexuality during the preschool years and continuing through adolescence.

The primary challenge is time. Typical church budgets are not able to afford the cost of a full-time family life educator. While pastors, youth ministers, and children's ministers may have degrees in family studies, their chief role is to fulfill the duties for which they were hired. Thus, the number of classes that can be taught is limited because of the time and energy that needs to be devoted to administration, worship preparation, and member care visitation. However, FLE cannot be compartmentalized from daily ministry. It is very easy to incorporate educational guidance about families into one-on-one conversations, as well as in group settings.

One answer to this challenge is to determine which congregational tasks can be accomplished through the use of lay volunteers. Training people to do visitation ministry and to assist with administrative responsibilities can be very helpful. The goal is to add flexibility to the schedule so that family life educators can have more time to dedicate to teaching. Although many congregations may be unable to bring on more paid staff, due to the involvement of volunteers they will be able to multiply the ministry and education efforts to better meet the needs of individuals and families.

Mark Heine, MS, CFLE

Family Life Pastor

Saint John's Lutheran Church

Napa, California

Private Sector: Corporate Settings and Entrepreneurs

The U.S. workforce has been changing as it is becoming more racially and ethnically diverse and getting older with a median age of 41.7 and a projected labor force growth that will be influenced in the coming years by the aging of the Baby Boomer generation. While there are still more men in the labor force than women, the growth rate for women in the labor force is slightly higher than that of men (Toossi, 2012). Whereas mothers still spend more time per workday caring for their children than fathers, fathers are "catching up" (Galinsky, Auman, & Bond, 2009). Work-life conflict for women has not changed significantly in the past three decades, although the level of work-life conflict for men has increased. Because greater stress and strain at home can negatively influence work performance, companies need to assure that both men and women are helped to succeed both at home and work. This means that companies are being more attentive to providing family life education programs for their diverse employees. In addition to corporations becoming more involved in family life education programs, some educators have seen the need for targeted services in their communities or states and have started their own consulting firms or educational organizations to provide services to families and communities.

■ CORPORATE SETTINGS

Lifetrack's Employee and Family Education Services provides FLE as part of corporate work-life initiatives. Work-life includes a specific set of organizational practices, policies, and programs, and a philosophy that recommends aggressive support for the efforts of everyone who works to achieve success both at work and at home (AWLP, 2005). The resources Lifetrack provides include in-person seminars, online webinars, e-newsletters, audio podcasts, and more. We support corporate work-life initiatives from a lifespan approach, offering topics in the areas of parenting, families, personal growth, money management, elder care, work-site issues, and health and wellness. By providing FLE to employees at the work site, employees are given the tools and information they need to efficiently utilize their flex time and paid time off to manage family demands, which often compete with workplace responsibilities.

Lifetrack uses the expertise of Certified Family Life Educators (CFLEs) to provide evidence-based information to individuals. Although a number of companies continue to schedule in-person seminars as part of their work-life initiatives, many are gravitating toward online delivery, so Lifetrack has created a unique resource in response to this trend. Customized online portal pages are available to companies for purchase. Each portal page is co-branded to coincide with the company's image, with content chosen by the company to reflect current business strategies. Many times the focus of these resources is on health and wellness. Through a strategic partnership with the Minnesota Department of Education, Lifetrack is able to provide a number of free online resources for working parents of young children. These resources automatically scroll into each company's online portal page as an added-value resource. By doing this, we are intentionally creating a holistic approach to work-life that includes FLE, even if FLE is not on the company's work-life radar.

The business case for work-life initiatives is very clear; 76% of companies say work-life balance programs increase worker productivity, and 70% say they have a positive impact on the recruitment of new workers. Employees at organizations where work-life programs are offered are much more likely to stay with their employer for at least the next five years and report higher job satisfaction and engagement (Kacher, 2013).

The challenges faced by providing FLE as part of our scope of resources can be extensive, but overcome with some clear communication. Privacy policies can inhibit any follow-up Lifetrack wishes to provide when promoting the free FLE resources. Company firewalls sometimes need to be overcome in order for employees to access the online portal pages and resources. In addition, many times companies do not see FLE as part of the work-life strategy. It takes perseverance and talking points that clearly demonstrate a business return-on-investment to overcome this hurdle.

The FLE programming we provide is influenced by a number of growing and evolving trends in the workplace. These include, but are not limited to, the evolution of work-life (previously referred to as work-family), flexible work arrangements, the global workplace, telecommuting, rising health-care costs, and the aging population. As these trends continue and new ones begin to surface, Lifetrack will adapt content to meet the ever-changing needs of employees, while making the business case for work-life initiatives to employers. A key component of an effective work-life initiative is and will continue to be family life education.

Beth Quist, MS, CFLE
Director, Employee & Family Education Services
Lifetrack Resources
St. Paul, Minnesota

■ ENTREPRENEURIAL SETTINGS

As an education consultant my area of expertise is family engagement. I currently work in five states, over 55 public school districts, and have facilitated over sixteen thousand clock hours of professional development. I train, consult, and mentor a variety of organizations that share the common goal of increasing parental involvement, or family engagement, in an effort to increase student achievement. My role consists of helping organizations conduct needs assessments for school districts, facilitating workshops for administrators of Head Start (a program of the United States Department of Health and Human Services) who work with families, providing in-home plans for post-adoptive families, creating one-year plans for federal program directors, modeling parenting classes for Dallas Housing Authority representatives, presenting workshops for incoming freshmen at colleges, and serving as a liaison for community-based organizations that partner with public schools.

Family life education can be integrated into a variety of settings during the initial stages of strategic planning for an organization. Organizations are encouraged to capture a realistic view of the families with whom they are involved in terms of their life stage, socioeconomic status, and education. Therefore, it is imperative that a needs assessment is conducted to ensure that programming and planning are relevant. If this is not done effectively, an organization may run the risk of not using resources wisely.

One of the biggest challenges in an entrepreneurial setting is communicating to administrators how family dynamics influence the success of families and children. It is normal to spend considerable time educating organizations on success rates, basics about family functioning, and helping them identify the actual needs of their families. Organizations often have a plan to help families already in place, but that plan may not be appropriate for the actual families with whom they are working. Many administrators are out of touch with what really affects families and how they function. Thus, they have difficulties perceiving families and their roles and values.

Convincing organizations to backtrack and invest time in a needs assessment can be difficult. As a consultant, budget is always a factor. Many times an organization already has an idea of what they want to accomplish and may not want to shift gears. This can pose a challenge as they have allocated certain funds for services and additional time for consulting may not be in their budget. This puts the organization in a situation in which they have to reframe what their outcomes may be. When consulting with an organization, you may need to help them redefine their vision. As an outside person engaging with an organization for the first time, this can present a barrier. The client may not feel you are able to help them accomplish their goals based on the fact that there may not be an established relationship. Connecting with the client and asking key questions can help to avoid this problem.

Current trends include graduation rates, unemployment, and global issues exposure for families. These areas can have a major impact on the outcome of a program and can have a direct effect on families and children. As a consultant, you never want to become stale, so you must stay current and relevant. One way to do this is to continue to volunteer and offer services in a variety of settings that share the same focus.

Some recommendations for being a FLE consultant are:
- Remember to meet the families where they are.
- Stay open-minded when choosing clients—family is family no matter how you view it!
- Be mindful that it is all about relationships.
- Choose more volunteer options as they reflect your true passion.

- Organizations, families, and children find value in consultants being transparent.
- Sustainable programs have partnerships.
- Just like scaffolding, every family's experience helps you to connect with another.

Kimberly Hunt, MA, CFLE
Educational Consultant
Dallas, Texas

Government and Military Settings

There are three types of mandated family life education although only two are mandated by the court system: *mandatory education for a "voluntary" role*, such as caring for a foster child, adopting a child, or accepting a foreign exchange student; *education for risky family situations*, such as mandated education for divorcing parents or parents taking a child home after a medical procedure; and *mandated education for parents or families judged as inadequate*, such as parents who have been found to be abusive and/or neglectful (Myers-Walls, 2012). It can be difficult to identify the strengths of parents and families mandated to participate in family life education, but this can be a positive turning point for families and provide hope for making a difference. In addition, mandated programs have linkages among courts, agencies, and educators to assist families in need.

Military families face multiple challenges such as geographical separation, isolation, and relocation. These changes affect family roles, spousal employment, stress, mental health, and social support networks, as well as children's education and relationships (Carroll, Smith, & Behnke, 2012). In addition, there is the risk of injury or death, traumatic brain injuries (TBI), and post traumatic stress disorder (PTSD). Military families have the advantage of living within a system that values and supports individuals and families. Improved family policies and support have increased the level of commitment to the military of both the soldiers and their families (U.S. DOD, 2009). Various programs exist for marriage and relationship education, family resource management, and parenting education (Carroll, Smith, & Behnke, 2012).

■ Court-Mandated Settings

Parenting Partnerships uses an educational, structured, curriculum-driven approach to work with families engaged in family law litigation, specifically divorce/separation or ongoing custody issues. We provide family life education services to businesses, families, schools, and any organization that needs and provides services to families. All of our curriculum is research-based and focuses on developing parenting, co-parenting, communication, and conflict-management skills.

We have created programs that focus directly on family restabilization and restructuring following divorce/separation. These programs include a court-mandated 4-hour course entitled *Children Caught in the Middle* and a 12-hour program called *Shared Parenting* that is designed for use in a group setting or individually. This program is a structured, educational program with flexibility to address unique family needs (age-appropriate information and/or information/support regarding special needs) when offered privately. We also utilize our curriculum when offering Parenting Coordination/Facilitation services and have developed comprehensive resources, booklets, and handouts to assist in our programming. All of our curriculum can be used to work individually with families and is often court-ordered, depending upon the assessed needs of the court. Within the next year we will be offering webinars and podcasts addressing parenting and co-parenting challenges.

Our greatest challenge is helping parents and their legal representatives understand the need for a minimum of 8 to 12 hours of FLE sessions to facilitate change. They think families fractured by litigation can mend the damage in one or two meetings. Another challenge is helping others understand the differences between our educational approach compared to counseling or therapy. Our competition is primarily licensed mental health professionals. Unfortunately, many are without additional training in family law support (mediation, parenting coordination/facilitation), parent education, and curriculum development. Our employees are not only CFLEs, but are also certified in mediation, parenting coordination/facilitation, interdisciplinary collaborative law, and have a minimum of 8 hours domestic violence training (as specifically stated in much of our state's legislation).

Family law professionals want to learn more about what it is that we do that appears to work with their families. Legislation was proposed this year to include *Crisis Marriage Education*, a mandated 12-hour course that all parents filing for divorce must be complete within 60 days of filing. This course includes a skill and research-based curriculum that addresses conflict management, communication skills, and the potential effects of divorce on children and parents, as well as forgiveness. Unfortunately this bill did not pass in 2013.

Dedicated family law professionals, such as judges and attorneys, have worked with us over the years to support our efforts to include CFLE language because they see the value of this credential, but so many legal and mental health professionals are struggling financially that their efforts to disqualify competitors keep us "on our toes." Luckily the families we serve offer our strongest support. While we have not yet been successful in getting the CFLE credential specifically recognized, we have been able to get marriage educators and those with degrees in family studies recognized as providers, which is a good step toward further recognition of the appropriateness and effectiveness of an educational approach. While licensed mental health professionals currently have more recognition as providers, the positive outcomes of parent education provided by family life educators is resulting in increased demand for professionals with training in family life education, as opposed to therapy. Hopefully this continued success results in the formal recognition of the CFLE credential to provide mandated parent education for divorcing parents.

We do not work with families that have identified domestic violence, as these families are referred to programs specifically designed to address those challenges. Therefore, we use a very effective screening process that works with highly litigious parents who want other professionals to think there might be a domestic violence issue to further their case in court.

Many of our clients come into our programs thinking they have been sent because they are "bad" parents. All courses and services are referred to as "parenting classes," which may have negative connotations. However, once they meet with us they appreciate the family education services we provide. When they understand they are not with us because they are bad parents, they are much more receptive to our skill and research-based programs. While we do not use our clients to advertise our services because we have to honor confidentiality, we do find that our clients are our greatest advertising. We often receive referrals from our own clients—some even convince their attorneys to make sure *Parenting Partnerships* provides their services, or they volunteer to attend on their own because of what friends have shared about their experiences.

Deborah Cashen, BS, CFLE
President and Founder
Parenting Partnerships, Inc.
Houston, Texas

■ MILITARY SETTINGS

Some of the most well-suited and rewarding employment opportunities for family life educators (FLEs) are those available in military family service centers. Military families face all the same challenges as non-military families, but because of frequent relocation, deployments, and other factors related to military service, these issues can be more frequent and sometimes exacerbated. They also face some unique challenges, so having a family service delivery system designed to address these challenges is essential. In an effort to mitigate these factors and maintain the highest possible level of mission readiness, all of the uniformed services provide a wide range of support programs for their members and families.

The family service centers for each service have somewhat different names, but the same basic programs are generally supported. The entire range of FLE practice applies directly to the services provided at these centers. While the individual program names can vary to some degree, the general programs provided through these centers include:

- *Transition Assistance Programs* provide information and assistance to all separating and retiring members to help them make an effective transition from military to civilian life. An integral aspect of this goal is to ensure that members leaving the service are made aware of, and have access to, the numerous programs and services available to assist them in the transition process.
- *Relocation Assistance Programs* assist members and families transferring to new duty stations become familiar with their new communities and the resources available.
- *Financial Education and Counseling Programs* help military personnel and family members develop sound financial skills. The programs focus on financial education, training, and counseling to promote sound personal financial management and freedom of choice for members and their families.
- *New Parent Support Programs* enhance parent and infant attachment, increase knowledge of child development, and provide connections to the support services that allow parents to become nurturing and capable caregivers. Staff members provide in-home parenting education, support, and resource linkage.
- *Exceptional Family Member Programs/Special Needs Programs* assist members by addressing the special needs of their exceptional family members during the assignment process. Special needs include any special medical, dental, mental health, developmental, or educational requirement; wheelchair accessibility; adaptive equipment; and/or assistive technology devices and services.
- *Family Advocacy Programs* identify, educate, treat, and monitor personnel engaging in spouse or child abuse/neglect (physical or psychological), and sexual abuse.

- *Employee Assistance Programs* provide confidential professional assessment, short-term counseling, and referral services to help employees with their personal, job, or family problems.
- *Sexual Assault Prevention and Response Programs* establish and ensure standardized procedures for responding to sexual assault victims and include reporting requirements, as well as initiation and continuity of care.
- *Deployment Readiness Programs* provide training and support to assist leadership, civilians, service members, and families to successfully manage the challenges of all phases of mobilization and deployment.
- *Life Skills Programs* offer activities designed to promote family strength and well-being. Classes and workshops may be offered for issues such as stress management, relationship enhancement, communication, parenting, and career development.
- *Health and Wellness Promotion Programs* strengthen and enhance mission performance by providing policies and promoting positive health habits. These programs help to ensure that members and their families have a variety of tools available to maintain fitness and wellness.

For Family Life Educators considering employment at a military family service center, you will need to do some research, such as where the installations are located, military-rank structure, organizational hierarchies, military customs and courtesies, and military terminology. One of the benefits of working for the military in any capacity is the opportunity to live and work in several bases within the continental United States, Alaska, and Hawaii, as well as working abroad in family service centers in England, Germany, Italy, Greece, Spain, Japan, Korea, Guam, and other countries.

Working at a military family service center is a great way to apply your FLE education and experience, support the efforts of our military services, and help military members and their families live happier lives. The opportunities are many, and they can also lead to other opportunities serving families within other federal agencies, as well as with contractors providing these services for the government. Opportunities exist for family life educators at any stage of their careers and are certainly worth considering as you formulate your career path.

Jon-Eric Garcia, MA, CFLE
Employee Assistance Program Coordinator for the U.S. Coast Guard
Boston, Massachusetts

Health-Care Settings

There are a variety of health-care settings that are amenable to family life education. Some of these may be collaborative with health professionals, such as nurses and health educators, since family development and functioning are an integral part of health and wellness. Family life educators may work in public health programs and services, hospital-based family support, nutrition education programs, prenatal and maternity services, holistic health centers, long-term care settings, and hospice programs. There is a broad range of health-related topics pertinent to individuals and families, such as managing stress, learning about sexuality and contraception, and understanding death in the family. In addition, some hospitals offer programs for new parents and new grandparents.

The Affordable Care Act (ACA) has the potential to dramatically increase employment opportunities for family life educators in health-care settings. The ACA mandates that prevention efforts address behavioral health. A number of family professionals and family-related organizations are advocating for the inclusion of evidence-based family education programs in the prevention efforts of the ACA. A majority of hospitals (65%) are non-profit and required to invest 85% of their profits back into the community. Historically, these funds covered the cost of caring for patients with no insurance. However, with the expansion of Medicaid through the Affordable Care Act, funds used to cover the care of the uninsured can be freed up to be invested elsewhere. Hospitals will be conducting needs assessments in their communities to determine how to best use these funds. Since according to the Affordable Care Act these investments must be focused on "prevention," this may create new opportunities for family life education programs and providers (Taner, 2013b).

■ UNIVERSITY TRAINING IN HEALTHCARE SETTING

Patient teaching and family education are essential components of patient care in every health-care setting. All health-care professionals are taught and expected to participate in informal and formal family life education. Nurses, in particular, believe that one of their primary responsibilities is to be a health educator to individual clients/patients, families as a whole, and groups of people in the community. This teaching reaches across a broad gamut of subjects related to medical assessment, diagnosis, treatment, and evaluation, which includes medications, procedures, laboratory results, self-care, illness prevention, signs and symptoms, health promotion, and much more. This teaching can occur as a spontaneous answer to questions from patients to more formal education that includes a plan and resource materials.

All professional nurses are expected to do some patient/family teaching, but some nurses are more prepared to fulfill this role. Nurse practitioners, nurse clinical specialists, or those who are Certified Family Life Educators have the advanced training in educational pedagogy to make this learning more effective.

Examples of programs for patient/family groups can include: First Aid Training, Prenatal Education, Care of Infants, Parenting/Parenthood, Care of Diabetes, Living with Chronic Illness, Family Caregiving, and Living with Mental Illness. As a nurse and family life educator, I have taught many individual patients about their issues of health and concern, and have worked with thousands of nursing students over the years in the classroom and clinical area, as well as taught workshops for continuing education for professional colleagues. There are many challenges that one faces in medical settings in terms of teaching and learning, but it is an exciting area in which to work.

There are trends in health-care settings that influence patient and family learning. One major change concerns the electronic and digital revolution. Patients are free to go online, track their medical care, and maintain their own medical records. In addition, there are large quantities of health information available over the Internet; however, not all this information is valid or reliable. The teacher who is patient, whether a CFLE or professional nurse, can help broker the best information available at a level that is understandable to the public.

Shirley Hanson, PhD, CFLE Emerita
Professor Emerita, OHSU School of Nursing
Adjunct Faculty, WSU College of Nursing
Spokane, Washington

■ **HEALTH CARE-HOSPITAL SETTING**

Working with families, children, doctors, clinics, other professionals, and communities to promote health and well-being is both rewarding and challenging. Our goals are to:

- Promote and develop printed and website resources on health, safety, and injury prevention in the community
- Work with Fire Rescue to present a burn education puppet show for all kindergarten students in public and private schools in the community
- Work with *Safe Kids* and other organizations to sponsor safety education programs in the community
- Conduct children's tours of the hospital with a health and safety focus
- Teach babysitting classes
- Serve as a media resource for interviews on health, safety, and parenting topics

We provide services to enhance parent education in the community by:

- Developing and teaching parent education classes
- Developing and teaching puberty education classes at our hospital and in surrounding communities
- Providing parent support by phone, e-mail, or personal consultation
- Providing parenting information at the discharge of newborns, along with information on child temperament through a grant from the United Way
- Developing printed and website resources on parenting
- Writing a blog on parenting issues (www.averastorycenter.org)

We give assistance to doctors, clinics, and other professionals in the health system by:

- Providing printed materials on child development, health, safety, and nutrition topics
- Providing parenting consultations for parents referred by physicians

We promote quality childcare in the community by:

- Developing and teaching childcare training classes in the community

Some of the programs we have developed include "Growing Up" Classes. *Let's Talk for Girls* is a puberty education program for girls ages 10–13 and their parent or other adult. The class covers female anatomy, changes in puberty, hygiene, communication, and self-esteem. The *TALK for Girls* is an advanced class for girls of middle-school age and up that includes frank discussions on male and female anatomy, how pregnancy occurs, what sex is, sexually transmitted disease, risk behaviors, and abstinence. We also consult with the local Catholic dioceses on their puberty education program *All in God's Plan*. Parenting information at discharge provides new mothers with a packet of information about hospital and community resources, information on safety issues like safe sleep and shaken baby syndrome, and a child development newsletter covering birth to six weeks.

Our biggest challenge is the shrinking dollars that health-care systems have in their budgets. As patient reimbursements continue to decline, funding, which was once available for community programs, no longer exists. Another challenge is the way people want to receive information. The first time we offered "Potty Training" as a parent education class 15 years ago, 70 people attended. Today, we average 5–10 people in a parenting class. Therefore, we have moved toward technology-based programs that are offered online. We also use a blog to post about parenting, health, and safety topics. A concern about the new trend toward technology-based information is how parents judge the validity and reliability of the sources they are accessing, and how should we market our online information as a reputable source.

Betty Barto-Smith, BS, CFLE
Doniese Wilcox, BS, CFLE
Avera McKennan Hospital and University Health Center
Sioux Falls, South Dakota

SUMMARY

Family life education exists, or can exist, in a variety of settings with multiple job titles. This means it might be difficult to find employment unless you can understand the range and potential of these settings and how being a family life educator fits into the domain and practice of the profession. Each setting has its specific characteristics and challenges, along with many opportunities for creative problem solving. Many times you will need to "think out of the box" when seeking a position by creating a niche within an existing setting or becoming an entrepreneur to fill a void in services in your community. However, the well being of families with varying needs is at stake.

QUESTIONS AND ISSUES FOR DISCUSSION

1. In what other settings could family life education be included? What content might be covered? How would you promote the inclusion of family life education within this setting?

2. In which institution/organization would leaders be most responsive to offering family life education programs: faith-based institutions, businesses, schools, military, or communities? What are the reasons for your response?

3. As family life education is becoming more collaborative with other professions, what additional preparation do you think family life educators need in order to be better equipped for their roles in this new paradigm?

4. Since family life educators are employed in a variety of settings, what kinds of job search strategies would you employ?

5

Program Design in Family Life Education

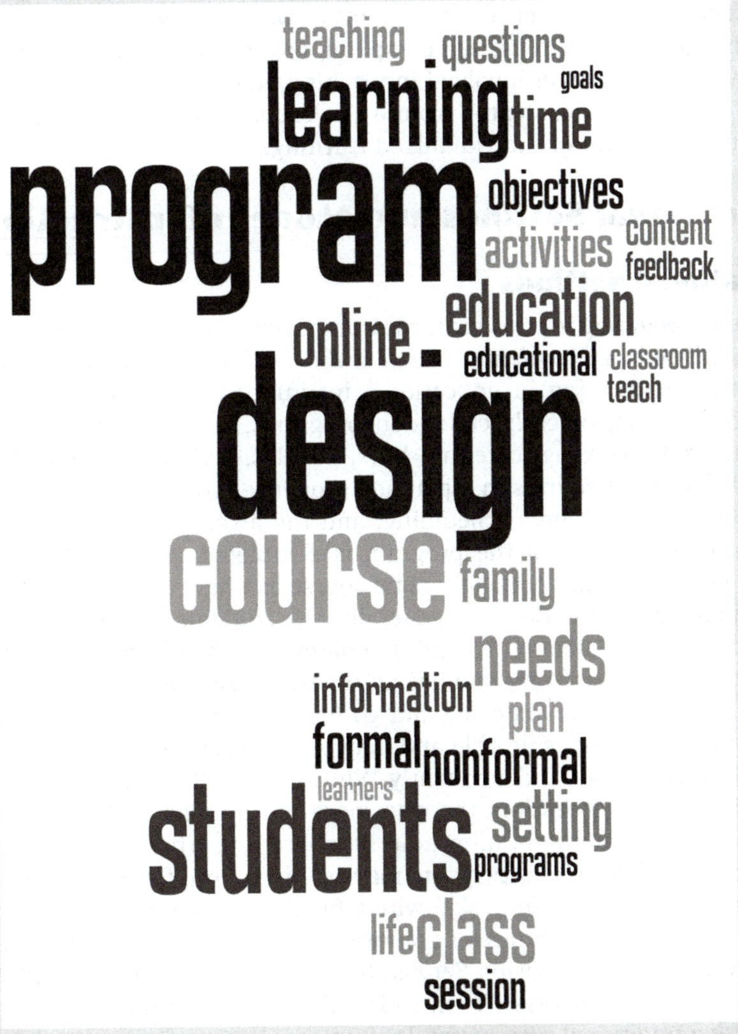

Congratulations! You have been asked to teach a course on a particular topic, and because you are qualified and have an interest to teach about this topic, you agree. Now what? Whenever you teach a new course, you engage in two related activities. First you design the course by gathering information and making decisions about the content and the way the course should be taught. You will need to analyze the nature of the problem that needs to be addressed by your course, as well as information about your target audience in order to develop a conceptual foundation that is based on relevant theory, research, and teaching methodology. Second, you engage in teacher-student interactions as you implement the course. Whereas this chapter will focus on the information you will gather and decisions you will make in designing the course, the following chapter will deal with the options you have in implementing your teaching decisions and design.

Everyone is a teacher in some informal way, whether you teach a child to ride a bicycle, a neighbor to use the computer, or a friend to plant a garden. However, when you have a career involved in teaching others, you do so in a "planned" way and in a variety of contexts—from a traditional classroom or online course to a community seminar or individualized learning.

Educational Settings and Modes of Instruction

Educational Settings

Before planning for this course it is important to consider if the structure of the course will be in a *formal, nonformal,* or *informal setting. Formal education* refers to teaching and learning in educational institutions, such as schools, universities, technical centers, or early childhood programs. It is systematic, structured, and administered according to certain laws, policies, and norms (Dib, 1988). There is usually a series of courses in a planned sequence, grades based on performance in those courses, traditional scheduling, and the awarding of a certificate, diploma, license, or degree when the program is completed (Chamberlain & Cummings, 2003). Granted an institutional online course can have student involvement at various times during the day, but generally, the students still follow the established time schedule of school terms and due dates for assignments and examinations. A *nonformal educational* program has an organized session(s) facilitated by a professional(s), but the learners come and go because attending all sessions is optional. Nonformal education is flexible and may better meet the needs of students, if they are motivated to learn independently. While there will still be a predetermined time to begin and end a session, the classroom setting may be located in a religious, health-care, community, or after-hour school setting. There are no exams or graded assignments, although participants may be given an informal assignment, such as trying a new communication skill with a family member. Self-help seminars and in-service training are examples of nonformal programs along with classes conducted by the Cooperative Extension Service (Chamberlain & Cummings, 2003). *Informal education* does not necessarily include subjects and "approved" objectives associated with a traditional curriculum. It often supplements both formal and nonformal educational programs and can include non-credit, independent projects in a university setting; visiting museums or science exhibits; attending lectures; or reading magazines, journals, or books. Informal education is a lifelong approach that may also occur when talking to another individual in a meeting or casual encounter.

Modes of Instruction

Another way to view family life education programs focuses on the mode used to reach interested persons, namely, the *mass, group,* and *individual* modes. The *mass mode* involves educational information provided to the masses, but not just through mass media sources. The audience is anonymous because there is no direct contact between the educator and the participants. Anyone with the interest, access, and means (e.g., television, computer, reading ability) to participate can do so. This may be a special lecture by a knowledgeable person in the community, media presentation including radio or television (organizational promotional spots, educational programs, after-school specials), the Internet (news programs, access to government Extension sites, YouTube), and print media (books, magazines, newspapers, newsletters, bulletins, pamphlets) (Harman & Brim, 1980). However, knowledge about families and parenting is not available to millions of people via the printed word because of illiteracy. Recent statistics show that 20% of high school seniors are classified as functionally illiterate, 42 million adults cannot read at all, and 50 million adults are unable to read above a 5th grade level. Moreover, the number of adults who are classified as functionally illiterate is increasing by 2.25 million each year (Blumenfeld, 2012; Boog, 2012). Because of this, making use of a variety of media sources is all the more important.

The *group mode* is oriented toward participants who are in learning groups organized around a particular topic. The group mode is *not* group therapy, but focused on instructional goals. The structure of groups can be formal or nonformal and vary in size, composition, frequency of meeting, and duration (Harman & Brim, 1980). Small groups are often used for parent and marriage education programs with people of similar interests and goals. The *individual mode*, which involves one-on-one interaction, may be associated with counseling and guidance, which are outside the realm of family life educators. However, educators often talk to parents individually about the needs and accomplishments of their children or may do a home visit to both learn about the child and teach parents educational activities they can use with them. At times educators may provide assistance or advice consisting of information and explanations to parents and families. For example, an educator working with young children may send home weekly letters to parents telling them of the upcoming week's activities and giving additional information to facilitate parent-child communication about the anticipated learning for the next week. If a family is in need of counseling and therapy, a family life educator should have a list of professionals and their contact information available for participants.

Instructional Planning: Structural Characteristics and Situational Factors

In previous chapters we have presented content on the diversity of participants (Chapter 3) and settings (Chapter 4) involved in family life education programming. This can be a guide in planning one's course or program. In future chapters we cover information related to implementation, evaluation, and examples of content for family life education programs. (See Figure 5.1.)

Figure 5.1   Elements of Program Design

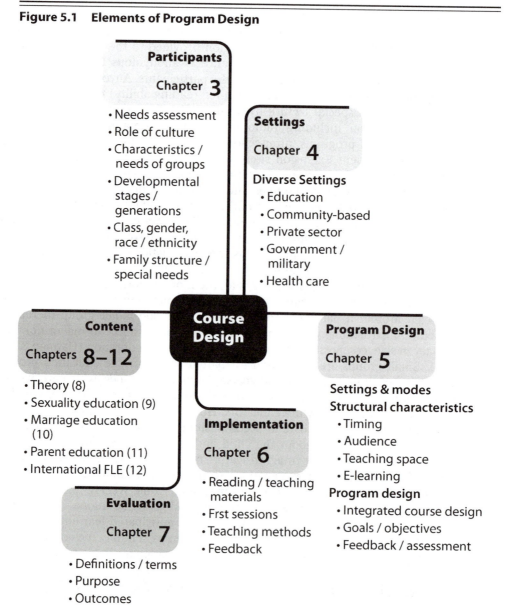

Before examining the specific content and activities that might be incorporated in a family life education course/program, there are *structural characteristics* and/ or *situational factors* to consider. Since using the group mode in formal and nonformal programs is commonly associated with family life education efforts, we will focus on these two types of programs and their structural considerations concerning timing, audience, teaching space, and e-learning issues.

Timing: Formal and Nonformal Education

When assigned to teach a class in a formal setting, you will need to look at the timing of the course. Timing varies each term depending on the days of the week you teach, break schedule, and the length of the term. Scheduling course content, exams, and assignments will be based on this time schedule. You may want to consider how the timing of course elements aligns with the schedules of you and your students. For example, do you want to schedule an exam the day before Thanksgiving? What about scheduling more than one set of papers from different classes to be due on the same date? If you are going to teach a course about public policy and your state legislature only meets during a specific period of time during the year, how can you schedule the class activities to best align with the legislative session? If you teach a course during the regular school year and are then asked to teach it during an abbreviated time period in the summer, will you alter the assignments in number and kind? Will there be fewer days for the students to complete projects and write papers, as well as fewer days for you to grade them? The class sessions may be longer to accommodate the summer schedule and while you still teach the same requisite content, you will have to alter the learning experiences to maintain student interest during longer daily sessions. The most important thing to remember about timing in both formal and nonformal settings is to keep an "eye on the clock." Pay attention to the time you are given and make sure to begin and end on time. If you cannot finish what was planned in the allotted time, acknowledge that there is much more that could be said and move to your concluding statements. Be respectful of the students' available time.

In nonformal education settings, you will be the person who decides how many sessions are needed, for what length of time, at what frequency, at what time of day, and during what season. If you have adults in this class who work during the day, when is the best time to schedule these sessions? More people might prefer to come to a one-time session rather than commit to a long-term course with multiple sessions, although a one-time session may be a catalyst for their return to a longer program at a later date. A frequent comment from adults is, "If we could only find the time." With the hectic lives of people with responsibilities for families, children, jobs, and educational goals that compete for their limited discretionary time, the timing of your session and program must be prioritized to make the best use of the time available to meet their needs. If you have more than one session, you might also want to plan "backwards." Determine what you want students to reasonably achieve at the end of the course and then plan how many sessions are needed to reach this goal. To entice people to attend the course, you may want to use food. Either plan a dinner session where they can eat and learn or have some other kind of refreshments. While formal education classes do not necessarily include food, nonformal sessions can incorporate food as a way to make the experience pleasant and provide opportunities for participants to connect with others in similar circumstances.

Audience: Formal and Nonformal Education

Students in a formal setting are often in high school or college or some other institutional setting. Their needs are often "ascribed" as institutions have some general idea about what the students need and have therefore designed their program of study, major, or curriculum to meet these perceived needs for the students and the profession. However, it is also up to you to note any specific needs related to the topic and students so you can alter the course accordingly, while not changing the "approved" goals and objectives of the course. For example, an issue may emerge in the news that relates to the course content or there may be a student who is blind, requiring you to talk about the appearance of any diagram you might display.

In a nonformal educational setting, students are often adults. But what is an adult? At various times individuals can be characterized as adults by certain qualities, such as their *age* (e.g., age to vote, drink, or join the army); *circumstance* (e.g., becoming a teen parent); social role (e.g., breadwinner or oldest male child if a father is not present); or *social or psychological maturity* (e.g., adapting to social norms of one's age cohort). *Adult education* is a "voluntary" process through which adults interact with their environment resulting in changes in their knowledge, skills, and attitudes. They typically are not only highly motivated to learn, but also have an increased complexity to their lives. The life expectancy of adults is increasing, along with concerns about health and wellness, more leisure time in retirement, and increased opportunities to take classes or seminars. They have greater knowledge and expanding experiences in all areas of life to add to discussions (Tippett, 2003). However, you may have to manage their input. While the contributions of your adult students may be valuable, their focus should be related to the main topic. You will need to be flexible in managing adult-student enthusiasm and comments so the course does not become solely a discussion group for mutual support, unless that is the goal.

When planning for adult students you need to consider physical/biological, social, and psychological differences. *Physically,* their size may be larger so that tables and chairs may be desirable rather than student desks. Some students may have physical limitations with their sight, hearing, or motor skills. When dealing with the location of the course, you may need to consider access to public transportation and handicapped parking. *Socially,* adults may have time and economic limitations that should be considered when determining the cost of any class. There may also be cultural factors, so attending a class may either be a status symbol, embarrassment, or a means to socialize. Previous bad or idealistic experiences with schools may also influence their willingness to participate. *Psychologically,* adult learners have high levels of personal and professional expectations of their learning experiences, but may want an informal learning environment. They want content that is practical, can be immediately applied, and will be relevant to their work or personal lives. Sharing the responsibility for learning and instruction with the instructor, as well as interacting with other participants will be of interest to them. Be aware of nonverbal cues regarding any confusion or lack of interest. This will allow you to vary the pace, change the activity, rephrase the question or statement, or regain the attention of the audience.

When teaching adults, try not to get too personal or treat adult participants as children by talking down to them or being condescending. They want to be respected for who they are and what they bring to the classroom setting. While it is common to do introductions at the beginning of a class, do not ask adult learners to identify their profession or work background. This may create a status differential among members in the class. Instead, ask them to communicate something nonthreatening about themselves or their children by giving suggestions of things to share, while providing the option to pass. Experimentation, practicing new skills, and not feeling like a beginner are important. It is also critical to allow autonomous and self-directed learning, and time to reflect and integrate new learning into their patterns of life.

Teaching Space: Formal and Nonformal Education

In formal education settings, you will most likely be assigned a classroom. It is good to visit this classroom before the term begins to determine the best arrangement of chairs/desks, lighting conditions, operational procedures for media equipment, and location of restrooms. Determine the optimal arrangement for the tables, chairs, or desks, so people can see and hear each other as much as possible. Whenever classrooms are renovated, technological enhancements also become updated so there may be little consistency within any particular institutional setting. The number of students in a classroom and the arrangement of seating can greatly influence the educational setting. Are you in an auditorium with raised seating or a large classroom that has considerable depth or breadth? Do you need a microphone and if so, is it stationary or portable? Is the classroom on a busy corridor so that there is considerable noise from outside the class? Where is/are the door(s) located and are you able to keep the door(s) open or will exterior noise affect student learning? Are all lights functioning in the classroom? Similarly, if a large number of students will fill the room to capacity, are all desks in working order? If not, it is good to report any problematic classroom conditions. Often times we see problems in a room and think someone else will mention it, but this is not usually the case. Some of these same issues are applicable to nonformal education settings and, again, visiting the classroom is essential before the class begins. If the class is taught during the evenings or a weekend, there may be no support person to assist with classroom issues, so making these contacts and checking out the room and equipment in advance are critical.

E-Learning: Formal and Nonformal Education

Greater access to personal computers and the Internet have increased educational opportunities in both formal and nonformal educational settings. Some elements of online design used in formal educational settings include the following, although many may also apply to nonformal settings: (1) Online courses should be instructor-led with a clear and consistent presence of the teacher who facilitates learning; (2) Learning should also be student-centered with challenging activities along with effective guidance and quality feedback; (3) Learning is collaborative with small-group activities and team projects to foster an online community of learners; (4) Coursework should maximize flexible participation within a paced framework; (5) Courses should foster information, communication, and technology skills for success in today's environment; (6) Course format, expectations, and instructions should be clear and concise; (7) Activities and evaluation should account for different learning styles; and (8) Courses should use the latest and best practices (NEA, 2003). Teaching an in-person class and transferring all the lectures, notes, and PowerPoint slides into an online course does not work, although you may be able to adapt some of the materials. In general, you will have to redesign the course to meet the needs of students within an electronic classroom. This format may also need pedagogical and technical support from the institution or other service providers.

There are advantages and disadvantages to online teaching and learning. The course material is available 24/7, so students can participate in lectures (if provided) multiple times. Since many students are working during the school year and throughout the summer, participating in an online course can help them learn while attending to personal financial needs. Time is also saved because students do not have to commute to campus, drive in rush-hour traffic if taking an evening class, or find parking. There is also greater anonymity that can facilitate clarifying misconceptions and increase the honesty and quantity of class participation. While in-class discussions may be uncomfortable to students because they may not want to speak in front of a group or need time to prepare a response, an online discussion allows time for thoughtful responses. The cost of online courses may or may not be an advantage. Since additional classrooms do not need to be built or maintained, there could be a savings to the institution and students. However, many online courses have higher tuition costs to cover technical support and teaching assistants for larger online courses that require ongoing individualized communication. One of the problems with online courses is that they require increased self-discipline and time management skills with no in-person reminders of assignments that are due. Teachers use cues from students to know when they are having trouble understanding and can then react by altering their approach to help them (Hill, 2008; Serlin, 2005). For both students and teachers, the face-to-face relationship is lost in an online class.

Some of the same issues for students are also relevant for teachers, such as flexibility, convenience, and commuting times. There is also a global reach for students and teachers in that you can travel hundreds of miles away from the institutional setting and still participate in class. Academic dishonesty can be a problem as well, although now exams can be taken worldwide at approved proctored testing centers. While grading class participation in an in-person class can be a problem especially in large classes, online courses allow you to keep track of the substance and quantity of student participation and facilitate grading. Electronic monitoring also allows for checks on plagiarism from other online sources, as well as the online submissions of papers from current and former students. It is hoped that the teachers have the knowledge and experience to manage virtual classrooms. The main disadvantage reported by teachers is not being able to connect with their students. This can be a problem when a recommendation is needed from a teacher, who may not have personal knowledge of the student, a clear notion of who the student is as a person, or his or her professional goals (Hill, 2008; Serlin, 2005).

The Internet has become an important tool for educating families in nonformal settings. People are no longer just viewing content passively, but through social media they are actively sharing ideas and answering questions about family issues. Thus, family life educators need to develop research-based programs that utilize a wide range of interactive strategies that will engage students. *Online family life education* can be defined as "any educational outreach primarily delivered via the internet that intentionally facilitates individual and family well-being by using online technologies that include programmatic educational strategies or structures" (Hughes, Bowers, Mitchell, Curtiss, & Ebata, 2012, p. 712). Because an online program reaches a wider audience than a traditional program, its content is essential to a successful program and must involve an integration of theory, research, practice, and context. If content is to be delivered in an online format, you must understand the online abilities and activities of your potential audience, as well as the way that families use the Internet to learn about family issues. It is helpful to provide students with brief and clear instructions at an appropriate reading level along with technical support to navigate the course, if needed. Incorporating various forms of media is encouraged with the use of pictures, video, animations, music, and audio segments that add educational value. It is often said, "A picture is worth a thousand words." Since online learners may not all be able to read, or like to read, incorporating media can facilitate learning with fewer words. In addition, interaction can promote retention as learners spend time processing information, getting feedback, and trying out various ideas. There are many family life education, web-based programs that are designed to educate individuals and families across the lifespan about various topics, such as marriage, divorce, and parenting. These programs are often voluntary, but may be court-mandated depending on family issues and state laws (e.g., Parenting Partnerships, www.parentingpartnerships.com). Although formal evaluations of online programs have been limited, as well as varied in terms of methodological rigor, increasing numbers of programs are including some form of program evaluation in addition to personal feedback and recommendations to others. Developing successful online programs is a process that involves ongoing evaluation of program design, content, teaching methods, and the effectiveness of online delivery methods (Hughes et al., 2012).

Another popular mode of electronic nonformal education is the use of a webinar, a *web-based seminar*, presentation, lecture, workshop, or training session that is transmitted over the web. A key feature is its interactivity—the ability to give, receive, and discuss information, which is in contrast to a *Webcast* in which data transmission is one-way and there is no interaction between the presenter and the audience. Webinars are usually hosted by an organization or company and broadcast through computers via the Internet. During the webinar a presenter may share PowerPoint presentations, videos, or other multimedia content. The participants may interact with the presenter by asking questions via a voice, video, or messaging chat line. Webinars can involve collaborative presenters along with polling, surveys, and question and answer sessions to allow greater participation. Organizations involved in webinars enlist the services of web conferencing vendors to facilitate connectivity. These webinars can be recorded and archived for later use with other groups. Webinars often require a fee to be paid to the vendor and organization. If you agree to teach a webinar, it is essential to have a practice session so that all technical issues can be resolved prior to the actual session. The advantages of a webinar are the ease of connection to others with similar interests anywhere there is a computer and Internet connection, interactivity with other participants in the meeting, and the reduced cost of learning compared to dealing with travel costs.

Instructional Planning: Program Design

Integrated Course Design

Fink (2005) in his model for *integrated course design* for significant learning proposed that one should first look at *situational factors* or *structural characteristics* and how they might influence the program design. Situational factors include what the students, department, institution, profession, and society expect of the course. You may also want to consider the class size or level of the course—lower or upper division or graduate level. What is the length and frequency of class meetings and how will instruction be delivered—in-person, online, in a classroom setting, or in the field? What are the characteristics of the learners (e.g., amount of time involved in parenting, work expectations, achievement of personal and professional goals) and what kinds of past experiences might students have had? In addition, what are the characteristics of the teachers regarding their values or beliefs about teaching and their knowledge of the subject matter? Many of these elements are similar to those discussed earlier in the section on structural characteristics. These factors influence the *learning goals and course objectives* along with the *teaching and learning activities* you will plan and the *feedback and assessment* you will create. In other words, all four elements are interrelated when planning your course; they are consistent and support each other. (See Figure 5.2, which is adapted from Fink, 2005.)

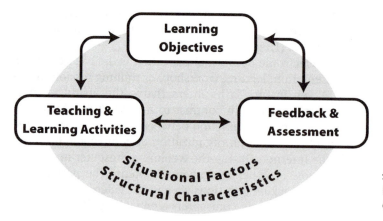

Figure 5.2   Integrated Course Design

Goals

Prior to planning the course, identify the real-life problem to be addressed or the reason for the course. What are current theories related to this content and what scholarly literature is available to address the audience, setting, and focus of the course? When you have a clearer perspective of what this course will entail, you may want to begin planning by using a backward design process and asking yourself the question, "What would you like your students to have learned by the end of this course that will still be with them two to three years later" (Fink, 2005, p. 5). Your responses constitute the learning goals for the course. A *goal* is a broad general statement of intention or direction for the program describing what you want to achieve through your efforts. It may be somewhat abstract, hard to measure, and encompass a longer time frame. For example, a goal might be that you want students to have a greater appreciation of the multiple roles of families.

To facilitate learning in a course consider the *interactive nature* of *six types of significant learning*. This means that each type of learning can stimulate other kinds of learning, and thus, has implications for the creation of learning goals for the course. While it might seem challenging to include all six types of significant learning, you will find that including as many elements as feasible will result in a more valuable learning experience for your students. These types of learning and some subcategories include the following (Fink, 2005):

- Foundational Knowledge—understanding and remembering information and ideas
- Application—skills, thinking (critical, creative, and practical), and managing projects
- Integration—connecting ideas, people, and realms of life
- Human Dimension—learning about oneself and others
- Caring—developing new feelings, interests, and values
- Learning How to Learn—becoming a better student, inquiring about a subject, and self-directed learning

When developing the goals for the course, ask yourself what you need to know to make the best teaching decisions. It is important to have information about the learners (demographics, backgrounds, needs, interests, and goals); the latest developments within the subject area (research and programs); available resources (material, financial, and human/personal); societal trends (local, national, and international, as well as state laws and policies); community contexts (attitudes, values, and resources); and learning theories (Chamberlain & Cummings, 2003).

Objectives

The next step in the planning process involves creating objectives for the course or program. An *objective*, compared to a goal, is specific, short term, and measurable. For some time Bloom's taxonomy of educational objectives, which is probably the most widely known educational taxonomy, has been used to categorize learning. It encompasses the *Cognitive* (knowledge), *Affective* (attitude or self), and *Psychomotor* (skills) *Domains* (Bloom, 1956; Krathwohl, Bloom, & Masia,

1973; Simpson, 1972). Most attention has been focused on the *Cognitive Domain*, which involves behaviors concerned with intellectual pursuits, thinking, using one's mind, and relational learning that can be thought of as the goals of the learning process. The behaviors are organized into levels from simple to more complex mental processes including *knowledge* (recalling information); *comprehension* (explaining information); *application* (using information); *analysis* (separating information); *synthesis* (combining information); and *evaluation* (making assessments). A former student of Bloom proposed wording changes to these categories so that the new names of the six categories are parallel to the former names, but are changed from nouns to verbs (Anderson, Krathwohl, Airasian, & Cruikshank, 2001). Thus, the suggested terminology is *remembering, understanding, applying, analyzing, evaluating,* and *creating.* (Note, compared to Bloom's configuration, there is a reversal in the order of the last two categories.) Nevertheless, Bloom's taxonomy has had a long history and popularity and is still widely used in creating curriculum objectives. Whether you use the original or revised taxonomy, the levels of cognitive domain should be considered when determining measurable course objectives for any course you design. See Table 5.1 for guidelines for these six levels of the cognitive domain regarding what is expected of learners, examples of objectives at each level, and verbs to reflect various levels of learning (Clauss, 2005.) This table can be very helpful in creating the course objectives.

Table 5.1   Creating Measurable Objectives (Syllabus Objective Guide)

	Learners are expected to:	Examples: Students will:	Verbs to use when writing objectives reflecting this level of learning:
Knowledge Can learners **recall** information?	Remember a fact, idea, or phenomenon essentially in the same form in which they learned it	**List** four functions of families **Name** the food groups of the food guide pyramid **Define** the terms "reduce," "reuse," and "recycle"	cite, count, define, find, identify, label, list, match, memorize, name, note, omit, point to, quote, recall, recite, repeat, say, spell, state
Comprehension Can learners **explain** information?	Communicate an idea in their own words (translate); grasp the meaning of an idea to be able to explain it (interpret); or project the effect of things (extrapolate)	**Explain** the process of divorce **Paraphrase** another's verbal and nonverbal message **Infer** the effect of a pregnant woman's smoking a pack of cigarettes a day on the fetus **Interpret** the phrase "You cannot not communicate"	annotate, clarify, describe, elaborate, explain, generalize, translate, infer, interpret, restate, review, reword, summarize

	Learners are expected to:	Examples: Students will:	Verbs to use when writing objectives reflecting this level of learning:
Application Can learners **use** information?	Use abstractions such as concepts, principles, rules, and generaliza-tions in specific and concrete situations	**Use** active listening skills **Calculate** the amount of carpet needed for a specific home **Give an example** of an effective discipline technique for a toddler **Show** foods appro-priate for a diabetic	apply, calculate, employ, give an example, illustrate, interview, operate, show, solve, survey, use, utilize
Analysis Can learners **separate** information?	Break things down into components; determine relation-ships among elements; dis-tinguish factors; or classify information	**Contrast** biological and environmental influences on human development **Classify** fast food into food groups on the food guide pyramid **Outline** the decision making process	analyze, categorize, classify, compare, contrast, diagram, differentiate, distin-guish, divide, examine, outline, relate, separate, take apart
Synthesis Can learners **combine** information?	Produce original plans; create new patterns or structures; or combine what is "known" into a new perspective	**Integrate** professional literature reporting results of research on consumer behavior **Plan** a house to meet a particular client's specifications **Propose** a family life education program for parents of "boomer-ang" children	blend, build, combine, compose, construct, create, design, form, formulate, generate, hypothesize, integrate, invent, modify, plan, predict, produce, pro-pose, rearrange, reconstruct, reorder, reorganize, revise, structure, write (compose)
Evaluation Can learners **make assessments?**	Judge the value of material based on definite criteria; rate ideas, conditions, or objects' or accept or reject ideas, things, or conditions based on standards	**Choose** the most energy-efficient appliances **Justify** discipline strategies as parents of adolescents **Evaluate** construction of a ready-to-wear garment **Rank** characteristics of an effective family and consumer sciences teacher	appraise, assess, choose, criticize, critique, debate, decide, defend, evaluate, grade, judge, prioritize, rank, rate, recommend, referee, reject, select, support, umpire, weigh, justify

Note: Some scholars believe "synthesis" is a more complex intellectual effort than "evaluation." Hence, the order of these two levels of learning can be interchanged. You decide!

(Clauss, 2005)

The customary practice in writing objectives is to specify the ultimate behavior of the learner. Behavior can be measured objectively because you have concrete evidence of achievement based on the wording of the objectives. Behavioral objectives are applicable to learners in both formal and nonformal settings and in a variety of contexts, such as classroom students, athletes, or in-service training sessions. One focus is to construct S.M.A.R.T. learning objectives (Drucker, 1954; Schmitt, Hu, & Bachrach, 2008). Consider whether or not your objective is . . .

S Specific—Does it say exactly what the learner will be able to do?

M Measureable—Is it quantifiable and can it be measured?

A Attainable—Can it be accomplished in the proposed framework with available resources?

R Relevant—Will it meet the needs of the participants and the organization?

T Time Frame—Can it be accomplished in the time available?

Whereas Table 5.1 has examples of objectives for each of the levels in Blooms Taxonomy, the terminology below should be avoided because the objectives would be difficult to observe or measure: Participants will...

- *understand* the importance of good parenting
- *become familiar* with family theories
- *learn* about the developmental characteristics of adolescents
- *appreciate* the value of relationship and premarital education

Feedback and Assessment

Throughout the course it is important to give formative feedback by providing information to students about their learning. At times this feedback may need to be corrective, and not just about their strengths and weaknesses. Students should also be given opportunities for self-assessment and reflection about their learning experiences. Peers can be encouraged to provide constructive feedback, whether it is on papers, assignments, or thought processes. Through effective feedback, students can identify where they are having difficulties and can make improvements in their future work. Of course, the degree and frequency of feedback are based on various situational factors, such as the number of students in a class, number of courses being taught by the instructor, and/or the nature of the class.

You may never truly know the impact of the course in the future lives of your students except for those who may write or see you in the community. So, during the course you will want to incorporate some current and "forward assessment measures" (Fink, 2005). Give students exercises, questions, and problems that have a real-world context for a given issue, problem, or decision they might have to address in the future. If you give them forward-thinking experiences in which they can "practice" for the future, students gain insight about how to integrate the content of the course into their future lives. For example, you can have them plan and implement teaching units in family life education, or (as noted in Chapter 11 on Sexuality Education) provide students opportunities in class to respond to sexuality pressure lines. This gives them practice so that when they encounter these situations in real life, they will be better prepared to handle them.

In formal education settings, it may be necessary to grade students' papers and give exams. Checklists, scorecards, and rubrics are instruments that can be used by learners to evaluate themselves or their peers, or by teachers to evaluate the learners' work. It is important to provide a grading rubric to assist learners in writing their papers. A *grading rubric* is a scoring tool that explicitly represents the expectations for an assignment. It separates the assigned work into component parts and provides clear descriptions of the characteristics of the work associated with each component at varying levels of mastery. Rubrics can be used for a wide array of assignments: papers, projects, oral presentations, student portfolios, and group projects. In addition, rubrics can be used as scoring or grading guides, to provide formative feedback to support and guide ongoing learning efforts, or both (Eberly Center, n.d.; Nilson, 2003).

Creating good test questions takes considerable time and effort. Thus, writing items as you progress through the sections of the course will allow time to reflect on the relationship of the questions to the stated course objectives. While test banks developed by book publishers are often available, they are not always accurate or appropriate for a given course or its objectives. Creating questions in proportion to their emphasis in class is a good policy. While there are several types of exam questions, generally in national exams, multiple-choice questions are preferred. Multiple-choice questions are not easy to construct, but they can objectively measure knowledge, determine the ability to apply concepts or principles, assess elements of problem solving, and are easy to grade (McKeachie & Svinicki, 2006). Some examples of guidelines for writing multiple-choice exam questions include the following:

ITEMS (The entire multiple-choice question) should . . .

- be appropriate for the course objective and level of performance (i.e., knowledge-based, application-oriented, or evaluation-level questions)
- focus on important aspects of content and not trivia
- have agreement of stem and options
- avoid negatives (no, not, except)
- avoid absolutes (all, always, never, only)
- avoid giving clues
- be independent of other items in the exam

STEMS (The first, sentence-like portion of a multiple-choice question) should . . .

- ask a question or pose a problem (desired response is evident)
- be written in a clear, precise, and unambiguous manner
- provide all pertinent information necessary to answer the question with no extraneous information

OPTIONS (all of the possible multiple-choice responses) should . . .

• have only one correct answer

• include plausible and attractive distracters

• avoid "all of the above," "none of the above," or other confusing options

• have a logical order of options

• have a minimum of 4 options

• make options grammatically and conceptually parallel

• be of similar length

Depending on the size of the class, long or short-answer essay questions may be a viable option. Problems can be posed for which students need to apply class content or use higher levels of Blooms taxonomy. Whatever type of questions you use, it is wise to carefully proof the exam prior to distributing it to the students and even have a colleague evaluate the test for clarity and content.

After the exam has been given and scored, conduct an item analysis and if it is based on objective questions, calculate the *Difficulty Index* and *Discrimination Index* for each item. The Difficulty Index is calculated by adding the number of students who chose the correct response for an item and dividing it by the total number of students who took the test. The Difficulty Index will range from 0 to 1 with a difficult item being indicated by an index of .5 and an easy item being indicated by an index of over .8. The Discrimination Index is determined by first calculating the percentage of students answering each item correctly within the upper third and lower third of the exam scores. Subtract the percentage of the lower group from the percentage of the upper group of students to get the index. The index will range from −1 to +1 with a discrimination over .3 being desirable, while a negative index will indicate a possible flawed item. How your students perform on well-designed exams provides important data assessing their learning, as well as insights about your teaching.

It is recommended that students within a family life education methodology class have an opportunity to plan and implement a unit they will teach, as well as create assessment measures, such as multiple-choice questions. This means students will create exam questions that will be aligned with objectives for their created unit or course. If possible, this unit can be presented to the class along with a discussion of the recommended questions. The teacher can take one question from every unit and prepare a "pop quiz" to be used as a subsequent learning experience. After the completion of the units, the instructor can bring the quiz to class and announce that there will be a surprise "pop quiz." Have the students discuss their feelings about this announcement. Then distribute the quiz, but have students put false names on the quiz, so that only they will know their results (e.g., Superman, Queen Elizabeth, Mickey Mouse, or Beyoncé). After taking the quiz, have it scored electronically with all possible analysis options. Then bring the quiz responses back to class and have the students anonymously examine their own individual performance and how others responded to their question. This is not to be used as an assessment of students, but a teaching and learning experience to understand the difficulty in creating good test questions and how flawed questions can be changed.

In nonformal education settings you will receive feedback from students in a variety of forms, such as casual comments; direct statements of praise or complaint; or nonverbal reactions such as facial cues, posture, or eye contact. Unfortunately, you may not accurately receive the messages that are being transmitted. One important form of feedback to pay attention to is whether or not learners return after the first class. In other words, the most important goal of a first class session is to create the desire for students to return for the next session.

SUMMARY

Designing a program or course has many interrelated elements, such as classroom settings and modes of instruction; structural characteristics; and creating program/course goals, objectives, and evaluation. As noted in Figure 5.1 participants, organizational settings, content, and implementation need to be simultaneously incorporated into course planning. The selection of teaching and learning activities will be influenced by your original research into the course topic and the situational factors, course objectives, and assessment plans associated with your course design. However, you will have to "stay tuned" for the next chapter for some suggestions on various teaching methods. Once you have designed your course, you will continually refine it with new course objectives, teaching activities, resources, and assessment measures. Your goal is to develop the best possible class, course, or program that you can, but inevitably, there will be changes during the course and afterward. Program design involves the joy of creating and meeting the challenges of change.

QUESTIONS AND ISSUES FOR DISCUSSION

1. What are some examples of formal, nonformal, and informal settings for family life education?
2. What are some examples of mass, group, and individual modes that can be utilized in family life education?
3. What are some positive and negative teaching locations that you have experienced and what contributed to your evaluations of that space?
4. What kind of experiences have you had with online courses? What contributes to a successful online course?
5. What types of exam questions do you like or dislike and why?

ACTIVITIES

1. If you have mature adults taking a family life education methodology class, determine if they would be willing to share what it is like to be a mature student who is taking courses while managing other work, family, and life issues.

2. Have speaker(s) come to class who are involved in technical or pedagogical support for online courses to share the range of possibilities in designing online courses.

3. Have each student or a group of students explore an unfamiliar technological tool for use with online learning. Present this technique to the class describing its features, advantages, and disadvantages.

4. Give small groups of students an "in-class" experience of designing a course on an innocuous topic, such as basket weaving, building a birdhouse, or learning a foreign language that is not commonly taught in schools. What would be the "backwards" goal(s) for students? What would be the objectives of the course, content, learning experiences, and assessment?

5. Assign individuals or small groups of students to plan and teach a unit applicable to one of the content areas within the Certified Family Life Educator program. Students should also create exam questions and some type of program evaluation so they can analyze the effectiveness of their unit.

6

Implementation of Family Life Education

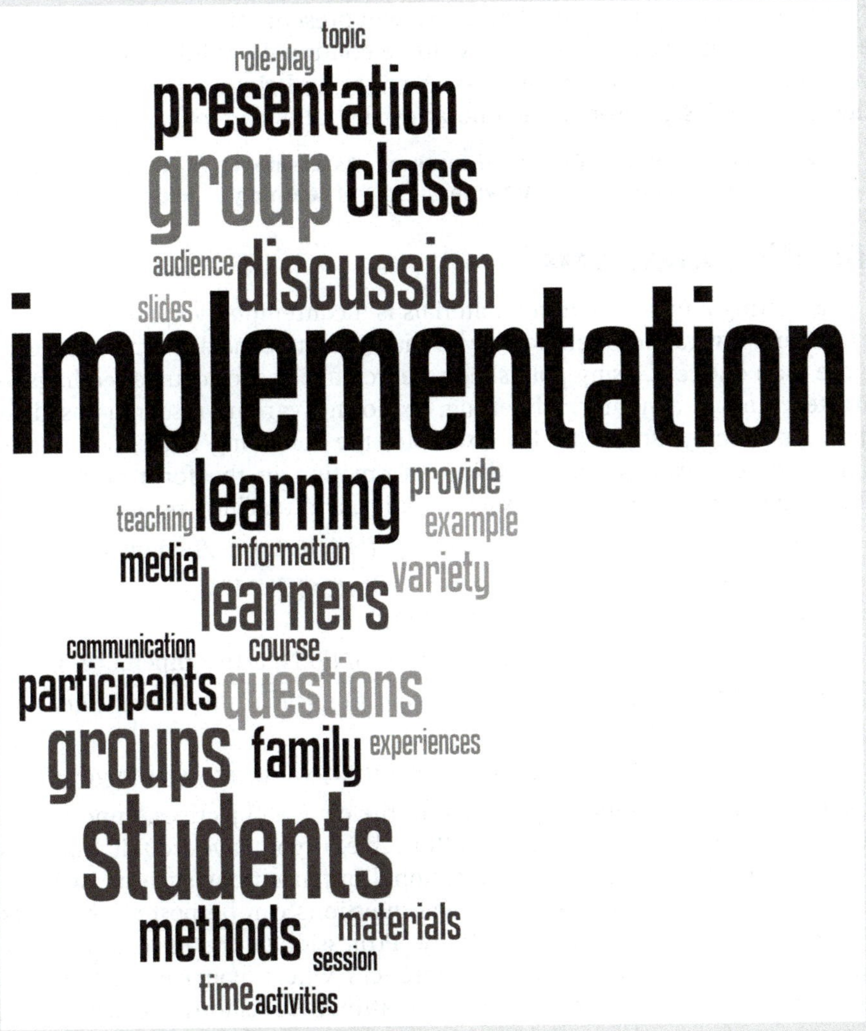

≡ Incorporating Effective Teaching and Learning Activities

Now that you have learned about designing your program (Chapter 5), it is time to *implement* your plans. You have already taken into consideration situational factors and structural characteristics while writing learning objectives and creating feedback and assessment measures (Fink, 2005). While most likely you have been thinking about teaching and learning activities to accompany your plans, it is now time to explore a variety of educational methods to assist in developing learning experiences for your family life education class or program. Some of you will go on to teach at the high school or college level (formal settings), whereas others will present workshops or learning experiences in the community (nonformal settings). In this chapter we will present information relevant to a variety of family life education settings. To be continually thinking of each element as you plan and implement your class, it might be helpful to create a *worksheet* for this ongoing design process incorporating the following four columns (Fink 2005).

Learning Objectives for Course/Session	Teaching-Learning Activities	Assessment of Learning	Resources Needed (e.g., people, materials)

≡ Reading Materials

Selecting a text or reading materials is a contemplative process. In addition to examining several pertinent texts, you may want to consider combining chapters of more than one text, using published research articles for course readings, or if you are teaching in a nonformal setting, exploring various research-based materials that can meet your needs. For example, the following sites and organizations, among others, can provide credible information in the form of tip sheets, fact sheets, pamphlets, sample program modules, and teaching resources.

- *National Council on Family Relations* (NCFR, http://ncfr.org)
- *National Healthy Marriage Resource Center* (NHMRC, http://www.healthymarriageinfo.org)
- *National Parenting Education Network* (NPEN, http://npen.org/)
- *Sexuality Information and Education Council of the United States* (SIECUS, http://www.siecus.org/)
- *Cooperative Extension Service* (CES, http://www.csrees.usda.gov/Extension/)

Reading materials should be pertinent to the course objectives, appropriate for the reading level of your students, and affordable. If you have trouble finding suitable materials for your class, many professional organizations such as NCFR or NPEN have an e-mail discussion list to which questions can be posted about resources, methods, or best practices to employ. Professional organizations also conduct national, regional, and/or state conferences where you can network with colleagues, obtain reviews of new books, or attend workshops and webinars. Having access to professional materials and resources is one of the benefits of belonging to a professional association.

Incorporating Teaching Materials and Equipment

Depending on the setting in which you will teach, some equipment and materials may be available in the classroom or placed online for student access, in other situations you may have to bring them with you. When doing a pre-check of the classroom, note if there are whiteboards, blackboards, and functioning markers, although it is always good to bring writing implements with you to class. If you need some technical equipment, you may have to request it in advance. While most classrooms have computers and teachers may be able to upload PowerPoint slides from another location to a teaching site, it is always good to have backup materials on a flash drive. Furthermore, you may need paper and pencils for small group activities or other teaching supplies, such as toys if they are enhancements to your child development lesson; examples of books on topics that might be of additional interest to students; or other handouts, objects, and props that may add to your class sessions. Keeping a list of needed materials, as indicated in the worksheet, can be a real asset when assembling the materials needed for any class session.

It is essential to have a backup plan. At times a DVD or computer will not work and you will need an alternate strategy. This might mean you highlight the points of your presentation on the blackboard or white board. With all the materials that one has to take to any class, at times, you may even take the wrong folder so your class notes and outline of content materials are not present. After that initial "sinking feeling," you realize that you have probably gone over these materials a few times before arriving at your classroom. Therefore, sitting down and reconstructing the highlights of the presentation can work, and at times your newfound freedom from the planned agenda can make the presentation even more effective—assuming you were thoroughly prepared before you arrived.

Managing the First Session

Depending on the length of the session or program, you will want to engage the learner as quickly as possible to "break the ice." Begin by introducing yourself. Without reciting your vita or resume, provide some credentials to support why you are qualified to teach this course, as well as a little personal background. You can pose some questions for your students (which you answer first), such as, who has been the biggest influence on your life, what is the hardest thing about being a parent, or what is a special memory you have from your childhood. It is important to get the participants talking, but you need to keep self-disclosure low so no one feels threatened. You can use general questions or some that are specifically related to your course content. For example, in a *Family Ecosystem* course ask how one part of their environment is affecting them today, or for a workshop on *Human Sexuality* ask what they learned about sexuality when in a school-based curriculum or what their parents or friends told them about sexuality. It is always good to give participants a choice of questions to which they might respond.

A multi-session course can provide an opportunity for more involved introductions, especially in a college setting where the first few days of the term are comprised of drop/add procedures and getting the enrollment established. However, if you only have a one-session class, time for extended introductions might be a lux-ury. Nevertheless getting to know the students and each other is essential. In a short seminar, at times you might ask students to raise their hands if they are members of certain groups or have certain qualities. For example, you could ask them to raise their right hand if they have siblings, rock their arms like a cradle if they have a child under six months of age, swing their arms if they exercise each day, circle their eyes if they watch television every day, or put their head on the table if they would like more sleep at night (Tippett, 2003). If the group is large, there can be some small group activities that involve introductions, or you can ask for volunteers or randomly call on students to share introductory information letting them know that you will be calling on other students later.

In the opening session you will set the stage for learning by creating interest in the content of the class and building rapport with your students. Since style of communication is important, keep the amount of information low and digestible, especially if this is the first of multiple sessions. As you present new ideas, get feedback and request examples, while also taking time to respond to student input. In a relaxed mode, with a sense of humor, and through interactions that are respectful, send the message that you are a person with whom they can be comfortable and trust. In other words, developing a rapport with your students is critical, but depends on the situation. In a single session, you may choose to greet participants at the door as they enter the classroom and then later link some of your background and personal information to the participants (Chamberlain & Cummings, 2003). In an institutional setting, building rapport is a continual process of personal contact. When students enter the classroom, ask questions, indicate an interest in them and their activities, and show a positive and enthusiastic attitude.

Selecting and Incorporating Teaching Methods

While considering the size of your group, select presentation methods that can work in either formal or nonformal settings. Giving lectures may not be an optimal approach because the potential for discussion is often limited. Nevertheless, discussion is still possible in small groups and even in large groups, although you may have to use a portable microphone and move around the classroom. You may also want to add elements (e.g., pictures, stories, videos) to your presentations to make them more enjoyable and engaging.

Presentations

Lecture

One of the common methods used by teachers in both formal and nonformal settings is a lecture—a carefully prepared oral presentation of a subject by a qualified expert that at times may seem somewhat structured and formal. A lecture is used to present factual material in a direct and logical manner, entertain or inspire, or stimulate thinking and further study on a problem prior to opening the subject up for discussion. "Simple lecturing" employs what is known as the "still" method of learning—"you sit *still*, while I in*still*." Lectures can communicate an intrinsic interest in the subject matter and convey material that is not available in another format, such as unpublished research. Furthermore, lectures can be used to reach many listeners at the same time, which is an advantage to those who learn well in this manner, but may be problematic for others who learn better from different methods. Since lectures primarily involve one-way communication with minimal feedback, they put students in a passive rather than active role. This format is not well suited to complex or abstract material, so the burden of organizing and synthesizing the content is primarily on the presenter. For lectures to be effective they need to "combine the talents of a scholar, writer, producer, comedian, showman, and teacher in ways that contribute to student learning" (McKeachie & Svinicki, 2006, p. 57).

Unless giving a lecture meets a clear purpose and is appropriately delivered, it might be better to consider this presentation type as facilitating a discourse, talk, and conversation rather than a one-way transmission of knowledge. Generally, lectures do not sustain attention, which diminishes in 15 to 25 minutes, and tend to be forgotten quickly. Because little information is absorbed or retained, it is a good idea to plan a variety of methods to add stimulation to your presentation. For example, break a lecture every 7 to 10 minutes with an exercise that involves students in some way, such as questions, anecdotes, personal experiences, problems, applicable current events, short quizzes, illustrations, discussion, and humor. While there are several types of humor, self-effacing humor is probably the safest and least offensive type to use in a classroom. It can demonstrate that, despite your credentials and education, you are fallible and human (Royse, 2003).

Clickers can be used to engage students and collect responses. Retention will be enhanced the more you exercise their brains and involve their senses. Remember that as a presenter you are the primary ingredient in a successful learning experience. If you are enthusiastic, committed to the concepts you are presenting, and realize that class participation is also an essential element, you can be successful.

Incorporating *PowerPoint slides* has become increasingly popular. While in the past, teachers often highlighted their points by writing on the black or white board, teachers now prefer to emphasize their content in colorful slides. When the teacher wrote statements on the board, they were done in "real time" during which students had an opportunity to digest the information, take notes, and ask questions. This process allowed time to think while writing. Since the days of writing on the board are mostly gone, below are some tips for incorporating PowerPoint slides (Chamberlain & Cummings, 2003):

- Begin by providing an outline of your presentation, possibly using bullets for your main points. This will give learners the intended direction of your presentation.

- Avoid wordiness by using only a few words, phrases, and bullets. Make sure you proof your slides for spelling mistakes, use of repeated words, and grammatical errors.

- Use a readable font. Whereas some fonts are easy to *read* in printed documents (e.g., Times New Roman, Verdana), others are easy to *see* projected across a room (e.g., Arial, Helvetica). Depending on the room size, use at least a 24-point font and only capitalize letters when necessary, because CAPITALS ARE MORE DIFFICULT TO READ (McKeachie & Svinicki, 2006).

- Use a background that is simple and attractive. For a well-lit room, use a light background and dark text with the reverse for a dimly-lit room. Use a font color that is easy to read and has sharp contrast. Use color to add interest and emphasize a point, as it is a good tool if used wisely. If possible, keep the lights on in the classroom and avoid showing slides in a dark room for more than 15 minutes (McKeachie & Svinicki, 2006).

- Use animation and transitions prudently to maintain a minimal level of visual disturbance. Overdoing can distract from your content.

- Use graphs and charts rather than tables to facilitate comprehension and retention of data.

- Incorporate multimedia clips to convey your message more effectively. Dynamic content from a brief video is a great way to engage your audience. Again, be careful not to overuse this format.

- Talk about your slides without reading the content verbatim. Slides are used to enhance a presentation and are not "the presentation."

- Pace the change of slides in your presentation to 1 to 2 slides per minute. If you change slides too quickly, learners have difficulty reading and assimilating the content, whereas if you change slides too slowly, learners have problems because the presentation drags.

- Provide slides electronically in a formal class through a course website or in paper format for learners in a nonformal setting. Since you may be including a variety of slides for interest and stimulation, you should only post or print slides with content that learners may want to revisit. Having handouts of your PowerPoint slides available at the beginning of a presentation facilitates student engagement in your presentation while allowing them to write additional notes on the handout. In all cases, one has to consider the cost of paper and ink and the effect on the environment of using multiple pieces of paper.

- Include an effective and strong closing slide/conclusion. You may want to summarize the main points and/or suggest future avenues for research or practice. End your presentation with a simple statement that welcomes questions from the audience and incorporates a visual aid to use during the question period.

- Use note pages at the bottom of slides to facilitate your delivery and be prepared for technical issues, such as a computer failure or power outage. Have paper notes and a set of printed PowerPoint slides available as a backup.

An alternate to PowerPoint is using *Prezi* (www.prezi.com), a web-based presentation tool for presenting ideas by allowing users to zoom in and out of their presentation to show contextual relationships. It works with a "canvas" that you use to create a path that is followed as you progress with your presentation. Each "area" becomes its own presentation, as you are able to delve deeper within the frame before you move onto the next area.

Panel

A panel presentation involves a group of 4 to 6 persons with special knowledge of a subject. It can be used to identify and explore a problem or issue, give learners an understanding of the various parts of the problem, and/or weigh the advantages and disadvantages of a particular course of action. As with a lecture, the goal of this type of presentation is to engage the audience in asking questions and giving comments. The panelists could each give a 5 minute introductory statement as to their current situation or position while being seated in a semicircle so they can see each other during the conversation and also be seen by the audience. Presenters then hold an unrehearsed, informal, and orderly conversation on an assigned topic in full view of the audience. This type of presentation has a moderator, who might be the instructor, whose tasks are to introduce the panelists, present the topic of conversation, incorporate prompting questions to begin the dialogue, keep the flow of communication moving, handle questions from the audience, manage disagreements, and bring the session to a close. A moderator may also have to deal with panelists who tend to ramble, are relatively silent, or are clearly wrong. If needed, the moderator can ask specific questions of some participants if they appear uncomfortable about speaking or have difficulty inserting themselves into the conversation. An example of a panel presentation, which could be meaningful to an audience, would be couples who are at various stages in the dating process or who have been married for varying lengths of time.

Symposium

A symposium presentation is a series of prepared speeches given by 3 to 5 experts on as many elements of an issue as there are speakers. The goal of a symposium is to help the audience gain an overall view of various aspects of a topic. The presenters' comments are directed toward the topic and kept short (approximately 10 to 20 minutes). The symposium can present new material in a concise and logical way; give several objective viewpoints to offer an impartial treatment to the subject under consideration; provide a fair analysis of several sides of a controversial issue; and/or clarify facets of a complex problem. There will again be a moderator, which could be the instructor, who will introduce the speakers; time the presentations; facilitate discussion among the presenters, as well as with the audience; and bring the symposium to closure. A symposium could be a viable option when dealing with professionals who are family life educators in different settings. They can present what their roles are along with the joys and challenges of their settings. When the series of presentations is complete, as with other presentation modes, engaging the class in questions and discussion is critical.

Interview

An interview is a presentation in which one or more resource persons respond to questioning by an interviewer. The purpose of an interview presentation mode is to share information. The interviewer serves as the moderator and before questioning begins, he or she can discuss with the resource person(s) the overall topic in order to reach agreement on the general line of questioning. Once the interview begins, the interviewer asks the resource person(s) questions that explore various aspects of the topic. An interview might be used to explore issues related to teen pregnancy and could involve a pregnant teen and her mother as resource persons. In this instance the informal dialogue is less threatening to the persons being interviewed, because they do not have to prepare a presentation.

Debate

In a debate, participants try to persuade others to see an issue from their perspectives. Thus, the topic must have certain positions that are either "for" or "against" a particular issue (Chamberlain & Cummings, 2003). Each team presents their position with their strongest possible argument. Afterward the participants can respond to statements of their opponents. Usually there are two sides, but there could be additional perspectives. Chapter 11 includes an example of a debate before a hypothetical school board by four groups who are stating their positions on various forms of sexuality education to be offered by the school district.

Workshop

A workshop consists of a group of persons with a common interest or problem who want to improve their ability or understanding of a subject. This method can be an effective means of explaining procedures, illustrating the learning process, and developing understanding by "doing," with the major ingredient being *active participation*. Although it is preferable to involve everyone, all members of the group may not need to be fully engaged in workshop activities and can observe others' participation. The workshop may be used to identify, explore, and seek a solution to a problem; permit extensive study of a situation; and provide a "hands-on" learning experience. It may range from one to several hours or to multiple sessions scheduled over several weeks. There may also be various centers to allow participants to rotate to different locations for a small group context within a larger setting. An example is a workshop for parents on creative learning experiences for their children that will involve the active participation of parents in various activities such as art, music, science, reading, mathematics, games, and outdoor activities.

Multimedia

Multimedia involves different forms of media that combine text, sound, animation, still images (e.g., cartoons, pictures, newspaper headlines), video (e.g., YouTube or news clips), or interactivity and can be accessed by computerized and electronic devices. In other words, this presentation mode encompasses all methods of instruction that utilize any form of media. Teachers are constantly looking for videos or print media to use in their classes to give examples or highlight certain concepts. Two challenges for teachers are students' short attention spans and a visual orientation to learning. Many of today's students spend "more hours watching television, playing video games, or surfing the net, than reading books" (Downing, 2008, p. 51). Being part of a "visual culture" contributes to the formation of limited attention spans because they are used to quickly moving, brightly colored, and rapidly changing segments. As a result the typical college lecture may seem bland, colorless, and dull (Downing, 2008). Therefore, in order for learners to receive the greatest benefit from this form of instruction, the teacher must incorporate a systematic plan, along with wise and skillful use of media materials and technology. This instructional form can be used for presentations to large or small groups or in situations that involve self-instruction. The materials do not stand alone and need to be introduced and utilized as a part of the whole organized presentation. They may be used to stimulate other senses—hearing and sight, supply a concrete example for conceptual thinking, and provide experiences not easily obtained through other materials.

Students are bombarded with so many visual images on a daily basis, from television to online videos to social media, that it is important to only incorporate visual stimuli into your sessions if they apply to the points you are trying to make, are followed by discussion, and are used in moderation. Full-length films or documentaries can be used, but may involve greater time expenditures than are needed or available for your course objective(s). However, video clips can provide the examples you need. To find clips, you can search the Internet or ask students, other colleagues from your community or institution, or colleagues on a professional e-mail discussion list. You can also create your own videos of guest speakers, developmental milestones of children, or examples of communication styles.

While hearing a lengthy recorded speech is not necessarily appealing to students, at times various other auditory materials can be used. For example, you can include music to illustrate different issues in relationships whether they pertain to dating, parenting, or marriage. You can also get music from previous eras to show how messages about relationships have changed over time. It may be wise to use clips that have been edited into one sound track to keep the pace of this learning tool appropriate to the students' level of interest.

Exhibits and displays

Using exhibits and displays allows groups of people to gather simultaneously in various areas of a room where they may see a demonstration, hear an explanation of an issue or program, or watch a media presentation. Exhibits and displays provide educational information to create interest in topics, as well as provide knowledge and resources. Visual media can help to attract attention, convey content, stimulate action and thinking, provide positive relations, and create affective changes (Chamberlain & Cummings, 2003). The variety within this style of presentation is limited only by imagination and productivity. Exhibits can be used to get attention; reach people who do not read and will not attend regular meetings; provide a dramatic impact; and/or create a casual, relaxed, and close environment in which to learn and potentially interact with others. When teaching about the use of visual media within an exhibit, you may want to provide some guidelines or resources about the characteristics for effective visuals such as color, texture, shape or form, space, proportion, balance, emphasis, and lettering. Childhood safety in many different areas of the home, school, and near environment could be an example of an exhibit and display presentation.

Facilitating Interactions

Questioning

Skillful questioning is an important key to stimulating purposeful learning. Prior to class you might formulate some questions to remind you of the questions you intend to ask and help start the process. Thus, you can more skillfully guide students toward attaining the intended objectives and exploring conceptual skills at higher levels of the *cognitive domain*. For example, you can ask questions that deal with *Synthesis* (e.g., If you were given this responsibility, what actions would you consider taking?) or *Evaluation* (e.g., What decision would be the best for you and why?). You can also ask probing questions that focus on:

- clarification (asking for more information about what their response means)
- justification (requesting students to defend their responses)
- refocusing (redirecting attention to related issues)
- prompting (providing hints to learners)
- redirecting (bringing additional learners into the discussion by asking for their reactions)
- connecting (involving attempts to link material and concepts that otherwise might not seem related)
- comparing (asking for similarities and differences related to various concepts, theories, communication styles, or teaching methods)
- critical questioning (examining the validity of an author's or researcher's arguments) (Chamberlain & Cummings, 2003; McKeachie & Svinicki, 2006)

If you are asking questions, make sure that the learners have sufficient background for a response, word questions clearly and concisely, and direct questions to the entire group. You also need to allow them time to respond, at least 10 to 15 seconds (Nilson, 2003). A beginning teacher often asks questions, but may be nervous and answer them before a student has an opportunity to react. If there is no response, give a hint or rephrase the question to make it easier to understand or incorporate a lower level of learning. If no one volunteers a response, you can call on some individuals by name. However, when calling on students, it is best to do so randomly and not in an organized manner down rows or around a circle. Students may be hesitant to respond to questions if they do not know the answer and perceive they will be "put down." You want to establish a positive climate for participation. Therefore, you can suggest that maybe your question was unclear or that they made an interesting point, and then continue asking students for input, as often times students have excellent ideas that their teachers have never considered (Chamberlain & Cummings, 2003).

How do you respond to questions that you are asked? First, it is important to *listen* to the question and ask for any clarification, if needed. Then *repeat* or *paraphrase* the question so you model this type of behavior to assist others in the class to hear the question. Watch students' *body language*, as this may also be part of their communication, and then *respond*. If you do not know the answer, *do not bluff* your response (Chamberlain & Cummings, 2003). Ask the class for their thoughts, brainstorm ways to determine the answer, and suggest that both you and the students attempt to determine the answer to share at the beginning of the next session, if there will be one. However, it is essential that you follow through with this suggestion during the next session. Use caution so that learners' questions and your responses do not extend too long or go beyond the interest of the entire class.

Discussion

Discussions are part of most educational experiences in all kinds of settings (formal, nonformal, and informal). They are often paired with lectures, but can also be used as the primary mode of learning. Discussions are dependent on the questioning skills of the leader. It is best to contemplate your questions in advance along with the main points you want to cover, but impromptu questions will occur that result from "teachable moments." It is helpful to set some guidelines for discussion, such as being polite, respecting other points of view, letting one person talk at a time, limiting the time one speaks, and letting others finish without interrupting. Discussion leaders should select a topic and present provocative statements, questions, articles, videos, or data to initiate the discussion with a summary of the main points at the end (Chamberlain & Cummings, 2003). Then be ready to make supportive and encouraging comments or ask pertinent questions. It is important to involve everyone, if possible, by noting who has not yet responded or might have difficulty entering into a conversation. You might then ask a question specifically directed to less-involved learners to give them an opening to offer their comments. Having learners sit in a manner in which they can see others is a good idea, if possible, but at times seats are not movable. It is also suggested that the leader sit on the side and not be the center of attention, which could put him/her in a perceived authoritarian position and reduce the flow of communication. While you may have personal thoughts regarding the discussion topic, it is best to refrain from adding your own ideas until the end, if at all.

Small group discussions may be a viable option for enhancing interactions that may not readily occur in large groups. You can ask students to form their own groups or you can create different options for forming groups related to a numbering system, birth month, alphabetically by name, or some symbol or color on a name tag. Depending on the assignment given to a small group, you may want students to select a facilitator and/or recorder if the group is to report back to the larger class. You will need some clear instructions for discussion on a meaningful topic that also involves the teacher moving around to interact with groups. This will facilitate any needed clarification, help them keep on task, and give input to their progress with the assigned task.

There are some *structured discussion techniques* you can employ depending on the circumstances. The size of the group and location would be important considerations.

Roundtable discussion groups involve a group of people that gather for a conference or session with each person having an equal status. The participants consider a specific issue and have a dialogue amongst themselves. The leader is usually the one who presides and moderates the discussion. He or she should have pertinent knowledge about the topic and may bring additional information, materials, and handouts. There may be a recorder to keep track of the group's deliberations and to report its progress, if this is a part of the intended purpose. Usually there are a variety of topics discussed in round tables, so that all individuals participate in the topic of their choice. At times a person has the option of selecting to participate in two or more topics during the scheduled roundtable presentation. Thus, a bell or flash of lights could indicate the time to move to another group. An example might be a series of roundtable discussions on topics, such as childhood nutrition; reading activities; or safety in the home, school, or recreation activities.

Brainstorming is a technique for encouraging a large quantity of viable solutions to a problem by involving all members of moderate to large groups. Members can feel comfortable and supported when contributing their ideas, which can facilitate an interaction of ideas resulting in a synergistic effect. It is a process used to create an environment in which participants can offer suggestions without criticism resulting in the production of a plethora of creative ideas. It involves collaborative thinking to focus on a specific problem. There are certain guidelines for brainstorming: (1) the ideas are expressed openly, rapidly, and recorded on a black or whiteboard; (2) all ideas are welcome; (3) "free-wheeling" is invited—not paying attention to conventional norms; (4) "hitchhiking" is encouraged—improving on an idea by saying that you have an addition to a former idea; and (5) evaluation of ideas should be postponed until all possible ideas have been mentioned. After the flow of ideas has ceased, the group can examine the list to see if there are commonalities, themes to pursue, or ideas that seem prominent. While some of this scrutiny may occur immediately after the session, a smaller group of persons involved in organizing the session may meet to do so later. Brainstorming may be used to create ideas for topics to be used in a series of family life education seminars in your community.

Reaction panels are comprised of a team of 3 to 5 members of the audience or group responsible for the presentation that will react to a speaker or other resource person. They may ask questions of the speaker and assist the speaker in meeting the needs of the audience. The reaction panel may be used to facilitate communication when the subject matter is likely to be difficult to understand and/or provide feedback to the speaker regarding the representative views of the audience when it is large. For example, a speaker from out of town is invited to give a speech to a community group on some aspect of parenting. A reaction panel, whose members are aware of the topic and the needs of the audience, can provide questions to the speaker after his or presentation rather than trying to obtain questions from a large group in an auditorium.

Buzz sessions directly involve every member of a large audience in the discussion process. The audience is divided into small groups (3 to 7 members) for a discussion that allows for all members to contribute their ideas. This method can be used to develop questions for a speaker, discover ideas for which the audience desires more information, determine areas of special interest for future programs, or evaluate a meeting regarding its value to the participants. If a speaker or panel was involved in a half or full day session, buzz sessions might occur after an initial presentation and before a break. A written summary of points could be brought forth to those involved in moderating the session so that pertinent comments could be addressed in the time available for discussion and interaction with the speaker(s). Depending on the size of the group, a leader can go around to provide encouragement to stay on task and provide assistance, if needed. When the leader senses that the groups are nearing completion of their task, a warning can be given such as "Take a minute or two to complete your task."

After a discussion, instructors need to evaluate its success in order to make improvements and plans for the future. Some questions to consider include the following:

- Was progress made toward meeting course objectives?
- Was the pace of the discussion fast enough to be interesting and slow enough to promote analytical thinking?

- Was the topic stimulating, challenging, realistic, relevant, and meaningful to the group?
- Did the participants have the background necessary to engage in the discussion?
- Were participants and their comments received in a positive manner and treated seriously?
- Did at least three-fourths of the group participate?
- Was the discussion summarized clearly and concisely?

Make sure you let your students know that you value their comments by using their ideas when feasible (Chamberlain & Cummings, 2003). By using discussion and eliciting feedback, you can better evaluate and improve your own teaching.

Fishbowl is a discussion strategy that involves a small group of 6 to 8 people having a conversation while seated in a circle. These *fish* are surrounded by a similar or larger group of observers in an outer circle (the *bowl*). A facilitator gives a brief introduction that outlines this method prior to the members of the inner circle beginning their discussion. Participants in the outer circle listen and observe, but do not interrupt persons in the inner circle. If someone from the outer circle wants to participate and move to the inner circle, someone from the inner circle must vacate a chair. The purpose of this discussion method is to observe, analyze, and learn from other thought processes. An alternative is a closed fishbowl in which all chairs are filled. In other words there are two groups—one in the inner circle and the other in the outer circle. At some point after about 10 to 15 minutes, the facilitator can suggest that the observers in the outer circle discuss what they heard and understood about the views of the participants in the inner circle. The persons in the two circles can switch their positions and continue discussing some additional factors not previously considered or discuss a parallel issue (McKeachie & Svinicki, 2006). For example, this method can be used to discuss gender roles and expectations of males and females in dating, love, or marriage issues.

Simulated Learning

Incorporating simulated learning experiences into the classroom provides an opportunity to explore the paradigm of "real life" experiences. It promotes active learning and interest in the learning environment and motivates learners. Simulated learning experiences provide a common and enjoyable experience that can be a catalyst for meaningful discussion. Some of the benefits of a simulated learning experience include seeing something from another point of view, sharing emotions, developing insight into human relations, improving communication skills, and using higher-order thinking skills (Chamberlain & Cummings, 2003). Although there are a variety of simulated learning experiences, we will share only a few, including different kinds of role-play (paired, sociodrama, and circular), case studies, and modeling.

Role-play

A role-play is an unrehearsed presentation during which participants act out a real-life situation in front of an audience of other class members. There is no script or set dialogue since participants create their parts as they go along after receiving some prompts from a facilitator. The group then discusses the implications of the interactions. A role-play is especially effective when the situation acted out involves some type of interpersonal conflict. It can be used to examine a delicate problem in human relations and explore possible solutions to an emotion-laden issue. A role-play, which can be both educational and entertaining, can involve adults or adolescents in formal or nonformal settings. At some point, the facilitator will stop the role-play to begin discussion. The facilitator may ask each member of the pair how it felt playing that role. This is especially important if you have an adolescent playing a parent role and vice versa. Getting a different point of view may be insightful to some of the issues each is facing. An example might be a role-play between an adolescent son or daughter and a parent who finds drugs in the child's room. In addition to discussing the issue of drug use among adolescents, parent-child communication can be observed.

One problem with role-play is that some participants may feel uncomfortable being the center of attention and speaking in front of a group. Rather than run the risk of asking for volunteers and having no one respond, prior to class ask a few people to participate whom you perceive to be outgoing and might be willing to play various roles. At times participants believe they have to play certain roles appropriately by saying and doing the right things. This adds pressure; so suggest that the roles can be played in any way that they choose. You can always ask the same pair or another pair of learners to role-play the scenario in a different way. Employing some other variations of role-play may be less stressful because more participants are involved and no one is the main focus.

Paired role-play

Have all students/participants form pairs and then present them with a situation that they role-play with each other. Later the facilitator can lead a discussion on the different ways the role-play was handled, what the students learned from the situation, and suggestions for how it could be handled in the future. For example, pairs of students could role-play a job interview with questions that the teacher puts on a PowerPoint slide. Students could alternate going first with questions. This gives them practice in responding to such questions, as "What are some of your good and not so good qualities?," and "Why should I hire you?" Another example would be to create a scenario of two young people who have been dating for some time and are nearing a point in their relationship when they are thinking of engaging in sexual relations. However, they are concerned about safety and want to know more about the intimate background of their potential sex partner. If after a few minutes a facilitator determines that students are having difficulty beginning this conversation, there may be a brief interruption to ask, "How might you begin this conversation." After the conversation has been underway for a period of time, the facilitator can stop the interaction to allow students the opportunity to talk about how they felt about the exercise and what helped to facilitate the conversation. These particular paired role-plays give students "practice" communicating about sensitive subjects, so that if these situations ever occur in their own lives, they will have had some previous experience in beginning and carrying out these important conversations.

Circular role-play

In this role-play format participants play two roles at the same time. Participants sit in a circle and respond in writing to a scenario that might take place between a parent and a child. They are asked to play the role of the parent with the person on their left and the role of the child in that same situation with the person on their right. In other words, any individual is simultaneously playing a parent and child in the same scenario, but with two different family pairs. After 4 to 6 or more exchanges between the parent and child, stop the interactions and begin discussing what was or was not effective in dealing with this situation and how simultaneously playing the parent and child gave insights into these two points of view. This activity leads to a lively discussion.

Sociodrama

A sociodrama can be used to involve multiple participants playing the same role at the same time. You could have roles being played by 2 or more family members and even include the entire class, if it is small. Again, you could have a scenario that involves a parent-child conflict, but for this example you would have the child interacting with both the mother and father. You would set up a triangle with five chairs on each side and ask participants to sit in any chair they desire. Then designate that participants on one side of the triangle will play the role of the mother, another side will be the father, and the third side will be the adolescent daughter. Number the participants on each side from 1 to 5. It is also helpful to put a sign on the floor in front on each group to indicate the role that these participants are playing (mother, father, or daughter). Then have the students who are mother, father, and daughter #1 raise their hands, as they are now family 1. Do the same for all five sets of families. Indicate that the sociodrama will begin with family 1, 2, 3, 4, or 5, but in general it is best to randomly select the family to participate and not do them in numerical order. Introduce a scenario, such as a daughter who finds out she is pregnant and comes home to tell her parents. After they interact for a while, change to a different family and then continue integrating each group, followed by repeating some that have already participated. When a new family is identified, that family picks up the conversation where the other family ended their conversation. Continue until many of the pertinent issues regarding the topic of the sociodrama have been portrayed.

If the size of your class results in students who will not be actively playing roles in the sociodrama, assign them to observe communication patterns of various family members. First provide them some *communication barriers*, such as not listening, interrupting, yelling, criticizing, name calling, being sarcastic, interrogating, making the other person feel guilty, negative non-verbal messages, "psychologizing," and being a "know-it-all." In addition, provide them with some *communication bridges*, such as picking a good time to talk, listening well and letting the speaker know you are listening, looking at the person's face and eyes, laughing at yourself or situation as appropriate, using "I statements" (see Chapter 10), trying to understand how the other person feels, examining possible ways to resolve the issue, and touch (e.g., giving a hug or showing affection). Have students observe each group of participants (mothers, fathers, and daughters) for their use of communication barriers and bridges and how responses were influenced by communication styles. Upon completion of the sociodrama, begin the discussion by asking for the insights of those observing the sociodrama participants. Then get input from the family members about how they felt in their roles. Note that you had the participants sit in the chairs before you indicated the roles to be played. In other words, you may have males playing the roles of the pregnant teen or mothers, along with females playing the role of fathers. Thus, part of your discussion entails asking the participants how it felt to play a role that was not typical of their gender.

Case studies

Case studies can be used in many ways. You can read them aloud to promote group discussion, use them in an individualized assignment, or assign small groups to analyze a family's situation. Each group could have the same scenario or different ones. In either case, the group(s)' conclusions can be shared with the entire class to elicit further discussion. Students can identify the problem, propose alternate solutions, examine and analyze the consequences of potential solutions, and decide on a course of action. See Box 8.1 (pp. 185–186) for examples of case studies that can be used to better understand family theory.

Modeling

Modeling can be used to demonstrate skills to be learned by others. Teachers can affirm openness, encourage listening, and/or reinforce positive behavior. Rather than replying, "OK," which is a neutral response, there are many positive alternatives, such as (Chamberlain & Cummings, 2003):

- That's right.
- Great, fantastic, terrific, excellent, super, wonderful, tremendous, marvelous, outstanding, very impressive, or WOW!
- You did that really well.
- Right on.
- Good thinking.
- I am proud of you.

Even though teachers may never actually comment on what they are doing, students can learn about professionalism and how to treat others. On the other hand, teachers may later want to follow-up with a discussion to see if students can identify the skills being demonstrated.

Games

Educational games are designed to teach learners of various ages about certain subjects, expand concepts, understand a culture, and assist them in learning a skill. Conceptual play facilitates students' engagement and enjoyment in learning by actively involving them in some type of competition or achievement in relationship to a course objective. Make sure you clarify the objective(s) and rules for the game so that students understand what is expected, and only include a game if it fits the curriculum and learners have the necessary background information. In addition, provide all materials for the game, have reference materials available as needed, monitor the group while the game is progressing, and expect some noise. There are several types of games including card games (e.g., BARNGA—explained in Chapter 3); board games based on class content (e.g., Bingo and commercial board games); word and pencil games (crossword puzzles and word searches); action games (e.g., charades and others that involve movement); and televised game shows (Chamberlain & Cummings, 2003). Television game shows such as *Jeopardy* or *Family Feud* can be replicated in a classroom setting to reinforce knowledge presented in a lecture or to review content for an exam.

Teachers can create games to facilitate collaborative learning, such as gaining information about contraceptives. When beginning a lecture about contraception, many students passively respond as if they "already know all there is to know." Thus, creating a contraceptive game may engage them in active learning. A teacher can create multiple game boards to be used in small groups of 5 to 6 students. The boards will contain a grid so that the top row lists contraceptives for students to learn (e.g., pill, condom, IUD, diaphragm, rhythm method, etc.). In the far left vertical column list certain characteristics (e.g., What is it, How does it work, How to use it, Contraindications, Side effects, Percent effectiveness, and Myths). Student groups will also receive a stack of small cards that fit into the empty rectangular boxes on the grid with the answers for the questions related to characteristics of the contraceptives. The task is to put the appropriate responses in the empty boxes. The students soon realize that they do not know all the answers, so they begin working together to complete the grid. After each group has placed all the cards in the empty boxes of the grid, provide the individual groups with a sheet of correct responses so students can evaluate their level of success. When a majority of the groups have completed the task, provide any needed additional information about contraceptives, initiate discussion, and respond to student questions.

Group Process

Groups are a "way of life" for educators. In addition to your entire class being a group that you will teach, you may be called upon to speak to all kinds of groups, become involved in various groups and committees to accomplish tasks, or use small group learning in your classroom. While groups are formed for various reasons, such as treatment groups, support groups, task groups or committees, subgroups, or Internet groups, we will only be focusing on *educational groups* that are designed to increase knowledge, teach skills, make decisions, or all three.

Group processes are especially notable in classrooms where group projects and teamwork are the foundation of effective teaching. Group projects can help students develop multiple skills that are important in their professional lives, such as tackling more complex problems than they could do individually, sharing diverse perspectives, pooling knowledge and skills, and developing new approaches to resolving differences. While the potential benefits of group work are considerable, there is no guarantee that groups will be successful unless they are well designed, supervised, and assessed (CMU, n.d.). Positive group experiences have been shown to contribute to student learning, retention, and overall student success (NSSE,

2006). Groups are also important in modern global communities where people need to work together for a safe and secure world (Schmuck & Schmuck, 2013). Thus, along with teaching the planned curriculum, teachers can help students to develop the attitudes, skills, and procedures needed to live in a democratic society.

Generally group members come together to talk; listen to each other; and share values, expectations and resources, and thus become interdependent. The intensity of the group can be low to moderate depending on the topic and the amount of time needed to complete its tasks. Groups can last for a few hours, days, or months and can range on a continuum from collaborative learning to cooperative learning groups (Royse, 2001). Collaborative and cooperative learning are similar in that they are both based on the educational advantages of a social experience, however they also have some differences. Whereas *collaborative* learning focuses on communicative knowledge and involves a loosely structured small-group format in which students work on a task (e.g., projects, discussion groups), *cooperative learning* is a more structured group effort focusing on the subject matter in which students thrive on interdependence and individual accountability to accomplish a task upon which student grades may be dependent (Chamberlain & Cummings, 2003; Nilson, 2003; Royce, 2001).

Groups, which are formed by being assigned or self-selection, go through a process of development to become cohesive. The first stage is *groping* during which members try to determine what they are really supposed to accomplish, followed by the second stage when there is some *griping*. In other words, "Why do we have to do this?" or "There is not enough time to get this task accomplished." The third stage is *grouping,* when members come together and begin to work cohesively with each other. Stage four involves *grinding* out the work, and for some groups, members evolve to stage five—*grieving*. In other words, the group work and bonding of members was such a positive experience that they grieve about no longer needing to meet to work on the project. Not all groups get to stage 5, but some groups do and report really enjoying their membership and work in this group.

One of the main tasks of an effective family life educator is to be able to lead groups. You will be expected to (1) provide learning experiences that will aid participants in expanding their knowledge and developing their skills, (2) maintain a balance between the presentation of information and the activities needed to assimilate the information, and (3) cope with interpersonal problems that may arise in groups. For teachers it is important to continually reflect upon what did and did not work well in the group experience. An effective educator needs to be a good administrator (group management and task focused) with affective skills (person-centered, feelings focused, and emotional "climate controller"). Teachers, who are aware of these needs, can help group members ease tension and keep differences of opinion minimal during complex communication interactions.

While there can be many different purposes for organizing *small groups*, one example is to supplement lectures by assigning students to small groups of different hypothetical families, with each student assuming the role of one family member. These groups are presented with real-life situations over the length of the course (e.g., job loss or promotion, illness, addition of a family member through birth or marriage, or extended absence of a family member). Students analyze and write about the effect of each new situation on the family member with whom they are affiliated, as well as the entire family, and bring those perspectives to their groups to discuss. Students using this activity can be introduced to diverse family structures, experiences, and resources, as well as the challenges families may face (Koropeckyj-Cox, Cain, & Coran, 2005).

≡ Obtaining Feedback on Learning Experiences

Whenever you design and implement a course, as well as incorporate learning activities, you have some idea of how students will respond to your creation. Following these learning experiences, you will get some feedback when discussing the activity and the learning that evolved.

One method is to use *One-Minute Papers*, although they may actually take 2 to 3 minutes. Ask students to share the most important or useful points they learned from the day's presentation, reading assignment, or discussion, along with any remaining questions (Nilson, 2003). These can be anonymous or used as an indication of attendance, if required by your institution. A similar method is called *Thought Bubbles*, which constitutes a way to get students to think about questions in class and facilitate discussion on that topic. The teacher will post a question and give the students 3 to 5 minutes to respond. Then students will be asked to share their responses. If this is done at the beginning of class, students are more willing to participate in class discussion, as they have had a chance to write their thoughts first. Again, this technique may be anonymous, ungraded, or used as a vehicle for taking attendance, if needed.

At the end of the course, you may want to know if the teaching and learning activities incorporated resulted in any *significant learning* for the students (see Chapter 5 for examples of significant learning). It is helpful to go beyond feedback from daily discussions, as well as teacher, program, and course evaluations, by asking students to list and rank order five things (1 to 5 with "1" being the most memorable or valuable) from the class that they are most likely to remember in the future and explain why they chose each item. In addition ask them what two new insights they gained about themselves, their families, or their profession and how these insights might influence them and their future interactions with others. The results are often quite varied but provide meaningful feedback on what impacted the lives of students. It also indicates that different methods and content can engage different learners.

SUMMARY

There are many things to consider when preparing to implement a course. Thus, it is helpful to have a plan for integrating learning objectives, teaching-learning activities, ways to assess learning, and helpful resources. One must also arrange for reading materials while considering the amount, reading level, and cost of materials. Selecting and incorporating different teaching methods add variety and interest, such as varying the types of presentations (e.g., lecture, panel, symposium, interview, debate, workshop, multimedia, and exhibits and displays).

Attention should be given to facilitating interactions through questioning, discussion, simulated learning experiences, games, and group process. During and after presenting course content in various ways, it is important to gain feedback on how you can improve your teaching and better involve learners.

QUESTIONS AND ISSUES FOR DISCUSSION

1. Why does the "still" method of presentation continue to be used in many classrooms if it is really so ineffective? Does this mean that a facilitator/teacher should never present a lecture to a group?

2. Should you use written notes when you present? If so, how should they be structured and used?

3. If you are a moderator, how will you deal with panelists or presenters who ramble, are mostly silent, or are clearly wrong? How will you deal with learners who are aggressive, defensive, or have personal problems and distract the flow of the presentation or question session?

4. When working with groups, how do you handle the discussion dominators, frequent interrupters, disruptive members, or persons in crisis who are dealing with deep emotions?

5. Would you be willing to participate in role-play? Which kind of role-play do you like the best or least and why?

6. Have you ever worked in a group for which members grieved after their group work was completed? What was the task of this group and why do you think that the group grieved at its conclusion?

ACTIVITIES

1. Have students find online video clips related to a content area in the Certified Family Life Educator program and discuss how they could be integrated into their teaching.

2. Have students or groups of students demonstrate some of the teaching and learning activities mentioned in this chapter using subject matter from the content areas of the Certified Family Life Educator program.

7

Evaluation of Family Programs

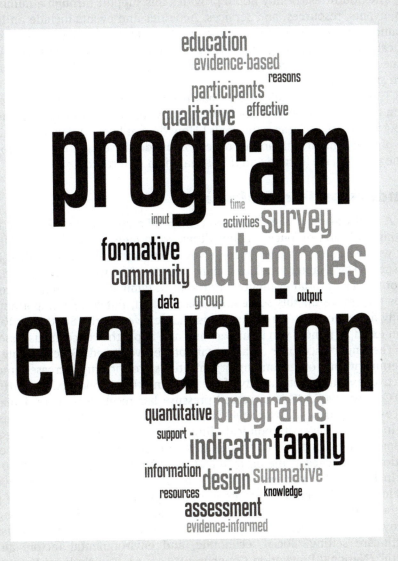

Imagine that you are the director of the Southwest Family Room, a neighborhood resource center located in a large metropolitan city. Funded by the United Way, the Southwest Family Room serves residents with children from before birth to age 6 living in the nine neighborhoods that make up the southwest section of the city.

The overall goal of the Southwest Family Room is to increase school readiness for children entering kindergarten. It was developed through the efforts of professionals at a lead agency and the input of community residents and business and service providers. The developers of the program have determined that one way to increase school readiness is to provide families with formal and informal support systems.

The Southwest Family Room provides this support through a number of activities, events, resources, and services. Activities and events include an Indoor Playground, a Family Fun Night, numerous baby and toddler classes, and parenting education and support groups. They also offer a resource and toy library, make home visits, and produce a monthly newsletter and calendar of events for families with small children.

The Southwest Family Room has been operating for 5 years. Overall, things seem to be going well. But how do you know for sure? How do you and your staff know if you are meeting your goals? How do you know if you are making the best use of your limited staff and resources? How do those funding your program know if the program is effective and if it is making a difference?

Understanding Evaluation

A family agency or organization can spend a great deal of time and money promoting and carrying out programs designed to meet the various needs of families. But without conscious, systematic evaluation efforts, it might be time and money misspent. This chapter provides an *introduction* to the topic of evaluation. The intent is not to make you an evaluator, but rather to familiarize you with the concepts and steps that make up this sometimes complicated, but always important, aspect of family life education. Throughout this chapter we use the Southwest Family Room as an example to help you to understand and apply the concepts discussed.

The importance of evaluation cannot be overstated. Federal, state, and local governments and other funding organizations are showing increased interest in the effectiveness and accountability of the programs they support (Cooney, Huser, Small, & O'Connor, 2007.) This increased pressure has resulted in more demand for evidence-based programs, which will be discussed in more detail later in this chapter.

In recent years, the political climate in the United States has become more accepting and supportive of preventative efforts compared to the service and intervention approaches of the past. In fact the Affordable Care Act of 2010 mandated the inclusion of a preventive approach to behavioral health and called for the development of a National Prevention Strategy to realize the benefits of prevention for the health of all Americans. The National Prevention Strategy recognizes that "many of the strongest predictors of health and well-being fall outside of the health-care setting. Social, economic, and environmental factors all influence health" (National Prevention Council, 2011, p. 6). The National Prevention Strategy includes seven priorities: Tobacco Free Living, Preventing Drug Abuse and Excessive Alcohol Use, Healthy Eating, Active Living, Injury and Violence Free Living, Reproductive and Sexual Health, and Mental and Emotional Well-being. All of these priorities can be positively influenced by family life education.

In light of this, program evaluations need to be designed to measure individual program effectiveness, as well as to collectively address questions on the minds of policy makers about which family support and education programs work, for whom, how, when, where, and why (Weiss & Jacobs, 1988). Especially where public tax revenues support parent and family education programs, taxpayers and legislators expect accountability and evidence of measurable benefit to the community. The development and recognition of effective prevention programs could serve to restructure the delivery of human services in this country. Although great strides have been made in recent years to increase the thoroughness and effectiveness of family program evaluation, there is still much to learn.

Beyond meeting the requirements of funders, evaluation is also important to those carrying out family programs and is an integral part of the program planning and implementation process. Without proper evaluation it is difficult to know if the programs being carried out are working. Family life educators must continue to conduct thoughtful and careful evaluations to ensure that family programs reach their goals in the most efficient manner possible.

Definitions

We begin the discussion by looking at the definition of *evaluation* as articulated by several contributors to the literature on program evaluation. One of the most commonly referenced definitions comes from Michael Patton (1997) who defines it as "the systematic collection of information about the activities, characteristics and outcomes of programs to make judgments about the program, improve the program effectiveness, and/or inform decisions about future programming" (p. 23). Littell (1986) considers program evaluation to be "the systematic collection, analysis, and interpretation of information designed for use in program planning and decision-making. It is concerned with the types of interventions used, by whom, toward what ends, under what conditions, for whom, at what costs, and with what benefits" (p. 17). Finally, evaluation is defined by Weiss and Jacobs (1988) as: "the systematic collection and analysis of program-related data that can be used to understand how a program delivers services and/or what the consequences of its services are for participants. . . . It is both descriptive and 'judgmental' of program merit, with the emphasis on designing an evaluation that fits the program" (p. 49). Though the definitions vary, they contain similar concepts, namely, that evaluation is a systematic collection of various types of information and that the results of the collection and analysis of information are used to modify programs, increase effectiveness, and aid in decision making.

Evaluation, which is different from research, is used to determine the value, quality, or effectiveness of a program. It is judgmental, and the results are usually program specific and often motivated by the program's needs. Information gathered can be subjective, however, the major reasons for conducting an evaluation are for planning, improving, or justification. An evaluation should result in some sort of recommendation.

Research, on the other hand, examines the relationships among variables and is nonjudgmental and conclusion oriented. One purpose for research is to contribute to knowledge building through the dissemination of findings. The intent is to have information that can be generalized, rather than specific to any one particular program. Evaluation answers the question of *what*, whereas research answers the question of *why*. Box 7.1 describes two scenarios; one involving research and the other, evaluation.

Box 7.1   Evaluation or Research?

The staff of the Southwest Family Room wants to know if toddlers who regularly attend a program like the Indoor Playground (which includes opportunities for climbing and exercise on playground equipment) show more advanced motor skills than toddlers who do not attend such a program. This type of study would be considered *research*. The staff of the Southwest Family Room also wants to know how the parents who attend the Indoor Playground feel about the program and if they find it to be a good opportunity to connect with other parents in their community. This type of study would be considered *evaluation*.

Reasons for Evaluation

For many family life educators, evaluation provides quite a challenge. Thorough evaluation takes planning, time, and money, often beyond the capabilities and resources of the average family education program and the technical expertise of the staff. Moreover, there can be resistance to evaluation. Program directors and staff may be concerned that evaluation will divert resources away from the program's activities, will increase the burden for program staff, and/or be too complicated. Some fear that it may produce negative results that will jeopardize program funding.

So why bother with evaluation? The reality is that evaluation is imperative to the success of a program. According to the National Registry of Evidence-based Programs and Practices (NREPP), evaluation can serve three purposes: (1) it can be used to assess a program by providing a way to verify, document, and quantify programming activities and their effects, (2) it can assist in program improvement by identifying what is and is not working, and (3) it can be part of a strategic management plan that provides information that can help you make better decisions about the best use of resources in order to meet the goals of the program and the mission of the organization (SAMHSA, 2012).

Evaluation can provide a way to improve the efficiency and effectiveness of your staff's efforts by identifying strengths and weaknesses. You can increase the likelihood that resources are used effectively and goals are reached. Evaluation can show those who fund your program, as well as community members, how your program is benefiting its intended audience. Also, when results are shared with others running similar programs, it can contribute to knowledge in the field. "It should be the charge of any social service organization to not only affect the children it serves, but to improve the lives of those who it will never serve directly. This goal is often done through advocacy" (Pizzigati, Stuck, & Ness, 2002). If consciously incorporated into the design and ongoing operation of a program, evaluation does not need to be overly complicated or time-consuming.

Types of Evaluation

Assessing Needs and Assets

Perhaps one of the most important concepts about evaluation is the need to incorporate an evaluation plan *into the development and initial planning stages of a program*. A well-developed program begins with a mini-study (sometimes referred to as a needs assessment, a feasibility study, or an assets inventory. See Chapter 3 for a more detailed discussion of needs assessment). These mini-studies often involve an examination of the current situation to determine if the proposed program is justified. Who is the target audience for this program? What resources are available? What are the strengths or assets of this community? Do similar programs exist in this community? Will the community support the program? What benefits are likely to be produced through the program? It is important to be clear about the need for, and goals of, a program. If you do not have a clear picture of what the program is trying to accomplish, you will not know how to tell if you've been successful. Think seriously about what it is you want to learn from an evaluation. Consider its place in the ongoing implementation of your program and integrate the evaluation into the ongoing activities. Remember that evaluation is a process, not an event.

Formative Evaluation

Evaluation efforts can have different goals and can be conducted at different points throughout the development and implementation of a program. Evaluations may be formative or summative in nature. *Formative evaluations* generate information for the purposes of planning, monitoring, and improving programs and are sometimes also referred to as *process evaluations*. Formative evaluations describe a program and provide feedback on how it is doing *while the program is still in progress*, often prompting changes in timing, approaches, etc. Formative evaluation can also assess progress toward objectives (Level 4 of Jacobs' Tiers which will be discussed later in this chapter). Therefore, formative evaluation might include surveying participants midway through a scheduled program to see if the program is meeting their expectations. If participants are not learning what they should, outcomes might not be reached. Formative evaluation can provide an opportunity to reteach or reinforce information.

As an example of formative evaluations, imagine that your agency holds a monthly meeting to provide education on infant development to mothers of newborns. Although the participants seem very enthusiastic about the meetings, attendance has been sporadic. By surveying the participants, you find that availability of transportation is a defining factor in whether or not they attend. Therefore, a car pool is arranged that provides rides for everyone who wants to attend the meeting, resulting in a dramatic increase in attendance. If surveying the participants had been delayed to the end of the program, it would have been too late to implement the car pool and a number of possible program participants would have missed out on the program. The use of formative evaluation throughout the program facilitates making changes that will increase the likelihood of better implementing the program and reaching intended goals.

Box 7.2 gives an example of a formative evaluation of the Indoor Playground program. With this information the staff can determine if the program is meeting the needs of the participants and make any needed changes in scheduling and format. They can also determine which marketing efforts are working best. This formative evaluation will provide them information that can be used to modify the program while it is still in progress.

Box 7.2   Formative Evaluation

The Indoor Playground is held each Friday at the Southwest Family Room. Once each month staff members distribute a survey to the attendees. The survey includes questions such as:

- How many times have you attended the Indoor Playground?
- What is your main reason for attending?
- Is this a convenient day for you to attend?
- Is this a convenient time for you to attend?
- If not, when would be better?
- What changes would you like to see in the Indoor Playground?
- How did you hear about the Indoor Playground?
- Do you attend any other Southwest Family Room events?

Summative Evaluation

Summative evaluations, sometimes referred to as *outcome evaluations*, are concerned with the end results of a program. How did the program affect the people it served? Were the program goals met? Summative evaluations can be used to determine if a program should be replicated, expanded, or perhaps discontinued. In the example given in Box 7.3, a summative evaluation carried out at the end of the program cycle could determine if participants in the New Parents program had increased their knowledge of infant development.

Box 7.3   Summative Evaluation

The Southwest Family Room sponsors a New Parents support group for parents of newborns. The meetings are facilitated by parents in the community who have completed a 16-hour small group-facilitation training program and provided with resource materials. Parents enter the program before their babies are born or just afterward. The program meets twice a month for 2 hours over a 2-year period. A summative evaluation of the New Parents program would be conducted at the end of the 2-year period with participants being interviewed or asked to complete a questionnaire. The intent of the survey or questionnaire would be to determine how the parents benefited from the program. Did they learn new knowledge about child development or new skills regarding parenting? Did their participation help them feel more confident about their abilities as parents? Did they feel less alone and less isolated? Do they feel more connected to their community, having met other families in a similar situation? Results of this summative evaluation will help the staff of the Southwest Family Room know if their goals have been met. The results may determine if the program will be replicated and/or may influence how future programs are conducted.

Commonly Used Terms in Evaluation

Although the specific terminology varies, some common terms and concepts are used in the literature on evaluation. Both the W. K. Kellogg Foundation (2004) and the United Way of America (Hatry, van Houten, Plantz, & Greenway, 1996) offer publications that provide a conceptual framework for understanding evaluation, including discussion of the following measurement terms.

Logic Models

Programs can be developed and outcomes identified with a *logic model* or an *if-then* method of looking at a situation. Logic models can facilitate thinking through the progression of steps taken by program participants and provide a more realistic view of what to expect of the program. Logic models also help identify key components that must be considered in order to determine if the program is effective. Logic models include inputs, activities, outputs, and outcomes. An example of a logic model might be: *If* funding (input) can be provided, *then* parenting classes can be offered. *If* classes (activities) can teach about child development and parenting skills (output), *then* parents can acquire knowledge, gain skills, and change their attitudes about how to care for their children (initial outcomes). *If* they learn new approaches in dealing with their children, *then* they will change their behavior to reflect these new methods (intermediate outcomes). *If* they change their behavior, *then* they will increase the likelihood of positive childhood outcomes such as healthy emotional development. Applying this method can help identify the steps needed to reach intended goals and link activities to program outcomes.

Inputs

Inputs include resources dedicated to or consumed by the program. Examples are money, staff and their time, volunteers and their time, facilities, equipment, and supplies (see Box 7.4).

Box 7.4   Inputs

Inputs at the Southwest Family Room include financial support provided by the sponsoring agency, staff members and their time, and members of the community who volunteer their time to various programs and services offered through the Southwest Family Room. Additional inputs would be the site where the Southwest Family Room is located, including meeting space, materials, supplies, playground equipment, and toys available through the Indoor Playground.

Activities

A program uses inputs to fulfill its mission through *activities*. Activities include the strategies, techniques, and types of treatment that make up the program's service methodology. In our example of the Southwest Family Room, activities would center on providing education and support to families with small children. These activities would include the Family Fun Night, the Indoor Playground, the community calendar, and other events and services intended to provide education and support to parents of small children.

Outputs

Outputs are the direct products of program activities. They are usually measured in terms of the volume of work accomplished, such as the number of classes held, brochures distributed, and participants served (see Box 7.5).

Box 7.5   Outputs

How many people attended the Indoor Playground? How many sessions of Family Fun Night were held? How many people used the toy library? How many brochures or flyers about the Southwest Family Room were distributed at neighborhood festivals and community events? These questions attempt to gather information about outputs. In addition to attendance, further quantitative information might reveal meaningful results. Program observers could tally specific parent-child behaviors.

Outcomes

Outcomes are the benefits or changes to individuals or groups that come during or after participation in program activities. Outcomes are influenced by outputs and reflected through modified behavior, increased skills, new knowledge, changed attitudes or values, improved conditions, and other attributes. They represent the changes in the participants from the time they started the program until the time they completed it. For example, outcomes of the program described in Box 7.6 would be a better understanding of toddler development and a resulting change in parenting behavior, such as the use of more appropriate discipline strategies. Program evaluation should include consideration of initial outcomes, intermediate outcomes, and long-term outcomes.

Box 7.6   Outcomes

Parents attending a monthly class, called "Discipline and Your Child," learn new techniques for directing the behavior of their toddlers. The staff hopes that providing comprehensive information about child development and discipline alternatives will expand parents' understanding of these topics. Staff members perceive that by increasing parents' knowledge, they will make better choices about discipline including approaches to preventing misbehavior. The goal is for parents to use less punitive means and employ more appropriate choices with their children. By preventing misbehavior, parents can have a more positive attitude about discipline, feel more confident about being able to prevent misbehavior, feel more successful as parents, and enjoy their child even more. A positive change in the behavior of the parent will result in a better relationship with the child. Additionally, the child will be more likely to experience positive outcomes relevant to physical, social, and emotional development because he or she is being raised in an optimal environment. These are all examples of outcomes.

Indicators

An *indicator* identifies the factors that are being measured to track the program's success of an outcome. An indicator is observable and measurable (see Box 7.7 on the following page).

Qualitative Data

Qualitative data describe and interpret happenings or emotions. They are verbal or narrative comments that can be collected by observing or interviewing participants. Methods for collecting qualitative data include focus groups, interviews, questionnaires, case studies, and direct observation. Although qualitative data are difficult to analyze, they address what effects positive human behavior and what family programs hope to influence. Qualitative data might include descriptions of how parents teach children to play with a new toy; stories about how a support group changed a parent's perception of a crisis situation; or a series of excerpts from a parent's journal that describe what was learned during a year of being involved in a home visiting program. Qualitative data can be important for communicating with stakeholders and providing a way to share success stories (see Box 7.8 on the following page).

Box 7.7   Indicators

One of the goals of the Indoor Playground is to provide opportunities for parents in the community to connect with each other. Staff at the Indoor Playground events might systematically observe parents to see if they are interacting with each other and if relationships are forming. This interaction between the parents, especially if the same parents sit together and talk to each other at subsequent events, could be considered an indicator of parents' connection with each other. Staff could also observe other Southwest Family Room events to see if some of the same parents attend and if they interact with other families.

An overall goal of the Southwest Family Room is to increase learning readiness of children entering kindergarten. One indicator of learning readiness is having received all recommended shots before entering kindergarten. Another indicator might be that children have been screened for hearing, vision, or speech problems and have received the appropriate intervention, if needed. If these problems are identified early enough for actions to be taken, children will be ready to learn by the time they enter kindergarten.

Box 7.8   Qualitative Data/Evaluation

If the staff of the Southwest Family Room wanted to gather *qualitative data* or carry out a qualitative evaluation, they could interview or survey the participants of the programs to collect information on how they feel about the programs and how they think they have benefited. Another option would be to observe parents at various events and record information about their interactions with their children or other parents. Another option is to hold a focus group meeting of parents of 4-year-olds to determine what issues are of most concern at this stage in their children's lives. This information could be used to help them design future classes or determine what resources might be most helpful.

Quantitative Data

Information gathered through quantitative methods is typically reported numerically and can take less time to analyze than qualitative data. Age, education level, and attendance records for various events would all be considered *quantitative data*. However, quantitative data can also include participant's perceptions, perhaps identified through a Likert-type scale (e.g., range of options from 1 strongly disagree to 5 strongly agree), regarding their perceived knowledge gains, comfort levels, or satisfaction. These data can be gathered through questionnaires, tests, surveys, counting the number of participants in the program, and/or observation (see Box 7.9). For example, one measurement of a quantifiable change in the parent-child relationship may be an improvement in parenting skills observed by the use of appropriate communication methods with the child or the correct implementation of guidance strategies.

Although evaluators are likely to continue to debate the best approach to evaluation, design, and data collection methods (i.e., qualitative vs. quantitative),

---

Box 7.9   Quantitative Data/Evaluation

At each event held by the Southwest Family Room, a sign-in sheet with the participant's name is provided. Staff members use this information, in addition to attendance, to monitor how many people are attending each event—an example of an output in Tier Two of Jacobs' model (see Appendix D). They may also collect data on how kindergartner children that have attended the program score on developmental assessments. These would be considered *quantitative data*.

---

many evaluators believe the questions that focus the evaluation study should lead to a discussion about which types of approaches are used. It is also important to note that many studies employ a mixed-methods approach, that is, a design using both qualitative and quantitative methods. The needs and interests of the stakeholders in your program may also influence the evaluation design and methodology. Stakeholders, which include anyone who is affected by the results of the evaluation, can include decision-makers and policy makers as well as staff, people in the community, and the clients themselves (Rader & Cooke, 2005).

Levels of Outcomes

In some instances there is just one desired outcome for a program. However, in many cases there is a series of outcomes, each of which can contribute to the accomplishment of another and, ultimately, to the final outcome goals of the program. Different programs use different terms to describe these same levels. The important concept to consider is that there are varying levels of outcomes.

Initial Outcomes

Initial outcomes are the first changes or benefits that a participant experiences as a result of the program. It may be a change in attitude, knowledge, skills, or all of these. In most programs these initial outcomes would not be ends themselves, but important steps toward reaching the desired ends.

Intermediate Outcomes

Intermediate outcomes connect a program's initial outcomes to longer-term outcomes intended for its participants. Intermediate outcomes are often exemplified by changes in behavior as a result of the new knowledge, skills, or attitudes.

Longer-Term Outcomes

Longer-term outcomes are the lasting outcomes that a program wants to achieve. These are usually significant changes that are often longitudinally apparent and related to condition or status. An example of a longer-term outcome might be that since the program began, parent attendance at parent-teacher conferences in the community has increased significantly. See Box 7.10 on the following page for an example of the various outcomes of a Southwest Family Room class. Unfortunately,

Box 7.10   Levels of Outcomes

Initial Outcomes—After attending the "Terrific Threes" and "Fabulous Fours" parent education classes, there is a measurable increase in subsequent classes in the number of minutes that most parents spend reading to their child in one-on-one parent-child time.

Intermediate Outcomes—Several months into the program, the staff member who oversees the program's lending library notes that the library is busier. When she checks her records, the librarian determines that library usage has more than doubled for most parents.

Longer-Term Outcomes—Two years into the future, as kindergarten teachers collect information about their students' preschool experience, they discover that children who participated in "Terrific Threes" and "Fabulous Fours" scored significantly higher on all school readiness assessments.

many programs only have the resources to measure initial outcomes. The cost of conducting evaluations to include intermediate and longer-term outcomes is sometimes prohibitive for organizations operating on limited budgets.

The Evaluation Process

Five-Tiered Approach to Program Evaluation

There are a number of methods and techniques involved in carrying out a program evaluation. The *Five-Tiered Approach to Program Evaluation*, (see Appendix D) is a widely used evaluation approach (Jacobs, 2000). It provides a useful rubric for family life educators to ensure that a program is evaluated comprehensively. It prompts evaluators to think about the purpose of evaluation, its audience, and the procedures for collecting and analyzing data. The step-by-step tiers serve as a guide for a systematic strategy for evaluation. Tiers one through three guide users through assessing needs and ensuring accountability, quality, and clarity. Tiers four and five explain the process of translating data into new outcomes, applying findings to further research, enhancing the program, and determining areas for public policy action. In addition to Jacobs' Five-Tiered Approach to Program Evaluation there are many resources available to assist you in the evaluation of your family program. See Box 7.14 for a list of organizations and resources that can guide you in preparing for and conducting a program evaluation.

Evaluability Assessment

There is another step that can be implemented prior to an evaluation process: an *evaluability assessment* (EA). This is "a systematic process that helps identify whether program evaluation is justified, feasible, and likely to provide useful information" (Juvenile Justice Evaluation Center, 2003). An EA can include questions about both the design and the implementation of the program. Does the program have a design or model with clearly articulated, realistic, and measurable goals and objectives? An EA might compare the program design to the program that is actually being implemented. It could also ask if the program is serving the population for which it was designed. Are the resources identified in the program design actually in place? Is the program being carried out as originally planned and described? Are resources in place to provide for collection of data needed for program evaluation? Conducting an evaluability assessment prior to carrying out a full program evaluation can minimize the risk of determining part way through an evaluation that certain necessary components are missing or unobtainable.

Cultural Considerations in Evaluation

Regardless of the method of evaluation chosen, it is important to keep cultural contexts in mind. Most standardized instruments were designed for white, middle-class populations. These are often inappropriate when English is not the primary language of the individuals who will complete them or if Western cultural concepts would not be well understood or do not carry the same value. The issue of language is complex. For example, not everyone from a particular ethnic group can read and write even in their native language. Not only do dialects and regional language differences exist, but also communication skill-levels differ among generations, across socioeconomic groups, and among people with different educational histories.

Some Western concepts are difficult to translate and require data collectors to clarify survey items for study participants. For example, self-esteem is not only a concept that is challenging for U.S. researchers to define and measure, but it may also be a concept unfamiliar to new or recently arrived immigrants. In addition, evaluators should be mindful of any participant's reluctance to fill out a form. In the situation of undocumented immigrants, participants may be fearful of revealing any identifying information that might be available to immigration enforcement. Carrying out pretesting interviews and surveys or setting up advisory group review committees can determine the best approach for examining questionable words or concepts. This procedure is sometimes referred to as *pilot testing*.

It is important to be aware of *cultural response sets*. In some cultures, professionals may be seen as authority figures deserving of respect. Participants in this situation may feel uncomfortable or unwilling to provide any negative feedback even if encouraged. In some cultures, asking for help or appearing needy is inappropriate. Participants from such cultures may not feel comfortable revealing what they consider to be weaknesses. There may also be cultural taboos against revealing too much personal information. Other things to consider within varying cultures might be gender, age, and socioeconomic status. Are family programs experienced differently by men than by women or by people of different economic levels? Awareness and sensitivity to such factors will increase the effectiveness of your information-gathering strategies.

In order for family life educators to be successful they must have, in addition to knowledge and skills relevant to family life education topics, an understanding of the specific cultural beliefs and practices of the population with which they are working (Taylor & Ballard, 2012; also see Chapter 3). It is important for this awareness to carry over into any evaluation processes put in place.

Evidence-Based and Evidence-Informed Programs

The issue of *evidence-based programs* is increasingly prevalent when considering family life education programs and practices. As discussed earlier in this chapter, many funders are requiring that programs be identified as "evidence-based" in order to receive financial support (ASPE, 2013; Cooney et al., 2007). This attention and support has resulted in an increase in information and resources relevant to identifying, designing, and evaluating evidence-based programs.

A program can be identified as being evidence-based if "(a) evaluation research shows that the program produces expected positive results; (b) the results can be attributed to the program itself rather than to other extraneous factors or events; (c) the evaluation is peer-reviewed by experts in the field; and (d) the program is "endorsed" by a federal agency or respected research organization and included in their list of effective programs" (ZERO TO THREE, 2011). The Substance Abuse and Mental Health Services Administration (SAMHSA), defines evidence-based programs as having been "reviewed by experts in the field according to accepted standards of empirical research, are conceptually sound and internally consistent, have sound research methodology, and can prove the effects are clearly linked to the program itself and not extraneous events" (Kyler, Bumbarger, & Greenberg, 2005, p. 2).

Evaluation Design

In order to be recognized as evidence-based, a program must undergo an evaluation study. There are a number of different ways to design an evaluation study with some designs considered to be more rigorous than others. Differences in design include the presence or absence of a control group, the method by which participants are assigned to groups, and the frequency with which outcomes are measured (SAMHSA, 2012). *Experimental* designs (Tier Five of Jacob's model) are considered to be the most rigorous followed by *quasi-experimental* and *pre-experimental*.

Experimental Design

An *experimental design*, sometimes referred to as a *randomized controlled trial*, involves the comparison of a randomly assigned treatment and control group. Members of the treatment and control groups should have similar traits and characteristics. Both groups are measured or observed prior to implementation of a program, and after the program is completed the outcomes of the two groups are compared. The random assignment of the subjects to the groups helps to ensure that any differences in outcome are likely the result of the program. Repeating the experiment multiple times with several different control and treatment groups helps to increase confidence in the outcome of the study. While often the best way to accurately measure program effectiveness, experimental design is typically more expensive and can be more time-consuming. Box 7.11 provides an example of an experimental design.

Quasi-experimental design

Given that it is not always practical or feasible to create a control group, a *quasi-experimental design* can be conducted (see Box 7.12). A quasi-experimental design uses two or more pre-existing or self-selected groups that share some common variable. The most important issue with a quasi-experimental design is the lack of a random assignment to treatment or control groups. Because of the lack of randomization, quasi-experimental designs tend to have lower internal validity than experimental designs because it is difficult to know for sure if the comparison groups differed in any important way that might account for differences in outcomes.

Box 7.11   Experimental Design

Let's revisit the scenario in Box 7.3:

The Southwest Family Room sponsors a New Parents support group for parents of newborns. The meetings are facilitated by parents in the community who have completed a 16-hour small group-facilitation training program. Parents enter the program before their babies are born or just afterward. The program meets twice a month for 2 hours for a 2-year period.

In this situation an Experimental Design would involve the random assignment of the parents of newborns born in a community hospital during an identified time frame into two groups. One group of parents would be enrolled in a "New Parents" support group and identified as the "treatment group." The other group would be identified as a "control group." Both groups would be given a pre-test measuring their knowledge of infant and toddler development. The treatment group would participate in the New Parent program over the course of the next two years. The parents in the control group would not participate in the program. At the end of the two year program, both sets of parents would be given the same test again. If the parents in the New Parents support group demonstrated greater knowledge of infant and toddler development it could be concluded that participation in the program resulted in increased knowledge, especially if this same study was repeated with subsequent groups of parents and demonstrated the same results each time.

Box 7.12   Quasi-Experimental Design

A Quasi-experimental design could be achieved through a delayed intervention. If all parents interested in attending a class could not be accommodated, a wait list could be created. Those on the wait list could complete the pre-test and post-test at the same time as those in the class but without the benefit of having completed the class. Initially those on the wait list would be part of a comparison group, but would eventually be able to attend the class. This can be a more ethical way to carry out a quasi-experimental design because it does not deny anyone the program or services that could be beneficial.

Pre-experimental design

A pre-experimental design is considered the least rigorous because it lacks a control group and does not involve random assignment. Only the people participating in the program are involved in any kind of measurement. There may be a pre-test and a post-test or just a post-test. A post-test only approach will only tell if the participants have reached a specific outcome, such as learning a new skill, since there will not be a baseline to assess. Incorporation of a pre and post-test enables comparison of the participants' knowledge or attitudes before and after they enter the program, making it easier to measure how the participants have changed. However, because there is no control group it is difficult to attribute any change to the program itself.

Box 7.13   Pre-Experimental Design

Parents participating in a *New Parents* support program would be selected as the study group. All participants in the group would be given a pre-test about infant and toddler development upon entering the program. They would be given the same test at the end of the second year. It might be determined that the knowledge demonstrated on the post-test was the result of participation in the class. However, because there is no control group for comparison, it is difficult to say for sure if the increased knowledge was attributable specifically to participation in the class. There is no way of knowing if parents who did not participate in the class demonstrated a similar knowledge gain just by virtue of having been parents for the past two years.

Benefits of Evidence-Based Programs

There are numerous benefits to implementing an evidence-based program. It can help to ensure that the program is based on solid research and proven theories and increase the likelihood that the results or outcomes can be attributable to the services received from the program. Additionally, using a program that has been tried and tested adds to the likelihood of success. It can facilitate the most efficient use of resources because money is spent on proven programs rather than invested into the design of a new program. Another benefit of using evidence-based programs is that the program is likely to have undergone a cost–benefit analysis. This can demonstrate that the benefits of the program outweigh the costs, making it easier to obtain funding and support from policy makers, community leaders, and participants. Moreover, many evidence-based programs offer packaged materials, instruction, or staff training so that the program will be taught as intended by the developer. Finally, using well-implemented evidence-based programs can help assure that families receive the best services available.

Where to Find Evidence-Based Programs

While there is no universally accepted definition of what it means to be evidence-based, there are a number of clearinghouses and registries that have established guidelines, standards, or criteria for inclusion. Many of these registries focus more on target populations and the prevention of negative outcomes over the promotion of positive ones (Cooney et al., 2007) but increased interest in primary prevention promises to result in advancements in the field. Box 7.14 includes a partial list of resources and organizations relevant to evaluation and evidence-based practice.

Box 7.14   Resources for Evidence-Based Programs and Practices and Evaluation

American Evaluation Association
  www.eval.org

Blueprints for Healthy Youth Development (Annie E. Casey Foundation)
  www.blueprintsprograms.com

Centers for Disease Control Framework for Program Evaluation in Public Health
  www.cdc.gov/eval/framework/index.htm

Child Welfare Information Gateway
  www.childwelfare.gov/preventing/evaluating/tools.cfm

Children, Youth, and Families Education and Research Network (CYFERNET)
  www.cyfernet.org

Coalition for Evidence-Based Policy
  www.coalition4evidence.org/

Community Toolbox (Work Group for Community Health and Development—University of Kansas)
  www.ctb.ku.edu/en

FRIENDS - National Resource Center for Community-Based Child Abuse Prevention—Evaluation Toolkit Resources
  www.friendsnrc.org/evaluation-toolkit

Harvard Family Research Project
  Evaluation Exchange www.hfrp.org/evaluation/the-evaluation-exchange
  Evaluation Publications and Resources www.hfrp.org/evaluation/publications-resources

Home Visiting Evidence of Effectiveness (HomVEE)—U.S. Department of Health and Human Services
  http://homvee.acf.hhs.gov/

Institute of Education Sciences (IES) What Works Clearinghouse—U.S. Department of Education
  www.ies.ed.gov/ncee/wwc/

National Parenting Education Network (NPEN)
  www.npen.org/resources-for-parenting-educators/evaluating-parent-education-programs/

National Registry of Evidence-Based Programs and Practices (NREPP) from Substance Abuse and Mental Health Services Administration (SAMHSA)
  www.nrepp.samhsa.gov/

RAND Corporation Promising Practices Network
  www.promisingpractices.net/

U of Wisconsin Extension—Program Development and Evaluation
  www.uwex.edu/ces/pdande/evaluation/evallinks.html

Wisconsin—What Works, Evidence-Based Programs
  www.human.cornell.edu/outreach/upload/Evidence-based-Programs-Overview.pdf

Challenges for Evidence-Based Programs

While the value of implementing evidence-based programs is widely recognized, a number of challenges exist regarding their wide-spread and consistent use. Additionally a lack of consensus over the criteria used to determine or define evidence-based programs can make it difficult for a program developer or user to know what standard to pursue.

Cost

It can be expensive to conduct the research needed to identify a program as evidence-based. In addition, many smaller agencies and organizations may not have the funds necessary to purchase the rights to use the materials needed to implement an existing evidence-based program and may not have the capacity to conduct the program exactly as a developer intended, which could jeopardize the program outcomes.

Lack of programs for targeted populations

An agency may have difficulty finding a program that meets the needs of its specific population. A program that must be implemented exactly as designed may not allow adaptation for cultural values or local conditions compromising fidelity to the program model.

Importance of provider expertise

The effectiveness of a program is as much a function of *how* it is delivered as *what* is delivered (Ballard & Taylor, 2012; Small, Cooney, & O'Connor, 2009). It is important that the person(s) delivering an evidence-based program, or any family program for that matter, be qualified, trained, and supported by the agency. Program leaders play a major role in program outcomes through their efforts in selecting, supporting, and training staff; overseeing data collection; and communicating with stakeholders. The efforts of program leaders can contribute to a positive working environment influencing staff retention, which has a positive impact on program success. Additionally, oversight of program implementation by involved leadership increases the likelihood that the program is carried out as intended (ZERO TO THREE, 2011).

Principles of Effective Programs

While it may be preferable to use a proven evidence-based program, it is not always an option, typically due to funding and staffing issues. Incorporating principles of proven programs into existing programs can provide a way to increase the effectiveness of prevention programs. Small, Cooney, and O'Connor, (2009) developed an approach called "evidence-informed program improvement" (EIPI) based on what they had learned about the common traits of evidence-based prevention programs. The EIPI approach provides a framework for considering the principles of effective programs. The authors identified 11 principles of effective programs and organized them into four categories: (a) program design and content, (b) program relevance, (c) program implementation, and (d) program assessment and quality assurance (Small et al., 2009).

Principles within *Program Design and Content* include being theory driven, of sufficient dosage and intensity, comprehensive, and actively engaging. In comparison, principles within *Program Relevance* include being developmentally appropriate, appropriately timed, and socioculturally relevant. For *Program Implementation*, a program should be delivered by well-qualified, trained, and supported staff and focused on fostering good relationships. Finally, within the category of *Program Assessment and Quality Assurance*, a program should be well-documented and committed to evaluation and refinement.

Providers can incorporate these principles when developing new programs, even if the programs are not able to include measurements or be conducted in a way that would allow them to be defined as evidence-based. The principles can also be used as criteria to evaluate existing programs and influence program redesign. The application of the EIPI approach can enable family program practitioners to increase the effectiveness of the services they provide.

Framework for Best Practices in Family Life Education

The value of using an evidence-based or informed approach to program development and implementation is widely recognized, but there are other important factors to consider. *The Framework for Best Practices in Family Life Education* moves beyond a focus on content and methods to include program format and features (Ballard & Taylor, 2012). The Framework considers program content and design, as well as the family life educator presenting or developing the material. All components are considered within the context of the strengths, needs, and culture of the population.

Best practices can incorporate what is known about the audience and what will work for them in terms of content and methods. Additionally, the skills and experiences of educators are paramount to the process. "Good family life education programs based on best practices may be a combination of empirically supported content and program design along with experiences and skills of the family life educator. The key to meeting the needs of a diverse audience is to pay attention to all of these components and to recognize that these components are interrelated and interdependent. . . . Therefore, these three components (program content, program design, and the family life educator), set in the context of culture and needs and strengths of the population provide the Framework for Best Practices in Family Life Education" (Ballard & Taylor, p. 5).

SUMMARY

This chapter has provided a brief overview of many concepts and issues involved in evaluation. As you have surmised, evaluation can be a complicated issue. However, its value and importance cannot be underestimated. If you find yourself involved in family programming in any way, you will be directly or indirectly involved in evaluation. It is imperative to take time to carefully carry out the necessary steps for an effective evaluation plan including assessing the needs and strengths of your audience, identifying existing resources, considering stakeholders and their expectations, and developing a logic model that thoughtfully considers the relationship between actions and results, along with program activities, inputs, outcomes, and indicators. It will be important to build formative evaluation into the design of your program, as well as summative evaluation at the end of your program or class to help you determine what worked and what could be improved. By following these important steps and considering the multiple aspects of evaluation, you will increase the likelihood that your program will improve and enhance the lives of its participants.

QUESTIONS AND ISSUES FOR DISCUSSION

1. How would you do a needs assessment, formative evaluation, and summative evaluation for a one-night, 3-hour workshop on *Balancing Work and Family*?

2. What are some possible inputs, activities, outputs, outcomes, and indicators for the same program?

3. How would you gather qualitative and quantitative data in the above scenario?

4. What are the possible initial, intermediate, and long-term outcomes that could occur as a result of attending the *Balancing Work and Family* workshop? Could all outcomes be realized by the end of the workshop, that is, at the end of that same day?

ACTIVITIES

1. Identify a large federal grant opportunity that focuses on prevention rather than intervention. How would evaluation be different for a program that focuses on prevention?

2. Read Appendix D, "The Five-Tiered Approach to Program Evaluation," and provide examples of evaluations performed at each tier.

3. Your 6-week workshop, *Sexuality and Your Teen*, has not been going as well as you had hoped. Attendance has been dropping, participants seem distracted, and it has been difficult to engage them in group discussion. How can you find out what the problem is and the reasons for their discontent?

PART III

Content of Family Life Education

8

Relating Theory to Practice

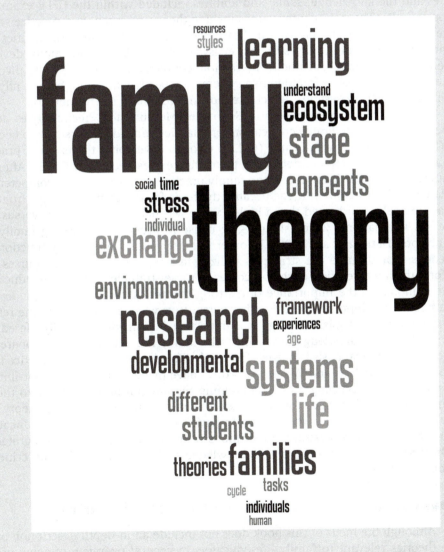

Need for Theory in Family Life Education

Theories contribute to our understanding of families by providing reasonable explanations of individual and family behaviors. Because families are so complex, there is no single theory that can explain all family behaviors, thus, we need several theories from various disciplines to understand family structures and functions. The incorporation and integration of multiple theories are essential because we are affected by many different elements within our childhood, family, gendered and socialization experiences, and cultural beliefs.

The Content and Practice Guidelines for the Certified Family Life Educator (CFLE) program were derived from the University and College Curriculum Guidelines and the knowledge, skills, and abilities included within the CFLE exam (see Appendix B). These 10 content areas include theory, research, and practice within the field of family life education. Examples of some of these core theories and frameworks include family systems, ecosystems, individual and family development, social exchange, symbolic interaction, conflict, feminist, and stress theories. Family life education is founded in a systems perspective including both family systems and larger ecosystems, which are woven throughout the framework.

In 2007 NCFR colleagues and Schroeder Measurement Technologies developed an exam to facilitate certification for qualified individuals desiring to become a Certified Family Life Educator (CFLE). Prior to developing the exam, a practice analysis was conducted to determine the competencies needed by CFLEs. After the data were collected from CFLEs and family practice professionals, 76 competencies related to the 10 content areas became the basis for the exam. Findings from the practice analysis indicated that a higher value was placed on strategies versus theoretical foundations, which should give pause to programs educating family life educators (Darling et al., 2009). In order to better understand family functioning, theories should guide the strategies utilized in family life education courses and inform the interpretation of the outcomes of these strategies. Family life educators often emphasize the importance of a strong theoretical foundation to guide programmatic development, however that perspective was not apparent in the results of the practice analysis. Although it is important for entry-level family life educators to have the knowledge and skills to be family life educators, it is apparent a stronger theoretical basis is needed for family life educators to better practice their profession. Bredehoft and Walcheski (2009) have made an important contribution to the field by publishing a book containing the integration of theory into the 10 content areas with implications for practice. Their theme of integrating theory and practice resonates well with our goal to have well-prepared family life educators. Since theory is more abstract, applications of the theory need to be integrated to help students go beyond facts and knowledge about families and think critically about how families function.

Overview of Theories Used to Study Families

Although the focus of this book does not include an in-depth description of all the theories relevant to family life educators, a general overview of some of the main theories will be shared. For some readers these highlights will be a review of concepts previously learned, whereas for others, it will introduce theoretical concepts for further exploration. In addition, activities, assignments, or suggestions for application will be provided. When individuals have an opportunity to experience the theoretical concepts in an applied manner, they can more readily incorporate that knowledge in their work with families. Thus, the second section of this chapter will provide examples of ways to use these theories when learning about and working with families.

Family Systems Theory

Evolving from general systems theory, viewing the family as a system provides an important paradigm when analyzing human and family behavior (Chibucos, Leite, & Weiss, 2005; Ingoldsby, Smith, & Miller, 2004; White & Klein, 2008). The family as a whole is viewed as greater than the sum of its parts and as a social system with rules, roles, communication patterns, and a power structure. A *system* can be viewed as a collection of elements with interrelated and interdependent parts so that what affects one person in a family also influences other members. The family system is maintained by a boundary that can be perceived as occurring on a continuum ranging from *open* (allowing elements outside the family to influence it) to *closed* (becoming self-contained and isolating the family from its environment). However, no family is completely open or closed. There are two key elements of family systems theory: (1) *structural characteristics* involving *boundaries* and their *permeability, subsystems*, and *hierarchies* and (2) *process characteristics* comprised of establishing boundaries; establishing connectedness and separateness; and establishing congruent images, themes, messages, and rules. There are a number of other key concepts, such as *inputs, outputs,* and *feedback; circular causality; family rules, routines,* and *rituals;* and *equilibrium* and *dynamic equilibrium.*

Concepts from the *Couple and Family Map (Circumplex Model)* (Olson, Russell, & Sprenkle, 1989; Olson & DeFrain, 2006; Olson & Gorall, 2003) help us to understand (1) family *cohesion* or the emotional bonding within families ranging from *enmeshed* to *disengaged* and (2) family *flexibility* regarding the amount of change in its leadership, role relationships, and relational rules ranging from *chaotic* to *rigid* and how these characteristics can change through the family life cycle and across cultures. The third element is *communication*, which is considered essential to facilitating movement on the other two dimensions. Having a balanced family system between the extremes of cohesion and flexibility tends to be more functional across the life cycle. The notion of cohesion can be further understood by examining *vertical attachment* to a previous or subsequent generation and *horizontal attachment*—connectedness within your same generation. Moreover, couples and families try to maintain their separateness and connectedness by balancing *centrifugal forces* that push family members away from the family and *centripetal forces* that pull family members together (Goldenberg & Goldenberg, 2003).

Using this model, theoretical clarifications can evolve from discussions of boundaries and distance regulation along with cohesion and flexibility. What types of boundaries exist for persons of varying ethnic, age, or gender backgrounds or

when dealing with various crises? What kinds of expectations for family togetherness and flexibility exist for different ethnic and religious groups? For example,
cohesion can have different meanings in cultures that value familism vs. individuality. A discussion of family stories, rituals, and rules can also provide understanding and meaning about differing families and groups.

Family as an Ecosystem

Family ecology is a general theory that can be used to examine a wide range of
issues related to individuals and families within various environments. Since it is
not based on any particular family configuration, it can be used with families of
diverse structures, backgrounds, and life circumstances. An ecosystems approach
can be quite useful to add understanding and context to family life education
(Andrews, Bubolz, & Paolucci, 1981; Bubolz, Eicher, & Sontag, 1979; Bubolz &
Sontag, 1993; Bronfenbrenner, 1979, 2005; Darling, 1987; Darling & Turkki,
2009). With individual and family issues becoming increasingly complex, a framework is needed that can handle the task of incorporating a holistic view of multifaceted issues. Whereas human beings in interaction with their environments
comprise the human ecosystem, a family ecosystem focuses on the family's interaction with its environment. There is increasing awareness that we are interdependent creatures and not independent organisms. This is not only true in our
relationships with each other, but also with the total environment in which we live.

There are several basic premises that underlie the ecosystems framework. The
first and most basic premise is that individuals and families are viewed as being in
interaction with their environment, which constitutes an ecosystem (Andrews et
al., 1981; Bubolz et al., 1979; Bubolz & Sontag, 1993; Darling, 1987; Darling &
Turkki, 2009). In such an ecosystem, the parts and wholes are interrelated and
interdependent. A second premise is that the family carries out certain essential
physical, biological, economic, psychosocial, and nurturing functions for its members, for the family as a collective, and for the larger society. Thus, the unique and
powerful value of an ecological perspective lies in its potential to examine these
multilevel functions and systems in relation to each other over time. The third
premise consists of the interdependence of all persons worldwide along with their
resources. A core value in an ecosystems framework is the survival of humans,
other living species, and the resources of our planet. The overall well-being and
health of the planet and of all people cannot be viewed in isolation or outside the
context of the whole ecosystem. Thus, the underlying value of an ecological framework is grounded in a balance between demands of the ecosystem for cooperation
and integration versus demands of the individual for autonomy and freedom. The
basic values of an ecosystems perspective focus on the complementary needs of the
individual and the needs of the global ecosystem. Ideally, this complementarity
facilitates the development and well-being of the individual and family, as well as
the ecosystem.

The family ecosystem model is built on three major concepts: the *organism* or
human environed unit (*HEU*), the *environments* encompassing societies' families, and
the *interrelationships* between the family system and its surrounding environments

(Darling, 1987; Darling & Turkki, 2009) (see Figure 8.1). The *organism* or *human environed unit* can be a single individual or plurality of individuals who have some feelings of unity; share some common resources, goals, values, and interests; and have some sense of identity. While many times the group of interest is the family, the focus of the human environed unit could be on an individual or any bonded group. The environments can be categorized into three types: (1) the *natural environment* (NE) is formed by nature and includes space-time, physical, and biological elements; (2) the *human-constructed environment* (HCE) is that which is altered or created by human beings and includes sociocultural, sociophysical, and sociobiological elements; (3) the *human-behavioral environment* (HBE) is socialized by human beings

Figure 8.1   Family Ecosystem Model

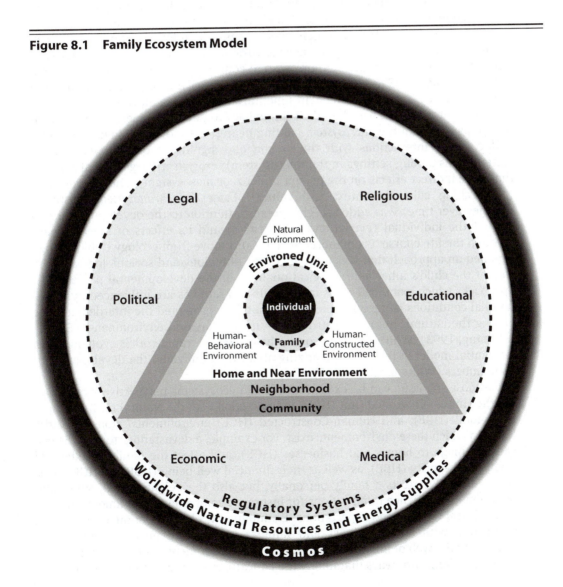

and their behaviors including psychological, biophysical, and social dimensions. The *regulatory systems*, which are part of the HCE, include the legal, political, economic, religious, educational, and medical systems. One should not forget the role of *worldwide natural resources and energy* supplies, as well as the *cosmos*. With our need for natural resources and energy, along with the influence of changing weather systems, these elements of the natural environment should be examined in context of the worldwide ecosystems of families. While the *cosmos* is not often part of common discussions about the ecosystem, recent attention to global warming, solar flares, and meteors falling to earth make us mindful of this environmental element. *Interaction* can occur within the environed unit, between environments, and between the environed unit and the environments. The family is continually adapting to changing social, economic, political, and biological elements in the environment.

The NE, HCE, and HBE and their interactions with individuals and families can occur at many levels including the near environment, within the home, and externally in the neighborhood, community, state-country, world, or cosmos. Similarly, Bronfenbrenner (1979, 2005) in his ecological approach described the individual as influenced by a set of nested environmental structures. He incorporated levels of environmental systems based on their immediacy to developing persons in the ecological paradigm of the *microsystem* (setting nearest the individual involving direct and concrete interactions with the person and significant others); *mesosystem* (interactions among settings in the microsystem); *exosystem* (larger social systems that have indirect effects on the person's micro- or mesosystem); and *macrosystem* (overarching cultural context and values). Later the *chronosystem* (systemic changes over time) was added to give greater attention to the developmental history of the individual (events and experiences) and its effects on development through the life course. Bronfenbrenner's (2005) move from ecology to bioecology signaled an approach that was more inclusive of biology and sociobiology and the role of the child's inherited biological qualities in the developmental process. His approach, which examined ways individuals and families are influenced by extra-familial conditions and environments, has not fully promoted the interdependence among the natural, human-constructed, human-behavioral environments (Bubolz & Sontag, 1993). While still in its youth, the ecological framework is evolving as an influential model in regard to theorizing about the family and the development of its members (White & Klein, 2008).

Almost any issue can be examined from an ecosystems perspective incorporating the Human-Environed Unit (HEU) in interaction with the Natural (NE), Human-Behavioral (HBE), and Human-Constructed (HCE) environments, along with the levels in which these environments exist. For example, a devastating storm (NE) can cause damage to homes and businesses (HCE), and affect the family's feelings of safety and security (HBE), as well as their financial well-being (HBE and HCE). This storm not only affects a family personally, but also the neighborhood, state, and nation may experience ramifications for insurance companies, government support, and political realities and expectations. Examining the elements of the ecosystem in interaction with an individual's and family's multifaceted environments is like examining the web of life. It brings greater clarity for student understanding of family issues, along with ways that family life educators can teach and serve families.

Family Developmental Theory

Incorporating a developmental framework for both individuals and families can provide a longitudinal perspective to understanding families (Chibucos et al., 2005; Ingoldsby et al., 2004; White & Klein, 2008). Although change is ever present, gradual, and a part of individual aging, it is occurring in families and society at an even faster rate. Along with media influences, alternate lifestyles, and advances in biotechnology, family life has also evolved. Family developmental theory was one of the first family-oriented theories and it still holds value in today's analysis of families.

Family developmental theory, like individual development, focuses on stages of development and the changes in internal development that occur at various stages across the lifespan. From the family developmental perspective, a *family* is an arena of interacting personalities organized into *roles* (expectations for a kinship position over time); *positions* (role arrangement over time such as husband, wife, father, mother, son, daughter, brother, and sister); and *norms* (cultural expectations or guidelines that set behavioral limits). Examining the students' current roles (e.g., caretaker of younger siblings, sharing in household responsibilities, contributor to family communication), positions (e.g., daughter, son, brother, sister), and cultural norms (e.g., cultural expectations of a son or daughter at current age) can help them relate to these concepts. While it may be difficult for students to verbalize the cultural norms of various family members' roles, one might call attention to mothers and fathers in the news, who have violated the perceived cultural norms for parents so that their behavior became newsworthy. We commonly refer to the *family life cycle* as having eight stages including: (a) *Married couple* (without children); (b) *Childbearing families* (oldest child from birth to 30 months); (c) *Families with preschool children* (oldest child from 2.5 to 6 years); (d) *Families with school-age children* (oldest from 6 to 13 years); (e) *Families with teenagers* (oldest from 13 to 20 years); (f) *Families as launching careers* (first child gone until last child leaves home); (g) *Middle years* ("empty nest" to retirement); and (h) *Aging families* (retirement to death of both spouses) (see Table 8.1) (Duvall & Miller, 1984). Other options may include two stages—expansion and contraction, or a ninth stage, the *Expectant Family Stage*. Stages evolve because of the addition or subtraction of a family member through birth (age of the oldest child), leaving home, and death. Research has indicated that when examining variables associated with the presence and ages of children, the family life cycle continues to be a useful predictive tool (Kapinus & Johnson, 2003).

Within the stages of the life cycle, various *developmental tasks* are proposed based on normative expectations. If the task is completed, one will be adequately prepared to move to the next stage. However, failure at a task does not necessarily mean that an individual will not move to the next stage, but it may result in unhappiness, disapproval by society, and difficulty with optimal functioning in the next stage. (Some of these stage-critical tasks are noted in Table 8.1 on the following page.) To apply the concept of "developmental task," you might provide an example of an individual task that needs to be completed successfully at a certain time in life (e.g., the task of learning to read). If children learn to read at the expected time in their lives, they have a sense of happiness and accomplishment, but if they do not accomplish this task and have reading problems compared to others, they may feel inadequate and embarrassed as reading is fundamental to moving forward with other school learning experiences. This illustration can be used to stimulate discussion of other examples of individual or family developmental tasks that are milestones in one's development.

Table 8.1   Stage-Critical Family Developmental Tasks throughout the Family Life Cycle

Stage of the Family Life Cycle	Positions in the Family	Stage-Critical Family Developmental Tasks
Married couple	Wife Husband	Establishing a mutually satisfying marriage Adjusting to pregnancy and the promise of parenthood Fitting into the kin network
Childbearing	Wife-mother Husband-father Daughter-sister Son-brother	Having, adjusting to, and encouraging the development of infants Establishing a satisfying home for both parents and infant(s)
Preschool age	Wife-mother Husband-father Daughter-sister Son-brother	Adapting to the critical needs and interests of preschool children in stimulating, growth-promoting ways Coping with energy depletion and lack of privacy as parents
School age	Wife-mother Husband-father Daughter-sister Son-brother	Fitting into the community of school-age families in constructive ways Encouraging children's educational achievement
Teenage	Wife-mother Husband-father Daughter-sister Son-brother	Balancing freedom with responsibility as teenagers mature and emancipate themselves Establishing post-parental interests and careers as growing parents
Launching center	Wife-mother-grandmother Husband-father-grandfather Daughter-sister-aunt Son-brother-uncle	Releasing young adults into work, military service, college, marriage, etc., with appropriate rituals and assistance Maintaining a supportive home base
Middle-aged	Wife-mother-grandmother Husband-father-grandfather	Rebuilding the marriage relationship Maintaining kin ties with older and younger generations
Aging family members	Widow/widower Wife-mother-grandmother Husband-father-grandfather	Coping with bereavement and living alone Closing the family home or adapting it to aging Adjusting to retirement

From Duvall, E. & Miller, B. *Marriages and Family Development* 6/E © 1984. Printed and electronically reproduced by permission of Pearson Education, Inc., Upper Saddle River, NJ.

One criticism of family developmental theory is its assumption that all families develop in the same manner (Laszloffy, 2002). Thus, you might ask students if these family life cycle stages fit their families. Some will respond positively and some negatively, however, they may have to "think outside the box" to better understand their unique family circumstance. For example, there may be a remarriage involving one person who is in the *Aging Family Stage* with someone who is in the *Launching Young Adults Stage*, yet as a couple they are in the *Establishment Stage*. Realizing that this newly married couple is trying to accomplish the developmental tasks of three different stages simultaneously facilitates understanding the various issues this family is facing. No wonder this new stepfamily has some challenges. For various reasons many families may not progress through the family life cycle stages in an orderly manner. Moreover, while generally one focuses on the age of the oldest child, some researchers find the age of the youngest child should be considered, especially when dealing with single and blended families, as it provides information about the role and time demands facing parents with young children (Kapinus & Johnson, 2003). Another criticism of family developmental theory is its focus on a single generation. Families are complex multigenerational units, so integrating systems theory with a multigenerational approach to family developmental theory can be helpful. (See Family Spiral Analysis in the application section of this chapter.)

Social Exchange Theory

Most gratifications, such as a happy family life, contentment in love, and need for acceptance, result from the actions of others. Thus, some of the rewards in life that people seek can only be obtained through social interaction. Whereas elements of social exchange theory can have various names, such as exchange theory, reciprocity theory, or equity theory, the basic premise is that humans form interpersonal relationships in light of the rewards, costs, or profits that they might be expected to bring. *Rewards* are anything that meets our needs, whether they are personal, familial, or community needs. We also obtain some general rewards from social approval, financial success, marital relationships, or children; however, these relationships can also have costs. *Costs*, which are the opposite of rewards, make a behavior less likely to occur. These costs may come from loss of opportunities as a result of any choice one makes. Within families, these costs may also come from additional responsibilities, as well as loss of autonomy, spontaneity, and/or freedom. When experiencing exchanges, the outcome of the exchange is based on the difference between the *rewards* and *costs* resulting in either a *profit* or *loss*. Evaluations of social exchanges may also be conducted using *comparison levels*—the general standards upon which a person evaluates an outcome (rewards and costs) based on what is perceived to be deserved. One might consider comparison to other possible outcomes and relationships (past or present), along with comparisons to the other available alternatives. Other important concepts in exchange theory are *reciprocity*, the mutual giving and receiving involving the equalizing of exchanges, and *equity*, the fairness or justice of the exchange (Chibucos et al., 2005; Ingoldsby et al., 2004; White & Klein, 2008).

Exchange theory assumes that people are goal oriented and want to gain an advantage in social exchanges. Thus, the *resource hypothesis* may be employed in which the person with greater resources has more power and can gain the most benefit. The *principle of least interest* suggests that the person with the least interest has more power. Exchanges in families are seldom clear due to the informality of family behavior. However, it is important to consider that family exchanges are not necessarily always returned in-kind (same resource, such as money or services, is not mutually exchanged) and one can also build up equity over time. Children whose parents do things for them when they are young may reciprocate later in life by doing things for parents to meet their needs at that time of their lives. While the theory originally may sound calculating and manipulative, in actuality, the emergent quality of social exchange or successive social exchanges has been related to friendship intensity, satisfaction with interpersonal relationships, and intimacy (Chibucos et al., 2005).

Exchange theory can be applied to understand the rewards and costs of various upcoming decisions such as selecting a major, dealing with housing options, going to graduate school, getting married, or returning home to live as a "boomerang" young adult. Exchange theory assumes that individuals are generally rational about determining the costs and rewards of social exchanges in their lives, however that may not necessarily be the case. Applying the *principle of least interest* and *resource hypothesis* can also be useful when dealing with interpersonal, dating, marriage, and parental relationships. Analyzing relationships that may not have been successful regarding who had the most power in a relationship and who had the least interest can bring insight into current and future relationships.

Family Stress Theory

"In this world nothing can be said to be certain, except for death and taxes."
—Benjamin Franklin

In reality, a third thing that is certain is family stress. *Family stress* is a state of tension that arises when demands tax a family's resources. If adjustments do not come easily, family stress can lead to a *family crisis*, a situation in which typical coping strategies are ineffective and new ones are needed. Family crisis involves three interrelated ideas: a crisis involves change, a crisis is a turning point with the potential for positive or negative effects or both, and a crisis is a time of relative instability (Boss, 2002).

When dealing with family stress theory, the *ABC-X Model of Family Stress and Crisis* (Boss, 2002; Weber, 2010) is often incorporated. Within this model "A" refers to the *stressor* or *crisis-precipitating event*. These events, which are influenced by the family's context, can be normative (expected during the life cycle) or nonnormative (unforeseen events or situations); internal or external to the family; brief or prolonged; ambiguous or clear; or can affect family configuration or status shifts in the family. There are several types of stressors, such as addition or loss of a family member, sudden change in family income or status, conflict over family roles, caring for a disabled or dependent family member, ambiguous loss, or stressor overload/pile-up. Small events may not be enough to cause any real stress, but can take a toll when they occur simultaneously or consecutively. The family's personal or collective strengths (ability to cope) at the time of the stressor event are referred to as *stressor/crisis-meeting resources* (B) (Boss, 2002; Weber, 2010). Resources can be physical, economic, relational, social, or psychological characteristics that a family can use to respond to one or more stressors. How families *perceive, define,* and *assign meaning* to an event (C) is key to understanding how they *manage the degree of these events* or *the crisis* (X). The integration of stressor(s) (A), resources (B), and perception of the event (C) leads to the level of stress or crisis (X) and the response the family experiences ranging from bonadaptation to maladaptation. Family stress is not necessarily bad, but can become a problem when the status quo becomes overwhelming or a change occurs that is so acute that the family ceases to function and becomes debilitated.

The *Roller Coaster Model* of family adjustment after a crisis is another important component of family stress theory (Boss, 2002; Hill, 1949). According to this model, after a family experiences a stressor event it may go into a period of disorganization during which previous methods for managing and solving problems become inadequate. Depending on the amount of time needed for the family to reorganize, the family reaches a turning point and enters a period of recovery. This turning point can result from a change in the "stressor," availability of "coping resources," and/or change in the "perception" of the stressor and resources. The family will reach a new "level of organization," which may be lower, equal to, or higher than their previous level of functioning.

Ambiguous loss is an important stressor to highlight (Boss, 1999). Negotiating family boundaries is difficult when the loss of a family member is ambiguous. There are two types of ambiguous loss: One type is having a family member who is *physically absent* but *psychologically present* as exemplified by unexpected catastrophes, such as war, natural disasters, imprisonment, desertion, and more common types, such as migration, adoption, divorce, and family members leaving home or being institutionalized. The second type is *physical presence* but *psychological absence* as noted by some unexpected occurrences of brain injury, Alzheimer's and dementia, stroke, depression, and affairs, along with some more common types, such as preoccupation with work, computers and TV, or homesickness. Paying special attention to ambiguous loss is important, as youth and family members examine concerns about war, terrorism, and PTSD being experienced, as well as the aging of our society and the potential for a greater incidence of Alzheimer's disease and dementia. This discussion can be meaningful for those who know someone who is experiencing these kinds of losses. According to Boss (www.ambiguousloss.com), "With ambiguous loss, there is no closure; the challenge is to learn how to live with ambiguity." Understanding family stress theory, the ABC-X model, and the roller-coaster model as they apply to normative and nonnormative stressors, including ambiguous loss, can provide insight into family adaptability and resilience (Boss, 2002).

Application of Family Theories in Family Life Education Settings

At times learning about theory can be challenging because it is abstract and students do not perceive how it is connected to themselves personally or their environmental context. Thus, creating meaningful learning experiences and assignments can help students better understand theory and how it applies to their lives. Examples include using analogies, case studies, news reports, personal reflections, "doing" theory, mini research projects, and family spiral analysis.

Using Analogies to Understand Theory

To help students understand the idea of developmental influences in one's life, a teacher can use an analogy of baking chocolate chip cookies. As the process of making these cookies is discussed, one can find that some people use different kinds of shortening, sugar, salt, nuts, chocolate chips, and eggs and may mix, bake, and store the cookies in a variety of ways. If each student were to bake a batch of chocolate chip cookies, they would all be tasty, but there would be similarities and differences in appearance, texture, and flavor. Using the cookie analogy, an educator can discuss cultural differences regarding prenatal development, early childhood experiences, adolescent changes, adult development, and family socialization experiences that can all influence the development of individuals and families (Darling & Howard, 2009). The cultural context can be incorporated by examining the role of different environments related to the analogy of baking cookies involving accessibility of ingredients (raw materials), using different ovens (temperature, time, and altitude), or values placed on foods for sustenance versus pleasure. Just as all people develop differently based on various values and conditions in their cultures, so do our cookies. While some people and cookies may be quite different due to their development and culture, others may be similar, yet all have value.

Applying Theory to Case Studies

Students may listen to lectures on theory, but applying these theories to family situations will add some additional stimulation and practice. Providing a case study to small groups of students along with some general questions related to the theories presented can create an experience where group participants can work together cooperatively while using their notes and class materials to better understand how families function. While a case study may be brief, students can brainstorm what things might be like within that family and then report back to the class how they applied the theories to these families. In an academic setting, this activity was positively received and not only facilitated application of theories, but also became a review of theories prior to an exam.

Each case study in Box 8.1 represents a family at a different stage of the life cycle. (*Hint*—the families in the case studies have been given a color as their family name. Then handouts are printed on colored sheets of paper that coincide with the family name. These sheets are collated by color so distributing them to the class helps to create groups of students from different class locations. By relating the family name to the color of the handout, the teacher can easily move among the groups, as needed, and readily know the family's situation.) A handout of questions might include some of the following questions depending on what theories and concepts were incorporated into the class.

Box 8.1   Family Case Studies for Different Stages of the Life Cycle

Provide each group with one case study and questions for application of the theories discussed in class.

The Green Family—Tom and Jeannie Green have been married for 27 years and are both employed full time. Tom is a car salesman, whereas Jeannie is an engineer. They have three grown children: Ken age 26, Kim age 21, and Jordan age 18. Kim and Jordan are both in college. In the past few years, Tom's father, Henry, who is 80 years old, has had some cardiac problems and has become weaker and less able to care for himself. Tom and Jeannie have noted that Tom's father can no longer care for himself and have reluctantly decided that Henry should come to live with them. What might affect how this family is functioning?

The Teal and Blue Family—Jake Teal and Chris Blue, a gay couple, have been married for 2 years. Because they always wanted to have children, they enlisted the help of a surrogate to give birth to their child. However, the ultrasound indicated a surprise because they are going to be parents of twins. Jake has been working as a mechanic, whereas Chris has been employed as an office manager. Chris had planned to take some family leave time to be with their newborn baby and was not supposed to go back to work until the baby was 3 months old. However, now with the birth of twins, they feel that Chris needs to stay at home with their newborn babies. What might affect how this family is functioning?

The Redmond Family—Sheila Redmond is a single mother with four children: Martin age 18, Jenny age 15, Kristin age 14, and Alex age 10. Jenny is pregnant and wants to keep the baby. While Sheila has mixed feelings about this pregnancy, she is insistent that Jenny should complete her education. What might affect how this family is functioning?

The Orange Family—Jill and Justin Orange graduated from college and got married two weeks later. They had planned to work for a few years and then go to graduate school, but conceived a child on their honeymoon. They are seven months into their pregnancy and making plans for the future. What might affect how this family is functioning?

The Gray Family—John and Maria Gray have been married for 10 years and have three children: Adriana age 8, Elena age 6, and Carlo age 4. John is a science teacher in the public high school. Maria, who used to be a nurse's aide, has stayed home taking care of their children since the oldest child was born. Now that their children are older, she wants to go back to school to become a registered nurse. What might affect how this family is functioning?

The Garnet and Gold Family—Eric Garnet and Lisa Gold fell in love on their very first date three months ago. They knew that they were right for each other and just got married. In two weeks they will graduate from college with Eric getting his degree in nursing and Lisa getting her degree in chemistry. Both Eric and Lisa want to move to another state away from their parents and are looking for positions elsewhere. They both definitely want a professional position in their respective fields since they have worked hard to get their degrees. What might affect how this family is functioning?

The LaVender Family—Ken and Tonya LaVender have 3 children—Yolanda age 4, LaShanda age 3, and Dexter age 2. Since both Ken and Tonya are elementary school teachers and wanted to be home with their children, they decided to share one teaching position after the children were born. Whereas Ken teaches a third grade class in the morning, Tonya teaches the same third grade class in the afternoon. They also try to do various tasks for neighbors to help with their income, but the children take a great deal of time. What might affect how this family is functioning?

(continued)

The Violet Family—Jessie and Tom Violet have been experiencing some stress since they retired. Jessie makes trips twice a week to visit her mother in a nursing home 60 miles away and her husband just had a mild stroke and is going through physical therapy. In the meantime their children and grandchildren want them to visit more often, but flying across the country is expensive. What might affect how this family is functioning?

The Beige Family—Dave and Jennifer Beige have three children who are grown, married, and living in three different cities. The two oldest children have children of their own, while the youngest is unmarried and in graduate school. Dave and Jennifer have been looking forward to their retirement next year so they can travel, but their oldest daughter is thinking that they will be babysitting for the child they are expecting. What might affect how this family is functioning?

- **Family developmental theory**—Identify the developmental stage in which this family is currently involved and the information used to determine the appropriate stage. Explain one task with which this family might be struggling and one that is being successfully completed.

- **Family systems theory**—Identify and discuss the permeability of one physical and one psychological boundary in this family. Describe a subsystem within this family and compare the rules and boundaries of this subsystem with those of the system as a whole. Where would this family be placed in the Circumplex Model: (Cohesion—disengaged to enmeshed: Flexibility—chaotic to rigid)? Give one example of each of the following for this family: routine, ritual, relationship rule, and procedural rule.

- **Ecosystems framework**—What is an example of the natural environment, human-behavioral environment, and human-constructed environment related to this family? What are examples of two different interactions between the Human Environed Unit (HEU) and one of its environments (NE, HBE, or HCE) or between two environmental elements?

- **Exchange theory**—Select one family member and evaluate the current outcome of his/her relationship with another family member. What is a cost and reward associated with each member of this dyad? What is an example of reciprocity within this family?

- **Family stress theory and ABC-X model**—What is the stressor (A) in the family and is it normative or nonnormative? What resources (B) does the family have for coping? How does the family perceive the stressor (C)? How is the family adapting to this stressor (X)?

It might be beneficial for groups to begin with a different theory and series of questions if the time is short and some groups cannot fully complete their group assignment. After most of the groups have completed their theory applications, the educator can facilitate a discussion of theories using some of their examples. Family groups would not need to present on all theoretical questions, but each group would present some insights about their families by demonstrating the application of theoretical concepts to their case studies.

Incorporating Current News Reports to Demonstrate Theory

The family ecosystem is easily applied to current events. By going online to find video clips of news items from any of the major news channels and showing the clips in a classroom setting, it is easy to get students involved in discussions to find examples of the Human-Environed Unit (HEU)/Organism, Natural Environment (NE), Human-Behavioral Environment (HBE), or Human-Constructed Environment (HCE) and the interactions between the HEU and its environments or interactions between various environmental elements. There are a myriad of examples in news clips involving weather and natural disasters, the economy, legal issues, and family or human interactions in the U.S. or abroad that can lead to some insightful discussions and applications. By paying attention to news items in newspapers, magazines, television, and on the Internet, the educator and/or students can frequently bring examples to the teaching environment to provide ongoing application and reinforcement of theoretical content.

Using Personal Reflections to Understand Theory

While at first glance a theory may seem abstract and not applicable to one's life, asking reflective questions can provide personal insight moments. When teaching about exchange theory, some of the concepts of rewards and costs may seem to be cognitively based and not personally applicable. However asking a simple question such as, "Have you ever felt 'used' or taken advantage of?" provides an "a-ha" moment. Most students reply that they have had these feelings, so looking at the equity of exchanges becomes personally relevant.

Teaching Theory by Doing Theory

While teachers often "teach" theoretical concepts, one suggestion is to have pairs of students "do" theory by observing perceived family groups in public settings, such as a grocery store or mall to glean information about family systems (Whitchurch, 2005). When students return to class, they report the locations of their observations, which can be used to show the ecosystems in which families are involved. They also can share the comments they overheard, which might pertain to finances, parenting, or interpersonal communication and can be used to exemplify concepts, such as boundaries, subsystems, feedback, family rules, cohesion, and or flexibility.

Applying Theory to Life Changes in a Mini-Research Project

Because one's life is comprised of a series of interactions with others and their environments, have students change a significant element of their life for three to five days and ecosystemically analyze the results of this change. After briefly orienting the students on developing a research problem and their methodology, students can do a variety of things to alter their lives. However, caution should be given so they do nothing that is injurious to their health. Examples of changes might be to go without television, cell phones, e-mail, iPods, Facebook, and/or Twitter; go without electricity or certain appliances; go without certain cosmetics or grooming products; get 8 hours of sleep; change eating behaviors or clothing patterns; start exercising; study in a different environment, add or remove the use of a car, activity, or implement; share sincere compliments with others and/or try different interactional patterns in their lives. Students should review pertinent literature, apply theoretical concepts, and analyze their findings. It is preferable to have them quantify their findings in some way (e.g., number of e-mail messages received or missed, number of hours slept, cost of new eating pattern). Finally ask the students what they learned about their ecosystem from this exercise. Doing these projects in small groups (2 to 3 students) and presenting them in class can provide further awareness of the application of the ecosystems framework.

Using Family Life Spiral Analysis to Demonstrate Integration of Theories

In order for students to recognize that multiple theories can be used simultaneously to gain meaningful insights into families, a family life spiral analysis assignment can be used as the basis of an in-class demonstration and discussion. This analysis integrates concepts from systems theory and developmental theory.

- Figure 8.2 contains 3 concentric circles. The *inner circle* begins with stage 1 (birth/early childhood) and goes clockwise to stage 4 (mate selection). Then move out to the *middle circle* beginning with stage 5 (parenthood) and going to stage 8 (middle adulthood). Next, transition to the *outer circle* with stage 9 (grandparenthood) and go to Stage 12 (late adulthood). For some families with members who are living longer, extrapolate beyond stage 12 and add stage 13, which might be called "senior or elderly adulthood."

- Figure 8.2 is also comprised of four quadrants. The top quadrant with stages 1, 5, and 9 is squeezed into a smaller formation to represent centripetal forces in a family system. In other words, when there is a birth of a baby in stage 1, the family boundaries are more closed and parents are focusing on their new child, as are grandparents, who are spending more time in family activities during the grandparenthood stage. There is a reconnection among family members across generations within this quadrant. In comparison, stages 3, 7, and 11 are spread further apart to represent centrifugal forces in the family system. Adolescents are becoming more involved with peers and looking forward to gaining independence. Their parents are renegotiating their marriage and dealing with career issues, while the older generation is newly retired and looking forward to travel, hobbies, and possibly a second honeymoon. The quadrant with 2, 6, and 10 represents movement toward centrifugal, whereas stages 4, 8, and 12 represent movement toward centripetal.

- At the bottom of Figure 8.2 are the approximate ages at which one transitions into any of these 12 stages. For example, the birth/early childhood stage is entered at birth or age 0, middle childhood/school stage at age 6, adolescence/puberty stage at age 12, and so forth.

- Table 8.2 (on p. 190) contains a chart with 6 columns to accompany the spiral diagram. The 2 columns on the left indicate *Period* (centripetal to centrifugal) and its corresponding location within the Circumplex Model. For example, in stages 1, 5, and 9 one experiences centripetal forces, which in the Circumplex Model means high cohesion and low flexibility.

• The third column focuses on *Generations* or *Stages* in the life cycle.

Figure 8.2   Family Life Spiral Diagram

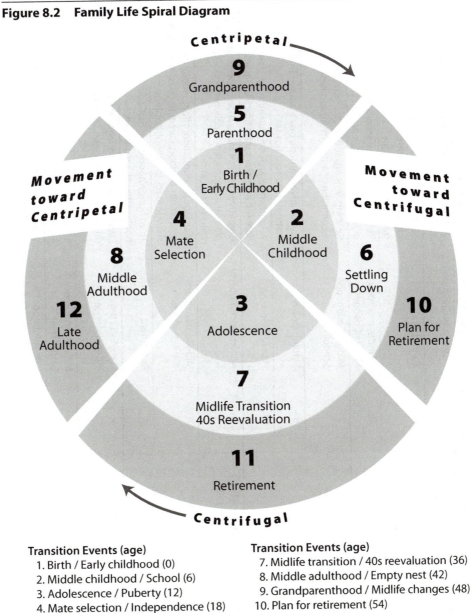

Transition Events (age)
1. Birth / Early childhood (0)
2. Middle childhood / School (6)
3. Adolescence / Puberty (12)
4. Mate selection / Independence (18)
5. Parenthood (24)
6. Settling down (30)

Transition Events (age)
7. Midlife transition / 40s reevaluation (36)
8. Middle adulthood / Empty nest (42)
9. Grandparenthood / Midlife changes (48)
10. Plan for retirement (54)
11. Retirement (60)
12. Late adulthoood / Pass the torch (66)

Table 8.2   Family Life Spiral Analysis

Period	Circumplex	Generation	Transitional Event[1]	Other Characteristics[2]	Age Range[3]
Centripetal	Cohesion—high Flexibility—low	1	Birth/Early Childhood	Walking; talking; potty training; preschool	1–6 (8)
		5	Parenthood	Start career; religious exploration; graduate school; buy first house; mother/child love affair; establish traditions; seek advice from parents (reconnection)	24(26)–30(32)
		9	Grandparenthood/ Midlife Changes	Relived memories; menopause; focus on tradition; practical advice to generation 2 (reconnection)	48(50)–54(56)
Movement Toward Centrifugal	Cohesion—low Flexibility—low	2	Middle Childhood/ School	Reading, writing, arithmetic; separation anxiety; recognition of authority figures besides parents	6(8)–12(14)
		6	Settling Down	Career advancement; buy a house (2nd); religious commitment; routines set	30(32)–36(38)
		10	Plan for Retirement	Volunteer work; clubs; philanthropy; travel; retirement date set; assess/organize financial situation	54(56)–60(62)
Centrifugal	Cohesion—low Flexibility—high	3	Adolescence/Puberty	Cognitive/physical maturation (new mind/body); plan for independence; college/work exploration; values clarification	12(14)–18(20)
		7	Mid-life Transition/ 40s Reevaluation	Marriage renegotiation; affair; separation; divorce; second honeymoon; career reassessment; career change; back to school; hobbies	36(38)–42(44)
		11	Retirement	Third honeymoon or marital isolation; recreation/ hobbies/travel; second career	60(62)–66(68)
Movement Toward Centripetal	Cohesion—high Flexibility—high	4	Mate Selection/ Independence	Dating/courtship; renegotiation of parent-child relations; more interests/peer-like; engagement/ marriage	18(20)–24(26)
		8	Middle Adulthood/ Empty Nest	Reevaluation of marital relations (with stability); instilling values; loss of parents	42(44)–48(50)
		12	Late Adulthood/ Passing the Torch	Illness; widowhood; storytelling (archival function); instilling values	66(68)–72(74)

[1] **Transitional Event**—Event which marks entrance into a given period of the family life cycle
[2] **Other Characteristics**—Other events or family traits which tend to occur during a given period of the family life cycle.
[3] **Age Range**—typical ages (social norms) of individuals in a given period. Number in parentheses allows for two year lag.

- The fourth column contains some potential *Transitional Events*, which would be the events that mark entrance into a given period of the family life cycle.
- The fifth column has *Other Characteristics*, which are events or family traits that tend to occur during a given period of the family life cycle.
- The sixth column includes the approximate *Age Range* of the life cycle stage. Note that the age range for Stage 1 is years 1 to 6 with an 8 in parentheses. This includes the typical ages or social norms of individuals in a given period. The number in parentheses is for a 2-year time lag. Thus, parenthood may begin at age 24 to 26 and end at age 30 to 32.

Individuals place their extended families into two spiral diagrams: one is based on the ages of their family members and the other is based on their characteristics. They then analyze them according to the integration of two theories used as a basis of this assignment—developmental theory and systems theory. Further details about the incorporation of this analysis as an assignment or a potential voluntary demonstration can be noted in Box 8.2 on the following page. The students who have participated in the family spiral analysis have had some incredible insights about their family's functioning as noted in the following themes and comments:

Family Change

- I can see that my family is changing dramatically. I have learned that different periods in the life of my family bring it together or spread it apart.
- Life changes are to a certain extent predictable. These diagrams provide a general picture for me to look at and notice how each family member's age and transition affect others in the family.
- The spiral diagrams helped me to see more clearly the reasons why our family seems to be constantly changing. We are all getting older and facing different problems and new challenges every day of our lives.

Closeness vs. Separateness

- I have learned how my family functions and more importantly why it functions that way. I never understood before why at some times one family member would not seem as close as the others, while at other times they would be very close to the rest of the family. I now know that one family member can feel detached from the family if they are a period ahead or behind the rest of the family.
- I have learned that pushing people away isn't always the answer, even though it may seem so at that stage of one's life.

Understanding Others

- I can better understand why my father has become isolated. He has moved into a period much later than the societal norms for his age and the centrifugal forces in some ways are pulling him away from us.
- I realized how different families are if there are no children. My sister and I have often visited my father and stepmother. But, they have never had the responsibility of raising any children in their home. They are in one stage of

Box 8.2   Family Life Spiral Analysis Assignment

To demonstrate spiral family analysis either use a volunteer in class or incorporate it as a student assignment by asking individual students to plot their family members on 2 separate family life spiral diagrams: an Age Spiral and a Transitional Period Spiral.

1. **Age Spiral:** Place yourself and your family (your siblings, your parents, and your grandparents) into the family life spiral diagram based on your *current ages*. Insert a family member in only one segment of the age spiral diagram that most closely relates to his/her age. In other words, if a category ranges from age 6 to 11 and your family member is 7 years old, place him/her closer to the age 6 demarcation. Place an X in the diagram to represent the family member and include their name, family position, and age.

2. **Transitional Period Spiral**: Place yourself and your family (your siblings, your parents, and your grandparents) into the family life spiral diagram based on *current transitional events and other characteristics* (see Family Life Spiral Analysis Chart). Place a family member in only one segment of the transitional period spiral diagram. It might be that a family member has characteristics of more than one stage, so place that member in the stage that best describes what is most like him or her.

Students may have questions about what to do if some family members are no longer living or if their parents have remarried. Have students create diagrams involving the members of their family to describe as best they can their immediate and involved family system. If a grandparent has just died, he or she may or may not still be emotionally connected to the family and may or may not be included in the diagram. Depending on the student's perceptions of sibling and stepsibling relationships or living arrangements, the diagrams could be drawn in various ways.

Potential Discussion Points:

- After completing these two diagrams, discuss and analyze what it is about *each* family member and his or her characteristics (within the chart) that caused placement of him/her in a particular transitional period? Did you have any difficulties placing family members according to the characteristics? What were these difficulties, if any? Discuss what changes in the characteristics column of the Family Life Spiral Analysis Chart should be made to accommodate these difficulties?

- To what degree do individual members compare to each other *within each spiral diagram* (Compare age and transitional period spirals *separately*). Discuss issues related to any member(s) who are lagging behind or getting ahead of the general period of your family. Who is in or out of sync with the rest of the family and what does that mean for interpersonal relations and closeness in the family? You may have all members within the same quadrant, or you may have some members in one quadrant and a few that are in another quadrant. What does this mean for the functioning of your family?

- To what degree does the *"age spiral"* fit or match the occurrences of the "transitional period spiral"? (Compare *both diagrams together*.) For example, you may have a family member who has retired early. In other words, for his age, he is doing different things or has different characteristics compared to others of that same age. Therefore, he may be in different positions in the 2 diagrams. Discuss your family's positions in the spiral diagrams according to centripetal and centrifugal forces.

- How can you apply this family life spiral analysis to better understand your present or future family life? What have you learned about families?

the spiral, whereas my mother, stepfather, and siblings are in different stages. Not having children puts less stress on the marriage and on finances. This could be why my stepfather has not retired and why my father and stepmother have not had as many marital problems.

- I now understand why my grandparents are so involved in our family and why other members of the family are not as concerned with it. This spiral has also shown me that perhaps I should talk more often to my grandparents because of how they might be feeling at this time in their lives.

General Family Insights

- I have a tendency to see my family as being slightly messed up, but I learned that what I thought was messed up is really perfectly normal.
- I have learned that my family is pretty normal after all. The insight that this assignment has given me has proved most useful and definitely will be considered in the future.

This assignment and discussion were perceived by the students as not only being meaningful and insightful, but also an enjoyable way to apply theory to understand their families.

Overview of Learning Theories and Styles

"Tell me and I forget. Teach me and I remember. Involve me and I learn."
—Benjamin Franklin

Learning is a complex process that varies for different learners and can be viewed from a range of *theories/conceptual frameworks* that describe how information is absorbed, processed, and retained (Newman & Newman, 2007). There are three traditional categories of learning theory: *Behaviorism* focuses on learning as reacting to external stimuli and is founded on the belief that behaviors can be trained, changed, and measured (Ertmer & Newby, 1993); *Cognitivism* attempts to focus on the process of acquiring, storing, and constructing new information (Steele, 2005); and *Constructivism* views learning as a process of creating new knowledge based on a learner's prior experience when information comes into contact with existing knowledge that has been developed by previous experiences—an approach that has worked well for adult learners (Adams, 2006; Koohang, Riley, Smith, & Schreurs, 2009; Ruey, 2010; Spigner-Littles & Anderson, 1999). Other learning theories have also been developed, such as *connectivism*, which has evolved in the digital age to focus on learning by making connections between specialized information sources and interpreting patterns (Tschofen & Mackness, 2012). Learning theories have added to our understanding of change and how new learning is acquired and maintained. However, they do not consider the developmental level of the learner and his or her physical or cognitive maturation, changing values and goals, and capacity or motivation (Newman & Newman, 2007).

Since people respond differently to the learning materials that are presented to them, a relevant approach for students and teachers has been the examination of learning styles. *Learning style* refers to an individual's natural or habitual pattern of acquiring and processing information. The focus is not on what students learn, but how they choose to learn. Individuals have preferred learning styles that can be identified at an early age and remain relatively constant through time (Royse, 2001). Educators need to be aware that their selection of learning experiences may favor the bias of their own learning styles and thus, they should strive to create a variety of educational experiences that would not consistently disadvantage certain students. It is impossible to incorporate every student's favorite learning style, but by teaching in different ways, students can recognize their preferences while developing their ability to learn using other styles. Students need stimulation from many different dimensions. Everyone has a mix of multiple learning styles, but may favor some more than others or use certain ones in specific circumstances.

Incorporating learning experiences to engage multiple learning styles is becoming increasingly popular. Two such learning styles are included in this chapter with a sample application of each that could be used in a nonformal or formal educational setting. It should be noted that older learners, who have years of life experiences, are different from those who are younger, and thus learning styles and methods need to be adapted accordingly.

One seminal perspective is Kolb's (1984) Experiential Learning Theory and his learning styles model, which have helped educators understand human learning behavior and facilitate student learning through the lifespan, and have been particularly influential in the field of adult education (Newman & Newman, 2007; Stokes-Eley, 2007). According to Kolb, learning occurs in a cycle consisting of four modes. Learners can enter the learning cycle at any point and will learn best if they practice all four modes. These learning styles can be conceptualized as forming two intersecting axes (continua) that form a quadrant: the *Processing* continuum ranging from active experimentation (doing) to reflective observation (watching), and the *Perception* continuum ranging from concrete experience (feeling) to abstract conceptualization (thinking). A matrix containing these four modes is noted below (see Figure 8.3).

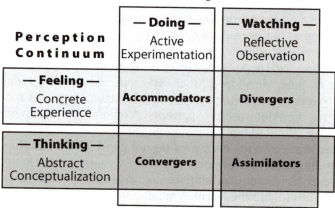

Adapted from Kolb, D. (1984). *Experiential learning: Experience as the source of learning and development.* Upper Saddle River, NJ: Prentice-Hall, Inc.

Figure 8.3   Experiential Learning Styles

Kolb's learning theory incorporates four learning styles: *Accommodators*, who are doers and feelers, rely heavily on concrete experiences and active experimentation and benefit most from group work and experiential methods, such as field trips, role-plays, and simulations; *Divergers*, who are feelers and watchers, utilize concrete experiences and reflective observation and readily respond to discussions; emotionally moving lectures; and experiential methods such as case studies, service learning, and simulations; *Convergers*, who are doers and thinkers, rely on their skills of abstract conceptualization and active experimentation and enjoy demonstrations, computer-aided instruction, and objective homework problems and exams; *Assimilators*, who are watchers and thinkers, combine abstract conceptualization and reflective observations to excel in organization and synthesis and prefer logical factual lectures, textbook reading assignments, and independent or library research (Nilson, 2003). To assist with determining your learning style according to Kolb's conceptualization, an inventory of Kolb's learning styles can be found online in various locations. As with any learning style, this is a guide and not a strict set of learning strategies, but can be useful to educators as they design their courses and plan for varied learning experiences.

An example of incorporating experiential learning styles into a nonformal parent education setting might focus on the topic of parent-child communication. After introducing a few general guidelines regarding communication, two parents would role-play being parent and adolescent who are attempting to resolve an issue in their relationship, such as getting a cell phone, driving a car, or sharing household responsibilities in a relationship. The participants can portray these roles in various ways displaying constructive and destructive communication styles. Afterward parents can discuss what they felt, thought, and learned playing these roles and what suggestions they might have for engaging in similar conversations with their own children. There could be a series of parents doing various scenarios. Since some parents would be playing the part of an adolescent, remembering similar conversations and roles from their own adolescence would provide insight and empathy to how their children feel. These practice sessions can facilitate better communication and reduce tension in the conversations they have with their own children. This activity involves *concrete learning experience (feeling)*—learning from a specific experience and relating it to others' feelings; *reflective observation (watching)*—viewing the role-play and looking for meaning in the interactions; *abstract conceptualization (thinking)*—involving a logical analysis of ideas and acting on the intellectual understanding of the situation; and *active experimentation (doing)*—getting things done by influencing people and their behaviors through action.

Another pertinent and accessible educational theory is Gardener's Multiple Intelligences (2006, 2011). He claims that rather than a singular measure of intelligence, there are multiple intelligences—we are all intelligent in different ways. While Gardener first reported on seven different kinds of intelligence, he later added an eighth and ninth. People generally possess all of these intelligences for solving problems, but these capacities vary for individuals. The kinds of intelligence are noted below along with some suggestions for teaching strategies:

- **Linguistic Intelligence** (Word smart): Language skills including sensitivity to the subtle meanings of words and written or verbal communications. Incorporating letters, poems, stories, and descriptions might be applicable.

- **Logical/Mathematical Intelligence** (Number smart): The ability to use mathematics and complex logical systems of thinking. Incorporating facts, data, and experiments might be applicable.

- **Musical/Rhythmic Intelligence** (Music smart): The expressive medium and ancient art form of music with its own rules, language, and thinking structures. Incorporating songs, musical games, and song titles might be applicable.

- **Bodily/Kinesthetic Intelligence** (Body smart): Bodily control and skilled handling of objects or tools involving fine or large motor skills. Incorporating dance, role-play, or movement exercises might be applicable.

- **Visual/Spatial Intelligence** (Picture smart): The ability to comprehend the visual world accurately. Incorporating charts, posters, videos/video clips, and cartoons might be applicable.

- **Intrapersonal Intelligence** (Self smart): Understanding one's own feelings and using these insights to guide behavior. Incorporating journals, diaries, and self-assessment measures might be applicable.

- **Interpersonal Intelligence** (People smart): Reading the moods and intentions of others, as well as working well with groups. Incorporating cooperative learning, interactive learning experiences, and giving feedback to others might be applicable.

- **Naturalistic Intelligence** (Nature smart): The ability to recognize and classify living things (plants, animals, and minerals) and sensitivity to other features of the natural world. Incorporating nature walks, plants, and animals, as well as observing changes in the weather might be applicable.

- **Existential Intelligence** ("Big Picture" smart): The ability to use collective values to understand others; see the world around them; and ponder questions about life, death, and ultimate realities. Incorporating different points of view, connections of classroom learning to the outside world, and teaching others might be applicable.

To help students understand the essence of multiple intelligences, assign them to take a Multiple Intelligences Survey to determine some of their more prominent intelligences. (See Multiple Intelligences Survey www.surfaquarium.com/MI/inventory.htm.) Students in a formal educational setting, such as a family life education class, have often reported their strengths to be Linguistic, Intrapersonal, and Interpersonal Intelligences. To give them experience with a broader range of intelligences, provide small groups a topic such as dating, contraception, communication, or any topic from the 10 family life education content areas. Then have them create two learning experiences to teach that content using two different intelligences. This cooperative learning experience will help them verbalize their individual perceptions about multiple intelligences and how to apply these concepts to a potential classroom setting. Sharing these varied activities with the rest of the class can provide insight to other students in the class about the different ways they can incorporate a range of learning experiences that meet the needs of a variety of students.

SUMMARY

Using family and learning theories in family life education programs can assist students to better understand family behaviors and functioning. Rather than use one theory, it is good to consider the integration of various theories to gain a broader perspective of the topic being examined. Some basic theories/frameworks central to family studies include family systems, family ecosystem, family development, social exchange, and family stress theory, although there are others that can also be incorporated, such as symbolic interaction, feminist, and conflict theory. In addition to providing the basic concepts of the theory, being able to apply theories in classroom activities and assignments can facilitate student understanding.

Because people have different styles of learning, there are numerous theories about how individuals learn. Some favor experiential learning, reading, writing, watching demonstrations, videos, or listening to lectures. While the research on learning styles is inconclusive regarding the effectiveness of any one style, knowing that teachers and students have different learning styles can facilitate curriculum planning and enhance learning in your classroom. Students may prefer certain learning styles, but all participants learn better from the incorporation of multiple educational methods. By developing new approaches that will better meet the needs of learners, we can help a wide range of individuals understand their strengths and identify strategies that will stimulate their learning and feelings of success.

QUESTIONS AND ISSUES FOR DISCUSSION

1. In your study of theories, which theory best helps you to understand your family and why?

2. What stage of the family life cycle best fits your family and why? If your family does not fit any stage, why is that the case?

3. How would your life change if your family experienced a natural disaster and your home, possessions, and livelihood were lost? Analyze this event using one of the theories/frameworks mentioned in this chapter (family systems, family ecosystem, family development, social exchange, or family stress).

4. Recall the best teacher you have had and why you perceived him or her to be the best?

5. What are 2 to 3 multiple intelligences that best fit your learning style? What are 2 to 3 multiple intelligences that do not fit your learning style?

Approaches to
Sexuality Education

Definitional Issues

Sexuality education is a lifelong process of acquiring information and forming attitudes, beliefs, and values (SIECUS, n.d.b). In the past when we heard the term *sex education*, its meaning was unclear because the word "sex" is often used ambiguously to either indicate sexual behavior, reproduction, or being male or female. It all depends on the circumstance; if you are completing a survey, you might see a demographic question asking for your sex, but in reality the researcher wants to know if you are male or female. It is now more common to use "sex" to mean sexual anatomy that is biologically determined, whereas *gender* refers to being male or female, which is something we learn or construct for ourselves based on our social and cultural experiences.

Rather than "sex education," most educators use the term *sexuality education*, because it is a broader term than what you do sexually with another person. It encompasses the sexual knowledge, beliefs, attitudes, values, pleasures, and behaviors of individuals. Sexuality is not just about having sex or taking part in sexual behaviors, but also the feelings you have about your body; being male or female; the persons to whom you are attracted and love; and the ways in which you dress, move, speak, and act. Sexuality is a natural and healthy part of who you are, how you live, and how you express your sexuality, which will change depending on your age and stage of life (SIECUS, n.d.c). According to the Family Life Education Framework (see Appendix A) by the National Council on Family Relations (NCFR), *human sexuality* is defined as "an understanding of the physiological, psychological, and social aspects of sexual development throughout the lifespan, so as to achieve healthy sexual adjustment" (Darling & Howard, 2009, p. 142).

Another definitional issue regarding sexuality education evolved out of public controversies in the 1960s over the increasing inclusion of sexuality education in the schools. While human sexuality is one of the 10 content areas within family life education, previously some educators and administrators tried to hide the real focus of sexuality courses by using the terminology "family life and sexuality education," to provide some political safety by including a family context. As a result, the terminology of "family life education" became synonymous with sex education to some groups who objected to it being taught in schools (Darling, 1987). As a result, schools dropped courses in family life education and called them "parent education." While parent education also had components of human sexuality, there was less opposition because the incorporation of parenting terminology did not cause alarm for political groups. Through time and cultural change, this controversy dissipated and sexuality education courses became labeled as such to describe their actual content. However, controversies about "how" sexuality education courses should be taught continue to be part of our educational culture.

Adolescent Sexuality and Sexuality Education

Adolescence is a time of physical and hormonal development associated with puberty, as well as other psychological, emotional, social, and cultural changes. During their transition through adolescence, teenagers try to avoid many pitfalls such as pregnancy and sexually transmitted infections; however, they also receive several conflicting messages—more than any other age group. Whereas our cultural influences through movies, music, advertisements, and social media provide us with an allure and excitement about sexuality, the dangers and problems associated with sexual interactions are often communicated through news programs, public policies, school messages, and parents. Thus, the youth in our culture must find their way in a world of contradictions. While popular media scream, "always say yes," many adults admonish, "just say no," but the majority "just say nothing" (Brown & Taverner, 2001). To deal with this issue some parents, schools, churches, and politicians have encouraged abstinence, which means there is no need for education about sexual behavior and interactions, sexually transmitted infections (STIs), or contraception. It is as if we live in a bipolar culture in which individuals and families are pulled in many directions, at times making it seem like we are walking on a tightrope when it comes to teaching about sexuality.

Sexuality is a hot-button issue in our schools, homes, and culture because it is closely tied to parental, social, and political perceptions of right and wrong and peoples' feelings about religion and personal freedoms. Most adults agree on what is "not" healthy for teenagers as they share a deep concern about coercive or violent sex, sexually transmitted infections including HIV/AIDS, and unintended adolescent pregnancy (Collins, Alagiri, & Summers, 2002; Darling & Howard, 2009). However, the perception of health goes beyond the absence of disease to autonomy and the ability of individuals to integrate sexuality into their lives, derive pleasure from it, and reproduce, if they so choose. Parents have indicated they hope their children will have a good sex life in which they will be able to appreciate their bodies, express love and intimacy in appropriate ways, enjoy sexual feelings without necessarily acting on them, and practice health promotion. In other words, sexual pleasure also includes the ability to understand the risks, responsibilities, outcomes, and impacts of sexual interactions (McGee, 2004).

Approaches to School-Based Sexuality Education

Generally there are four approaches used for teaching sexuality to young people that can be distinguished by the way they teach about abstinence. While sexuality education for adolescents promotes abstinence as a way to deal with sexual urges with some constraints on complete sexual freedom, it does not advocate that adolescent sexuality should mean abstaining from all sexual feelings, thoughts, and interactions. Adults do not want youth becoming prematurely involved in sexual interactions, but total abstention and over-control of sexual feelings and expression can create both current and future problems for adolescents in terms of repression, denial, and isolation from social interactions. Consequently, we must examine if abstinence is being taught as a contraceptive method or a total avoidance of one's sexuality.

It may be useful to involve students of varying ages in a discussion of abstinence and its meaning. You could ask the entire class or small groups to define sexual abstinence and specify what behaviors would be included. How is sexual abstinence similar or different from abstaining from smoking, drinking, drugs, or over-eating? Participants could be asked to rate their agreement (strongly disagree to strongly agree) with various statements that arise regarding abstinence, such as "young people think sexual abstinence is a joke," "nothing we do educationally can impact sexual behavior," "abstinence means no sexual contact at all," or "there are ways to teach about abstinence without preaching." Reacting to these statements can elicit some meaningful conversations. There is no one correct definition or perspective about abstinence, but controversies exist about how it is taught. Hopefully young people can develop their own personal definition and be able to communicate it to an intimate partner. These definitions can be influenced by their gender, age, parents, religion, culture, and school sexuality education programs that are approved and funded by local school boards, communities, states, and/or the federal government.

Abstinence–Only Programs

These programs emphasize abstinence from all sexual behaviors as the only approach that is moral and safe. Advocates believe that adolescents should be protected from the details of sexual interactions and told of harmful outcomes. In addition, they are strongly urged to abstain and are provided with information to promote the benefits of abstinence. Discussions of abortion are avoided, while preventing STIs and HIV is promoted as the reason to remain sexually abstinent (Collins et al., 2002). Because these programs do not acknowledge that many teenagers will become sexually active, they do not include content about contraception or condom use. Therefore, students who get into intimate situations are left stranded regarding knowing how to have safer sex. Some of the abstinence-only and abstinence-only-until-marriage programs avoid certain discussions, such as same-gender sexual attraction, the sexual nature of persons with disabilities, diverse and non-traditional family structures, and pregnancy options (Kempner, 2004; Kenny & Sternberg, 2003; SIECUS, n.d.a). Furthermore, they have been designed to control young people's sexual behavior by using inaccuracies and instilling fear, shame, and guilt. Some of these programs:

- use inaccurate information about the spread of HIV/AIDS (e.g., "AIDS can be transmitted by skin-to-skin contact." "HIV can be spread via sweat and tears." "Any kind of sexual activity can spread STDs from one person to another.");

- discourage condom use (e.g., "Condoms can never protect someone from the emotional problems that can result from multiple sexual partners and premature sexual activity.");

- use biased language about abortion (e.g., "A 43-day-old fetus is a "thinking person." "Possible effects of abortion include increased risk of breast cancer and infertility.");

- incorporate negative consequences of sexual behaviors (e.g., "The consequences of premarital sex include guilt, disappointment, worry, depression, sadness, loneliness, and loss of self-esteem.");

- contain medically inaccurate information and distort facts (e.g., "Reassure students that small lumps in breast tissue are common in both boys and girls during puberty. This condition is called gynecomastia and is a normal sign of hormonal changes." (Gynecomastia refers to a general increase in breast tissue in boys.) "Twenty-four chromosomes from the mother and twenty-four chromosomes from the father join to create this new individual." (Human cells have 23 chromosomes from each parent.);

- promote gender stereotypes as fact (e.g., "Girls need to be aware they may be able to tell when a kiss is leading to something else. The girl may need to put the brakes on first in order to help the boy." "Girls need to be careful with what they wear because males are looking! The girl might be thinking fashion, while the boy is thinking sex. For this reason girls have a responsibility to wear modest clothing that doesn't invite lustful thoughts."); and

- incorporate catchy slogans for students to repeat in class (e.g., "Do the right thing, wait for the ring," "Pet your dog, not your date," or "Sex on credit, play now pay later.") (SIECUS, 2008, 2009; Waxman, 2004).

Sexuality educators for all age groups need to be aware of these messages and be able to clarify misconceptions, remove stereotypes, and promote the use of accurate information.

Abstinence-Only-Until-Marriage Programs

These programs are similar to abstinence-only programs by not including any information about contraception or disease prevention methods while emphasizing abstinence from all sexual behaviors prior to marriage. They may include inaccurate information and the use of fear. However, they also make a distinct point that marriage is the only morally acceptable context for all sexual activity. For over two decades the federal government has invested millions of dollars into abstinence-only-until-marriage programs. While these programs often replaced comprehensive sexuality education courses, they rarely provided information on even the most basic topics in human sexuality, such as puberty, reproductive anatomy, and sexual health, and they have never been proven effective (SIECUS, n.d.a).

Some believe it is reasonable to wait until marriage before having a sexual relationship and then be faithful to that partner for life, but this may be somewhat unrealistic for many young people because it fails to reflect the nature of modern societies in which people marry later in life, if at all. Moreover, with the high frequency of marital dissolution, people are very likely to have several sexual partners over their lifetime. While the age that people first marry has been increasing to the upper twenties, the age when they first have sexual intercourse has decreased to approximately 16 years of age. In addition, a diminishing minority of people report that their first sexual partner was also the person whom they married (AVERT, n.d.). These programs also do not account for gay, lesbian, bisexual, or transgendered (GLBT) relationships in which marriage may not be a legal option in some states.

Abstinence-Based and Abstinence-Plus Programs

Abstinence-based programs emphasize the benefits of abstinence. However, they also include information about noncoital sexual behavior, contraception, safer sex, and disease prevention methods. They do not rely on fear and shame and often help young people to develop skills they need to postpone sexual involvement. These programs explore the context for and meanings involved in sexuality. While they promote abstinence from sexual interaction, they acknowledge that adolescents may become sexually active. Thus, they include content on condom use and discussions of contraception, abortion, and STIs, such as HIV/AIDS. *Absti-*

nence-Plus Programs educate about contraception and condoms in the context of strong abstinence messages (Advocates for Youth, 2001).

Comprehensive Sexuality Education Programs

A vast majority of American parents support comprehensive sexuality education that is medically accurate, age-appropriate, and includes information about both abstinence and contraception. They also believe that young people should be given information about how to protect themselves from unintended pregnancies and STIs (SIECUS, 2007). These programs begin in kindergarten and continue until 12th grade and beyond. However, at times sexuality education may also be introduced into preschool programs with content related to naming body parts and enhancing self-esteem. Within comprehensive sexuality programs, age-appropriate information is included on a broad range of topics related to sexuality, such as STI/HIV and pregnancy prevention, as well as opportunities for students to develop interpersonal skills to exercise responsibility regarding sexual relationships. Abstinence is encouraged as the safer choice with sexuality being viewed as a natural and healthy part of living. There is respect for the diversity of beliefs about sexuality that exist in a community. Advocates of comprehensive sexuality education believe youth should have the knowledge they need to make informed and responsible decisions about their lives. Moreover, more than 80% of Americans believe that comprehensive sexuality education programs, which not only emphasize abstinence, but also encourage the use of condoms and contraception, should be taught in the schools (Kirby, 2007). In addition, young people should be learning about personal power, as well as negotiation and communication skills to help them delay sexual interactions if they believe that this is what they should do.

The guidelines for comprehensive sexuality education programs are based on four primary goals: (1) providing accurate *information* about sexuality, (2) providing an opportunity for young people to question, explore, and assess their sexual *attitudes* and develop their own *values* and *insights*, (3) helping young people develop *relationships* and *interpersonal skills* and (4) helping young people exercise *responsibility* regarding sexual relationships, including addressing abstinence, resisting pressures to prematurely become involved in sexual intercourse, and encouraging the use of contraception and other sexual health measures (SIECUS, 2004). These guidelines are based on values that reflect the beliefs of most communities in a pluralistic society (see Box 9.1). Which values are more important to students, their parents, and their communities?

The *Guidelines for Comprehensive Sexuality Education* are based on teaching six key concepts including: Human Development, Relationships, Personal Skills, Sexual Behavior, Sexual Health, and Society and Culture (SIECUS, 2004). These concepts are taught at each of four age levels with age-appropriate materials. The age levels are as follows:

Level 1: Middle childhood, ages 5–8; early elementary school

Level 2: Preadolescence, ages 9–12; later elementary school

Level 3: Early adolescence, ages 12–15; middle school/junior high school

Level 4: Adolescence, ages 15–18; high school

To illustrate that the concepts are designed to be developmentally appropriate, we can examine the key concept of *Human Development* and the sub-concept of "reproductive anatomy and physiology." The following are examples for each level:

Level 1: Each body part has a correct name and function.

Level 2: During puberty, internal and external sexual and reproductive organs mature in preparation for adulthood.

Box 9.1   Comprehensive Sexuality Education Values

The *Guidelines for Comprehensive Sexuality Education (SIECUS, 2004)* are based on a number of values about sexuality, young people, and the role of families. While these values reflect those of many communities across the country, they are not universal. Parents, educators, and community members will need to review these values to be sure the program that is implemented is consistent with their community's beliefs, culture, and social norms. The values inherent in the guidelines are:

- Every person has dignity and self worth.
- All children should be loved and cared for.
- Young people should view themselves as unique and worthwhile individuals within the context of their cultural heritage.
- Sexuality is a natural and healthy part of living.
- All persons are sexual.
- Sexuality includes physical, ethical, social, spiritual, psychological, and emotional dimensions.
- Individuals can express their sexuality in varied ways.
- Parents should be the primary sexuality educators of their children.
- Families should provide children's first education about sexuality.
- Families should share their values about sexuality with their children.
- In a pluralistic society, people should respect and accept the diversity of values and beliefs about sexuality that exist in a community.
- Sexual relationships should be reciprocal, based on respect, and should never be coercive or exploitative.
- All persons have the right and obligation to make responsible sexual choices.
- Individuals, families, and society benefit when children are able to discuss sexuality with their parents and/or trusted adults.
- Young people develop their values about sexuality as part of becoming adults.
- Young people explore their sexuality as a natural process in achieving sexual maturity.
- Early involvement in sexual behaviors poses risks.
- Abstaining from sexual intercourse is the most effective method of preventing pregnancy and STD/HIV.
- Young people who are involved in sexual relationships need access to information about health-care services.

SIECUS. (2004). *Guidelines for comprehensive sexuality education: Kindergarten through 12th grade,* 3rd ed. New York: SIECUS. Retrieved from http://www.siecus.org/_data/global/images/guidelines.pdf

Level 3: The sexual response system differs from the reproductive system.

Level 4: Hormones influence growth and development, as well as sexual and reproductive functions.

Another illustration would be from the key concept of *Relationships* and the sub-concept "families." The following are examples for each level:

Level 1: There are different kinds of families.

Level 2: Family members have rights and responsibilities.

Level 3: Relationships between parents and children often change, as they all grow older.

Level 4: One purpose of the family is to help its members reach their fullest potential.

Other key concepts and detailed content can be found within the *Guidelines for Comprehensive Sexuality Education* (SIECUS, 2004).

Program Effectiveness

A recent national study found that students in abstinence-only sexuality programs compared to those who were not part of the program were "similar" in their abstinence from sexual relations, involvement in unprotected sexual relations at first intercourse and over the last 12 months, number of sexual partners, and age of first intercourse. Moreover, students in abstinence-only programs were less knowledgeable about their potential health risks from STIs, less likely to report that condoms were effective in preventing STIs, and more likely to report that condoms are never effective in preventing STIs (Trenholm et al., 2007). While friends' support for abstinence may have protective benefits, maintaining this support can be difficult as these adolescents become older and change their perceptions and behaviors regarding abstinence and sexuality. When the impact study began, nearly all youth had friends who had attitudes and behaviors that supported abstinence, but four years later, only 40% of their close friends remained supportive of abstinence. Regarding programs in which students take a pledge not to have sex until marriage, the majority did not stick to the pledge. In fact, in one study 82% of the pledgers denied having taken a pledge five years after doing so. Not only did the sexual behavior of pledgers not differ from non-pledgers, but also those who signed a pledge were less likely to protect themselves from pregnancy and STIs (Rosenbaum, 2009).

Evaluations of comprehensive sexuality education programs found that no programs hastened the initiation of sexual relations or increased its frequency. Comprehensive programs were effective for both genders, all major ethnic groups, sexually experienced and inexperienced teens, and in different settings and communities. In addition, some programs' positive impacts lasted for several years (Kirby, 2007). Nearly all comprehensive programs had a positive influence on one or more factors affecting sexual behavior, such as improved knowledge about the risks and consequences of pregnancy and STIs, values and attitudes about sexual involvement and use of condoms or contraception, perception of peer norms, confidence in the ability to say "no" to unwanted sex, insistence on using condoms and contraception, and communication with parents or adults. When studies were replicated in different communities there were similar positive effects. However, if programs were shortened or certain content removed (such as the use of condoms) the original positive results were not replicated.

Public Controversy Regarding Sexuality Education

There are several public controversies about sexuality education. The U.S. ranks first among developed nations in rates of teenage pregnancy and STIs. Therefore, the federal government funded abstinence-only sexuality education programs for more than a decade. However, data have indicated that abstinence-only education is positively correlated with pregnancy and birth rates (Stangler-Hall & Hall, 2011). When the funding expired in 2009, a bill was passed later that year for "research and evidence-based" teenage pregnancy prevention programs. Although there was accumulating evidence that abstinence-only programs were not effective, the abstinence-only funding was restored and authorized in 2010 (Stangler-Hall & Hall, 2011; Trenholm et al., 2007). Increasingly, individual states have refused federal funding for abstinence-only education due to concerns about the accuracy and efficacy of these programs (Raymond et al., 2008).

Because there is no federal law or policy requiring sexuality education, individual states decide which type of sexuality education and funding option will work best in their states to reduce teen pregnancy and STI rates. In some states there are *mandates*, which are *requirements* that all school districts provide sexuality or AIDS education to their students usually with suggested curricula to be implemented at the local level (Guttmacher Institute, 2013). Whereas some states require schools to provide both sexuality and STI/HIV education, others require only STI/HIV education and some do not require local schools to provide either. Some states require abstinence-only education programs, while others require the inclusion of information about contraception along with pregnancy and disease prevention. Other states have *recommendations*, which are provisions by state legislatures or state departments of education that *promote* sexuality and/or STI/HIV/AIDS education, but do not require it. While curricula may be suggested, it is up to the local school districts to design and implement these programs. Thus, it is important for all students, parents, educators, and voters to fully understand the characteristics of programs that use the term "abstinence." Do they mean abstinence-only, abstinence-only-until-marriage, abstinence-based or abstinence-plus, or "abstinence preferred" for safer sex to delay the onset of sexual intercourse (e.g., Comprehensive Sexuality Education).

To help students understand the similarities and differences of approaches to sexuality education, a debate before a hypothetical school board can be implemented. Inform students they will be participating in an in-class debate on four approaches to human sexuality education programs that could be offered in their school district. This cooperative learning experience has engaged students in the learning process regarding the issues involved in school-based sexuality programming. While all students would prepare a position statement as an assignment and share ideas with the person presenting their designated approach to the school board, the actual presenter may be given some additional credit for making the presentation (see Box 9.2 for further details).

Box 9.2   School Board Debate Activity

Create a debate assignment and print it on four different colors of paper to distribute to students. These four colors represent *Comprehensive Sexuality Education Programs, Abstinence-Based Programs, Abstinence-Only Programs,* and *Abstinence-Only-Until-Marriage Programs.* Rather than have students self-select a program, have one member of each color group randomly select the type of program their group will support in the debate. In this way, each group has equal representation and their own personal preferences and views on this approach will be unknown to the rest of the class.

Students will prepare a position statement for their type of sexuality education program. You may give them some assigned readings, but also have them search for other sources on their topic in order to defend their assigned approach.

Some potential elements for this assignment might be the following:

- Prepare a position statement for your assigned approach to human sexuality education including key arguments for using this approach while integrating sources to support your statement.
- Identify one other approach of your own choosing. What are the pros and cons of this second approach? What questions would you ask the proponents of this approach during a debate?
- Who are the key supporters of your assigned approach and what are their main arguments?
- How does your approach deal with the topic of contraception?
- Include references used for your position statement.

Prior to the debate, give groups time to organize and share some information. Each group should decide who will be the main presenter for their group and who will be on the school board.

On the day of the debate, the members of each approach will gather together for a few minutes to share any pertinent information with the presenter. While the instructor will be the superintendent of the schools and facilitate the debate, a student from outside the class can be asked to join the school board and be chairman of the board. Each group's presenter has 5 minutes to put forth its case after which the school board can ask questions of the presenter or group.

After all four groups have presented, each group will ask one of the other groups some questions about their approach with all four groups having an opportunity to ask and respond to questions.

Following the presentations and questioning, the teacher will process the debate with the class while the school board votes on the approach it will adopt for this school district. Note that the outcome of the debate is variable and based on the individual opinions of the school board members and/or the persuasiveness of the presenter for an approach.

Through involvement in this debate, students not only learn the characteristics of each educational approach, but can also use this knowledge as parents, public officials, consumers of news media, and voters.

Model of Sexuality—Organizing Sexuality Education Content

The content covered in sexuality courses varies depending on the needs and ages of the students, settings, and length of courses. A *Model of Sexuality* (see Figure 9.1) can be used to help organize the content of your class or program and adjusted to meet the parameters of your course. This model includes the interac-

Figure 9.1   Model of Sexuality

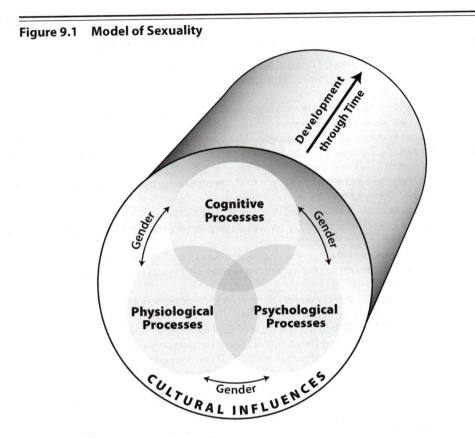

tion of changes through time of cognitive, psychological, and physiological processes; gender; and cultural influences.

Development through Time

Time, as it relates to sexuality, has two parallel dimensions—*historical time* and *personal time*. There have been numerous historical changes regarding our culture; interpersonal relationships; and science related to love, gender transitions, and understanding the physiology of sexuality. Box 9.3 shows some of the changes in the last 100 years or so. Within our culture we have seen evolving laws and court decisions; increasing openness to GLBT issues; and technological/scientific advancements, such as in vitro fertilization, RU-486 to facilitate abortions, and highly active antiretroviral therapy (HAART) for persons with HIV. In addition, the role of cell phones in relationships, social media, "sexting" (the sending of sexually explicit messages and/or pictures by cell phone), and "twerking" (dancing in a sexually provocative manner with thrusting hip movements and a low squatting stance) have infiltrated our cultural milieu. These changes affect the age cohorts of people that are moving through the life cycle during time periods when that particular cultural change is of interest to them developmentally and can affect their lives.

Box 9.3   Timeline of Significant Events in the History of Sexuality

1846   U.S. patent was issued for first diaphragm contraceptive device.

1905   *Three Essays on Sexuality* was published and provided some questionable ideas (Sigmund Freud).

1914   The *American Social Hygiene Association* was formed due to professional interest in sex education, prevention of venereal disease, and prevention of prostitution.

1916   Margaret Sanger was arrested and jailed for opening first birth control clinic in Brooklyn.

1923   John Kellogg became president of *Battle Creek Sanitarium* and promoted plain foods such as corn flakes to prevent sexual feelings and discourage masturbation.

1948   *Sexual Behaviors in the Human Male*, a study incorporating interviews of 5,300 males, was published (Kinsey, Pomeroy, & Martin).
        —First panty raid at Augustana College in Rock Island, Illinois.

1950   Existence of erogenous feeling on wall of vagina was suggested by Ernst Grafenberg, later became known as G-Spot.

1952   First sex reassignment surgery of a European-American, George Jorgensen, in Denmark
        —Lucille Ball, the first to play a pregnant woman on TV, was not allowed to say the word "pregnancy."

1953   *Sexual Behavior in the Human Female*, a study incorporating interviews of 5,940 females, was published (Kinsey, Pomeroy, & Martin).
        —Hugh Hefner published the first issue of *Playboy* (first Playboy Club opened in 1960).

1956   Elvis Presley appeared on *The Ed Sullivan Show*, but was only shown above the waist.

1957   *Society for the Scientific Study of Sexuality (SSSS)* was formed.

1960   Birth control pill was approved by the Food and Drug Administration.
        —Bikini introduced into U.S. after being initiated in Europe in 1946.

1962   *Sex and the Single Girl* was published and became best seller (Helen Gurly Brown).

1963   *Feminine Mystique* was published (Betty Friedan).

1964   *Sex Information and Education Council of the United States (SIECUS)* was founded.

1965   *Griswold v. Connecticut*. The Supreme Court established the right to privacy and married women's right to contraception.

1966   *Human Sexual Response*, an observational study of the physiology of sexual response, was published (Masters & Johnson).
        —*National Organization for Women (NOW)* was founded.

1967   *American Association of Sexuality Educators and Therapists (AASECT)* was founded.

1968   Opening of *Hair* (with onstage nudity) on Broadway in New York City.

1970   Title X Family Planning Program was established.

1972   *The Joy of Sex* was published and on *New York Times* bestselling list for 8 years, longer than any other book in history (Alex Comfort).
        —Title IX establishes sex equity in education.
        —*Open Marriage* was published (O'Neill & O'Neill).

1973   *Roe V. Wade*. Supreme Court established women's right to abortion.
        —*Our Bodies, Our Selves* was published (Boston Women's Health Book Collective).

1974   *American Psychiatric Association* removed homosexuality from list of mental illnesses.

1978   Birth of Louise Brown, first in vitro fertilization.

1979   Moral Majority was founded.
        —Hysteria about herpes began with media campaign in late 1970s and peaked in early 1980s

1981   First cases of unexplained infections among gay men in San Francisco.

1982   Reagan administration proposed "squeal rule" to notify parents of teens who have received contraception.

1983	*Dr. Ruth's Guide to Good Sex* was published, followed by 26 other books (Ruth Westheimer).
1984	Identification of the virus causing AIDS results in explosion of research.
1986	Surgeon General C. Everett Koop publicly advocated that sex education, including AIDS education, be directed toward preadolescents and adolescents.
1990	*The Kinsey Institute New Report on Sex* was published based on national statistically representative sample (Reinisch & Beasley).
	—Title X of Health Service Act and Family Adolescent Family Life Act mandated that sex education content promote abstinence as the primary sexual value for adolescents and was required for agencies receiving federal funds for sex education.
1993	First female condom approved by Food and Drug Administration (FDA).
1994	The *Social Organization of Sexuality* was published, which reported on the National Health and Social Life Survey and incorporated interviews of 3,432 people (Lauman, Gagnon, Michael, & Michaels).
	—*Seventeen*, a teen magazine, first used the words "oral sex" and indicated "masturbation was a normal part of life."
	—Jocelyn Elders, Surgeon General of the U.S., was removed because of her positive comments about masturbation.
1996	Section 501b of Title V of the Social Security Act was passed, the state entitlement for abstinence-only-until-marriage programs in public schools.
	—The Defense of Marriage Act (DOMA) enacted, prohibiting the federal government from recognizing same-sex marriages and allowing each state to refuse recognition of same-sex marriages performed in other states.
1997	Ellen DeGeneres "comes out" to the media that she is a lesbian.
1998	AIDS public education mandated in 42 states; 23 states and the District of Columbia mandate sexuality education programs in public schools.
	—Viagra, an oral medication to treat impotence, approved by FDA.
	—Matthew Shepard was beaten to death in Wyoming for being gay.
	—*Will and Grace* premiered on TV; lead male character was gay.
1999	Human Papilloma Virus found to be leading cause of cervical cancer.
	—RU-486, a pill to facilitate abortions, became available in the U.S.
2001	Surgeon General David Satcher issues *Call to Action to Promote Sexual Health and Responsible Sexual Behavior*, which underscored importance of comprehensive sexuality education programs.
2002	"Rape-drugs" became popular on college campuses.
	—New forms of hormonal contraception (patch, vaginal ring, and monthly injections) entered the market.
2003	*Lawrence v. Texas* struck down the sodomy law in Texas making same-sex sexual activity legal in all states.
2004	Youth Risk Surveys concluded that significant declines in adolescent risk-taking behavior occurred between 1991–1997, but did not continue to decline significantly after that time.
	—The *International Encyclopedia of Sexuality* was published (Francoeur & Noonan).
	—Cialis and Levitra, two new male impotence drugs, approved by FDA.
	—Massachusetts became the first state to legalize same-sex marriages.
2006	House of Representatives Committee declared the majority of abstinence-only programs provided false and misleading information.
2011	End of "don't ask, don't tell" policy for gays in the military (began in 1993).
2013	U.S. Supreme Court struck down the Defense of Marriage Act (DOMA) that prohibited the federal government from recognizing same-sex marriages.

Personal time, as noted by our aging and development, is another element of change. Participants in sexuality education courses are more interested in the issues affecting them at their particular personal age. For example, students in a college class on sexuality education may not be interested in the sexual activities, changes, and concerns of older people and vice versa. However, parents who have children in the home may not only be interested in their own sexuality issues related to being an adult who is a parent or single parent, but also those issues their children are facing at the developmental period of time in which they are situated. These areas of sexual interest will change and evolve through time as individuals and families move through the life cycle.

Cognitive Processes

While we do not often talk about the cognitive dimensions of sexuality, the brain is nevertheless commonly perceived as our biggest sex organ (Berman, n.d.). Cognitive processes pertain to acquiring knowledge and understanding through the thought processes of perception, memory, judgment, and reasoning as they relate to various decisions we make. We make decisions about sexual behavior regarding when to initiate a sexual relationship or interactions, with whom, and under what circumstances. Our thought processes can also affect our reasoning when dealing with moral and ethical decisions, such as sexual harassment. Although sexual harassment can appear in diverse guises and in many different environments, it is quite common, widespread, and can occur in educational settings or at work. In fact, a current study reported that 48% of surveyed middle and high school students indicated they were sexually harassed at least once during the 2010–2011 school year, and that girls (females) were most targeted and harmed by it (AAUW, 2011).

Within the cognitive dimension, ethical decisions about sexuality are important to consider. How does self-interest interact with moral demands when making life choices, especially regarding sexuality? In other words, what is good for me versus what is good for all? An ethical theory has two parts. The first part deals with elements that are fundamentally valuable, or the rationale behind decisions. In addition to some universal values such as honesty, fairness, freedom, tolerance, and helping others, we also have personal values related to love, pleasure, and feelings of self-esteem. Values not only serve as a basis for decision making (with each person having his or her own hierarchy of values), but can also generate guilt if particular actions conflict with one's values and prioritization of values. The second part deals with morality or how we treat others, as we have some limits on what we can do to others. While we have some general rules to guide us, we also have specific situations for which no one set of rules applies. In these instances, we have to analyze and evaluate each situation to determine which ethical principles are relevant. Some principles that can be applied to different sexual and moral issues involving others include the following:

- *Principle of noncoercion*: People should not be forced to engage in sexual expression unless they voluntarily consent to do so.

- *Principle of nondeceit*: People are not to be enticed into sexual expression based on deceit.

- *Principle of treatment of people as ends*: People are not to be treated as a means only; they should be treated as ends. In the sexual domain, this means that another person should never be viewed solely as a means of one's own sexual satisfaction.
- *Principle of respect for beliefs*: People must show respect for the sexual values and beliefs of others. This means that one person should not pressure another to act in a way not in accord with his or her sexual values and beliefs. This does not prevent one person from attempting to rationally persuade others that they are mistaken in their beliefs (Darling & Mabe, 1989).

Using these four principles to analyze various sexual issues, such as gay marriage, abstinence, sexual relations between a teacher and student, and the use or non-use of contraception can be enlightening. Are these principles adequate? Are they applicable to other areas beyond human sexuality? Are there any principles that should be rejected or additional principles that should be considered?

Psychological Processes

Thoughts of sexual intimacy may produce a wide range of emotional reactions including love, pleasure, and joy, as well as emotions such as fear, anxiety, guilt, jealousy, and embarrassment. Emotional responses to sex are primarily learned throughout one's life. *Social learning theory*, which identifies learning as a dynamic interplay between the person, environment, and behavior, proposes that societal reinforcements and punishments shape attitudes and behaviors that influence cognitions, observations, perceptions, ideas, beliefs, and attitudes about sexual behaviors (Chibucos et al., 2005; Gibson, 2004). As children, we use our siblings and parents as models of how we should interact with others, while later we incorporate teachers, peers, and social media as models and indicators of socially normative behaviors.

Three words that have a great psychological impact on the lives of men and women in our culture are "I love you," although the word "love" may be often misunderstood. Love, which is a strong emotion or feeling arising without conscious mental or rational effort, motivates people to behave in certain ways. Moreover, it often provides the basis for pairs to commit themselves to each other. For some people, love is an essential ingredient for emotional survival and may be a prerequisite to engaging in sexual relationships. One of the best known explanations of love is the *Triangular Theory of Love*, which is comprised of three critical elements at three corners of the triangle—*intimacy, passion,* and *commitment* (Sternberg, 1986). A loving relationship can be composed of any one component or combination of two, or all three to differing degrees. Love, which can bring pleasure and pain, at times results in some people feeling unhappy if any one of the three components is weak or missing. While both men and women may express their love for another, they may do so in different ways. Understanding the feelings, relational processes, and communication styles of men and women is essential to facilitate their interpersonal relationships and sexual interactions, along with the perception that the experience and meaning of love change over time.

Physiological Processes

Biological changes and explanations are only one aspect of sexuality, as sexuality also involves our growth and development, reproductive functioning, and sexual arousal and response. It is important to remember that sex is more than intercourse. Thus, there is a wide range of sexual behaviors that can be included in the content of a specific program, as appropriate. A few of these topics may be uncomfortable to some educators, so they may rely solely on discussing human reproduction; however, the physiological processes of sexuality are much broader than puberty and reproduction. To ease these feelings of insecurity, sexuality educators may need to do some self-study and incorporate research findings to add a basis to what they teach. Journals such as the *Journal of Sex Research*, *Archives of Sexual Behavior*, and *Journal of Sex and Marital Therapy* are a few good sources to aid your desire to seek further research-based knowledge. Moreover, what one teaches about sexual physiology will vary according to age, developmental level, and the culture of your community. For example, the physiological curriculum for adolescents would be far different than that provided for senior adults. In addition to examining suggested content in the *Comprehensive Sexuality Education Guidelines for Kindergarten through 12th grade*, check out NCFR's Family Life Education Framework (see Appendix A) regarding sexuality, which suggests various topics to be covered during childhood, adolescence, adulthood, and later adulthood within the context of the family system (Darling & Howard, 2009).

Gender

The cognitive, psychological, and physiological processes involved in sexuality all interact with *gender*—the psychological and sociocultural characteristics associated with being male or female. The clearest gender difference is anatomical; however, prenatally the genitals of the male or female fetus are indistinguishable until about 12 weeks when the genitals begin to differentiate. We have often focused on gender differences based on stereotypical beliefs, but research has indicated that some of these beliefs are true while others are false or changing (Fisher, 2012). Moreover, when gender differences are found, the size of the difference varies based on factors such as age and culture.

In general, males of all ages are more likely to engage in masturbation, especially during childhood and adolescence. Thus, most males experience sexual pleasure initially through self-stimulation, while females may experience sexual pleasure for the first time with another person. Whereas past research showed that males initiated sexual activity at younger ages and engaged in sexual behavior more frequently, recent research has indicated that these differences are changing. Although men have a gradual decline in responsiveness over the lifespan, for women, menopause results in some noticeable changes in bodily functioning and lubrication. Though the frequency of sexual activity declines for both men and women, they still continue to engage in sexual activities throughout their older years (Schick et al., 2010). In regard to sexual attitudes, men tend to be more permissive regarding their attitudes toward sex, are more accepting of casual sex, and perceive of sex as not having to take place within a committed relationship. In comparison, women are more inclined to have negative emotional reactions to sexuality, which is known as "erotophobia" (negative response to sexual cues) (Fisher, 2012).

These differences can result from various reasons based on biology, social roles, and especially cultural influences, as many cultures still have some form of a double-standard and/or an interaction of biology and culture (DeLamater & Hyde, 1998). Because of changes in culture and historical time frame, there are currently fewer significant differences in recent research. Gender role expectations are not only culturally defined, but depend on the era or historical time in which they occur. Unfortunately, much of the research is done with college students when males are at their peak of sexual development compared to women, which may exaggerate gender differences (Fisher, 2012).

Cultural Influences

A large part of our sexual learning occurs as defined by our cultural environment. Within any cultural setting, we learn various sexual scripts, which are analogous to a script for a play or movie. *Sexual script theory* suggests that sexual interactions between partners are socialized not only through the behaviors of peers and family members, but also through the influence of mass media, such as books, television programs, websites, and social media. In other words, our sexual behaviors are learned from culturally desired normative outcomes that define what sex and sexuality are, how to recognize certain sexual situations, and how to behave in them. Additionally, sexual scripts are progressively learned throughout life and are always changing due to social influences.

Scripts are ideas that people have about what they are doing and going to do (Gagnon, 1990; Gagnon & Simon, 1973). Whereas *cultural scripts* are based on collective meanings of a culture, *interpersonal scripts* relate to social interactions by individuals in a specific social context, and *intrapsychic scripts* involve the mental activity and management of the desires experienced by the individual (Simon & Gagnon, 1984). Scripts involve the *who, what, when, where,* and *why* of our sexual behaviors. The "who" part of our sexual script tells with whom we may or may not have sex and may involve limitations regarding age, gender, marital status, ethnicity, social characteristics, or blood relatives. The "what" provides us with the moral, immoral, normal, or abnormal guidelines of what cultures approve, such as an approved guideline in many cultures for heterosexual intercourse, but disapproval of rape and evolving cultural and legal disapproval of marital and acquaintance rape. "When" refers to the timing of sex related to time and age. Whereas time for sexual interaction is perceived as a private time when children are asleep or no one is in the house or apartment, age refers to the appropriate time to begin sexual relations, usually in adolescence or adulthood. "Where" focuses on the place where sexual activities occur and is often concerned with privacy. Traditional places in American culture for sexual relations are a bed in the bedroom or a hotel. "Why" refers to our motivations, explanations, or justifications for sexual activities, such as being in love or wanting to please oneself or someone else.

Many sexual scripts have portrayed males and females in traditional roles, but more contemporary scripts have evolved, such as the need for both partners to learn to take ownership in the couple's sexual experiences; communicate openly and honestly about their feelings; and meet each other's desires, needs, and wishes while trying to meet their own needs (Hammond & Cheney, 2009). The *who, what, when, where,* and *why* of sex need to be congruent with our values to engage in sexual behavior. An interesting example of scripting is a woman's visit to a gynecologist. While her genitals may be exposed and digitally penetrated, it is not necessarily arousing because one's cultural script of a visit to a doctor defines the setting (where), limited time of an office visit (when), individuals involved including a physician and nurse who is watching (who), activities (what), and reason (why).

The cultural dimension of sexuality is not readily apparent because the enculturation and socialization of our sexual beliefs and interpersonal relations limit our ability to perceive the role of culture in shaping our sexual selves. However, thoughtful observations from scholars in approximately 60 countries have provided some cross-cultural perspectives on the role of culture in our sexual lives (Francoeur & Noonan, 2004b). Kissing, which is one of the most common intimate activities in most Western cultures can be used to exemplify cultural scripts (Tieffer, 2004). While in some cultures, kissing accompanies sexual intercourse; in others it does not. There are also interesting variations of kissing such as sucking the lips and tongue of partners, kissing the nose and mouth at the same time, sticking one's tongue into a lovers' nose, or placing lips near a partner's face and inhaling. In Japan, intercourse is normal, but kissing can be perceived as pornographic. In Western cultures a kiss can be a greeting or farewell, sign of affection, religious or ceremonial symbol, or deference to a person of higher status. Thus, when teaching about sexuality within the U.S., one needs to be aware that there may be different interpretations of cultural scripts among the diverse students in your class. Culture influences one's sexual behaviors, feelings, and interactions with others.

Application of Model

Incorporating the *Model of Sexuality* into the design of a sexuality education curriculum varies according to the setting, length of educational program, gender and age of students, and cultural background. While the three overlapping circles of processes are portrayed as the same size and same perceived importance, they may actually vary in size and importance at different points in one's life. In other words, the *physiological processes* might be of greater interest and importance to individuals who are beginning to explore various kinds of sexual interactions. The *cognitive processes* may be more prominent with young people who are in peer groups that promote activities and interactions that might be in violation of their values. The *psychological processes* involved in love and companionship could also vary during the life cycle. Additionally, there is an overlap of content. For example, love, which might be considered as a highly charged emotion, may also be a critical element for some people in their physiological interactions and cognitive processes. The emotion of love also involves certain chemicals in the brain such as oxytocin, adrenaline, and vasopressin that can be released when we see someone to whom we feel attraction (Fisher, 2004). When designing a program, conceptually take a slice of the cylinder of the model to match the development stage of your students. What is most important for them to learn at that point of their lives? While the model can be incorporated as a perceptual tool for students to gain a broad perspective of sexuality and overview of the course, depending on the time available for teaching sexuality content, you may only be able to focus on a few elements of the model.

Learning Strategies for Sexuality Education

Teaching about sexuality needs to be planned and thoughtful, yet spontaneous. Because of cultural and personal sensitivity related to the topic of sexuality, it is important to plan learning strategies that can facilitate creating a safe environment for your students. In addition, it is helpful for students to clarify their own values and for teachers to sensitively become aware of what they are thinking in ways that do not push them into self-revelation, unless they choose to do so. Providing learning experiences in which students can practice refusal skills can be meaningful, so that if they ever find themselves in situations that require them to say "no," they can readily do so with self-confidence. While these are planned activities, it is important to be alert for teachable moments, whether they occur in the classroom setting or in the media. Sexual issues are continuously evolving and becoming prominent in the media and surrounding environment, so being able to readily integrate them into class discussions is important.

Creating a Safe Environment

A safe environment is especially important when teaching about sexuality. People have so many issues and concerns about sexuality that feelings of safety are critical. There are several ways to create a safe environment, such as providing *Class Guidelines* for participation and incorporating class activities—the *One-minute Squirm*, *Class Contract*, and *Question Box*.

Class guidelines

To make the students feel at ease, class guidelines can be discussed or provided to the participants electronically or in a hard copy. The degree of incorporation of these guidelines depends on the nature of the course and its length—one hour, one week, several weeks, or one semester. Some of these guidelines include the following:

- Full participation is expected: *Class will be successful if everyone participates; however you can only participate and share as openly as you feel comfortable doing.*
- Class Discussion Guidelines:
  - Any question is OK: *Don't be afraid to ask a question during or after class.*
  - Use terminology that is socially acceptable: *Some words can be offensive to others.*
  - Respect different values and points of view: *It is OK to disagree, but not tease someone.*
  - Do not use "put-downs:" *Do not give anyone a negative label.*
  - Remember that everyone has feelings: *We have feelings about topics and about what others may say about us.*
  - You do not have to speak: *Everyone has a right to "pass" on a question or activity. No one has to say anything he/she does not want to share.*

- The sessions will be confidential: *Do not share what others have said outside of class.*
- Do not use proper names during discussions: *Use expressions such as "my friend," "a person I know," or "someone I saw."*
- The teacher and students should respect diverse views of sexuality.
- Listen before you form an opinion: *Have an open mind. NO opinion deserves a put down.*
- Remember that no one's opinion is right or wrong: *Everyone is entitled to his or her opinion.*
- We all have a right to change our opinions: *As we become more knowledgeable about a topic, we may change our minds. This is a sign of growth.*
- Some topics are beyond the content of this course. *Sexuality education covers a broad range of topics; however we may not be able to cover them all.*

One-minute squirm

Often times sexuality educators design activities, create assignments, or discuss topics that students find embarrassing because they are expected to divulge more about their personal beliefs and behaviors than they desire. This could be due to their age, comfort with public speaking, religious beliefs, or level of sexual involvement and experience. While you can share this concern with students, learning by experience may have a more lasting effect. Thus, you can mention to your class in a beginning session that in a few minutes you will be calling on various students to share some of their early sexual experiences. Then go on to mention some general class information. Within a minute or two, return to this topic and tell them you will not be asking them for personal information, but wanted them to experience what some students might feel if asked to communicate something that was too personal to share publically. Ask how many "squirmed" when it was mentioned that various students would be asked to share their early sexual experiences. How many were hoping that their names would not be called? How many would have refused if asked to do this and why? Then reaffirm that this is something that they will NOT have to do in this class. The students' sigh of relief is readily apparent. This experience is designed to help future or current teachers think about how their own students might feel if a learning experience was created that was not within their students' comfort zone.

Class contract

Students may "hear" that the environment of a sexuality class is safe when class guidelines are discussed and they may "feel" a teacher's concern for their well-being by incorporating the "one-minute squirm" activity; however, integrating a class contract allows them to read and physically sign a statement that they have heard and understood a teacher's concern for their feelings of safety. Therefore, distribute a contract, such as the one below, for students to complete and sign on the same day the concept of safety is presented. This contract not only provides a safety net for the instructor in case someone later says that they had to do something against their values or beliefs, but also facilitates feelings of relief that your classroom is indeed a safe environment in which to learn about human sexuality.

Human Sexuality Education: Class Content Disclosure Statement

I, _Name of Student_, hereby acknowledge that I have been told by _Name of Instructor_ that this class will include explicit readings and discussions about sexual behaviors. Furthermore, I understand that my decision to participate in any of these pedagogical activities is voluntary, and I have the right to refuse to do any activity that is in conflict with my personal values, and that if I do, an alternative assignment will be designed for me. Furthermore, I realize I will not be penalized for exercising my rights as stated above.

Signed _____   Date _____

Question box

Over the years using a "Question Box" has been a common strategy for providing a safe environment in which students can ask questions. While some students have no problems asking questions, others may feel discomfort or embarrassment that they do not know the answer or that their question might reveal something too personal. Thus, distribute to the entire class identical pieces of paper. Instruct students to anonymously write a question about sex/sexuality, or write something else, such as the words to their favorite song, if they do not have a question. Then, pass around the question box for them to insert what they have written. Since all students will be instructed to put their papers in the box, no one will know which question belongs to any individual student. While some instructors may want to respond immediately, a suggestion is to read these questions after class and organize them according to the content to be covered in subsequent class sessions. Since many questions may be similar, respond to them all at one time and include related elements that may emerge. A question box may be included toward the middle or end of the course, because if incorporated too early most of the questions will relate to content planned for a later date, so answers to their questions may be unnecessarily postponed. If you do not know the answer to a question, this delay gives time to prepare a response. Depending on the size of the class and the relevancy of questions, you may not be able or choose not to respond to all questions. At times students' questions may be inappropriate for an in-class response because they are too personal or out of the context of your class and would be better asked of a physician or sex therapist. Other students may submit questions that are outrageous just to get a reaction from the teacher. A question box can be integrated at various times during a class to stay attuned to emerging questions and issues of concern.

Values Clarification

Fundamental issues in sexuality are intertwined with personal value systems. Beyond needs and drives, sexual behavior reflects the individual values and attitudes toward self, peers, parents, and life. Understanding a person's values and value hierarchy is important in establishing relationships, sexual activities, and sexuality education. One can teach about values, but introducing a variety of introspective exercises and discussion starters will enable students to examine their values more critically, and therefore, potentially increase self-awareness, catalyze individual thought, and promote critical self-analysis. Although there is no single value or value hierarchy that educators are promoting, they are trying to have students identify their values and decide whether or not to keep these values and how to behave accordingly. Two examples of exercises to assist with value clarification include *Hierarchy of Perceptions* and *Values in Relationships*.

Hierarchy of perceptions

Create a list of terms, activities, and situations to distribute to students. Without any identifying information on these papers, have students rank order the items from those they "like least" to those they "like most." Suggestions for these items can be any of the following or others you might choose to add depending on the age, setting, and interests of your audience:

- Abstinence
- Single parenthood
- Gay marriage
- Sex without a condom
- My body
- Female masturbation
- Male masturbation
- Oral sex
- Being a male virgin at age ____
- Being a female virgin at age ____
- Unmarried sex
- Sex between senior adults
- Sexting
- Twerking
- Sex relations between a teacher and student
- Best friend is single and pregnant

After students put these items in rank order, have them fold their papers to give to the teacher. The teacher can randomly redistribute them back to class members who now speak for the individual whose paper they have before them and NOT their own paper. In a discussion, determine the items of highest and lowest rank and what the values associated with those items might be. Note that some of these items may result in positive or negative reactions with the participants.

It is interesting to call attention to a few items for additional discussion. Ask students to compare the responses for male and female masturbation or the age of male or female virginity as noted in the paired items. If there is a higher ranking for one gender, ask students to raise their hands if this situation applies to males (or females). Thus, students can gain a perspective on how their response, which has been anonymous, compares to the culture of the other students in the class. Then discuss how far apart the paired responses are based on gender. In other words, is there a gender issue related to the values associated with this behavior?

The last item of "best friend is single and pregnant" is also of interest. Discuss their feelings about this issue. While many may feel concern for the young woman and indicate their support, others may feel sorry for the woman because being pregnant may negatively affect her future plans. Then ask if "age and circumstance" would make a difference. In other words, if a woman, who was in her mid to late 30s and a professor in family life education, chose in vitro fertilization (IVF) because she wanted a child, would that make a difference? This activity helps to clarify values, examine gender and context, and highlight value hierarchies. The teacher can suggest that there are many different value hierarchies displayed in this activity and similarly, there will be different values and value hierarchies that will emerge when dealing with the content of the course. There are no right answers, just something to ponder as students learn about themselves and from others.

Values in relationships

This activity helps to identify, clarify, and verbalize personal values regarding relationship issues. Moreover, one can examine some of the assumptions underlying judgments and values and then compare them to the perceptions and value hierarchies of others. (See Box 9.4 for this activity.)

Box 9.4   Value Differences in Relationships

Write the following names for participants to view. Depending on the cultural context in which you are teaching, change the names as appropriate. (e.g., John or José or Johan)

- John—Beth's fiancé
- Beth—John's fiancée
- Carl—Beth's classmate
- Anna—Beth's close friend
- Edward—Beth's new acquaintance

Explain that you will read a story and afterward you will ask them to rank these 5 persons from 1 (person you like best) to 5 (person you like least). There are no right answers—only their opinions.
Read the following statement, which you may have to do twice.

> John and Beth are engaged to be married, but John is away in the service stationed in Alaska. Beth is still in school and shares a class with Carl. She and Carl become friends and sleep together. Beth decides she doesn't feel right about having intercourse with Carl and tells him they'll have to stop, and they do.
> Some time passes and Carl tells Beth he is driving to Alaska. Beth asks Carl to take her along so she can see John. Carl says, "OK, if you go to bed with me."
> Beth is uncertain what to do and asks her close friend Anna. Anna says, "Do what you think is best." So, Beth decides to go to bed with Carl.
> Meanwhile, John has been dating, on a casual basis, a nurse stationed near him in Alaska. When Beth gets to Alaska, she feels obliged to tell John about her relationship with Carl. John ends the engagement saying he can't trust Beth.
> Beth returns home and meets Edward. She is upset and tells him everything and Edward asks her to live with him.

(continued)

When the participants have completed their rankings, form small groups of 4 to 6 individuals. Within these small groups, students are to discuss the issues involved in their rankings and come to a group consensus. This is not an average of individual rankings, but a thoughtful analysis of the factors needed to establish a group ranking.

While the small groups are working, create a grid on a board listing the names of the story participants on the vertical axis and the numbers of the groups on the horizontal axis. Get the attention of the class even though some groups may not have reached consensus. Have a member of each group report their rankings explaining why they ranked them in the manner they did or if they had problems in reaching consensus. The grid will most likely have a wide array of rankings for each of the story characters.

Discuss the issues that emerged such as:

- The role of honesty in a relationship
- The relationship between emotional commitment and sexual intercourse
- When intercourse is appropriate
- The meaning of engagement
- The meaning of "sleeping together"
- Exploitation in a personal relationship
- The role of a friend
- The double standard

Other points to discuss include what might be different if the names of the participants were changed to the other gender. In other words, what would happen to their rankings if Beth would be Bob and John would be Diane, etc. In addition, how might this values clarification exercise be applied to a current sexual issue in the media (e.g., Clinton-Lewinsky situation or some other more current sexual controversy). To conclude this discussion, call attention to the variations in rankings for the story participants. We all have values, but we value things differently. Thus, these varying value hierarchies are an indication that they will also value class content differently during the remainder of the course.

Adapted from Morrison, E., & Price, M. (1974). *Values in sexuality: A new approach to sex education.* New York: Hart Publishing Company.

Refusal Skills

An important skill for individuals of all ages is learning how to say "no." Resisting peer pressure at any age is not easy, but is especially difficult among today's youth. Begin this exercise by asking students what kinds of situations are problematic and what factors are involved (e.g., alcohol/drugs, numbers of peers, perceived status in a group). A mini lecture might be helpful for dealing with the topic of assertiveness (and nonassertiveness) versus aggressiveness. However, students may need some "practice" to implement refusal or resistance skills in a calm and positive manner so that they can maintain their friendships with the person, if they so choose. You can structure some role-play scenarios in your class, but some people may be uncomfortable in front of a group. Therefore you might divide the class into 2, 3, or 4 groups depending on the size of the class. Give each group in rotation a "pressure line" for their collective response and then have a student panel score the responses using numbered cards from 1 to 5. Someone can keep score to see what group gains the greatest number of points. This activity helps students to practice saying "no," while maintaining a relationship with their friends and peers. At the end of this activity, students might discuss how comfortable they were when reacting to these statements. Did it become easier to respond as the activity progressed? Since alcohol consumption is frequently part of sexual encounters, how would alcohol or other substances affect an individual's pressure for sexual interactions and the other individual's reactions to pressure lines?

The following are some sexuality pressure lines, although it is better to ask students to provide some lines that they have heard:

- If you love me, you'll have sex with me.
- I don't want to do anything. I just want to lie next to you.
- Come on. I'll be the best you have ever had.
- Have something to drink; it will make you more relaxed.
- Sex will help our relationship grow stronger.
- If you don't say "yes," I will find someone who will.
- I have never been with anyone else, so there is no chance you will get AIDS.
- I don't have a condom with me.
- When I stop to put a condom on, I'll lose my erection.
- Condoms are for people with diseases. Do I look sick to you?

A suggested refusal skill from a colleague dealt with his daughter and her mother. If the daughter was with her peers and an activity or relocation to another event was suggested that was against her values, she would say she had to call her mother first to get permission to stay out later or move on to another location. She would explain it to her mother and say, "Please, please can I _____." Saying "please" two times was the code for her mother to say, "No" and the daughter could ease out of a situation in which she did not want to be. Granted this does not work for all peer pressure situations and may not help this young woman to be direct in saying "no" to her peers, but it was effective for this mother and daughter. The young woman had considered her values and value hierarchies and acted upon that hierarchy. She might value honesty of peer friendship, but in this case it was of lower priority to her. In addition to leaving the situation, other things she could have done include suggesting an alternate activity, giving a reason why it was not a good idea, just saying "no," or saying "thanks, but no thanks."

Sexuality Educators

Becoming a sexuality educator may sound exciting, interesting, scary, or challenging. Unfortunately, there are few academic programs to train sexuality educators, but we offer some suggestions for gaining pertinent knowledge and assistance, as well as the importance of knowing oneself.

Training to Teach Sexuality

Many sexuality educators lack professional training to teach sexuality education, yet effective preparation for teachers in this area is critical (Cohen, Byers, Sears, & Weaver, 2004; Walters & Hayes, 2007). Because of its potential for controversy, people may feel vulnerable and are scared away from teaching sexuality courses. Although there are increasing numbers of sexuality programs in the public schools, educators may not only lack preparation in the content and methods of teaching about sexuality, but may be forced to teach material with which they are not personally knowledgeable or comfortable (Goldfarb, 2003). This lack of training exists for educators in both public schools and universities. Most sexuality educators at the university level have advanced degrees, but have no specialized training in the field of human sexuality. Some have taken a course in sexuality, but many have not because they were not offered in their departments. In fact, there are few academic programs from which one can get a degree in sexuality. Some university departments such as psychology, sociology, social work, medicine, health, and family sciences have a single sexuality course; however they can vary considerably based on the perspectives of the discipline. This means that there is little cross fertilization among the disciplines on campus or in their professional organizations regarding teaching strategies, sharing in research projects, and reading literature from other disciplines.

Teaching sexuality should be from an ecological context, evidence-based, needs driven, and evaluated. Because teacher preparation about sexuality is minimal in academic programs, it is important to provide teachers with in-service training, applicable research, and clearly documented teaching activities that have been found to work well in classrooms. Teachers have reported that even a two-hour in-service workshop provided some needed tools to help them teach about human sexuality (Buston, Wight, Hart, & Scott, 2002). When these courses or programs are available, teachers learn from each other, develop camaraderie with other sexuality educators, and acquire the confidence and skills to teach this subject matter. Additional suggestions are to network with other sexuality educators, become well read, and add yourself to e-mail discussion lists of sexuality educators who share information and teaching ideas (Taverner, 2006). It is also helpful to become familiar with teaching materials for various levels of students, from early childhood (Brick et al, 1989) to adolescence (Brick & Taverner, 2001; Taverner & Montford, 2005) to mid and later life (Brick & Lunquist, 2003). There is also a range of topics from teaching sexuality education to high-risk youth (Brown & Taverner, 2001) to power and consent in adult-teen relationships (Montfort & Brick, 1999), and hard-to-teach topics in sexuality education (SIECUS, 1998). Many of these teaching materials are available from the Sexuality Information and Education Council of the United States (SIECUS) and The Center for Family Life Education: Planned Parenthood of Greater Northern New Jersey. High quality preparation is required for high quality sexuality education in the classroom.

The Certified Family Life Educator (CFLE) program does not take for granted that students can assimilate knowledge about sex and sexuality from portions of classes, such as family relations or human development. Therefore, the CFLE program includes human sexuality as one of the 10 content areas, with this content commonly covered within a course specifically in human sexuality. There is a wide range of subject matter within this content area that is needed to become a CFLE, including biological elements, such as sexual functioning, family planning, and health, along with psycho-social aspects of human sexuality, such as healthy and ethical sexual relations, dynamics of sexual intimacy, and risk factors that are all addressed from a value-respectful position (See sexuality content in Appendices A and B). The American Association of Sex Educators, Counselors, and Therapists (AASECT) has also established a program to certify sexuality educators (see www.aasect.org/certification.asp). If you recognize that you are in need of assistance to become a sexuality educator or enhance your knowledge, skills, and abilities to teach about sexuality, various organizations and courses can help you to feel more comfortable in this role.

Knowing Oneself

While parents should be the primary sexuality educators for their children, expecting all parents to handle the complexity of this task is unrealistic in today's society. They are often embarrassed about discussing sexuality and there are a number of things they may not know. Thus, they turn to others, namely schools, for support, resources, and expertise and some may also simultaneously take comparable sexuality courses so that they may engage in meaningful discussions with their children. While parents and teachers are sexual beings, it is important that both understand themselves and the feelings about their own sexuality before becoming a sexuality educator to their own children or the children of others. The teacher is the key element to a good human sexuality program. No matter how carefully teachers design their course and implement their plans, unprepared teachers who are fearful, anxious, tentative, or embarrassed can defeat the entire effort. Instead, sexuality educators need to feel comfortable interacting with others about sexuality and committed to sexual responsibility (Bruess & Greenberg, 2009).

Personal Traits

Those who teach human sexuality often have some similar characteristics. They tend to be open, interactive, able to teach within the affective domain, and take an interest in students (Bruess & Greenberg, 2009; Timmerman, 2008). Sexuality educators may not have had personal experiences associated with different groups, but they can still be effective as long as they are open and willing to learn about sexuality among married persons, singles, gays and lesbians, disabled persons, or within diverse cultures by studying the research and literature on these topics (Wilkenfeld & Ballan, 2011). It is particularly important to understand the cultural context of students, especially if their backgrounds are affiliated with another country. If you are not aware of the environmental contexts of the student(s), become familiar with their cultures through readings or discussions with others from similar backgrounds. Students' beliefs about gender, homosexuality, body image, religion, contraception, and/or sexual health may be related to their cultural socialization. Thus, a goal for sexuality educators is to be aware of and accept other cultural viewpoints while simultaneously representing the societal context of the culture in which they are teaching.

Sexuality educators need to be comfortable with their femininity and masculinity. Since we all have both feminine and masculine qualities, being aware of them and free of societal stereotypes and misperceptions are essential. Having a positive body image is also important, along with being able to accept one's appearance. In order to discuss body development effectively, you have to be positive about your own. It is also hoped that sexuality educators have a sense of humor. At times, humorous situations will occur in educational settings, so a light-hearted and playful reaction to these circumstances will let students know that you can relate to the real world. Humor heightens the students' interest, makes it easier to discuss class topics, and provides a positive image of sexuality that at times results in some laughter, at no one's expense (Bruess & Greenberg, 2009; Timmerman, 2009).

Having good communication skills when dealing with groups and individuals is an important quality. While some teachers require the use of scientific terms, they may become cumbersome and awkward to students and thus inhibit their comments in class. As long as the terminology is socially acceptable and understandable, you can proceed. If a term is used that is not acceptable, then it is the teacher's responsibility to identify the correct terminology without embarrassing the student (Bruess & Greenberg, 2009). At times the student may also state a misperception that is clearly inaccurate. For example, a student once said, "you cannot become pregnant the first time you have sexual intercourse." Rather than publically and emphatically telling the student that he or she is wrong, you could say that this is something that many think is true, but actually, people can become pregnant the first time they have sexual intercourse. While you do not want to embarrass any student, it is important to correct any myths.

Sexuality educators should be at ease when communicating with students who come to talk about issues that are of concern. When students are upset, a teacher may be the person with whom they can share their feelings, such as distress over a mother just diagnosed as being HIV positive, anxiety over a personal diagnosis of breast cancer, or the trauma of being beaten by a sexual partner. They may perceive a teacher as approachable with sensitive topics and want to share their concerns. In these situations you should spend time with the student, listen, and refer him or her to help when needed. Be prepared with a list of accessible therapists and relevant contact information to distribute. Some teachers may also be therapists, but it is unethical to fulfill a dual role with students.

Challenges of Teaching Human Sexuality

Teaching about sexuality is like walking a tightrope between school, state, and federal mandates or recommendations, while also meeting the students' needs whether they are sexually active or not. Although sex and sexuality are almost everywhere in the media and campus environments, honest and knowledgeable conversations about sexuality are not. One of the challenges concerns "academic freedom." Whereas public colleges and universities often have academic freedom, some private colleges, which are funded by private foundations and tuition, may be concerned about the topics covered in courses. Curriculum may be more controlled in the public schools where elected school officials are held accountable for what might be taught about sexuality. One suggestion for teaching students beyond high school age is to let them know that this human sexuality course will occur in a pluralistic setting in which multiple voices will be heard, so students are allowed to make comments on all sides of an issue, but in no instance should students be disrespectful. The challenge is to keep an open dialogue, build bridges, and keep administrators and others informed.

Selecting textbooks and reading materials can be another challenge. Depending on the educational setting, the use of certain content, diagrams, and photos could be an issue. Some students say that they would not dare take their books home to their parents, while others say their sexuality books have been stolen from their dorm rooms or lockers. Others share that this was the first time a significant other or spouse looked at their text and actually read it before the student did. In the current environment, it is easy to make readings available to students along with a text or partial text. Some book companies are quite willing for teachers to select chapters from the texts they publish to create a reader that best meets the educational needs of the students.

Teaching about sexuality means having to navigate the emotional domain of students. Some students have experienced sexual violence, teen pregnancy, racist comments about sexuality, or have a nontraditional sexual orientation. Because it is important for teachers to understand their students, you could initiate a class with an activity called "Insight." Students are given a piece of paper, with no identifying marks, and instructed to inform you if there is something you need to know about them regarding the topic of sexuality and/or if there is a question they particularly want answered during the class sessions. Whether or not they have a response to these questions, they are to write something on the paper so others cannot identify who does or does not have an issue or question. Some of the responses received from an undergraduate class on human sexuality exhibited a wide variety of concerns, such as:

- I was date raped and had to have an abortion. I am slightly sensitive about this topic.
- I feel like I am promiscuous at times because I am not in a relationship, but have sex with strangers. I am also kind of questioning my sexuality.
- When I was six years old, the carpenter/gardener took advantage of me.
- I think it is important for people to know that you can still get STIs when using condoms. Most sexuality education classes imply that by using a condom you are completely safe and that is simply not true.
- Sex was hardly discussed in my home at all. I would like to be more open with my family regarding sexuality.
- I want to learn more about sexual arousal.
- How does being pregnant affect one's sex life?
- I have herpes and want to know if there is a treatment that can prevent my outbreaks from occurring as often as they do.
- My partner has never had an orgasm during sexual intercourse. How can I help change that? She enjoys intercourse, but I would like for her to enjoy it more.

This range of responses gives a teacher some anonymous *insight* into students' backgrounds and identifies some of their needs and issues of concern. Whereas the topics from some of these comments can be integrated into the content of the course depending on the level and length of time allotted for the class, other topics may require professional assistance from alternate sources, such as referrals to counselors, therapists, or physicians.

When teaching about sexuality, you teach in a vacuum. It is difficult to be gone from class because there are usually no qualified substitutes to teach this course. Speakers can also be a problem if a teacher does not know what they will say, their presentation content cannot be readily integrated into the course, or they make an insensitive remark. Therefore, careful planning and preparation for speakers are essential. Teaching a human sexuality course takes considerably more energy because you are always on guard. You also need to be sensitive with assignments by not asking students to reveal their personal thoughts and feelings related to sexual issues or behaviors. They may volunteer these opinions in class, but some do not choose to share on certain topics. Moreover, be careful to never lose a set of papers, especially with student names on them. In fact, some teachers have students identify their papers with a preassigned number.

People often have a lot of misguided perceptions about sexuality educators. Some may perceive that sexuality teachers are quite sexually adept or have more sexual dysfunctions than others. In addition, they perceive that sexuality educators would be capable of diagnosing and resolving sexual issues with a few well-chosen words or suggestions during a brief interaction at a social event. Gender and age also may influence others' perceptions of a sexuality educator. Whereas older males may be perceived as perverted, younger males may be looked to with a level of sexual interest. Some female students may have difficulty talking with a male teacher if they have had past experiences with victimization and feel vulnerable in the presence of male authority figures, especially those teaching about sexuality. In contrast, younger women may be presumed to be sexually available and interested in sexual freedom and experimentation. Older married and less physically attractive sexuality educators appear to encounter fewer problems. Moreover, married educators with children seem more conventional and less threatening. For example, Dr. Ruth is older, maternal, and outspoken, which are prerogatives permitted to a woman of her age. Teaching across gender lines with both a male and female educator would be great, if it can be funded. In general, sexuality educators continually work to be beyond reproach in their demeanor, dress, and what they say. It is very easy for a student to share something that was said or done in a sexuality class that is misperceived by the listener and passed to others as a rumor. In addition, some students may become distressed when teachers do not endorse or condemn certain behaviors about which the student may have a strong opinion.

Joys of Teaching Human Sexuality

One of the joys of teaching about human sexuality is the incredible range of topics that relate to so many different disciplines and aspects of life. There is always something new occurring in contemporary life that touches the area of sexuality. There are issues in the media and current events that can be added to class almost on a daily basis, so the element of creativity is always present. One does not become bored teaching about sexuality because new ideas are energizing. There is also camaraderie among colleagues who are teaching about sexuality. This may occur across fields, which facilitates an interdisciplinary excitement and sharing. A major joy is the opportunity to help others. Students are happy to find out what sexuality educators know while being given a license to talk about sexual issues that they have been thinking about for some time. This provides an opportunity to be involved in some life-altering situations, as shared by other colleagues:

- A victim of impotence from acquaintance rape had post-traumatic stress disorder (PTSD) and learned a lot about sexuality that helped her understand her situation and seek help.
- Within some students' cultural backgrounds, sexuality was not discussed so one young woman came to the teacher after class to get more information on sexual pleasure.
- Following a lecture on "Why young women don't use contraception," a woman informed the teacher that she had just made an appointment with her gynecologist.
- It is common that teaching about breast exams or various health exams results in preventing health problems.
- A discussion of testicular cancer resulted in one mother talking to her son about a self-exam. He found a nodule and needed to have one testicle removed, but it saved his life.

Sexuality is an important area of human development and family relations, so please do not ignore it or say "no" to teaching in this field. While at times teaching about sexuality can be difficult, there are many who enjoy the challenge. In the words of Katherine Graham, "To love what you do and feel that it matters—how could anything be more fun."

SUMMARY

Sexuality education is desired by youth, parents, and other adults for a variety of reasons, including gaining knowledge; enhancing relationships; and preventing premature, unprotected, and unwanted sexual involvement among young people. Many resources are available for information and education, but getting them to the persons in need is not always easy. While there are a variety of approaches to school-based sexuality education programs, they vary in effectiveness. The *Model of Sexuality* can be used to organize the content for a sexuality education course. Potential topics include the integration of development through time; cognitive, psychological, and physiological processes; gender; and cultural influences. Various teaching strategies can be incorporated that involve creating a safe environment, values clarification, and refusal skills. While there is minimal training available in academic settings for sexuality educators, along with several challenges that other fields do not have, there are also some incredible joys, especially teaching content that can have a major impact on the lives of others.

QUESTIONS AND ISSUES FOR DISCUSSION

1. Why does sexuality education continue to be a controversial issue? What can students, teachers, parents, and administrators do to promote sexuality education?

2. How can family life educators promote nonschool programs and culturally diverse programs on sexuality education in the community?

3. What should be taught about sexuality at different ages—young children, tweens, adolescents, young adults, mature adults, and seniors?

4. How can parents become more involved in teaching about sexuality to their children?

5. What did you learn about sexuality when you were in the public schools? What changes would you have liked, if any?

6. What are some examples of websites for teens that have accurate and positive messages about sex and sexuality?

ACTIVITIES

1. Using a specific entry or time period from the sexuality timeline (Box 9.3), have students examine the particulars of those historical changes to bring to class for discussion. How or why did that change affect sexual behaviors?

2. Find quotes about love and analyze what they are saying and if it is part of today's culture.

3. Have students find a popular press article to critique by examining named or unnamed sources, visual representations (if any), and research on the topic to refute or substantiate its claims.

4. Have students examine various chapters in the *International Encyclopedia of Sexuality* (Francoeur & Noonan, 2004b) to determine the role of culture in the sexual behaviors and interactions within other countries.

WEB RESOURCES

Advocates for Youth
www.advocatesforyouth.org
Advocates for Youth promotes efforts to help young people make informed and responsible decisions about their reproductive and sexual health. Advocates for Youth believes it can best serve the field by boldly advocating for a more positive and realistic approach to adolescent sexual health.

American Association of Sexuality Educators, Counselors and Therapists (AASECT)
www.aasect.org
AASECT is a not-for profit interdisciplinary professional organization. In addition to sexuality educators, counselors, and therapists, AASECT members include physicians, nurses, social workers, psychologists, allied health profes-

sionals, clergy members, lawyers, sociologists, marriage and family counselors and therapists, family planning specialists, and researchers, as well as students in relevant professional disciplines. These individuals share an interest in promoting understanding of human sexuality and healthy sexual behavior.

American School Health Association (ASHA)
www.ashaweb.org

ASHA is the leading membership organization for school health professionals. It is concerned with all health factors that are necessary for students to be ready to learn, including optimum nutrition, physical fitness, emotional well-being, and a safe and clean environment. This broad spectrum of topics makes ASHA unique among health and education organizations and sets the stage for collaboration among its membership and partners.

Centers for Disease Control and Prevention (CDC)
www.cdc.gov

CDC is a federal agency that collaborates to create the expertise, information, and tools that people and communities need to protect their health through health promotion, prevention of disease, injury and disability, and preparedness for new health threats. It provides links to information about STIs including HIV/AIDS, resources, prevention and available treatments.

Guttmacher Institute
www.guttmacher.org

Guttmacher Institute continues to advance sexual and reproductive health and rights through an interrelated program of research, policy analysis, and public education designed to generate new ideas, encourage enlightened public debate, and promote sound policy and program development. The Institute's overarching goal is to ensure the highest standard of sexual and reproductive health for all people worldwide.

Planned Parenthood
www.plannedparenthood.org

Planned Parenthood believes in the fundamental right of each individual, throughout the world, to manage his or her fertility, regardless of the individual's income, marital status, race, ethnicity, sexual orientation, age, national origin, or residence. They believe that respect and value for diversity in all aspects of their organization are essential to their well-being. They believe that reproductive self-determination must be voluntary and preserve the individual's right to privacy. They further believe that such self-determination will contribute to an enhanced quality of life and strong family relationships.

Sexuality Information and Education Council of the United States (SIECUS)
www.siecus.org

SIECUS has been a leader in the fight to ensure that everyone has access to information and education about their sexuality. SIECUS provides countless resources to help educators, advocates, and parents secure supportive public policies, provide high quality education, and help our youth become sexually healthy.

Society for the Scientific Study of Sexuality (SSSS)
www.sexscience.org

SSSS is dedicated to advancing knowledge of sexuality. To acquire that knowledge the Society requires freedom of inquiry, support for research, and an interdisciplinary network of collaborating scholars. The Society believes in the importance of both the production of quality research and the application of sexual knowledge in educational, clinical, and other settings. The Society also sees as essential the communication of accurate information about sexuality to professionals, policy makers, and the general public.

Approaches to Relationship and Marriage Education

Marriage Relationships and Well-Being

Healthy marriages have positive effects on men, women, and children. Married couples are not only happier, healthier, wealthier, and better educated (Amato, 2000, 2010; Fincham & Beach, 2010; Proulx, Helms, & Buehler, 2007), but also children who reside in married families are less likely to be poor, suffer abuse, experience depression, or be involved in risky behaviors, and more likely to do well in school (Amato, 2000, 2010; Amato & Cheadle, 2005; Heatherington, 2005; Kelly & Emery, 2003). Married persons indicate they are very happy with life compared to those who are not married. These findings are consistent for men and women, both old and young, who also report greater psychological well-being, lower rates of depression, and a stronger sense of personal growth (Proulx et al., 2007; Taylor, Funk, & Craighill, 2006). However, it is unknown whether marriage influences a more positive outlook on life or if people who are happier are more likely to marry. Several researchers have noted the connection between marriage and health, but since the issues are complex it is only an emerging area of research (Staton & Ooms, 2012). People who are married have greater financial well-being and accumulate greater assets than those who are single, which could be attributed to a motivation to work in order to support others and/or pooling of resources, health insurance, economy of scale, and/or retirement benefits (DeNavas-Walt, Proctor, & Smith, 2012; Fagan, 2009). When considering education, individuals with higher education have an increased probability of getting married. Moreover, persons with college degrees tend to have more stable marriages than those with high school degrees or less education (Bramlett & Mosher, 2002).

As we age, marriage has a greater effect on adult health, in that older married persons are more mentally and physically healthy with a delayed onset of physical limitations in carrying out their daily activities (Bookwala, 2005; Coyne et al., 2001; Rohrbaugh, Shoham, & Coyne, 2006; Umberson, Williams, Powers, Liu, & Needham, 2006). Married couples live longer and are less likely to die from the leading causes of death. It is generally perceived that those who are married have a health advantage due to greater social support, decreased isolation, and incentives to act in healthier ways. However, it is not simply marriage that is associated with greater health, but a "satisfying" one. Although long-lasting marriages come in various forms, some of the core characteristics include the following (Staton & Ooms, 2012):

- Long-term commitment
- Positive communication
- Resolution of disagreements and conflicts nonviolently
- Emotional and physical safety
- Sexual and psychological fidelity
- Mutual respect
- Enjoyment of time spent together
- Provision of emotional support and companionship
- Mutual commitment to children by parents

There is no clear blueprint for a happy marriage because people bring a number of personal and family background factors to their relationships. Nevertheless,

Americans believe that faithfulness, happy sexual relationships, and shared household chores are the top three characteristics of a successful marriage (Taylor, Funk, & Clark, 2007). The way couples communicate and spend time together also affects marital satisfaction, as well as their compatibility. After couples are married, personality becomes increasingly important in maintaining a happy relationship (Luo & Klohnen, 2005), along with being adaptable and able to compromise. Flexible partners often accommodate the other's needs and enjoy doing so (Schwartz, 2006).

Marriage has been identified as the optimal context in which to create families and raise children. The knowledge and skills needed for healthy marriage are widely known. Therefore, there has been increasing emphasis on providing relationship and marriage education to many people in a variety of settings. The benefits of marital health and satisfaction for couples, families, and children provide positive incentives for marriage and family life educators to continue developing programs as times and relationships change.

Marriage: Past and Present

Many changes in marriage have occurred over the years. For example, the term "traditional marriage" has often been mentioned, but we have to ask when, where, and how it is used. It has had many different meanings through time, such as heterosexual marriages or marriages in which the male partner worked outside the home while the female partner stayed home caring for the children. Now there are alternative configurations for marriage and relationships such as *peer marriages* (partners who have equal status in relationships including finances, housework, and child-rearing roles), *alone together marriages* (couples whose mutual friends and activities together have declined, but still remain happy in their relationships) and *LAT relationships* (Living Apart Together—couples in committed marital or nonmarital intimate relationships, but living in separate homes) (Amato, Booth, Johnson, & Rogers, 2007; Amato & Hayes, 2014; Levin, 2004; Schwartz, 1994; 2001). The number of spouses has also changed over time in that some societal and religious traditions have permitted polygamy or marriage to multiple partners (nonspecified gender). Having multiple wives (polygyny) is more common and can be found in Africa, the Middle East, Southern Asia, and North America, but is a diminishing phenomenon worldwide (Adams, 2004; Darity, 2008). Love, which has evolved for many as a basis for marriage, was originally condemned as too fragile of an emotion on which to base a marriage; however, as people took control of their destiny and love life, they began to demand the right to choose their own mate and to end unhappy marriages (Coontz, 2005).

Marriage laws have continued to change over time. Whereas 40 states once prohibited marrying outside one's race, California became the first state to declare a ban on interracial marriage to be unconstitutional, followed by the U.S. Supreme Court striking down the remaining interracial marriage laws in 1967. For many centuries women had no legal rights when they married, but over time these laws have evolved at the state and federal levels to reflect the equality of spouses. Divorce has also become easier to obtain with many states creating no-fault divorce laws, although some states have mandatory divorce and parent education (e.g., Arizona, Florida, Iowa, Kentucky, Minnesota, New Jersey, Tennessee, Virginia) (Gardiner, Fishman, Nikolov, Glosser, & Laud, 2002). Similarly, laws are in flux regarding same sex-couples' access to marriage, as the U.S. Supreme Court struck down the Defense of Marriage Act (DOMA) that prohibited the federal government from recognizing same-sex marriages and more states are passing laws to legalize gay marriage. Marriage laws evolve through time based on shifting societal attitudes and needs of families (Gardiner et al., 2002; GLAD, n.d.).

As a culture, we are obsessed with marriage. Whether it is the $50 billion we spend annually on marriages ($28,400 average per wedding); television programs about finding the right partner, dress, or wedding venue; focus on celebrity weddings; or the political interest in gay marriage, marriage is a central part of our way of life (Fairchild Bridal Group, 2002; The Knot, 2012). However, trends indicate that Americans have become less likely to marry. While our interest is strong, generally the interaction of economic, technological, cultural, social, and legal factors has contributed to the decline in marriage (Ooms & Wilson, 2004). From 1990 to 2010, there was a decrease in the number of households with married couples from 55.2% to 48.4% (Lofquist et al., 2012). Some of this decline could be due to a delay in first marriage, as the typical age of marriage has continued to rise to 29.0 for males and 26.6 for females (Vespa et al., 2013). There has also been an increase in unmarried cohabitation and a small decrease in the inclination for divorced persons to remarry. Between 1990 and 2010 more people showed a commitment to remaining single with the number of single persons increasing from 24.6% to 26.7%. Marriage data for those between the ages of 35 and 44 suggest a trend toward permanent singlehood, since usually persons who marry do so by the age of 45 (NMP & IAV, 2012). However, many unmarried Americans do not identify with the word "single" because they are parents, have partners, or are widowed (U.S. Census Bureau News, 2012).

While stable, happy marriages are almost universally desired, social, legal, and economic changes over time have led to the increased instability of marriages (Halford, Markman, & Stanley, 2008). The U.S. has one of the highest divorce rates in the world with a lifetime probability of divorce between 40% to 50% (Amato, 2010; Cherlin, 2010; Kreider, 2005; Kreider & Ellis, 2011). However, the overall risk of divorce has actually declined somewhat from its peak of approximately 50% during the 1980s, which is probably due to the increase in age and educational level of people who marry for the first time. Females are more likely to be divorced than males, because males are more likely to remarry and do so sooner than females (NMP & IAV, 2012). While the marriage rate is relatively stable among the affluent, marriage continues to be fragile and weak for the poor (Marquardt, Blankenhorn, Lerman, Malone-Colon, & Wilcox, 2012). Among middle-class Americans or those with a high school degree (almost 60% of the nation), the rates of divorce are higher along with decreasing marital happiness. In other words, although marriage is still valued in America, moderately-educated couples have become less likely to form stable unions (NMP & IAV, 2012; Wilcox, 2010).

Most children of divorced parents generally have lower levels of well-being, with some of these problems continuing into adulthood, such as poverty, troubled marriages, weak ties to parents, and symptoms of psychological distress (Amato,

2000, 2010; Amato & Cheadle, 2005). Some young people also expressed painful memories following their parents' divorce and wished they had spent more time with their absent parent (Kelly & Emery, 2003). The effects of divorce for children vary depending on the context of the divorce. For some children there could be improvements in well-being, whereas others show little change or have problems that either improve or continue into adulthood (Amato, 2010). In addition, with divorce there could be long-term implications of family problems that persist across generations, as well as other problems related to risks for children and future grandchildren (Amato & Cheadle, 2005). Divorce education for parents and children has become more prominent in the U.S. in the past decade. Programs that were research-based and focused on skill development showed more promise for parents and children than those that were didactic or affect-based (Kelly, 2002)

Marriage Education

Due in part to a growing national marriage education movement, there are a number of resources and programs available to help couples have a happy, healthy marriage. Minimizing divorce with better education before and during marriage can potentially result in more stable relationships. Marriage and relationship education provides information to couples about relationship knowledge, attitudes, behaviors, and skills to assist individuals and couples in sustaining healthy, mutually satisfying relationships, and reducing relationship distress. This includes making wise partner choices and managing or leaving abusive relationships (Halford, Markman, Stanley, & Kline, 2003; Hawkins & Ooms, 2010).

In the past, marriage enrichment programs were popular, such as the *Association for Couples in Marriage Enrichment (ACME)*, developed by David and Vera Mace (Mace, 1982). Their goal was to take an educational rather than therapeutic approach and make a good marriage even better. Often there were weekend retreats devoted to revitalizing one's marriage within the context of spiritual renewal (Doherty & Anderson, 2004). Because of the perceived importance of stable marriages for children and families and the costs of marital instability to individuals and society, various efforts have been made to provide relationship and marriage education. In fact, the field of marriage education has experienced a notable resurgence since 1995 and especially in the last decade when federal legislation allocated funds to support promising marriage and relationship education programs and initiatives targeted at lower-income couples (Doherty & Anderson, 2004; Hawkins & Ooms, 2010). In most cases, marriage education takes a preventative approach before difficulties occur, rather than a remedial approach to help couples who have severe relationship problems (Larson, 2004a). Over time other marriage education programs have been established that are research-based, focus on couples' relationship skills, and are often of interest to premarital couples and couples with long lasting relationships. Although further research is still needed to determine the effectiveness of marriage and relationship education for diverse and disadvantaged populations, there is evidence that skills-based relationship education for couples enhances maintenance of healthy and committed relationships and should be disseminated (Halford et al., 2008; Hawkins, Blanchard, Baldwin, & Fawcett, 2008).

Relationship or marriage education can occur at many different times, settings, and circumstances in one's life, such as when one is single, either in one's youth or young adulthood, or returning to singlehood after being in a relationship. Couples can also engage in relationship or marriage education at any stage of their relationship. They may need to reconnect, understand what makes their relationship work, or learn practical skills to improve or enrich their relationship (Squires & Smith, 2006). Skills and insights can be learned in marriage education to avoid unhealthy relationships; build a healthy, committed, and growing relationship; maintain and enrich a marriage; and/or rescue a struggling marriage. Other key relationship skills include communication, conflict management, developing realistic and shared relationship expectations, and promoting positive connections and commitment (Halford et al., 2008). Premarital prevention programs can produce immediate and short-term gains in interpersonal skills and relationship quality (Carroll & Doherty, 2003). While the findings from several evaluation studies have indicated mixed results, they are nevertheless encouraging. Because of the limitations and gaps within these studies, we need long-term data on family stability, child outcomes, parenting, and the spillover effects of marriage relationships into the work place and vice versa (Ooms & Hawkins, 2012).

Research on the prevention of marital distress has led to evidenced-based programs that help alter the course of marriage and prevent divorce. If negative interactions can be improved, couples can enhance their odds of staying together. Examples of programs used to help strengthen relationships and marriages include the *Prevention and Relationship Enhancement Program (PREP)* (Stanley, Markman, Jenkins, & Blumberg, 2009); *Within My Reach* (Pearson, Stanley, & Kline, 2005); *Couples Communication* (Miller, Miller, Wackman, & Nunnally, n.d.); and *Practical Application of Intimate Relationship Skills (PAIRS)* (Gordon, 2000).

Model: 5 Cs of Relationship and Marriage Education

To better understand and show the breadth of the multifaceted elements of relationship and marriage education programs, one can incorporate the *5 Cs of Relationship and Marriage Education Model*: *Consumers, Content, Changes, Context,* and *Culture*. Although counseling and therapy can be implemented to strengthen or repair marriages, the 5 Cs Model stresses a preventive approach. The elements of the model include the Consumers (demographics and stages during the lifespan); Content of the program (theory, Relationship Assessment Questionnaires [RAQs], and the *Marriage Triangle* of factors related to marital satisfaction); Changes in circumstances that influence the marriage (e.g., remarriage and stepfamilies, military deployments, and family stress); the Context of the program (educator, setting, and educational strategies); and the influence of Culture on love, marriage, and divorce (see Figure 10.1).

Consumers—Characteristics of the Participants

Understanding the characteristics of participants in relationship and marriage education programs can help educators more effectively plan, teach, and market

Figure 10.1   5 Cs of Relationship and Marriage Education

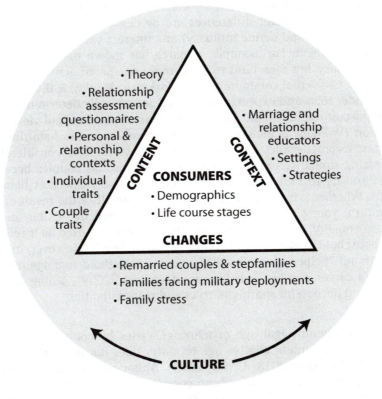

their programs. In general, little is known about the individuals and couples who participate in relationship and marriage education programs. Whereas some participants are students in educational settings, others are couples in various developmental stages of their relationship. Pertinent elements to consider include *demographic characteristics* (e.g., *gender, age, income level*, and *race/ethnicity*) and *stages during the lifespan.*

Demographic Characteristics

Gender

In a sample of 7,331 couples in a relationship formation, mate selection, and prediction of relationship quality study (Duncan, Holman, Yang, 2007), gender was a factor regarding the likelihood of couples attending a marriage preparation course. In particular, the greater the value that females placed on marriage, the more likely the couple was to participate in a marriage preparation course. A popular book, *Men Are from Mars, Women Are from Venus* (Gray 1992), suggests that men and women are quite different socially and psychologically. While some biological differences exist and some evidence of gender differences can be found in the research literature, they are outweighed by the similarities in gendered interests, abilities, and activities. The characteristics of men and women are not totally different or identical. We cannot say that all men and all women behave in a certain manner, because gender differences are by degree (e.g., ability to communicate, express feelings, and define intimacy) and interact with the culture and context of one's environment. For example, research has shown that both men and women value intimacy, but men tend to focus more on shared activities, whereas women relate more to verbal communication (Markman, Stanley, & Blumberg, 2010).

Gender roles and expectations, which are typically determined by society, play an important role in couple interaction, decision making, and views of marital satisfaction (Williams & McBain, 2006). However, because of shifting norms within the past several decades, these expectations have changed considerably in the U.S. Increasing similarity has occurred in gender roles, as couples become less structured and try to find a balance between work and home that better meets their needs. Whether it is a general freedom to be oneself or the result of the economic downturn, young adults do not want to be defined by gender and are working toward equality. In the past the term "help" was often used as it related to parenting, household chores, and providing for one's family. However, in today's society there is no "helper spouse" or "director of household management," nor is one spouse's career more or less important (Jayson, 2009). Young adults want conscious and purposeful sharing of roles and responsibilities.

Age

The minimum legal age of marriage varies by country and state; however, meeting the minimum eligible age to marry does not mean that one is ready for marriage (FindLaw, 2013; UNSD, 2008). Although some teen marriages are successful, they frequently suffer from complications, such as lack of education and poverty, and often lead to divorce (Dahl, 2010). Marriage education is available throughout the lifespan, although younger couples are more likely to participate. It is probably easier for couples with little to no relationship stress to become involved in enhancing their future or current marriages (Doherty & Anderson, 2004). In addition, more programs are available for younger participants and couples in school settings, religious settings, and state-approved premarital programs, which offer a reduction in marriage license fees for completion of a premarital education program.

Race/ethnicity

Research shows that African American couples experience some challenges in forming and maintaining marriages (Fein, Burstein, Fein, & Lindberg, 2003). However, there is considerable diversity among African American marriages that needs to be considered, such as in African, Caribbean, Hispanic, and interracial marriages (Fincham & Beech, 2010). Overall, even after taking financial resources into account, compared with whites, African Americans have a reduced likelihood to marry, if at all; lower quality marriages; more children outside marriage; higher levels of conflict; and if they marry, their marriages are more likely to end in divorce (Amato, 2011b). Gender roles are important in African American marriages. African American couples tend to be more egalitarian than white couples with both spouses sharing equitably in work outside and inside the family, as well as in child care. Most African American couples, however, would prefer a traditional division of labor, with husbands being the primary source of income and wives taking care of the family. Thus, there is a discrepancy between the ideals and realities that creates tension in many marriages. African American couples are less likely to support the lifelong norm of marriage and are also more likely to have experienced parental divorce and been part of a single-parent family while they were children. Religiosity is a major strength upon which to build marriage education programs for African Americans. Having couples form social networks in which they participate together and also address gender roles may be important themes for marriage and relationship education (Amato, 2011a).

Hispanics are diverse in their countries of origin, level of acculturation, length of U.S. residency, social class, religion, education, and other environmental factors that influence couples and families (Bean, Perry, & Bedell, 2001). Because Hispanics are the largest and fastest growing minority group in the U.S., it is important that marriage educators are prepared to work collaboratively with them (Bouchet, Torres, & Hyra, 2013). Whereas 45% of Hispanic women are married compared to 51% of white and 26% of black women, overall Hispanic women have the highest cohabitation rates at 13% compared to 10% of African Americans and 8% of whites (Bouchet et al., 2013). Hispanic family stability is influenced by immigration with 13% of immigrant Hispanics living apart from their spouses. Marriage among Hispanics may also entail different cultural traditions. It is important to understand *familismo*, a cultural value in which family relations are held with high esteem, along with respect for father figures, which is based on the conceptualization of *machismo*. Generally, Hispanic families are more likely to have traditional gender roles and a patriarchal structure. It is wise for educators working with this population to be bilingual, if possible. Although Hispanics function biculturally, their ability to be bilingual may vary. In addition, there are various groups of Hispanics who speak indigenous languages and may not be proficient in Spanish or English. The heterogeneity of the Hispanic population, along with their considerable needs, creates challenges for delivering relationship and marriage education.

Income level

Some marriage education programs developed for middle-class committed couples may not be relevant for low-income populations (Ooms & Wilson, 2004). While marriage may be declining for those who have fewer economic resources, they still desire to be married and are interested in learning how to improve their relationships through educational programs. However, many lower-income couples decide not to marry so they will not lose their government assistance (Edin & Kefalas, 2005). Regardless of race or cultural background, being poor adds considerable stress to relationships. Some of these stressors include shortage of finances, increasing debts, low levels of literacy, high unemployment, incarceration, substance abuse, depression, domestic violence, inadequate housing, and unsafe neighborhoods (Ooms, 2002; Seefeldt & Smock, 2004). Since low-income individuals and couples encounter daily challenges that interfere with their ability to make progress in their relationships, comprehensive intensive economic and support services are needed to stabilize their marriages. These challenges must be addressed in a sensitive manner. Low-income populations are often disproportionately people of color, so programs should be designed to be relevant to many different populations. Low-income persons may also have difficulties with literacy, lectures, and reading, so activities requiring responses to written materials should be kept to a minimum. Instead, programs should provide opportunities for honest dialogue, skill building, and enjoyment (Ooms & Wilson, 2004). One of the best known skill-building programs is *Prevention and Relationship Enhancement Program* (PREP), which is being gradually modified to address some of the challenges faced by low-income couples (Stanley, Markman, & Jenkins, 2004).

Consumers of Marriage and Relationship Education across the Lifespan

Various relationship and marriage education programs have been targeted for consumers at key *stages during the lifespan*. As people go through different stages of development, programs can be modified to meet their changing needs, while maintaining core values and principles. The following are some examples of issues and programs for adolescents, emerging adults, couples entering marriage, married couples, and older couples.

Adolescents

Adolescence is a time for involvement in relationship development including romantic attachments, coupled with an increasing independence from family influence. Because adolescents are also conscious of the dilemmas of marital distress and divorce, they may be more ambivalent toward relationships and generally unaware and unprepared for marriage (Popenoe & Whitehead, 2003). Almost all teens date at some point; however, teenage dating has become less common in recent years, along with a delay in sexual activity as compared to 15 years ago (Wood, Avellar, & Goesling, 2008). Teens that live with both biological parents express strong support for marriage and also consider their parents' marriages to be high quality. In addition, they increasingly approve of cohabitation before marriage and support the delay of their own marriages. Teenage boys have more positive attitudes toward marriage than teenage girls and are more likely to want to delay marriage.

As adolescents enter their dating years, some will experience relationship problems including relationship violence (Adler-Baeder, Kerpelman, Schramm, Higginbotham, & Paulk, 2007). Some conflict in adolescent relationships is common, so learning communication and relationships skills can help them negotiate a balance between closeness and independence. Healthy relationships can assist adolescents to develop self-confidence and self-esteem, provide opportunities for conflict resolution, and offer lessons on how to maintain and end relationships (Collins, 2003). Therefore, many professionals believe that adolescents should be taught relationship skills and marriage readiness when they are still in school rather than waiting until they are considering marriage (Gardner & Howlett, 2000) supporting the belief that treating a problem is more complicated than preventing one (Small & Memmo, 2004).

Emerging adults

While traditionally relationship education has more commonly been provided to couples that are preparing to marry, focusing on emerging adults helps to link early parent-child relationships to later romantic relationships and healthy marriages. Emerging adults (those approximately between the ages of 18 and 25) are becoming more independent from their parents, but do not yet have adult roles and responsibilities (Arnett, 2000, 2004, 2007). This is also a period during which risky behaviors, such as increased alcohol and drug use, "hooking-up," "friends with benefits," and involvement with multiple sexual partners can occur (Owen, Rhoades, Stanley, & Fincham, 2010). Researchers have shown that individuals in committed relationships experienced fewer mental health problems and engaged in less risky behavior than those who were single (Braithwaite, Delevi, & Fincham, 2010). Programs for emerging adults have the potential for long-term impacts in dealing with choice of partner and communication issues, which are easier to manage when being open to learning about relationships. Thus, providing relationship education to emerging adults may not only improve their current and future relationships, but also have long-term health benefits (Fincham, Stanley, & Rhoades, 2011). College students can participate in relationship education through academic course work, but it is also important to provide opportunities to emerging adults who do not pursue higher education.

An important topic in relationship education for emerging adults, as well as older adults, is commitment and its relationship to cohabitation, which has become an integral part of the marriage process (Manning & Cohen, 2012). In the U.S. cohabitation has become normative with about 60% of couples living together, and more than half of all recent marriages preceded by cohabitation. Cohabitation before engagement has been associated with an increased risk of marital distress and divorce, although this risk may be receding especially among recent marriage cohorts (Kennedy & Bumpass, 2008; Kuperberg, 2014; Manning & Cohen, 2012; Stanley, Rhoades, & Markman, 2006; Stanley, Whitton, & Markman, 2004). Taking into account the age that people begin living with someone is important because it has a considerable effect on the observed relationship between cohabitation and divorce. Not having the maturity and experience to choose compatible partners and conduct themselves in ways that will sustain long-term relationships can be problematic for emerging adults. Delaying settling down and forming coresidential unions until their mid-20s is recommended (Kuperberg, 2014). Considering context is also critical, because women who cohabited with future spouses had lower divorce rates than those who were serial cohabiters (Lichter & Qian, 2008). Moreover, marital commitment (e.g., wedding plans) prior to cohabitation was related to lower risks of marital instability among women, but not men (Manning & Cohen, 2012).

The phenomenon of cohabitation has been described as "sliding versus deciding." In other words, some couples that may not have married without first living together do so because of the inertia of cohabitation; they "slide" into marriage without making a conscious decision to marry (Stanley, Rhoades, & Markman, 2006). When examining commitment there are forces that motivate connection: *dedication* or a strong sense of couple identity with a long-term view to maintain and improve the relationship for the mutual benefit of both partners, versus *constraint* or the costs or pressures of leaving, which helps explain why some people remain in unhappy relationships (Markman et al., 2010; Stanley, 2002; Stanley et al., 2006). Research has suggested that cohabitation may be riskier for females compared to males, because husbands who cohabited were less dedicated to their wives than spouses who had not cohabited (Kline et al., 2004). Understanding relationships and commitment is important for emerging adults.

Couples entering marriage

Couples preparing to marry are often good candidates for marriage education. They are aware of the changes that are about to occur in their lives and motivated to make a smooth transition into their marriages. While the average cost of a wedding is close to $30,000 and premarital education can reduce the risk of divorce by 30%, less than a third of couples entering a first marriage seek premarital preparation (Stanley, Amato, Johnson, & Markman, 2006; The Knot, n.d.).

There are four key benefits of premarital education. Couples can (1) slow down and deliberate on elements related to marriage, (2) understand that marriage matters; (3) learn options if they need help in the future, and (4) lower their risks for subsequent marital distress or termination (Stanley, 2001). However, couples that become involved in premarital education often have a high level of satisfaction with their relationship and perceive little room for improvement. Previous research found that premarital education programs are generally effective, however, additional research involving a greater number of unpublished studies suggested that the results are more complex (Carroll & Doherty, 2003; Fawcett, Hawkins, Blanchard, & Carroll, 2010). Whereas the larger sample indicated that premarital education programs do not improve relationship quality, they do appear to improve couple communication, especially when observational measures were employed. However, couples with a higher risk of divorce were less likely to participate in premarital education. In addition, evaluation research rarely included random assignment, control or comparison groups, or long-term follow-up of participants.

Although second marriages are more likely to result in divorce compared to first marriages, they represent an understudied population. Nevertheless, a recent study noted that individuals in second marriages were less likely to receive premarital education (Doss, Rhoades, Stanley, Markman, & Johnson, 2009). Lower rates of premarital education for second marriages were attributed to a lower level of education and a lower probability of being married by a religious leader, along with a higher probability of cohabiting before marriage and having children from previous relationships. Thus, other types of support should be examined along with novel ways to recruit participants.

Married couples

Several marriage education programs encourage couples to understand and value the importance of spending time together. Economically disadvantaged couples, compared to nondisadvantaged couples, spend slightly more time together, mainly involved in leisure activities, such as watching television (Fein, 2009). While this advantage is lost when considering the differences in the number of hours they work, it persists after controlling for time devoted to work activities outside and inside the home. Couples with preschool children spend more time together, but less time alone compared to couples without young children (Fein, 2009). Thus, time use is an important factor in marriage education programs for married couples with and without children.

It is not just the quantity of time couples spend together, but the quality of time. With the natural rhythm of married lives, including busy schedules, endless tasks, and child care, it is easy to lose focus on one's marriage, resulting in less connection, spark, and intimacy. However, when partners are conscious, deliberate, and purposeful about maintaining and building a sense of connection over the years, they can create an *intentional marriage* (Doherty, 2000). *Rituals* of connection and intimacy have emotional meaning for both partners, such as romantic dinners, long talks, going for walks, and doing special activities together, and they are different from *routines*, which are things done repetitively with little emotional meaning. Rather than being on automatic pilot, Doherty suggests creating *rituals of intimacy* (e.g., dates for a special time together); *connection* (e.g., good-byes in the morning and greetings in the evening); and *community* (e.g., couple activities involved in giving and receiving support in their larger world). Talk rituals are also important, as couples need time to talk every day—uninterrupted, nonlogistical, and nonproblem-solving communication. Marriage classes can also be intentional. In the busy lives of married couples that are working and caring for children, it can be challenging to find time to attend marriage classes. Thus, marriage education programs need to be fun, couple or family oriented, flexible, and provide quality child care, if needed.

Older couples

While many older adults are divorced or have remained single, a large portion are involved in intimate relationships (Calasanti & Keicolt, 2007; King & Scott, 2005). The benefits of marriage may not be as great for older couples due to the challenge of merging households, lack of support from adult children, and the potential loss of social security (Sassler, 2010). Therefore, the proportion of older Americans who live in an intimate relationship without marriage has increased in past decades (Calasanti & Keicolt, 2007; King & Scott, 2005).

Marriage programs for older and retired couples need to focus on the issues faced by this age group. Generally, older people rate their relationship quality as high, but experts disagree on the connection between relationship quality and retirement. Whereas retired couples have greater satisfaction because of reduced pressures from other roles, some perceive that increased marital interaction after retirement can result in a loss of privacy, resulting in tension or disruption. Although there may be some lifestyle changes with retirement, it does not typically disrupt long-term behavioral or communication patterns. However, having adult children at home is inversely related to marital satisfaction for both men and women (Chalmers & Milan, 2005).

≡ Content

The content of relationship and marriage programs can vary according to the age of consumers (e.g., adolescent, young adult, or senior citizen), circumstance (e.g., first marriage or remarriage), or the state in which they live. In 2009, Florida was the first state among many to enact legislation that reduces marriage license fees for couples that complete a premarital education course either separately or as a couple. The content of this course can include instruction in conflict management, communication skills, financial responsibilities, children and parenting responsibilities, along with issues reported by married couples who seek marital or individual counseling (Florida Statutes, 2009).

Other suggestions for content include identified risk factors for relationship or marital distress. A greater number of risk factors means couples will need to work more on their relationships (Markman et al., 2010). Although understanding the following issues is important for relationships, they may not all be appropriate for marriage education settings:

- A personality that reacts strongly or defensively to problems
- Divorced parents
- Cohabitation with no clear commitment to marry
- Previous divorce of self or partner
- Children from a previous relationship
- Different religious backgrounds
- Marrying at a younger age (e.g., 18 or 19)
- Knowing each other for only a short time
- Financial difficulties
- Discrimination based on race, ethnicity, or religion

Some of the following issues are more amenable for marriage education programs:

- Negative styles of talking and fighting
- Difficulty communicating, especially in disagreements
- Trouble working as a team
- Unrealistic beliefs about relationships
- Different attitudes and expectations about important elements in life
- Low commitment to the relationship

The content in marriage and relationship education programs involves the integration of pertinent theories and *Relationship Assessment Questionnaires* (RAQs). Additionally, various *personal and relational contexts, individual traits,* and *couple traits* can be included (Larson, 2003).

Incorporation of Theory

An important component of marriage education is the incorporation of theory to guide program development. As noted in Chapter 8, theories contribute to our understanding of marriages by providing reasonable explanations of individual and family behaviors. Theories should guide the strategies utilized in marriage education courses and inform the interpretation of the outcomes of these strategies. Various theories can be integrated into marriage education programs such as the following:

Individual and family developmental theory can examine the developmental tasks of both individuals and families through the life cycle as they pertain to relationships. *Systems theory* can facilitate understanding boundaries, equilibrium, and morphogenesis. An *ecosystems approach* can clarify environmental/contextual factors influencing individuals, couples, and families. *Social exchange theory* can be used to examine the rewards, costs, and equity involved in relationships, as well as family power and family violence. *Social learning theory* suggests that patterns of behavior can be acquired through direct experience or observing others. *Attachment theory* can facilitate understanding long-term relationships between parent and child and then later adult relationships. It is believed that those who do not initially experience secure attachments may develop sensitivity to rejection in later relationships. Thus, attachment theory can be used to understand the role of attachment style with mate selection choice, commitment, jealousy, separation, or divorce (Chibucos et al., 2005; Darling & Turkki, 2009; Gibson, 2004; Ingoldsby, Smith, & Miller, 2004; Mikulincer & Shaver, 2012; Nakonezny & Denton, 2008; White & Klein, 2008).

Using Relationship Assessment Questionnaires (RAQs)

Often relationship and marriage programs in academic, faith-based, or secular settings incorporate the use of RAQs, which based on the participant's results, can help guide the planning and selection of specific course content. Since early detection, prevention, and education are important for relationships, using RAQs and having partners share their results can facilitate understanding the factors influencing a relationship (Olson, Larson, & Olson-Sigg, 2009). These questionnaires enhance awareness and facilitate subsequent discussions between partners about their strengths and weaknesses, readiness for marriage, and goals to accomplish before marriage. Predictors of marital satisfaction and stability include (1) *background and contextual factors*, such as family of origin issues, education and income, and relationship support from parents and friends; (2) *individual traits and behaviors*, such as self-esteem, interpersonal skills, and physical and emotional health; and (3) *couple interactional processes*, such as similarity of race, religion, socioeconomic status, values and attitudes, and couple communication and conflict resolution skills (Larson, 2004b). One of the biggest predictors of marital success is the compatibility of shared meaning, core values, and goals (Gottman & Silver, 1999). Examples of widely used surveys include:

- Couple Checkup (Olson et al., 2009; Olson, Olson-Sigg, & Larson, 2012)
- Premarital Preparation and Relationship Enhancement (PREPARE) (Olson, Fournier, & Druckman, 1996)
- Relationship Evaluation (RELATE) (Holman, Busby, Doxey, Klein, & Loyer-Carlson, 1997)

These questionnaires measure 85% or more of the relationship factors previously mentioned, can be completed in about an hour, and provide detailed reports on individual traits, couple traits, and relationship issues. RAQs also include information about remarriage issues. Some can be completed online or with the assistance of someone trained in using these instruments. Factors to consider in using RAQs include how you plan to use the results, the financial cost of the survey, number of class sessions for inclusion of survey findings, settings for the course, supplementary materials to be used, and the need for instructor training.

Personal and Relational Contexts

While using RAQs can show areas of similarity and dissimilarity between partners, to facilitate understanding these issues within a relationship or marriage education program, the *Marriage Triangle* can be incorporated to examine three factors that can predict future marital satisfaction. These three factors deal with *personal and relationship contexts*, *individual traits*, and *couple traits* (Larson, 2002, 2003).

Personal and relational contexts that can affect marriage relationships include age at marriage, parents' and friends' approval of the relationship, the quality of an individual's parents' relationship and other family relationships, previous marriages, children, parenting stress, and in-laws. However, we will only briefly highlight a few family of origin issues as an illustration.

Relationships are influenced by role models, particularly parents, who helped shape our views about marriage. We bring past experiences into a marriage setting (e.g., happy marriage, bitter divorce); functional or dysfunctional family dynamics (e.g., abuse, neglect, poor communication); extended family dynamics (e.g., grandparents, in-laws); and/or family stresses (e.g., death, financial difficulties, stepfamilies). Other family issues to consider include: Was the parent-child relationship satisfying, affectionate, and close, or cold, detached, and neglectful? Was family communication open and honest without being hurtful? Does an adult have a healthy sense of independence from his or her parents? Some of these situations can have more indirect than direct effects on marital satisfaction. In other words, family of origin processes (A) influence personality, self-esteem, and communication skills (B) that subsequently influence marital satisfaction in the next generation (C) (A → B → C) (Larson, 2003). Gaining a deeper understanding of one's family of origin can assist in understanding oneself and a partner better and is essential to building and maintaining a relationship. A good beginning can include sharing each partner's preferences for leisure activities; who their friends are; and how they felt in their families, schools, and communities. Further discussions could involve views about work and family, financial management, and how couples will manage the addition of children to their relationship (Larson, 2003).

Individual Traits

Individual traits can include personality and emotional health, as well as the values, beliefs, and attitudes of each partner in a relationship. Understanding oneself facilitates real sharing with a partner that can be helpful in the ongoing development of the relationship.

Personality and emotional health

Personality traits influence behaviors in relationships across one's entire lifetime, and while some traits can be relatively enduring, others may change over time (Allemand, Steiger, & Hill, 2013; Roberts, Kuncel, Shiner, Caspi, & Goldberg, 2007; Roberts & Mroczek, 2008). Generally, as people age they have increased self-confidence, warmth, self-control, and emotional stability. These changes predominate in young adulthood (age 20–40), but can also change at any age. The *Big Five Personality Traits* appear to be influential in intimate relationships. They include (1) *Extraversion*—being outgoing, enthusiastic, and social; (2) *Agreeableness*—being compassionate, cooperative, and trusting; (3) *Conscientiousness*—being industrious, dependable, and orderly; (4) *Neuroticism*—being volatile and prone to worry, anxiety, and anger; and (5) *Openness to experience*—being imaginative, unconventional, and artistic. While the first four traits make a difference in relationships, the last one seems to have little to do with success and satisfaction in close relationships (Costa & McCrae, 2003; DeYoung, Quilty, & Peterson, 2007). In addition to using scales from the *Big Five Personality Traits*, other personality measures can be incorporated into both formal and nonformal settings, such as the *Primary Colors Personality Test*, which has been adapted and published by PREP for individuals (Billings, 2004; www.prepinc.com). Along with personality, partners should consider emotional health (e.g., presence or absence of high anxiety, depression, and anger) for which insight can be gained by incorporating results from the RAQs subscales (Larson, 2003). As in personality determinants, a mutual discussion to compare similarities in personality traits and health issues can open a dialogue on what needs to be faced in the future and how to best deal with these issues.

Values, beliefs, and attitudes

A *value* is a measure of the worth or importance we attach to something that often is reflected in the way we live our lives. Values cannot be seen, but can be recognized in behaviors and actions and used to set standards of conduct, make decisions, resolve conflicts, motivate behaviors, and judge the behavior of others (Bristor, 2010; Moore & Asay, 2013). Values develop slowly throughout the lifespan and are influenced by many things, including one's culture, leaders, family members, friends, television, media, and more. While some values can change, core values do not shift much after our early twenties. Not having common core values can be a major problem for a relationship (e.g., one partner values having children and the other thinks children will impose on their lifestyle, or one partner believes that a successful career is highly desirable, whereas the other has family as a top priority [Vogt, n.d.]). While talking about differences is vital, if each partner's values are vastly different, communication may not be enough. Having these discussions before marriage is essential, because value differences are not easy to resolve after marriage. However, at times values may change due to a personal or familial experience with stress or crisis, such as a serious illness or accident that can elevate health and/or family to be a main priority and value. Values are often rank-ordered in importance, consciously or subconsciously, although one's hierarchy of values can change over time. Values that can benefit relationships are commitment, respect, intimacy, and forgiveness (Markman et al., 2010).

A *belief* is an internal feeling that something is true, even though it may be unproven or irrational. Some beliefs are dysfunctional, such as that disagreement is destructive, partners should be mind readers, a partner cannot change, sexual perfection is possible, and men and women are completely different (Larson, 2003). Core beliefs about oneself, marriage, and families can be valuable to a relationship or a risk factor if each partner has divergent beliefs (Markman et al., 2010). Individuals apply their beliefs and values through their attitudes, which can be expressed through their words and behaviors.

Participating in values clarification activities can help individuals and their partners better understand each other. Examining personal values and sharing the results with a partner, who has completed the same exercise, can be an opportunity to compare similarities and differences and then discuss what is important. Finding shared meaning can help couples discover deeper and more meaningful relationships. See Box 10.1 for *20 Things I Like to Do* and Box 10.2 for *Comparing Couple Values in Relationships*.

Box 10.1   Value Clarification Activity: 20 Things I Like to Do

Very few persons can overtly express what they value, so incorporating value clarification activities and sharing the results with a partner can provide for meaningful communication. One activity is to list *20 Things You Like To Do*. Then make a grid to one side of your list with the following headings indicating on the grid if any of the activities matches one of these categories

$ An item or activity that *costs* more than $25

A   An activity done *alone*

P   A *people*-oriented activity

I   An activity that involves *intimacy*

3   An activity that would not have been on your list *3 years ago*

R   An activity that requires some kind of *risk* (physical, mental, or emotional)

F   An item that would not have been on your *father's* list at your age

M   An item that would not have been on your *mother's* list 3 years ago

D   *Date* (approximate) when you last did this activity

After completing the list and grid, contemplate how readily you were able to list 20 things you like to do. What activities are similar to your mother and/or father, or what do you do alone, with others, or with an intimate partner? Do you participate in activities that cost money or involve risks? Have you done any of these activities recently? If not, what does that mean for you? How have the activities you value changed over time and why do you think that is the case? After you contemplate your list, share it with a partner and examine what values these activities express and what you have in common.

Adapted from Simon, Howe, & Kirschenbaum, 1972.

Box 10.2   Value Clarification Activity: Comparing Couple Values in Relationships

To understand your values and those of your partner, separately draw two concentric circles. In the inside circle list the beliefs and values that you hold dear or your core values. In the outer circle, list the beliefs and values for which you might be flexible when dealing with issues in your relationship. Think of this diagram as an egg with the inner circle as the yolk and the outer circle as the white. After you have individually completed this diagram, share it with your partner. Where do you have some commonalities and agreements? What feelings and goals do you have in common? Can you honor each other's point of view? Will you be able to compromise?

Couple Traits

Along with cohesion, intimacy, control or power, and consensus, two major couple traits include couple communication and conflict resolution skills. Communication, which is the heart of a marriage, determines how well the rest of the marriage is functioning. It involves a loving and cooperative attitude toward a partner and good communication skills. *Conflict resolution* involves effective speaking and empathetic listening skills to better resolve issues for which partners have dissimilar views (Larson, 2003).

Communication

Communication is a broad topic that includes elements such as listening vs. hearing, types and styles of communication, gender differences, and guidelines for fair fighting. There are three types of communication in which couples engage: *casual talk* when sharing details of life; *conflict talk* when dealing with inevitable disagreements; and *friendship talk*, which builds and maintains intimacy, connection, and security (Markman et al., 2010). Couples often have filters affecting what they hear and say, as well as how they interpret messages. These filters include *distractions* (lack of attention); *emotional states* (moods); *beliefs and expectations* (thoughts and expectations of the relationship); *differences in style* (being expressive or reserved); and *self-protection* (fear of rejection). Everyone has filters, which is not necessarily bad unless they distort communication. The goal is to be aware of filters and not let them hinder communication.

Marital communication is perceived as an important predictor of outcomes for newly married couples, because over time communication difficulties can erode intimate relationships. Using Gottman's four problematic ways of interacting with partners, also known as the "Four Horsemen of the Apocalypse," may be helpful in marriage education programs. They are criticism, contempt, defensiveness, and stonewalling (Gottman, 1994; Gottman, Gottman, & DeClaire, 2006; Gottman & Silver, 1999).

- *Criticism* involves attacking someone's personality or character rather than a specific behavior, usually with blame (e.g., saying "you always" or "never ____").

- *Contempt* focuses on attacking a partner's sense of self with the intent to insult or psychologically abuse him or her and is the worst of the "Four Horsemen" (e.g., name-calling, sarcasm, belligerence).

- *Defensiveness* means seeing oneself as the victim to ward off a perceived attack (e.g., cross-complaining or whining).

- *Stonewalling* involves withdrawal from the relationship to avoid conflict. Partners try to be "neutral," but stonewalling conveys disapproval, distance, separation, and disconnection (e.g., no verbal cues are given that the listener is affected by what he or she hears. In other words, it is like "talking to a stone wall").

A continuing cycle of discord and negative interactions can be difficult to stop without awareness of what is happening. Gottman, who has interviewed and studied numerous couples over the last few decades in the development of his research-based marriage education programs, has found that these behaviors identify those who would divorce with an accuracy of about 90% (Gottman et al., 2006). Compared to marriages that dissolve, lasting marriages generally have a ratio of five positive interactions between partners for every negative one (Gottman, 1994). Four strategies to facilitate positive communication are suggested: *calm down* when feeling overwhelmed; *speak non-defensively* by listening and not feeling it is necessary to defend yourself; *validation* by letting your partner know that he or she is understood; and *overlearning*—try and try again so that new skills become part of your repertoire. Creating intimacy in your relationship can be facilitated by self-disclosure. When sharing inner thoughts and dreams with a partner, there are opportunities to learn not only about oneself, but also about a partner due to the reciprocal effect of sharing inner thoughts and feelings (Gottman, 1994; Olson & Olson, 2000). Daily compliments to a spouse help to focus on his or her strengths and provide good feelings for each partner. Practicing these skills can help to improve a marriage, as well as spill over to communication styles with children and work colleagues. This is a common topic in marriage education programs with several exercises for helping partners work on improving their communication skills (Gottman et al., 2006; Gottman & Silver, 1999; Markman et al., 2010).

Conflict resolution

Conflicts are a normal part of relationships, but it is important to deal with them in a positive and constructive manner. Happily married couples behave like good friends and handle their conflicts in gentle, positive ways (Gottman et al., 2006). There are two types of conflict—either it can be *resolved* or it is *perpetual* with approximately 69% falling into the latter category (Gottman & Silver, 1999). The key to conflict resolution is listening and understanding. In other words, before asking a partner to change, he or she needs to feel understood. People can change only if they feel that they are basically liked and accepted as they are. One suggestion is to begin in a *gentle manner*. Each conflict has two points of view, so by beginning gently the core of the issue can be reached without defensive barriers. A recommendation is to use *I statements* rather than *you statements* to share a complaint. This removes blame, disarms the partner, and focuses on the primary issue and emotions of the situation. For example, partners might have a disagreement about household chores. Rather than beginning a statement saying "You didn't clean up the kitchen after you cooked dinner," an alternative would be "I get frustrated when I come home from work and the kitchen is not clean." It is also good to describe what is happening without judging; being clear, polite, and appreciative; and not storing things up like bonus miles that are cashed in all at once.

Another skill to learn when communicating about conflict is *active listening*, which is the ability to listen accurately and repeat the message that has been received. It is important to listen when a partner is speaking rather than formulating a response. This will facilitate a better understanding of each partner's point of view. To give participants some practice, a marriage educator might create some situations in order to incorporate a *gentle startup* along with the use of *I statements* and *active listening*.

There are various ways that couples manage and resolve conflicts including (1) Avoiding—stay away from arguing and refusing to challenge your partner in any meaningful way; (2) Yielding—relinquish your own goals and desires in consideration of your partner; (3) Compromising—search for a fair solution that satisfies some of both partners' needs and desires; and (4) Collaborating—consider each partner's goals and opinions and use creative problem solving to address the needs of both partners. The latter option involves seeking the partner's opinion, keeping communication open, brainstorming, and being supportive (Guerrero, Andersen, & Afifi, 2007). By incorporating meaningful communication and understanding, problems can be identified resulting in a satisfactory outcome for both partners. Using the activity in Box 10.3 on *Conflict Resolution and Change* in relationships might be helpful in a classroom or between partners.

Resolving conflict can be facilitated through the use of good communication skills. It can be helpful to set a time and place for discussion, focus only on the problem or issue that is causing tension, and talk about how each person contributes to the problem. Partners should brainstorm, analyze, and evaluate ways to resolve the conflict, agreeing on how each of them will work toward this solution, and then later sharing individual perceptions about the progress that may have been achieved (Olson & Olson, 2000). Consider asking participants to share how they saw their parents deal with conflict. In addition, participants can practice resolving a hypothetical conflict using these communication skills. Dealing with a situation that is not at the core of a couple's problems can provide good practice for other issues they suggest. Areas of conflict for partners often include managing finances, child rearing, sexuality, religion, sharing of household duties, and decision making. For example, how often and when might a couple engage in sexual relations? Will there be separate or joint checking accounts or a combination of

---

Box 10. 3   Activity: Conflict Resolution and Change

Have participants fold their arms, as they would normally do. Then ask those who have their left hand pointed upward to stand (the others would have their left hand pointed down). Look around to see how many fold their arms the same way. Ask them to describe how it feels to fold their arms the way that is normal for them. *(They usually describe it as comfortable, safe, relaxed, and the right way to do it.)*

Have participants fold their arms the opposite way and ask them to describe how it feels. *(Usually it is described as uncomfortable, strange, awkward, the wrong way to do it.)*

The point is that "my" way feels right and I will resist doing it "your" way because it feels wrong and uncomfortable. It demonstrates how our differences or preferences can become a point of conflict in relationships. It leads one person to try to change the other, because of an individual's perceptions of who is doing something the "right way." With their arms folded the uncomfortable way, ask how they think it would feel if they did it that way for a month. Would it feel different? *(They usually agree that doing it the other way would feel okay if they tried it long enough.)*

The point is that we may be able to change some things for the sake of the relationship if we care enough for the other person. Change is hard and uncomfortable because it calls us out of our comfort zone, but we can do it. Change also leads to personal growth and growing together as a couple. It is love and commitment that keep a couple together long enough to do the hard work of change.

both? How will general household chores be approached, such as child care and food preparation? (See Box 10.4 for an activity to stimulate discussion on household chores.)

Box 10.4   Division of Labor: Managing Household Tasks

Write various household tasks on ping pong balls and place them in a box. Some tasks may be written twice as both partners do them, such as working or spending quality time with their spouses and children.

Ask for two volunteers to participate in this activity. They may be two unrelated students in a class or an established couple. Read the following scenario.

> The two individuals in this relationship both have careers. Whereas one partner is an engineer, the other is a firefighter who works varying shifts. They have two children ages five and ten.

Select a ping-pong ball from the box, ask which partner will do the task indicated on the ball, and give the ball to that partner. At times, the rest of the participants may also suggest who might perform the task. (*If a ball falls to the floor, a task then "slips through the cracks." Note the task and discuss it, but do not pick up the ball.*) After the balls have all been distributed, provide an additional challenge.

> *One partner has a parent living in another city, who is having a health issue and needs assistance. Thus his/her tasks (balls) must be given to the partner remaining at home.*

Since it is most likely that the partner who has had to assume all the tasks cannot manage them all as noted by the balls falling to the floor, discuss how they can better manage these tasks by helping each other, eliminating or simplifying tasks, or getting additional assistance. Note the time involved in tasks, sharing of tasks, and gender-related preferences or assignments of tasks.

Examples of Household Tasks Indicated on Ping Pong Balls

Budget	Cook breakfast	Medical appointments for children
Pay bills	Prepare lunches	
Make investments	Cook supper	Stay home with children when they are sick
Handle insurance issues	Grocery shopping	
Repair cars	Take out garbage	Pick children up from school or child care
Wash cars	Take care of pets	
House repairs	Plan family entertainment	Bring children to school or child care
Do laundry	Children's daily homework	
Clean house	Involvement in children's school activities	Spend quality playtime with children*
Vacuum carpets		
Mop floors	Facilitate children's involvement in extracurricular activities	Spend quality leisure time with spouse*
Do dishes		
Yard work or outside work	Maintain connections with extended family birthdays, anniversaries	Maintain career*
		Community involvement
Purchase children's clothing	Care for aging parents	Shop for family presents for birthdays/holidays

*Note asterisk indicates potential duplicate tasks.

Changes

Changes occurring in couple and family circumstances can influence marriage education curricula. For example, programs have been created for those who are remarrying and forming stepfamilies, dealing with military deployments, and/or handling stress in their lives.

Changes for Remarried Couples and Stepfamilies

Remarried couples with stepchildren represent a considerable portion of the married population and have unique needs that can be addressed in marriage education programs (Adler-Baeder & Higginbotham, 2004). Approximately 75% of those who divorce will eventually remarry with approximately one-third of all weddings in the U.S. forming stepfamilies (NCFMR, 2010; U.S. Bureau of Census, 2006). While 90% of stepfamilies are created after a divorce and remarriage, some stepfamilies evolve from marriages involving a single parent after an out-of-wedlock birth or someone who is widowed. As a result, 42% of adults have a step-relationship with either a stepparent, a step or half sibling, or a stepchild (Parker, 2011). Remarriages are at a slightly greater risk of dissolution compared to first marriages. Compared to first-time married couples, remarried couples used less positive discussion, were much less negative, but were more likely to withdraw from interaction or avoid potentially difficult topics, such as negotiating parenting (Halford, Nicholson, & Sanders, 2007).

Stepfamilies are complex and have developmental differences compared to couples and families in first marriages. Whereas divorce, cohabitation, and serial transitions in and out of marriage are now typical of family life in the U.S., there are significant consequences for children. The more parental transitions and partnerships children experience, the lower is their emotional, psychological, and academic well-being (Amato, 2010; Cherlin, 2009). Moreover, stepfamilies have few institutional supports; may face stigmatization; have issues regarding financial management; and deal with unique issues regarding family rules, boundaries, and parenting decisions. Because the quality of the stepparent-stepchild relationship influences conflicts and relationship quality, priority should be given to the marital relationship and building its strengths (Adler-Baeder & Higginbotham, 2004; Bray & Kelly, 1998). Unfortunately, most couples in stepfamilies do not seek premarital education. Furthermore, the unique issues faced by remarried couples are not often addressed in most marriage education courses (Ganong & Coleman, 2004). Design elements of remarriage courses include the incorporation of a theoretical framework and research-based information; a variety of teaching methods and aides for facilitators and participants; recruitment and implementation materials; and evaluation of programs including the use of control groups and effects over time.

Examples of programs include *Designing Dynamic Stepfamilies: Bringing Pieces to Peace* (Taylor & Taylor, 2003) (www.designingdynamicstepfamilies.com); *Smart Steps for Adults and Children in Stepfamilies* (Adler-Baeder, 2001; www.stepfamilies.info/smart-steps.php); and *Stepping Stones for Stepfamilies* (Olsen, 1999; www.ncsu.edu/ffci/publications/1999/v4-n3-1999-winter/showcase-usa.php). *Smart Stepfamilies* (Deal, 2006; www.smartstepfamilies.com) is a practical program to help couples dealing with the common struggles of stepparenting by providing information for successful family living and to train faith-based and other professionals to assist stepfamilies. Providing marriage education to couples forming stepfamilies and giving them additional content specific to their needs can reduce risks for couples and children after divorce.

Changes for Couples Facing Military Deployment

Since September 11, 2001, the U.S. military and their families have experienced an increase in the number and frequency of military deployments. While separations have become routine for military couples, they have not prevented military couples from experiencing happy, healthy, and successful relationships. However, it is clear that military relocations, separations, and reunions add stress to relationships with infidelity a continual concern for both spouses (NHRMC, 2007). Communication is a critical issue when spouses are deployed, with 17% reporting it as their primary challenge. While technology has greatly assisted communication, any lapse of communication can result in concern regarding the well-being of the soldier or family members at home. For some soldiers, access to communications technology may be an issue, while others do not want to communicate for fear that doing so will make them sad or homesick. Knowing what information to communicate or omit, so as not to create worry for the partner, becomes a dilemma. When one spouse is deployed, it creates stress for the spouse at home, who takes on additional roles (Everson, Darling, & Herzog, 2013). Moreover, when a spouse returns, roles shift to accommodate the returning soldier.

Changes for Couples Facing Stress

Stress, which exists both outside and inside relationships, can influence marital functioning. This can occur both directly and indirectly through the quality of marital communication, the partners' well-being, and the time the partners spend together (Bodenmann, Ledermann, & Bradbury, 2007). For example, work, financial, or health stress is known to have a negative influence on marital quality or satisfaction (Howe, Levy, & Caplan, 2004; Neff & Karney, 2004, 2007). However, this external stress can also influence marital communication, relationship stress, and relationship quality (Ledermann, Bodenmann, Rudaz, & Bradbury, 2010). One's own external stress can spill over into a close relationship by intensifying one's feelings of relationship stress. In other words, low relationship stress and a high level of positive communication are important in relationships. *The Couples Coping Enhancement Training Program* (CCET) has been designed to help both partners develop new adaptive behaviors and strengthen existing ones (Bodenmann & Shantinath, 2004). Programs for couples that incorporate stress and coping skills in distress prevention help to manage stress inside the relationship, enhance marital communication, and facilitate long-lasting relationships.

≡ Context

Knowing the "content" to include in a relationship or marriage education program is not enough; understanding the "context" of teaching is also critical. What does it take to be a *marriage/relationship educator*? What *settings* can be used to teach about relationships and marriage? What *programs*, *methods*, and *strategies* are helpful? In addition to knowing about marriage and relationships, an educator also needs to know how to develop and teach programs.

Marriage and Relationship Educators

Marriage educators offer programs, services, and resources to support pre-marital and married couples and other kinds of intimate partners in building healthy relationships (Boyd, Hibbard, & Knapp, 2001). At times marriage educators are also couple facilitators, which means they need to be able to facilitate a discussion about marital issues in a safe and respectful environment. It is important to be mindful of the *Domains of Family Practice Model* (DFP) (Myers-Walls et al., 2011). Relationship and marriage educators are not therapists and should not perceive that their role is to fix people's problems. Participants are there to create solutions for their own problems. Most educators are familiar with the issues of their participants, but also need training to enhance their competence in interacting with them. A marriage educator may need certain skills, such as making connections between partners, empathizing and validating feelings, staying real and specific (define problem issues so that the couple has something concrete to grasp), exploring different points of view, and recognizing cultural differences. It may also be necessary for educators to practice these skills to enhance their abilities to educate and facilitate (Gottman, 2007). Gender may also be an issue. Some participants, especially men, may respond differently to a male or female educator, so having a male-female team of co-educators may be helpful (Hawkins, Carroll, Doherty, & Willoughby, 2004). A male-female team should respect each other as equals and be role models for the attitudes, skills, and behaviors being advocated within the program (Ooms & Wilson, 2004). The religious background of the educator may also influence the transmission of information about marriage. In other words, messages can be enhanced or inhibited by the messenger.

The quality of leaders or facilitators is a major key to the success of a marriage education program, especially with low-income participants. It is important that they be genuine, caring, respectful, and positive, as well as realistic role models (Ooms & Wilson, 2004). Qualities of marriage educators or facilitators, which may relate to their personality and training, include individuals who are:

- Able to manage group dynamics and handle any negative energy, individuals, or couples who want to monopolize the sessions.
- Committed, dependable, prepared, and punctual.
- Creative and able to enhance the curriculum through materials and activities.
- Energetic and engaging over multiple sessions.
- Aware that adults have different learning styles.
- Open, honest, and self-aware, as well as able to connect and empathize with participants.
- Respectful of boundaries, able to establish ground rules, and keep participants focused on skill building and not problem sharing/solving.

- Able to deal with issues and people with a sense of humor.
- Humble about the personal acquisition of skills being a work in progress that continues to evolve (NHMRC, 2007).

While various professionals serve as marriage educators, some states have laws that indicate who can provide marriage education within specific settings. For example, in Florida individuals electing to participate in premarital education in order to receive a discount on their marriage license need to choose from certain qualified instructors including a licensed psychologist, clinical social worker, marriage and family therapist, mental health counselor, an official representative of a religious institution, or other providers, such as school counselors who are certified to offer these courses (Florida Statutes, 2009). Because each state has different policies regarding whom they perceive as qualified to teach premarital and marriage education courses, attention needs to be given within individual states to promote Certified Family Life Educators for this important role.

Settings for Marriage Education

Government initiatives

Governmental initiatives to strengthen marriages through a variety of programs have been increasing (Brotherson & Duncan, 2004). However, there has been considerable controversy over the appropriateness of government intervention in marriage. Some believe that government has no right to be involved in private family matters, whereas others believe that the negative effects of single parenthood on child well-being justify government involvement (Ooms & Wilson, 2004). Marriage education efforts, which have become increasingly popular, have evolved from policy initiatives related to poverty reduction. To promote healthy marriages and fatherhood, the Federal Deficit Reduction Act of 2005 made available $150 million for each year from 2006–2010 for competitive research and demonstration projects to test promising approaches to encourage healthy marriages and promote involved, committed, and responsible fatherhood (ACF, 2005). This funding has resulted in educational initiatives and the strengthening of marriage. In many states, legislators and governors have also become involved in efforts to promote premarital education, relationship education in high schools, and covenant marriage (Brotherson & Duncan, 2004). For example, three states (Louisiana, Arizona, and Arkansas) have passed covenant marriage laws to strengthen the marriage bond by promoting premarital education/counseling and making divorce more difficult to obtain (NHMRC, 2010). Only a small percentage of couples (1 to 3%) choose this controversial option.

Community marriage initiatives

Over the past decade there has been an explosion of community-based initiatives in marriage education programs with 40 states creating programs to support marriages and strengthen couple relationships (Dion, 2005). Family professionals have become partners in many community initiatives. Often when there are perceived difficulties in marriages and families at local, state, and national levels, various elements of the community, such as business, government, education, and clergy take the initiative to improve marriages and the lives of family members. Some of these nationally visible programs and their goals include (1) *First Things First*, to strengthen families and increase involvement of fathers with their children; (2) the *Oklahoma Marriage Initiative*, to reduce the divorce rate and strengthen families; (3) *Healthy Relationships California*, to teach couples and individuals communication and conflict-management skills with classes available in English, Spanish, Chinese, and Korean; (4) *Stronger Families*, to facilitate life-changing opportunities for couples and families by promoting healthy and loving relationships and providing support at each stage of the marital journey; and (5) *Marriage Savers*, to preserve, strengthen, and restore marriages. There is no one specific plan for individual programs, as they are dependent on the needs of the population, resources available, and expectations of those organizing the program. No single type of organization (e.g., non-profit, for-profit, education, faith-based, military) is the best option for providing marriage and relationship education, as each has strengths and weaknesses. Therefore, programs that create collaborative partnerships with community-based service providers have an advantage with recruitment, which is essential for voluntary programs (Hawkins & Ooms, 2010). Community marriage initiatives hold considerable promise for the future. Further information on programs in communities in your area can be obtained by contacting the National Association for Relationship and Marriage Education (NARME, www.narme.org).

Cooperative Extension Service (CES) initiatives

The Cooperative Extension Service, created by the U.S. Congress, has a long history of community-based involvement in family life education and has developed research-based resources in marriage and couples education to reach the population beyond college campuses (Goddard & Olsen, 2004). The CES generally has taken a pre-marriage approach to their programs, but recognizes that relationship education is also for already married and remarried couples or divorcing parents. CES has developed numerous resources in marriage and couples education including fact sheets, programs (e.g., *CoupleTALK: Enhancing Your Relationship* from Kansas State University; *Married and Loving It!* from the University of Idaho), web-based materials, models, and summaries of community and/or state initiatives (e.g., Oklahoma, Utah, Florida, Michigan, and Alabama) (Goddard & Olsen, 2004).

Academic initiatives

Research has indicated that high school students are just as likely as college students to perceive that preparation for marriage is important. However, they are less likely to be informed about marriage education programs (Silliman & Schumm, 2004). High schools and colleges often provide marriage education programs for their students, with programs for adolescents becoming more frequent as a prevention approach to strengthen current relationships and future marriages. Whereas adolescents preferred friends, parents, and personal experience as sources of knowledge about marriage, they indicated some interest in marriage and couple programs depending on their duration and cost, with a preference for programs during the engagement period. Programs should consider both *nonformal* youth development programs, as well as *formal* marriage education classes. A recent study of 340 diverse high school students who were involved in a marriage education program indicated that participants experienced an increase in their relationship knowledge and their ability to identify unhealthy relationships, more realistic beliefs about relationships, and lower levels of verbal aggression (Adler-Baeder et al., 2007).

Some examples of programs for youth include *Love U2: Increasing Your Relationship Smarts* (Pearson, 2004); *The Art of Loving Well* (Ellenwood, 1998); *Building Relationships* (Olson, Defrain, & Olson, 1999); *PAIRS for Peers* (Gordon, 2000); and *Connections: Relationships and Marriage* (Kamper 2003, 2011). *Connections* is a popular program for students in grades 11 and 12 with goals to promote self-understanding and self-esteem; healthy dating relationships and values; effective communication and conflict resolution skills; and awareness of skills needed for successful relationships and marriages (www.dibbleinstitute.org/connections-relationships-marriage). While students involved in the *Connections* program only improved slightly in their knowledge about relationships, their use of violence decreased, their communication with parents increased, and their attitudes toward marriage were more positive (Gardner, Giese, & Parrott, 2004). These programs offer students an opportunity to think deliberately about meaningful relationships and how they are developed and sustained, as well as how they dissolve. However, in general, these programs do not adequately cover premarital predictors of marital satisfaction and stability (Olson-Sigg, 2004).

College students may have certain advantages, such as education and income, but they experience multiple relationships issues (romantic and non-romantic) that can cause considerable levels of distress (Darling, McWey, Howard, & Olmstead, 2007). Various colleges and universities offer academic courses to prepare students to find compatible partners, face challenges, and experience greater relationship satisfaction (Nielsen, Pinsof, Rampage, Solomon, & Goldstein, 2004). Focusing on college students can be constructive, because they are more likely to have some dating experience, are nearing the age when they will seek a life partner, can have more open discussions of sexuality without parental concerns, and have not necessarily begun selecting a partner because marriage is not imminent. Many college courses are primarily academic and do not focus on the goal of marriage preparation. However, one such course, *Marriage 101: Building Loving and Lasting Partnerships*, integrates academic methods with experiential and self-discovery methods (Nielsen et al., 2004). The program includes lectures, discussions, readings, journaling, experiential exercises, video clips, mentor-couple interviews, parent interviews, term papers, and program evaluation. While students show enthusiasm for such a course, evaluation is often impeded due to a lack of control groups, the length of time prior to marriage, and the difficulty in showing the long-term benefits of a marriage education course.

Religious or spiritual initiatives

Relationship, premarital, and marriage education is frequently offered within religious or spiritual communities. In earlier years couples often went for an appointment with a clergyperson prior to their wedding ceremony. Whether it was one visit or a few, clergy were often the only persons engaged in guiding new couples in their transition into marriage. However, more programs in religious settings have developed over the years. *Christian PREP* (The Prevention and Relationship Enhancement Program) is one such program that has a clear commitment to teaching a Christian model of marriage while integrating research on marriage and relationships. CPREP focuses on teaching couples how to communicate effectively; solve problems; manage conflicts; and preserve and enhance love, commitment, and friendship. CPREP is based on safety in terms of how couples treat each other while developing a fundamental sense that the marriage has a secure base of commitment (Barnes, Stanley, & Markman, 2004).

Military initiatives

The military has recognized that the well-being of their soldiers is influenced by the quality of their home life, especially when military couples are at high risk for marital problems that are exacerbated by deployments and combat. Over the past decade, PREP was widely used with married couples in all branches of the military. An adaptation of the PREP entitled *Building Strong and Ready Families* (BSRF) was implemented by Army chaplains. Evaluation studies indicated that marriage education has been well received by military couples with significant improvements for both men and women (Stanley et al., 2005). Military couples showed reductions in negative communications and gains in overall confidence in the future of their relationships. Using trained Army chaplains was particularly effective, as they were known and trusted by the couples and could adapt the educational program to their participants with culturally appropriate examples and stories. After deployment, marriage education programs need to help couples renegotiate their relationship, as they may be struggling with communication, balancing responsibilities, decision-making in the relationship, or other mental health problems such as Post Traumatic Stress Disorder (PTSD) or brain injuries (Krill, 2010).

Strategies for Marriage Education

There are many organizations providing relationship and marriage education. Whereas some participants may prefer to go to a faith-based institution or school in their vicinity, others may reject going to either of these locations based on negative past experiences. Thus, having seminars and programs in the community, work place, health-care centers, or military settings may be helpful in reaching participants who might not engage in marriage education in more traditional settings. On the other hand, while having marriage education programs on military bases may be convenient, at times soldiers and their spouses or families prefer to go off the base for privacy reasons.

Effective, flexible delivery of relationship education is recommended. Some couples prefer face-to-face relationship education because they value group interaction, whereas others may prefer modes that are more convenient or private, such as online courses, DVDs, and self-directed materials (Halford, Moore, Wilson, Farrugia, & Dyer, 2004). Marriage educators need to be flexible and open to find the best educational settings and delivery modes within the societal context of their communities.

Marriage education can occur in individual, dyadic, group, or mass settings. Whether through public awareness spots on television, online courses, or community resource centers, the potential to reach a large number of participants can shape values, attitudes, and behaviors that promote healthy marriages. Classroom strategies should be varied to meet the needs and learning styles of participants. While some may prefer lectures, others value discussion or experiential learning activities. Depending on the culture and age of the audience, some may not want to engage in self-disclosure. Thus, culturally-aware educators will need to talk to community members to learn how to best integrate participants' needs into their curriculum. After completion of the program, various modes of contact may be required to sustain the learning that occurred. Using e-mail or social media with participants may facilitate ongoing contact, sharing, and support.

There are multiple designs and methods for marriage preparation and enrichment programs that integrate a variety of strategies. Many programs use RAQs in combination with other techniques such as the *Fit to Be Tied Program*, which not only includes didactic instructions/group exercises, but also mentor couples and homework communication exercises using PREPARE (Wages & Darling, 2004). In addition to program instructors, mentor couples (who were trained married couples within the church setting) were paired with premarital couples. These mentor couples were effective in identifying the problems premarital couples were facing and modeling how difficult issues could be resolved. They also encouraged and challenged prospective spouses to adjust some of their behaviors. Nearly 91% of the premarital participants indicated that interacting with their mentor couple provided them with a more realistic view of marriage. In addition to mentor couples and didactic sessions, participants were given homework exercises in which they applied the communication skills learned in class to resolve differences and areas of indecision. Of the participants, 80% indicated that these exercises helped them change the ways they related to each other. However, about one-third of the participants did not take the homework exercises seriously. Formative and summative evaluation methods were used to make changes during and after the program (Wages & Darling, 2004).

⬛ Culture

Culture is the total way of life of a group of people—the customs, beliefs, values, attitudes, and communication patterns that characterize a group and provide a common sense of identity. Taken together, these components form a way of interpreting reality that is shared among members of a culture. By exploring the role of culture, not only can different values be found, but a critical examination can also be initiated about how these values influence behaviors.

Globally, many dimensions of marriage and family life have changed over the past century. There has been an increase in the age of marriage, children's involvement in mate selection, premarital sex, and contraceptive use. Fertility rates have declined along with changing relationships between women and men. In general, an emphasis on freedom, equality, and individualism has continued to spread throughout the world (Jayakody, Thornton, & Axinn, 2008). Although families have experienced similar changes, these changes have not resulted in a single global family because there are so many differential shifts in beliefs, norms, and governmental policies.

Marriages or partnerships exist in all societies, in some form, but while it is mainstream in the U.S., it may be quite different in other cultures. Globally people marry for many reasons, including legal, social, emotional, financial, spiritual, and religious. While some cultures place a primary emphasis on the marital bond, others value the parent-child bond. Love, dating, marriage, and divorce vary in different cultures based on religion, as well as patriarchal or matriarchal traditions. While research on other cultural groups is important, we should not draw unwarranted conclusions about individuals based on their group membership. Cultural insight comes from awareness of individual differences within social constructs. Using an ecosystems approach to examine marriages and marital quality can facilitate understanding the systems related to one's individual context, couple context, family background, and sociocultural context (Darling & Turkki, 2009; Duncan, Holman, & Yang, 2007). (See Chapter 8 on the Family Ecosystems Framework.)

Culture is an important source of information about the value of relationships and marriage. Our American culture both values and devalues marriage in several ways. Although our value of marriage may be indicated by a majority of Americans eventually marrying, there is also a growing number of individuals who have chosen singlehood as a viable lifestyle, as well as couples who cohabit as an alternative to marriage. In addition, many marriages end in divorce. While many couples spend a considerable amount of time, effort, and money on weddings, much less time and energy are spent on preparing for the actual marriage. Often there is a belief that "love conquers all," but certain skills are also needed to maintain a healthy relationship (Williams, 2004).

We live in a world that generally values love; however, there are widespread international differences. When responding to a Gallop Poll asking a question about feelings of love during the previous day, 70% of the respondents in 136 countries said that they had experienced love the previous day, whether it might be from a child, parent, family member, or a good friend. However, feelings of love vary in different cultures. Whereas the countries with the greatest feelings of love were the Philippines (93%), Rwanda (92%), and Puerto Rico (90%), those countries with the lowest feelings of love were Moldova (46%), Azerbaijan (47%), and Tajikistan (47%). In the U.S., 81% perceived feelings of love the previous day (Stevenson & Wolfers, 2013). Across the world the widowed and divorced were less likely to experience love and married couples felt it more than single persons. Those people who cohabited reported greater feelings of love than those who were married. Since love is often a prerequisite to relationships and marriage, these cultural differences can be an indicator of bonds, reciprocity, resiliency, and support.

Marriage customs and practices vary quite widely across cultures. In some parts of the world, heterosexual marriages are the cornerstone of married life (e.g., Egypt and Turkey), while in many developed societies (e.g., U.S., Israel, Japan, Italy, Germany, and Norway), there is a mixture of family forms (e.g., single parent, cohabitation, blended families, extended families, and same-sex families) (Gore & Gore, 2002; Roopnarine & Gielen, 2005). Traditional marriage arrangements are being abandoned at a faster pace, as noted by the large increase in birth rates to unmarried mothers in 2007—66% in Iceland, 55% in Sweden, 54% in Norway, and 46% in Denmark with the U.S. rate of 40% (Friedman, 2009). In comparison, China, with its one-child policy and preference for sons, is experiencing a "marriage squeeze" in which young men are having a difficult time finding a wife. While some marriage customs change, the pace is varied. For example, arranged marriages are generally decreasing as young people are incorporating personal choice and pairing is increasingly monogamous (Adams, 2004). However, in some countries arranged marriages are still common (e.g., Asia, Middle East, and Africa), with either a dowry paid to future grooms (e.g., parts of Asia and Africa) and/or a bride price, which is paid by a groom's family to the bride's family (e.g., parts of Asia and Africa) (Francoeur & Noonan, 2004). While officially there is a law in India banning the payment of a dowry, it is still part of the custom resulting in numerous dowry deaths in India (8,391 in 2010). A woman is regarded as a goddess, but can also be burned alive if her family does not continue to satisfy the demands of her husband and his family (Bedi, 2012).

Divorce practices are quite variable in different countries and by gender. There have been some dramatic changes in divorce in Argentina (800% increase between 1960 and 2000) and China (500% increase since 1978) (Jelen, 2005; Singh, 2005; UN, 2008). These dramatic increases are due to changes in family economics, perception of marriage as no longer being a "sacred pairing" (e.g., India) and the institution of no-fault divorce (e.g., China in 1980) (Sheng, 2005). While in France a majority of divorces are mutually initiated, in the U.S. women typically initiate the divorce process. Divorce in Ireland, which only became legal in 1996, is possible only if a couple has been separated for four years after the breakdown of their marriage (Kelly, 2004). The divorce process in Islam is complex, so it is difficult to say whether the rate is low or high (Modo, 2005). Muslim countries allow no-fault divorce for men, but wives have to give specific justifications. A husband may divorce his wife by stating "I divorce you," three times even if there are no specific reasons for the divorce. This must be done during a three-month waiting period during which time the man must feed and clothe his wife, but have no sexual relations. However, a wife may ask for a divorce only under specific circumstances, such as her husband's absence for a year or more, imprisonment for three or more years, or mental or physical illness (Ahmed, 2005). In China, new tax laws on the sale of second homes, which would force married homeowners to pay sizeable taxes, have resulted in long lines of happily married couples at local divorce registries (Jiang, 2013). China's marriage law allows for divorce if couples sign an agreement, present themselves at a registry office, and pay $1.50. For some couples, saving thousands of dollars is worth getting a divorce, because many young couples have two homes (Jiang, 2013).

Learning about love, marriage, and divorce in other cultures is not necessarily considered part of the marriage education curriculum within the U.S. because focusing on other issues, such as communication, conflict resolution, and decision-making have a higher priority. However, educators must be vigilant in their consideration of the cultural context regarding consumers, course content, and context. We live in a pluralistic society in which there are many immigrants who bring relationship and marriage values, as well as customs, from other countries. There are also cultural variations in the U.S. based on geographical location, race/ethnicity, religion, age, and gender. Gaining the realization of the importance of culture is more effective when we examine other cultures. The role of culture and gaining a cross-cultural perspective can widen our understanding of others and ourselves and make us more effective educators.

SUMMARY

As noted by the 5 Cs of Relationship and Marriage Education Model, there are many factors that influence the design and implementation of marriage education programs including knowledge of the consumers, content, changes, context, and culture. While the glamour and excitement of getting married may occupy the thoughts of couples planning for a wedding, working to establish a healthy and stable marriage before and after the ceremony is an important goal. There are several marriage education programs that can help provide the knowledge and skills needed to sustain a happy and satisfying marriage. Marriage education can empower individuals and couples to form healthy relationships and maintain stable families for the well-being of adults, children, and communities. People may get divorced thinking that they chose the wrong partner, but then remarry and find themselves facing the same problems, but now with a different partner. Thus, it is important to understand the influence of demographic factors and stages of the life cycle, along with personal and relational contexts, individual traits, and couple traits. As cultural influences and the needs and circumstances in life evolve, staying attuned to changes in individuals, relationships, and their environments is critical. Saying "I do" is just the beginning as couple relationships involve a continual process of becoming "us."

QUESTIONS AND ISSUES FOR DISCUSSION

1. What are people at your stage of the life looking for in relationships?
2. What can universities, communities, faith communities, and health-care centers do to motivate individuals and couples to participate in relationship and marriage education?
3. What other settings could be used to provide relationship and marriage education?
4. Why is it important to have a trained leader for marriage education courses? Is having a satisfactory marriage sufficient?
5. How would you select a good time to communicate about sensitive issues with a partner? What factors would you consider and what time would you suggest?
6. What messages about marriage, love, and dating are portrayed in the media?
7. What are the laws in your state regarding marriage in general, gay unions/marriage, and divorce? Are there any initiatives for changing these laws?
8. What kinds of messages, traditions, and rituals will you take from your family of origin into your marriage relationship?
9. What are some issues couples might encounter in "Peer Marriages," "Alone Together Marriages," and "Living Apart Relationships"?

ACTIVITIES

1. Invite a panel of engaged couples to class to share what is important in relationships.

2. Invite a panel of couples at different stages of the life cycle to share what is important in relationships.

3. Discuss with a partner your feelings about a current event, an important event from your childhood, and a future goal about which you feel passionate. What did you learn about your partner from sharing these thoughts?

WEB RESOURCES

National Association for Relationship and Marriage Education (NARME)
www.narme.org

NARME is a national association formed to represent the interests and serve the needs of relationship, marriage, and family educators by providing ongoing professional training; hosting an annual conference featuring best practices in the field; disseminating timely and relevant research; facilitating collaboration among healthy marriage, responsible fatherhood, and other family allies; and supporting public policy that strengthens families.

National Extension Relationship and Marriage Education Network (NERMEN)
www.nermen.org

NERMEN provides research-based resources and promotes partnerships to advance the knowledge and practice in relationship and marriage education. It constitutes a nation-wide outreach through Extension Specialists and Educators in partnership with agencies and organizations at the national, state, and community levels that support individuals and couples preparing for, developing, and enriching healthy relationships and healthy marriages.

National Healthy Marriage Resource Center (NHMRC)
www.healthymarriageinfo.org

NHMRC is a clearinghouse for high quality, balanced, and timely information and resources on healthy marriage. The NHMRC's mission is to be a first stop for information, resources, and training on healthy marriage for experts, researchers, policy makers, media, marriage educators, couples and individuals, program providers, and others. With support from the Administration for Children and Families' Office of Family Assistance, Annie E. Casey Foundation, Johnson Foundation, Kohler Foundation, the WinShape Foundation, and others, the NHMRC helps those who want to learn more about healthy relationships, marriage, and marriage education.

Smart Marriages
www.smartmarriages.com

Smart Marriages: The Coalition for Marriage, Family, and Couples Education is a special interest group whose members believe that family breakdown can be reduced through education and information. Smart Marriages facilitates a network of marriage professionals that constitutes a coalition for marriage, family, and couples education. Their website contains an archive of the coalition's newsletters, a directory of programming resources, advocacy information, and general articles and information.

RESOURCES: PREMARITAL AND MARITAL ASSESSMENT QUESTIONNAIRES

Couple Checkup
www.couplecheckup.com

Couple Checkup is an online couple assessment tool for marriage and relationship enrichment, which can be used alone or in combination with enrichment books, seminars, or marriage retreats. It is a scientifically-based assessment that identifies relationship strengths and weaknesses across key relationship areas, including communication, conflict resolution, financial management, relationship roles, affection and sexual relationships, couple closeness and flexibility, family closeness and flexibility, and personality.

PREPARE/ENRICH (Premarital Preparation and Relationship Enhancement)
www.prepare-enrich.com

PREPARE/ENRICH is a customized couple assessment completed online that identifies a couple's strength and growth areas. It is one of the most widely used programs for premarital counseling and premarital education. It is also used for marriage counseling, marriage enrichment, and dating couples considering engagement. Based on a couple's assessment results, a trained facilitator provides 4–8 feedback sessions in which the facilitator helps the couple discuss and understand their results as they are taught proven relationship skills.

RELATE (Relationship Evaluation)
www.relate-institute.org

RELATE is a comprehensive premarital/marital assessment questionnaire. This new version of the questionnaire was designed for use with individuals or couples who are single and unattached, steady dating, engaged, cohabiting, married, or contemplating remarriage. Tens of thousands of couples and individuals have benefited from these questionnaires during the past 20 years.

Approaches to Parenting Education

It's 3:00 AM and your 3-week-old son has been crying and fussing since 11:00 PM. You have fed him, changed him, and rocked him. You are out of ideas and patience. What does he need?

Your day-care provider pulls you aside and informs you that your 3-year-old has been biting the other children. Is this normal? Why is she doing it? What can you do to stop it?

Your 13-year-old has started to come home after his curfew. He has become sullen and uncommunicative. When he does talk to you, it is usually with disrespect or annoyance. The more you push him, the more he pulls away. What can you do to best deal with the situation?

Your daughter has just started her first year of college at a school 500 miles away. How involved should you be in her daily life? Is it ok to text her every day?

How does a parent best respond to these situations? Are there books that have all the answers, or do parents just "know" what to do? Can you take a class to learn how to be a better parent?

The Importance of Parents and Parenting Education

Being a parent is one of the hardest jobs in the world. Imagine seeing this job description in the paper:

> Wanted: Caregiver to rear one or two children from birth to maturity. The job is a seven-day-a-week, twenty-four-hour-a-day position. No salary or benefits, such as sick or holiday pay, no retirement plan. The caregiver must supply all living expenses for self and children, and in the event of any absence, even for a few minutes with younger children, must supply substitute care. There is no opportunity to meet child or children in advance of taking the position to determine compatibility. Motivation for the job and satisfaction in it must come from within the applicant, as neither children nor society regularly express gratitude and appreciation. (Brooks, 2011, p. 3)

Despite the challenges, parenting can be one of life's most rewarding experiences, but the knowledge and skills needed for good parenting do not necessarily come naturally. Most parents do not instinctively know how to be a parent or what to do when it comes to discipline, nurturing, toilet training, adolescent mood swings, or any of the many other issues that arise through the child-rearing years. Societal changes have made it more difficult to rely on parenting techniques from the past. The rapid pace at which these changes occur leave children facing issues their parents never imagined. Fortunately, today's parents have the benefit of unprecedented access to parenting resources and supports. There is ample research identifying what children and parents need for optimal development and demonstrating the effectiveness of parent education in supporting and influencing child and parent-wellbeing (Bornstein, 2002; Child Trends, 2009; Holmes, Galovan, Yoshida, & Hawkins, 2010; Karoly et al., 2005; Mbwana, Terzian, & Moore, 2009; McGroder & Hyra, 2009; Weiss & Lee, 2009). Parenting education can help build the skills of parents. Parents have multiple options for accessing parenting information including books, in-person and online classes, websites, and even mobile apps.

Parents have tremendous influence on a child's cognitive, social, emotional, and physical development making parenting education all the more important. "Children are affected by who their parents *are* (e.g., gender, age, race/ethnicity, intelligence, education levels, temperament); what parents *know* (e.g., child development, normative child behavior); what parents *believe* (e.g., attitudes toward child rearing); what parents *value* (e.g., education, achievement, obedience, interpersonal relationships); what parents *expect* of their children (e.g., age/developmentally-appropriate expectations for behavior, achievement expectations); and what parents ultimately *do* (e.g., parenting practices, overall parenting styles) (McGroder & Hyra, 2009). Family characteristics and parenting in the first years of life (including sensitive caregiving, cognitive stimulation, and positive involvement) have been shown to predict pre-academic skills and socio-emotional development throughout the preschool years, with the estimated effects of parenting often larger than the estimated effects of child care (NICHD Early Child Care Research Network, 2003).

Parental behavior is directly correlated with outcomes for children (Reeves & Howard, 2013). Parents who score highly on measures of both warmth and control have children who are happier and more competent (Baumrind, 1991; Baumrind & Black, 1967). Children are more socially skilled later in life if they have secure attachments to their parents in infancy (Sroufe, 2002). Society benefits from parenting education as well. Effective parenting education programs can provide economic benefits in the form of tax saving by reducing the need for remedial education and social programs, while increasing productivity provided by a better-prepared workforce (McGroder & Hyra, 2009).

Federal, state, and local agencies often fund parenting education programs as a way to strengthen families and prevent costly and undesirable outcomes such as child abuse and neglect. The Substance Abuse and Mental Health Services Administration (SAMHSA) funds many family strengthening programs as a way to prevent substance abuse and mental health problems. Similarly, the Office of Juvenile Justice and Delinquency Prevention invests in parenting education as a way to prevent delinquency (McGroder & Hyra, 2009). These efforts are centered on the prevention of undesirable outcomes. While this is certainly a needed approach, it is important that attention and funding also be provided to programs and approaches that focus on primary prevention and the promotion of positive parenting practices. The primary prevention approach will be discussed in more detail later in the chapter.

═ Societal Changes and Impacts

The rapidly changing pace of today's society has caused modern-day parents to face challenges unparalleled in previous generations, increasing the need for both formal and nonformal parenting education. There are greater influences on children originating from outside of the home. The media is filled with images of sex and violence and promotes a culture that glorifies celebrity and beauty. Families are impacted by unemployment, substance abuse, and domestic violence. Parents also find themselves seeking guidance on how to explain terrorism and random violence to children following events like 9/11 and the shooting at Sandy Hook Elementary School.

Changing demographics have revealed other needs; increasing numbers of grandparents are raising their grandchildren during a time intended for retirement. The mobile nature of our society means that families are more likely to live away from extended family members, which weakens their support network. Work-life balance continues to be a struggle with 53% of working parents with children under the age of 18 saying it is difficult for them to balance the responsibilities of their families and their jobs (Parker & Wang, 2013). Given all these challenges, it is important to understand the changing demographics and characteristics of the U.S. population as it has implications for parent education.

Demographics of Today's Families

In 2012, children ages 0–17 in the United States represented almost 24% of the population. The racial and ethnic diversity of America's children is changing with almost half of the population projected to be comprised of children who are Hispanic, Asian, or two or more races by 2050. Also in 2012, 64% of children ages 0–17 lived with two married parents which is a decrease from 65% in 2011. Approximately 6 million children and adults have an LGBT parent (Gates, 2013). Four percent of children lived with their unmarried cohabitating parents. Twenty-four percent lived with only their mothers, 4% with only their fathers, and 4% with neither of their parents. Of those not living with their parents, approximately 55% lived with their grandparents. Twenty-two percent of children not living with their parents or grandparents lived with other relatives and another 22% lived with non-relatives (FIFCFS, 2013).

The composition of children in single-parent families by race in 2012 was as follows: 67% black or African American, 53% American Indian, 42% Hispanic or Latino, 25% Non-Hispanic white, 17% Asian or Pacific Islander, and 42% two or more races (Annie E. Casey Foundation, 2013b). The number of children with at least one foreign-born parent has risen to 24% in 2012 from 15% in 1994. (FIFCFS, 2013). In 2011, 22% of all children ages 0–17 lived in poverty, reflecting little change from the percentage in 2010. The percentage of children with at least one parent working full-time, year round, rose from 71% to 73% in 2011 (FIFCFS, 2013). These statistics reflect the changing face of America's families. The discussion of family life education audiences in Chapter 3 speaks to the need for family life educators to know and understand the life circumstances and needs of those participating in their programs.

Societal Issues

Parents have always had questions about typical parenting issues, such as child development, discipline and guidance, limit-setting, building self-esteem, health, communication skills, academic achievement, balancing work and family, family systems, family transitions, conflict resolution, and parenting children with special needs, but they are also impacted by new and emerging issues that draw media attention and influence culture. It is important for parents to stay attuned to changing issues that influence their children. The press is full of stories about such issues as bullying (e.g., *Fox News*, 2013), binge drinking (e.g., *USA Today*, 2013a), and the escalating use of synthetic drugs such as Molly, K2, Spice and bath salts (e.g., *USA Today*, 2013b). Some of the more prominent issues in the media today include technology and social media, and the issue of indulgent parenting.

Technology and social media

Technology is revolutionizing family life. As of May 2013, 91% of Americans had a cell phone, 56% had smartphones, and 34% of American adults owned a tablet computer (Pew Internet & American Life Project, n.d.). Technology and media has had less impact on the sources and methods that parents use when seeking advice and more influence on *how* they parent. Only 10% of parents of children 0–8 were very likely to get parenting advice from a website, blog, or social network, preferring instead to consult a spouse (52%), their mother (34%), a pediatrician (31%), friends (25%), or teachers (19%) (Wartella, Rideout, Lauricella, & Connell, 2013).

A parent's own media behavior appears to have a major influence on how much time the family spends watching TV or using mobile devices. Parents who were identified as having a *media-centric* parenting style (used media an average of 11 hours a day) were more likely to incorporate media as a parenting tool and family activity than were parents considered to be *media-light* (used media less than 2 hours a day) (Wartella et al., 2013). Parents of young children make use of media and technology as a way to keep a child occupied, as a reward or discipline, and as an educational tool, although they also rely heavily on books and toys. TV and DVDs tend to be used more than mobile devices (Wartella et al., 2013).

Parents have mixed feelings about the role of the Internet and cell phones in their children's lives. While they recognize that the Internet and cell phones can help their children access information and connect to others, they express concern regarding the material to which children are exposed and the fact that online activity results in less face-to-face interaction (Lenhart et al., 2011). There is also concern that time spent with a computer can take the place of physical activity, putting them at risk for obesity (Child Trends, 2012). Increased time and attention to computers and technology can also result in being disconnected with nature and outdoor activity.

Technology can be useful for helping parents to be connected with their children via texting and social network sites. The use of technology is higher for parents of teens than the general population (91% of parents of teens had cell phones vs. 84% of the general population) (Lenhart, Madden, Smith, Purcell, Zickuhr, & Rainie, 2011). Therefore, technology will continue to have a major impact on family life and the parent-child relationship. Parenting education can provide needed resources and support to help families avoid the pitfalls and take advantage of all that technology has to offer.

Indulgent parenting

Today's parents increasingly practice indulgent parenting, a phenomenon that has received considerable media attention over the past decade (e.g., *ABC News* 2007, 2009; *The New York Times,* 2010; *Time,* 2009; *The Today Show,* 2013; *USA Today,* 2012). Parents in the U.S. indulge their children by giving material goods, attention, and freedom to do what they want when they want to do it, causing problems for many adolescents. This indulgence has a variety of names and references including overparenting, helicopter parents, invasive parenting, hovering parenting, concierge parenting, and tiger moms. Although parental indulgence has sometimes been referred to as "over indulgence," in reality indulgence is a continuum with no demarcation between indulgence and overindulgence (Coccia, Darling, Rehm, Cui, & Sathe, 2012). As an example, tiger moms might not be thought of as being indulgent, but they fall within the continuum of indulgent parenting because they are overinvolved in scheduling and controlling the activities in their children's lives.

There are three different elements in indulgent parenting including *too much*, or giving children too many resources ranging from objects and food to entertainment; *overnurturing*, or doing things for children that they should be doing for themselves; and *soft structure*, or setting few rules or consequences for children's behaviors (Clarke, Dawson, & Bredehoft, 2004). For example, despite the economic downturn and a decline in the adolescent population, adolescent spending was projected to grow to $209 billion in 2011 compared to $190 billion in 2006 (Marketing Charts, 2007). Parents have been observed ghostwriting homework for their children, making every extracurricular decision for them, and preparing their application materials for college (Marano, 2008). Moreover, indulgent parents have few rules, do not enforce rules, have few expectations about responsible behaviors, and assist children in avoiding consequences for their behaviors. Parents want to give as much as possible toward the well-being of their children by providing for a variety of extracurricular activities, classes, lessons, and sporting events. This indulgence involves "overscheduled children" and results in the decline of family time (Anderson & Doherty, 2005).

Parents indulge their children for various reasons. Fewer numbers of children can provide increased potential for attention and resource investments; parents in distressed marriages want to gain advantage with their spouses or children; divorced parents desire to compensate their children for their separation and divorce; parents own indulgence experience in childhood; and the influence of consumerism, media, community, and other people (Clarke et al., 2004). Even in times of economic downturn when parents cannot afford to give children extra time and resources, parents seem to overcompensate by providing children with *soft structure* (few rules) and *overnurturance* (doing things for the child that they should be doing themselves).

Adolescents who have been indulged through *overnurturance* and *soft structure* report greater life stress (e.g., irritations, difficulties, and events beyond their control). When parents provide their children with too many resources (*too much*) it increases parental life satisfaction by allowing them to view themselves as "good parents" who provide for their children. However, for adolescents receiving *too much* there is no relationship to their life satisfaction (Veldorale-Griffin, Coccia, Darling, Rehm, & Sathe, 2013).

Parental indulgence involves various paradoxes. Although indulging children may be gratifying for parents and may be enjoyable for adolescents, indulgent parenting has long-term problematic effects for both parents and children. The disproportionate investment of parental emotions, finances, and time devoted to one's children can erode marital bonds and contribute to the potential for divorce. It also leads to a destructive culture of parenting that reaches into many societal institutions (Marano, 2008). While a majority of parents mean well, indulgence does active harm and/or prevents individuals from developing self-efficacy and achieving their full potential. Individuals who report being indulged as children have noted that they experienced a range of feelings such as love, confusion, guilt, sadness, and anxiety due to feeling they did not learn how to manage certain tasks or decisions well in comparison with peers who were not indulged (Bredehoft, Mennicke, Potter, & Clarke, 1998). Whereas youth feel greater life satisfaction when they are indulged, it also has a detrimental relationship to their well-being over time, specifically in relation to stress and overall health. Early experiences with stress facilitate the ability to handle stress later in life (Boss, 2002). In addition, adolescents who experienced greater parental indulgence are more likely to have unhealthy eating behaviors, such as eating anything they want and having greater fast food intake (Coccia et al., 2012). Overall, parental indulgence has important implications for children and families.

Definitions

Before moving to the history and practice of parenting education, a discussion of the definition of parenting education is needed. Following are three commonly referenced definitions:

- Programs, support services, and resources offered to parents and caregivers that are designed to assist them or increase their capacity and confidence in raising healthy children (Carter, 1996).
- An organized, programmatic effort to change or enhance the child-rearing knowledge and skills of a family system or a child care system (Brock, Oertwein, & Coufal, 1993).
- A process that involves the expansion of insights, understanding, attitudes, and the acquisition of knowledge and skills about the development of both parents and their children and the relationship between the two. (NPEN, n.d.).

The definition of the National Parenting Education Network (NPEN; www.npen.org) recognizes the reciprocal relationship of the parent and the child and the importance of the parent's development within the process. NPEN defines parents as "those who are so defined legally and those who have made a long term commitment to a child to assume responsibility for that child's well-being and development. This responsibility includes providing for the child's physiological and emotional needs, formatting a loving emotional relationship, guiding the child's understanding of the world and culture, and designing an appropriate environment" (NPEN, n.d.). The inclusion of "those who have made a long term commitment to a child" recognizes many adults who care for children to whom they are not legally or biologically related.

Brief History of Parenting Education

With these definitions regarding parenting education in mind, let us review a brief history of parenting education in the United States. Parenting education in the U.S. has some of its earliest roots in the colonial period, when church and state shared the goal of influencing parents to raise their children according to religious mandates (Schlossman, 1976). It can be traced back to fields as diverse as medicine, social work, home economics, education, and psychology. G. Stanley Hall was perhaps the first psychologist to bring the study of children to a university setting, but Freud, Watson, Adler, Piaget, Gesell, Erickson, and others had theories of their own. Hall's focus was on understanding the development of the child for the purpose of discovering how children learn. His methods were considered unconventional, and he eventually lost favor in the academic world, but his ideas were carried out among the women who gathered in 1897 at the first National Congress of Mothers, a nationwide parent-education organization known later as the Parent Teacher Association, or PTA (Schlossman, 1976). A lot has happened since then.

The PTA grew from that first meeting to an organization of 60,000 members in 1915 to 4.3 million members in 2013. The focus of the PTA shifted from early childhood to adolescence and then to an emphasis on helping children in trouble or at risk and on reeducating families in modern methods of child-rearing. Eventually its main objective centered on domestic science and the goal of preparing women in household management and child care—a goal presumably resulting in happier and more stable homes. Today the PTA has moved from the community mothers' club model into its current form as an organization "devoted to the educational success of children and the promotion of parent involvement in schools" (National PTA, n.d.).

A number of other organizations were involved in parenting education in various capacities. The Child Study Association of America initiated the National Council of Parent Education in 1925 to coordinate lay and professional groups. This group contributed to the development of instructional materials and sponsored the first university course in parenting education at Teachers College, Columbia, Missouri, in 1925. Likewise, in the mid-1920s the American Home Economics Association (AHEA) began to include parenting education in its educational and lobbying interests. These initial efforts focused on poor families and those considered to be in need (Carter, 1996).

Benjamin Spock's *Baby and Child Care*, first published in 1946, brought the literature of child care and parenting to the middle class. Grassroots parenting groups began to appear and provided parents opportunities to meet with each other. One grassroots mother-led organization was the La Leche League. Groups of women shared their experiences with breast-feeding via support groups and mentored new mothers with lactation consultation. With their efforts, breast-feeding was reestablished as the preferred infant feeding method in an era when medical interventions were thought to be superior and more modern. Despite the influence of the La Leche League, most parenting education followed traditional educational designs, with an expert serving as the source of information and answers.

Slowly the focus shifted away from the experts and toward enhancing parents' own knowledge and experience. The federally-funded Head Start program, launched in the mid-1960s, acknowledged the value and impact of parents in the education of their children (Carter, 1996). By the 1980s community-based parenting education programs were joined by state and federally funded programs and a growing number of non-profit and for-profit organizations.

In 1995 parenting educators began discussing the feasibility of creating an organization that could meet the needs of this growing field. The most notable discussions were held at Wheelock College in 1995 and at the Family Resource Coalition of America conference in 1996. The National Parenting Education Network (NPEN), evolved from these discussions. The mission of NPEN, which is to advance the field of parenting education, represented an important step in the evolution of parenting education as a profession. As discussed in Chapter 2, one step in the development of a profession occurs when those trained in the field establish an association (East, 1980). NPEN's existence speaks to the recognition of the unique needs and goals of the field of parenting education. NPEN continues to influence the field of parenting education through its work to establish professional standards and competencies, which, will be discussed in more detail later in this chapter.

Incorporation of Theory

The practice of parenting education is heavily influenced by theory. Theories contribute to our understanding of families and parenting by providing insight and reasonable explanations for individual and family behaviors (see Chapter 8). Theory consists of a set of logically related concepts that seek to describe, explain, and predict behavior within a family and/or parenting context. Many family studies students learn about theories in specific courses about theory or when they are incorporated into content-related courses (e.g., family relations, marriage, parenting, child development, sexuality, stress). Therefore, this chapter does not focus on major explanations of theories, but will highlight a few to include when teaching about families and parenting, so students can be mindful of theory as they study the content related to families and parenting. Theory can be a guide for our own parenting practices, help us understand our children's behaviors, and enable us to predict outcomes. A key component in parenting theories is the understanding that parents influence children, but also that children can influence parents and that parent socialization strategies are bidirectional (Pardini, 2008). Theories incorporated in parent education classes are often a combination of family theories and child and human development theories, which can integrate various concepts. Family theories such as systems theory, social exchange theory, family development theory, and family stress theory can explain the parent-child relationship in the context of the family.

- *Systems theory* can be used to facilitate understanding boundaries, systems, and subsystems, as well as roles and rules. There is a focus on wholeness (a family is greater than the sum of its parts) and interdependence (what affects one person in a family also influences other members).
- An *ecosystems* approach or *biological ecological* perspective can be used to understand the interaction of various parts of one's ecosystem at different stages of child growth and development. This theory can answer questions about the parent-child relationship taking into consideration other various internal and external systems that interact with the relationship. For example it can be used to answer the question: What are the roles of parents,

peers, schools, day cares, employers, culture, and other social systems in the development of children?

- *Social exchange theory* can be used to examine the rewards and costs of having children and parenting them during different stages of their development, such as the rewards and costs of parenting teens with regard to power and independence. Do the rewards of having the child outweigh the financial and emotional costs?

- *Family developmental theory* can be used to gain a perspective of individual and family developmental tasks during different stages of the family life cycle, as moving to a different stage is often based on the age of the oldest child. How families are able to handle different life situations depends on whether they are considered "on-time" or "off-time." A situation is considered to be "on-time" if it is consistent with societal views of normal timing, such as graduation from high school. However, an adolescent who becomes pregnant would be considered "off-time."

- *Stress theory* helps people to understand that parents can experience stress that is both *normative* (expected during the lifecycle—e.g., birth of a baby, entering teen years, graduating from high school) and *nonnormative* (unforeseen events or situations—e.g., childhood illness, bullying, substance abuse). See Chapter 8 for further details and references.

Other theories pertinent to parent-child relationships focus on the topics of child-human development and socialization.

- *Piaget's cognitive developmental theory* examines a tendency to create complex cognitive structures or schemes (basic building blocks—organized patterns of thought and behavior to think and act in various situations). Piaget proposed that children adapt to the world and handle information according to two processes—*assimilation* (incorporating new information into existing schemes) and *accommodation* (changing structures to include new information). These steps are balanced through *equilibration*, which is the force that drives the learning process and development. Children have four stages of development: *sensorimotor* (period of rapid growth based on reflexive movements when children use their senses to learn about the world around them); *preoperational* (thinking is intuitive and egocentric, distinguishing between self and the environment using symbols to represent their play and discoveries); *concrete operational* (beginning of logical thought); and *formal operational* (ability to use abstract reasoning) (Phillips, 1981; Piaget, 1950; Piaget & Inhelder, 1969).

- *Erik Erickson's lifespan view of development or psychosocial theory* describes growth as a series of eight stages each with specific physical and psychological needs based on socialization along with a developmental crisis to be met and resolved. These conflicts serve as turning points in the child's development and their capacity to resolve the conflict impacts their ability to develop the specific quality. These stages and the approximate ages include *Basic Trust vs. Mistrust* (0–1); *Autonomy vs. Shame and Doubt* (1–3); *Initiative vs. Guilt* (3–6); *Industry vs. Inferiority* (6–11); *Identity vs. Role Confusion* (adolescence); *Intimacy vs. Isolation* (early adulthood); *Generativity vs. Stagnation* (middle adulthood); *Ego Integrity vs. Despair* (late adulthood) (Erikson, 1950, 1963).

- *Vygotsky's social development theory* suggests that cognitive development occurs through interactions with others and is oriented to the individual's culture and society. There is a *zone of proximal development* (ZPD) in which a child finds a range of tasks too difficult to accomplish alone, but possible with the help of adults or more skilled peers. Using *scaffolding* (similar to ZPD) to help a child learn a new concept helps the child master the task, so the scaffolding can then be removed (Daniels, 1996; Vygotsky, 1978; Wood, Bruner, & Ross, 1976).

- *Attachment theory* examines attachment patterns and a sense of trust that develops with adults who are significant to the child's life. Attachment is thought to be a lasting connectedness between individuals with the infant/caregiver relationship providing the basis for these relationships. There are four types of attachment: *secure, resistant, avoidant*, and *disorganized/disoriented*. The attachment relationship is essential to the child's subsequent cognitive and socio-emotional development that will affect their relationships throughout later life by creating an internal working model for individuals as they approach new and existing relationships (Ainsworth, 1973; Ainsworth & Bowlby, 1991; Bowlby, 1969, 1988).

- *Behaviorism* suggests that all behavior is a learned response from the environment and that past experience accounts for all behavior. Desirable outcomes in children can be obtained through conditioning based on consistent reinforcement and punishment (Skinner, 1953, 1957, 1974; Watson, 1925).

- *Social learning theory* proposes that human behavior is learned observationally through modeling without necessarily needing to act in a certain way. Human behavior is explained by continuous reciprocal interactions between the person, behavior, and environment. Bandura (1986) relabeled his approach as "social cognitive theory" in recognition of the more comprehensive nature of his theory than what was traditionally viewed as "learning." (Bandura, 1977, 1986, 1999; Gibson, 2004).

Incorporating theoretical frameworks into parent education courses can provide insight for parents to better understand the development and behaviors of their children, as well as their interactions with them. Some of these theories also have various stages to accommodate different ages and periods of development. Whether teaching in a formal or nonformal setting, incorporating theory is meaningful to the understanding and examination of the parent-child relationship.

Parent Development

The concept of parent development is important to include in any discussion about parenting education. Becoming and being a parent can have a profound impact on the development of both the mother and father. Theory and research on the stages of parental development include consideration of parenthood as a developmental stage, the transition to parenthood, and stage theories of parenthood and the family life cycle. The stages of parenthood are considered as developmental changes in the experience and action of parents over the course of bearing and rearing children (Demick, 2002).

Certainly teaching new knowledge, skills, and abilities to parents has a positive impact on children's development. But more lasting and meaningful outcomes can be dependent on the cognitive and emotional development of the parents. Parent education programs that focus on parental development operate on the assumption that parents who are more advanced in their understanding of themselves, their family, and their environment, are better equipped to understand their children and their relationship with their children, resulting in more positive parenting experiences and child outcomes.

The theory of parental conceptions considers the impact of parental cognitive development on the parenting experience (Newberger, 1980). Cognitive structure refers to stable patterns of thought that define how an individual makes sense of experience and organizes his or her responses to it. By interacting with the environment, a person's thinking can be broadened to consider a wider scope of ideas, information, and perspectives as well as reflect more depth and flexibility. A parent with more advanced cognitive skills can pull from a wider repertoire when considering solutions to parenting situations and problems. Newberger also identified *Parental Awareness* as the organized way of thinking about a child's behaviors or responses that can influence how the parent chooses to react. This awareness is on a continuum from self-centered, egotistic views (egoistic orientation) to a system-oriented view of the parent and child as interdependent systems (analytic) (Thomas, 1996). Each of the levels builds upon the preceding one and reflects an increasing awareness of the psychological complexity of the parent, the child, and the parent-child relationship.

- Level 1—Egoistic. Parents are self-focused and see the child only in terms of the parent's wants and needs. The child is a projection of the parent's own experiences.

- Level 2—Conventional. The parental perspective shifts from self-centeredness to consideration of issues outside of themselves (tradition, culture, authority). The parent role is organized around socially-defined notions of correct practice and responsibilities.

- Level 3—Individualistic. The child is seen as a unique individual. Parents operating at an individualistic level are able to respond to the needs of a specific child within the context of the parent-child relationship.

- Level 4—Analytic. Parents at this level of cognitive awareness see their parenting, their children, and themselves, as being embedded in a larger, reciprocal system. The parent and child both grow through the mutual fulfillment of each other's needs within the context of the relationship.

Logically, parents operating at a deeper level of cognitive development (individualistic and analytic) would be more likely to demonstrate practices that would be considered to encourage development.

Parent education programs should be designed to support the development of parental awareness and themes supportive of children's development. Clearly, positive early childhood interaction has implications for the long-term nature of the parent-child relationship and the child's development over time. Research has identified qualities of parental behavior that influence the parent-child relationship and child outcomes (Brazelton & Cramer, 1990; Bromwich, 1981; Isabella & Belsky, 1991; Maccoby, 1980). Themes reflecting parental response regarding child development, parenting, and parent-child interaction have been identified (Thomas, 1996). Parental behaviors that reflect encouragement of child development, including patterns of *sensitivity, responsiveness, reciprocity,* and *support*, were identified as *encourage development themes*, whereas behaviors, such as *insensitivity, unresponsiveness, intrusiveness,* and *domination*, were labeled as *constraint development themes*.

Delivery of Parenting Education

Parenting education is provided in a variety of settings and formats to a number of different audiences. Variations in the goals of the programs and the audiences targeted are reflected in the settings and approaches used to deliver parenting education.

Formats

Three modes of instruction for parenting education are the *individual* mode, the *group* mode, and the *mass* mode (Harman & Brim, 1980). The *individual mode* involves one-on-one interaction. This type of parent education is often carried out via home visiting programs, but increasingly parenting educators are marketing themselves as coaches perhaps to portray an educational approach rather being therapeutic or remedial. The *group mode* is a widely used approach through which instruction is delivered to a group of people in classroom settings, workshops, seminars, or support groups. The *mass mode* refers to education provided to the masses, often carried out through the print media such as newsletters, books, and pamphlets; via radio and television programs; and through the Internet and technology. Contact through the mass mode can reach a larger audience but may be less personal. The audience is anonymous because there is no direct contact between the educator and the parent. Parent education is increasingly provided in a mass mode through online webinars and learning modules and even through mobile apps.

The National Extension Parenting Education Model identified 15 program delivery strategies for reaching out to parents including parenting education groups, radio programs, hospital programs, and newsletter articles (see Box 11.1 on the following page) (Smith, Cudaback, Goddard, & Myers-Walls, 1994). Many of these delivery strategies are carried out in the settings described above. A more detailed discussion on each of these strategies can be found at www.k-state.edu/wwparent/nepem/nepem.pdf

---

Box 11.1   Program Delivery Strategies for Parent Education

Parent Education Groups	Community Forums
Parent Education Resource Centers	Interagency Support/Collaborations
Newsletters	Support Groups
Radio Programs	Community Coalitions/Task Forces
Home Visits	Learn-at-Home Programs
Mentor Mother/Godparent Programs	Parent Advisory Groups
Hospital Programs	Social Change Groups: Liberation Pedagogy
Newspaper Articles/Tabletop Messages	

Smith, C. A., Cudaback, D., Goddard, H. W., & Myers-Walls, J. A. (1994). National Extension Parent Education Model. Manhattan: Kansas Cooperative Extension Service. [Online]. http://www.k-state.edu/wwparent/nepem/nepem.pdf

---

Prevention Approaches

Parenting education programs can vary in the approach and intensity of the program and in the particular parenting behaviors or child outcomes being addressed. In general most parenting education programs are preventive in nature, but the focus of the prevention can vary. As discussed in Chapter 1, there are three levels of prevention programs: primary, secondary, and tertiary.

- **Primary prevention** is focused on the protection and education of healthy people from harm *before* something happens.

- **Secondary prevention** involves protection and education *after* problems, conflicts, or risks have occurred so the progress of the problem can be halted or slowed as early as possible.

- **Tertiary prevention** centers around helping people manage complicated, long-term problems to prevent further harm.

The prevention approach used in a parenting education program is often dependent upon the audience addressed. All three levels of prevention programs can involve some level of parenting education. However, increased efforts at providing primary prevention to *all* parents beginning prior to birth and continuing throughout the lifespan could reduce the need for programs focusing on secondary and tertiary prevention.

Audiences

Common audiences for parenting education programs include parents of infants, toddlers, adolescents, or college-age youth, as well as teen parents, single parents, fathers, stepfamilies, military families, grandparents raising their grandchildren, parents involved in foster care and adoption, and incarcerated parents. Depending upon the situation, the audience might be participating in a *universal* (all parents), *selective* (specific at-risk populations), or *indicated* (problem-focused) prevention program and the approach taken might be considered primary, secondary, or tertiary prevention. For example, grandparents raising their grandchildren might participate in a program geared specifically for that audience. The approach might be considered primary prevention because the audience is not necessarily considered to be at-risk, but shares a common characteristic or circumstance. Parenting education programs for these audiences can include general parenting education content and discussion of issues unique to that population.

Parenting and family life education programs are often designed for a universal, targeted, or indicated audience. These categories reflect the prevention approach applied to each group. Universal prevention programs are designed for the general population and focus largely on primary prevention and the promotion of positive parenting practices. They are designed to inform and prepare parents regarding normative parenting responsibilities and experiences with the intention of preventing problems and promoting optimal development. These programs are typically shorter in duration and less intensive than selective or indicated programs. A universal prevention program can address a generally accepted purpose, such as preventing unwanted teen pregnancy or adolescent substance abuse (Doyle, 2006; McGroder & Hyra, 2009).

Selective prevention programs are targeted toward those with higher-than-average risk for problem behaviors by virtue of their membership in a particular population. The goal of selective prevention programs is to prevent the development of serious problems. Selective programs are typically fairly extensive in duration and intensity (Doyle, 2006; McGroder & Hyra, 2009). A selective prevention program might target a particular audience, such as those going through a divorce, as research shows that on average, children with divorced parents score lower on a variety of emotional, behavioral, social, health, and academic outcomes (Amato, 2010).

Indicated programs target those that are already engaged in high-risk behaviors, such as reported child abuse. The goal of indicated programs is to end problem behaviors and prevent severe problems. Therefore, indicated programs can be fairly intense and long in duration. (Doyle, 2006; McGroder & Hyra, 2009). Although problem focused, indicated programs, should not be confused with therapy. Parenting education differs from therapy in its emphasis on (1) normative development and the prevention of family problems rather than on individual personality and family dysfunction, (2) techniques that provide support rather than conflict and confrontation, and (3) goals that increase self-confidence and satisfaction rather than restructure personality or family dynamics (Wandersman, 1987).

Settings

Chapter 4 provided discussion of the many settings in which parent and family life education occurs. Similarly, parenting education programs are offered in a number of different settings and through a variety of providers, including schools, Cooperative Extension programs, family and human service agencies, neighborhood resource centers, community education, faith communities, and health-care settings. In addition, for-profit businesses are increasingly offering programs and services relevant to parenting to employees because they recognize the impact that personal issues and concerns can have on company productivity (Grzywacz & Demerouti, 2013). The government provides parenting education through a variety of programs including Head Start, family support and intervention programs through the child protection system, and programs aimed for military families. As discussed previously, many parent and family education programs are funded through grants, which can create an unstable environment for program planning and implementation. Stable funding sources and continued efforts to present parenting and family life education as an acceptable activity for all families will help to increase the outreach and positive impact of family life education in American society.

Models and Approaches to Parenting Education

The overall goal of parenting education is to foster children's safety and healthy development. Parenting education programs seek to help parents develop appropriate child management techniques and gain knowledge and understanding of age-appropriate behaviors. By targeting the knowledge, skills, attitudes, beliefs, and behaviors relevant to effective parenting, parenting education programs can give parents the capacity and confidence to meet their children's developmental needs and prepare them for adulthood (McGroder & Hyra, 2009).

When discussing the availability of parenting education programs, it can be helpful to consider the mission of the program. Programs can focus specifically on the parent, child, and/or the parent-child relationship. With some programs the focus is on the family or on the community or environment in which the family lives. Recently there has been an increase in the types of programs that include the entire family and engage both parents and children in skill-building activities. Some programs also offer parents support or referral to services to reduce the stress that makes it difficult for them to be effective parents.

Assumptions about Parenting Education

Most parenting education programs are influenced by certain assumptions regarding the nature of parenting, the growth and development of the parent, the environment in which the parent and child live and interact, the learning environment and circumstances, and the overall goals of the program. Assumptions influence the content included in parenting education programs and can also impact how the content is taught or addressed.

The National Extension Parenting Education Model includes nine key assumptions regarding parents and their relationships with their children (Smith et al., 1994):

- Parents are the primary socializers of their children.

- Parenting attitudes, knowledge, skills, and behaviors can be positively influenced by parent education efforts.

- Parenting is a learned skill that can be strengthened through study and experience.

- Parenting education is more effective when parents are active participants in and contributors to their parenting education programs.

- The parent-child relationship is nested within and influenced by multiple social and cultural systems.
- Programs should be responsive to diversity among parents.
- Effective parenting education may be accomplished by a variety of methods.
- Both the parent and the child have needs that should be met.
- The goal of parent education is strengthening and educating the parent (or caregiver) so that he or she is better able to facilitate the development of caring, competent, and healthy children.

When developing or selecting parenting education programs, parenting educators need to be mindful of both the content and the process of delivering this content. While there are a number of frameworks, guides, and models to assist in the development and evaluation of parenting education programs, this chapter will focus on two: The Parent Education Core Curriculum Framework and The National Extension Parenting Education Model.

Parent Education Core Curriculum Framework

The Parent Education Core Curriculum Framework provides a guide to planning curriculum for parent education programs (MNAFEE, 2011). The Framework is designed specifically for parents of young children, but it can be adapted to other audiences. The specific goals of the *Parent Education Core Curriculum Framework* are to provide a resource that:

- frames or defines the body of knowledge in the field of parent education;
- is applicable across the field of parent education with any type of parent education program, population, setting, and delivery mode;
- is a planning tool for development and delivery of parent education curriculum and lesson plans;
- identifies the intended content and objectives of parent education [originally designed for Early Childhood Family Education (ECFE) and Even Start];
- provides guidance for parent goal-setting in parent education;
- guides assessment of parent education outcomes and programs;
- promotes accountability in parent education programs and with individual parent educators; and
- informs practice in parent education.

The Framework contains four levels of information including *Domains* (Parent Development, Parent-Child Relationships, Early Childhood Development, Family Development, Culture, and Community); *Components* (areas of content within each domain); *Categories* (units of more specific learning content within each component); and *Indicators* (long-term learning goals in each category for parents participating in parent education). Potential uses of the Framework include:

- Planning curriculum and daily lesson plans—selection of content, teaching methods, and resources.
- Integrating parent education with children's education.

- Providing direction for assessing parent outcomes.
- Informing program standards and evaluation.
- Identifying and planning for staff development needs.
- Communicating with parents, sponsoring institutions/agencies, policy makers and the public about parent education and parent education outcomes.
- Providing direction for assessing parent and community needs.
- Providing direction for assessing the impact of public policy.

The Parent Education Core Curriculum Framework document also includes "Procedures for Using the Parent Education Core Curriculum Framework and Indicators" in curriculum planning and development, as well as implementation. The Framework is an excellent resource for anyone involved in parenting education program development or implementation.

The National Extension Parenting Education Model

The National Extension Parenting Education Model (NEPEM) provides a broad perspective on program content relevant to parenting education (Smith et al., 1994). It was developed to stimulate and conceptualize parenting education programs at state and county levels and to provide a content guide for parenting educators. In addition to the assumptions regarding parents and their relationships with their children discussed earlier, the model also includes eight underlying guiding principles relevant to the content of parenting education programs:

- parents' actions to enhance the well-being of their children
- priority parent practices that are significant across the full range of childhood and adolescence
- core priorities
- importance of skills and practices compared to arrangement of practices
- categories of parent skills with fluid, not rigid, boundaries
- model that is dynamic, not static
- emphasis on parent strengths and empowerment
- parent strengths sufficiently broad and flexible to be useful in developing programs across the cultural spectrum

In 2000, a group of Extension professionals met to outline the critical skills and practices of parenting educators. Their efforts combined the NEPEM "priority practices for parents" with their "priority processes for parenting educators" to create a new structure, the *National Extension Parenting Education Framework*, or NEPEF (DeBord et al., 2006). In the NEPEF, six categories of skills and content practices for parents were recommended: *Care for Self, Understand* (children, their developmental needs, and uniqueness), *Guide, Nurture, Motivate,* and *Advocate.* They are to be used alongside the six processes for parenting educators (*Grow, Frame, Develop, Educate, Embrace,* and *Build*). See Figure 11.1 for these approaches. The NEPEF provides an excellent format in which to consider numerous aspects of parenting education.

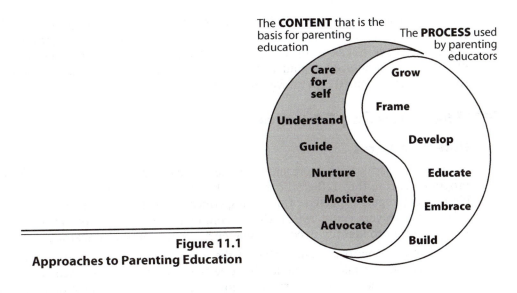

The **CONTENT** that is the basis for parenting education

The **PROCESS** used by parenting educators

Care for self

Grow

Frame

Understand

Develop

Guide

Nurture

Educate

Motivate

Embrace

Advocate

Build

Figure 11.1
Approaches to Parenting Education

Identifying Parenting Education Programs

Multiple parenting education programs cover a broad range of topics and use numerous formats and approaches. Therefore, it can be difficult to find appropriate curriculum or to know if the program will be effective with the intended audience. The ability to adequately evaluate parenting education materials and curricula is an important competency for the professional family life educator. Professional parenting educators must possess the knowledge and skills needed to determine what, if any, theory a program might be based upon and ensure that content is grounded in solid research. The literature regarding the evaluation of parenting curriculum and programs is increasing as the field becomes more firmly established. The Family Life Education Quality Assessment Tool (FLEMat QAT) was designed to help family life educators and those who work with families to judge the quality of written and online materials aimed at families (Myers-Walls, n.d.). See Chapter 7 for a more detailed discussion of evaluation.

Fortunately, there are a number of sources for evidence-based programs focused on multiple audiences (see Box 7.14 in Chapter 7 for a partial list of resources for evidence-based parent and family programs). The National Registry of Evidence-based Programs and Practices (NREPP), provided by the U.S. Department of Health and Human Services Substance Abuse and Mental Health Services Administration (SAMHSA) is a searchable online registry of more than 300 programs supporting mental health promotion and substance abuse prevention, (as well as mental health and substance abuse treatment). Some of the programs focused specifically on parenting education on the NREPP list include *Celebrating Families!*, *Children In Between* (for children of divorcing parents), *Nurturing Parenting Programs*, *Strengthening Families Program*, *Systematic Training for Effective Parenting (STEP)*, *Parents as Teachers*, and *Active Parenting*. Other registries include *Blueprints for Healthy Youth Development* and *Child Welfare Information Gateway*.

These registries can provide a helpful overview of the types of programs available to help strengthen families. While there are many quality parenting education programs that have not been officially designated as being evidence-based, funders often require supported organizations and agencies to use programs that meet some kind of identified criteria for efficacy.

The Parenting Educator

Role Paradigms

Parenting educators represent a crucial component in any parent education program because they reflect the goals and philosophy of a program. Three possible role paradigms expected of parenting educators include *expert, facilitator,* and *collaborator* (Myers-Walls, 1998). Understanding these varying expectations is necessary in order to identify needed competencies for parenting educators.

- The first role paradigm is that of the expert. Parenting educators acting in this role are knowledgeable about certain information and facts and share that knowledge with parents, who see the parenting educator as having answers they need and want.

- Parenting educators can also take a much less active role. In this situation, the parents are assumed to already have the information and knowledge they need, but parenting educators can provide a perspective or a setting for discussion and can access appropriate resources. In this role paradigm, the parenting educator operates more as a facilitator to guide group process than as a leader—a "guide on the side" as opposed to a "sage on the stage." The parents establish the agenda and goals. This type of approach is especially effective with disadvantaged or oppressed populations, but it takes an especially competent parenting educator who knows how to use evidence-based research and adapt it to diverse populations. "Liberation pedagogy" is one educational approach that has been used to nurture marginalized peoples. This approach seeks to empower the learner and encourages them to challenge and change oppressive systems and hierarchical power structures. (Shor & Freire, 1986).

- A third role paradigm falls between the expert and the facilitator. In the collaborator approach, the educator and the parents work together to determine the goals and agenda of the program. The parents are valued for their knowledge, and the parenting educator is recognized for his or her knowledge base, as well as his or her skills in group facilitation.

Three other similar roles and approaches include the following: In the *critical inquirer approach* the parent educator poses questions to encourage participants to think critically, following the assumption that parents have a social responsibility to be well-developed thinkers. The *interventionist approach* views the parent educator as a change agent helping parents to alter the way that they think and subsequently behave. Finally, a parent educator following the *eclectic* approach uses a variety of all of the approaches depending on the audience and situation (Duncan & Goddard, 2011).

The delivery philosophy of parenting education programs can fall within three delivery approaches, *transmission*, *transactional*, and *transformational* models (Thomas & Footrakoon, 1998). A program following the transmission model is designed to transmit knowledge, attitudes, or skills to improve the way that parents relate to their children. In this approach the parent educator would be seen as an expert sharing information and in control of the parent's learning. Programs incorporating a transactional perspective consider the parent as a person, as well as a learner. Transactional programs are designed to promote the learner's growth, development, and problem-solving capacities. The educator's role is to facilitate the learning of the parent. Transformational programs provide opportunities for parents to think very differently about themselves and their role in their community. They incorporate a social context and work toward collective social action and change. In transformational programs the parent is an active participant and may be largely responsible for the learning process, or they may work collaboratively with the parent educator.

Because the role of the parenting educator can vary depending upon the audience, setting, and goals of the group, a competent parenting educator should be capable of moving and adapting to whatever role is needed in the particular situation. A parent educator offering a one-day workshop may need different skills than someone facilitating an ongoing group or writing a newspaper column. Those currently working to define and establish the field of parenting education are faced with the difficulty of trying to move the field forward by defining content and competencies while still supporting the broad diversity of the profession.

Parenting Education as a Profession

Preparation and Training

The qualifications of parenting education providers can range from less than a high school diploma to a graduate degree, specifically in parenting education. Historically, parenting education has been conducted within the domains of a number of different disciplines, including medicine, social work, therapy, and education, and informally by parent-to-parent advising (Heath & Palm, 2006). This history has had implications for the formal recognition of parenting education as a profession, as many in the helping professions have been involved in parenting education without the benefit of formal training. For example, parents might ask a pediatrician how best to deal with their toddler's temper tantrums. Although this is not necessarily a medical question, the doctor may be inclined to offer advice. In some circumstances professionals in other related fields provide parenting advice as they are assumed to have expertise in parenting education by virtue of their role. Unfortunately, parenting is seldom directly addressed in training programs for many of the helping professions.

The formal recognition of parenting educators as professionals, and of parenting education as a profession in its own right, is increasing. There have been substantial advances in the identification of the knowledge, skills, abilities, and competencies needed to provide parenting education. There are more opportunities to provide parenting education within the context of education and prevention rather than as embedded within other practices and settings. Professionals in the field are working to formalize training and recognition opportunities for parenting educators, including those working as peer educators and paraprofessionals.

Packaged programs

Programs highlighting specific curricula often use paraprofessionals as presenters. Instructors may not have any formal training in child development or parenting, but receive a certificate or become certified upon completion of a prescribed training focused on a program's particular approach or curriculum. Continuing education may or may not be required. This approach can be limited, as the provider's expertise is confined to the specific program or materials. Packaged programs can be effective in certain situations or on specific topics, but parenting educators need the ability to deal with a variety of issues and be skilled in adapting to their audience. Training programs for specific curricula may not provide training in issues beyond the content of the program leaving the educator without the skills needed to deal with unique situations. However, this approach to parent education can be very effective, as long as the educator maintains fidelity to the program.

Peer educators and paraprofessionals

Some parenting programs involve the use of volunteers, usually experienced parents, (sometimes called peer educators or paraprofessionals), who offer support or facilitation. Peer educators share common life experiences with the audience members. Paraprofessionals are generally trained to assist professionals, but are not licensed or credentialed themselves. They may have some of the knowledge and skills and may be able to work independently, but do not meet the requirements for recognition as a professional in the field (Jones, Stranik, Hart, Wolf, & McClintic, 2013).

MELD (now merged with Parents as Teachers) is a good example of a program that uses peer educators. Experienced parents are trained in facilitation techniques and given supporting research-based material on child development and parenting issues. These trained parents then lead parenting groups with new parents. One of the strengths of peer-led programs like the MELD model is that it includes parents from the community in leadership roles as group facilitators. These parents often share the same cultural and socioeconomic status as the parents in the rest of the group. This shared background gives the facilitators increased credibility and acceptance and is sometimes used to provide parenting education via home-visiting programs.

There has been substantial work to include peer educators and paraprofessionals within the continuum of parenting education. A comprehensive discussion of the contributions and limitations of the role of peer educators and paraprofessionals can be found on the NPEN website in a white paper on the diverse roles of practitioners in parenting education (Jones et al., 2013).

Certificate and degree programs

While parenting education is often included as a topic or course within family and child development degree programs, there are growing opportunities for professionals to be trained specifically in parenting education and to consider parenting education as a primary profession. The number of degree-granting programs in parenting education is increasing throughout the United States. As mentioned in Chapter 2, a number of higher education institutions, such as North Carolina State University, Wheelock College, Plymouth State University, River College, University of Minnesota, and University of North Texas at Denton offer graduate certificate programs in parenting education (NPEN, 2013).

Competencies for Parent Educators

There is an emerging consensus on the parameters of parenting education and the knowledge and skills needed for effective practice. The discussion surrounding the establishment of parenting education as a field and parenting educators as professionals has led to consideration of competencies. What do parenting educators need to know to effectively practice? What skills should they possess? Campbell and Palm (2004) identified three stages of growth and development (novice, intermediate, and master) for parenting educators in five areas of development: knowledge, group facilitation skills, teaching skills, professional identity and boundaries, and understanding diversity. These levels of professional development provide insight into the depth and breadth of competencies needed by parenting educators as they increase their level of professionalism (see Table 11.1).

Table 11.1   Levels of Professional Development for Parent Educators

Novice Level	Intermediate Level	Master Teaching Level
Knowledge		
Aware of basic child development and parenting information. Some apprehension about being able to answer parents' questions.	Possesses broader knowledge base. Aware of a variety of resources on development and parenting issues.	Confident about being able to answer questions and/or able to find resources. Realization of being well versed.
Aware of basic stages and theories of family dynamics and development.	Able to identify individual families' circumstances in reference to stages and characteristics.	Uses holistic perspective to understand each family's journey. Able to link current challenges and successes to stages and cycles of development. Understands and provides insight into impact of family of origin as well as current family dynamics.
Beginning to understand community resources. Some uncertainty about what is available and how to refer parents to other services.	Aware of basic community services and some comfort with access. Understands referral process.	Able to access information and services easily. Comfortable approaching parents for referrals. Uses a holistic perspective with parents within a collaborative approach.

(continued)

Novice Level	Intermediate Level	Master Teaching Level
Group Facilitation Skills		
Understands group process but feels challenged with group leadership role.	Enjoys group leadership. Focuses primarily on content and plan for session.	Confident as a group leader. Able to blend support and possible intervention with content. Understands behavior and can utilize skills to respond.
Understands dynamics of conflict and behaviors. Uncomfortable with dealing with difficult group/individual dynamics.	Has some skills to address challenging behaviors, mostly to defuse them and refocus group.	Is comfortable with addressing challenging or difficult group dynamics. Recognizes and uses "teachable moments." Takes responsibility for healthy group process and development.
Teaching Skills		
Understands adult learning styles.	Plans and executes sessions with a variety of teaching methods but uses discussion as a primary method.	Able to assess parents' needs and styles and match methods accordingly. Shows insight in planning and leading to meet diverse needs of parents.
Able to develop and implement an appropriate parent education session plan.	Able to tailor a plan to an individual group. Able to access ongoing needs of group and modify plan, as needed.	Uses creative and varying strategies for group education and process. Has clear goals and objectives, yet uses flexibility as needed.
Professional Identity and Boundaries		
Shows basic self-awareness, but limited understanding of impact on relationship with group and role as facilitator.	Has insight into self, family-of-origin experiences, and their impact on the role as a parent educator.	Maturity and life experiences that reflect deeper understanding and self-awareness. Ability to separate biases and strong values from professional role.
Uncertain about skills and abilities as a parent educator.	Growing confidence from positive experiences with parents that affirm abilities as a parent educator.	Quiet confidence in abilities. Leadership role within the parent group, as well as within the profession as a mentor and a guide for other professionals.
Understanding Diversity		
Shows basic awareness and sensitivity to importance of diversity issues. Not sure how to integrate into practice.	Growing awareness of family and cultural diversity and the impact on family and parenting issues.	Values family structure and cultural diversity in programs. Willing to learn from parents; comfortable addressing differences and facilitating discussion to address differences respectfully.

Campbell, D., & Palm, G. F. (2004). *Group parent education: Promoting parent learning and support.* Thousand Oaks, CA: Sage. Table 11.1, pp . 206–207.

Reflective practice, which is relevant to the competencies of a parent educator, is a general term used to describe the attitudes and behaviors of practitioners to improve their own knowledge and skills and to understand how effective practice works (Campbell & Palm, 2006). Reflective practice can involve self-assessment to identify knowledge, disposition, and skills. Box 11.2 on pp. 294–295 includes a self-assessment checklist specific to parenting education in group settings.

The formal identification of competencies needed for the practice of parenting education is currently underway. A National Forum on Professional Development for Parenting Education was held in May of 2011 in an effort to work on the identification and establishment of credentialing, certification, and content knowledge and skills for parenting educators. A preliminary list of core competencies evident within different professional development systems was identified (McDermott, 2011):

- Child and lifespan development
- Dynamics of family relationships
- Guidance and nurturing
- Health and safety
- Diversity in family systems
- Professional practice/best practices in adult learning
- School and child care relationships
- Community relationships
- Assessment and evaluation
- Organizational and public policies/laws

Formal Recognition of Parenting Educators

There are several methods of recognition of parenting educators currently available including registries or directories, state licensure, and national certification. Professionals in the field are currently working to identify a formal recognition system.

Registry

The Texas Registry of Parent Educator Resources (ROPER) at the Center for Parent Education at the University of North Texas includes a parent educator database (www.parenteducation.unt.edu/roper) that registers parent educators from across Texas and provides them with newsletters, training, and a website which includes links to research, organizations, information on conferences, job opportunities, a forum for questions, and ideas and resources for parents. The searchable database can be used by parents, agencies, and parenting professionals to identify parent educators by location or area of expertise.

State licensure

Minnesota is currently the only state to require parent and family educators to be licensed. The license is for a specific statewide parenting education program. Originally, in order to be licensed, parenting and family educators had to have completed a specified number of credits in family structures and functions, family

---

Box 11.2   Parent Group Leader Competencies: A Self-Assessment Checklist

Instructions: Review each item in each of the three major areas and rate yourself from 1 (Not developed) to 5 (Exemplary).

Knowledge: This area outlines knowledge that is specifically related to understanding group dynamics and facilitating parent learning in a group context.

_____ 1. Understanding the developmental stages of group process as this applies to parent groups.

_____ 2. Understanding different theories of group dynamics and their applications to parent groups.

_____ 3. Understanding the roles and boundaries of the parent group leader.

_____ 4. Understanding the emotional nature of parenting issues and how this influences parent group learning.

_____ 5. Understanding different leadership styles and their effects on parent group behavior.

_____ 6. Understanding multiple ways to assess parent and family strengths and limitations in the context of parent groups.

_____ 7. Understanding a variety of active learning methods to assist parents in solving problems and making decisions.

_____ 8. Understanding and being aware of various community resources for parents and families and how to connect parents to these resources.

_____ 9. Understanding family and community diversity and how diverse values and beliefs influence parenting behavior as well as parent group dynamics.

Dispositions: This category of competencies refers to character traits and emotional attitudes that have been identified as important for parent educators (Auerbach, 1968; Braun et al., 1984; Clarke, 1984). These are different from general personality traits or types such as introvert and extrovert. Each individual will have his or her own unique blend of these dispositions.

_____ 1. *Maturity:* Parent group leader is clear about his or her own identity and able to clearly focus on the needs and issues of parents in the group.

_____ 2. *Caring:* Parent group leader is able to focus on the needs of parents and demonstrate understanding, compassion, and support for parents.

_____ 3. *Nonjudgmentalness:* Parent group leader appreciates the complexities of parenting and accepts parents without blaming them for their problems or mistakes. The focus is on helping parents and understanding that there are no easy answers.

_____ 4. *Sensitivity:* Parent group leader is able to perceive and respond to individual parents' needs and feelings.

_____ 5. *Organization:* Parent group leader is able to express goals clearly and provide direction toward parent learning.

_____ 6. *Flexibility:* Parent group leader is able to change direction as needed and balance between individual and group needs of parents.

_____ 7. *Creativity:* Parent group leader is able to design interesting and engaging parent sessions.

_____ 8. *Enthusiasm/Optimism:* Parent group leader has a positive attitude about people and the subject matter and is able to excite parents about learning.

_____ 9. *Honesty:* Parent group leader is clear about his or her own knowledge and limitations.

_____ 10. *Genuineness:* Parent group leader is honest and open in his or her relationships with parents.

_____ 11. *Humor:* Parent group leader is able to appreciate and express what is humorous without ridiculing people or their problems.

Skills: These are presented in general areas followed by very specific behavioral indicators of each general skill area.

1. Creates a warm and welcoming environment.

_____ a. Greets each parent or family member in a welcoming manner.

_____ b. Demonstrates a genuine interest in parent and child well-being.

_____ c. Uses effective openings for a session—involves parents in an engaging and non-threatening manner.

2. Creates a safe environment for parents to share ideas and feelings.

_____ a. Helps group establish and implement ground rules.

_____ b. Elicits a variety of opinions, values, and philosophies from parents.

_____ c. Affirms parents in a genuine and supportive manner.

3. Guides a discussion, giving it form and structure.

_____ a. Informs parents of agenda and goals for the session.

_____ b. Helps parents identify needs and concerns.

_____ c. Keeps the group focused on the group goals and the topic of discussion.

_____ d. Asks clarifying questions to better understand parent issues.

_____ e. Restates and clarifies parent ideas/issues.

_____ f. Summarizes important ideas/issues.

4. Models acceptance of each individual as someone to be listened to and respected.

_____ a. Listens carefully to parents.

_____ b. Gives nonverbal messages of acceptance.

_____ c. Accepts and acknowledges negative feelings and distress.

_____ d. Restates and/or acknowledges parent contributions to the discussion.

_____ e. Addresses diversity and facilitates discussion around differences in values, culture, and family structure.

5. Takes responsibility for establishing a positive and supportive learning environment.

_____ a. Helps parents to identify and set their own goals.

_____ b. Invites parent participation using a variety of methods.

_____ c. Challenges parents to evaluate and reconsider their ideas.

_____ d. Uses concrete examples to bring abstract concepts to life.

_____ e. Adapts information to meet different parent capabilities.

6. Fosters relationships and interaction among group members.

_____ a. Encourages participation of all of the group members.

_____ b. Connects parent comments and experiences to point out common themes.

_____ c. Engages the group in problem solving for individual group members.

_____ d. Addresses conflict directly and respectfully.

Campbell, D., & Palm, G. F. (2004). *Group parent education: Promoting parent learning and support*. Thousand Oaks, CA: Sage. Appendix A, Parent group leader competencies: A self-assessment checklist, pp. 223–225.

dynamics, child development, interpersonal relationships, parenting, and teaching methods (University of Minnesota, 1991). The criteria were later changed to focus on a competency-based model (State of Minnesota, n.d.).

National certification

Much of the conversation among parenting education professionals regarding professional standards has included the feasibility or need for national certification specifically for parenting educators. The National Council on Family Relations' certification program for family life educators requires knowledge in many of the areas deemed relevant for parenting education. The Certified Family Life Educator (CFLE) designation requires a minimum of a baccalaureate degree and work experience in family life education ranging from 1,600 to 4,800 hours, depending on the level and relevancy of the degree. Some argue that professionals practicing in parenting education should have preparation in the broad areas that make up the CFLE criteria. However many parenting educators who operate as facilitators, paraprofessionals, and volunteers, as well as many that consider themselves to be professional parenting educators, may not be able to meet all of the requirements of the CFLE designation. Others have argued that there is a level and depth of knowledge needed in parenting education that is not included within the CFLE standards.

The idea of required licensure and/or certification of parenting educators has been met with concern by those who support peer-educator/paraprofessional models and other grassroots community-based programs. Establishment of specific academic criteria could prevent many of these parents from practicing as parenting educators.

Framework for Understanding Parent Educator Professional Preparation and Recognition

Fortunately, efforts are underway to develop consensus around a set of core competencies for parenting educators; create a standard for states that are developing professional development and recognition systems; and clarify the roles of peers and paraprofessionals (Bowman, Rennekamp, & Wolfe, 2012). The NPEN Professional Preparation and Recognition Committee is working to identify guidelines for parenting educator competencies; provide information about professional preparation and recognition that promotes development of these competencies; and explore development of a national parenting educator recognition system within NPEN (Cooke, 2011). To that end, the committee is designing a *Framework for Understanding Parenting Educator Professional Preparation and Recognition* (www.npen.org/profdev/forum/tools/framework.pdf). The Framework considers preparation options for individuals entering parenting education from a broad range of experience and educational levels, from high school education/GED to doctoral degree. The NPEN website includes resources relevant to the profession of parenting education, competencies, and state and national models.

SUMMARY

In this chapter the important role that parents play in the lives of their children has been examined along with the value that parenting education can provide to families and society. In addition to some of the prominent pressures impacting today's families, there was a brief review of the history of parenting education as an approach to societal issues. Relevant theories have been suggested along with the concept of parent development and aspects of parenting education delivery including formats, approaches, audiences, and settings. A number of parenting education models and approaches have been presented. A discussion of parenting education would be incomplete without a thorough consideration of the role of the parenting educator, training and preparation options, and competencies for best practice. Finally, existing alternatives for the recognition of parenting education were presented along with the ongoing efforts to bring a more formal and established professional recognition framework to the field.

This is an exciting time for the field of parenting education. The growing number of professionals who consider parenting education to be their primary profession are actively discussing new ideas, approaches, theories, and criteria. Increased recognition of the value and impact of positive parenting on the well-being of individuals and society will no doubt result in continued discussion and growth in this important field.

QUESTIONS AND ISSUES FOR DISCUSSION

1. Can parenting educators be effective if they have never had children themselves?
2. Is parenting education a profession or a discipline within the profession of education?
3. Should parenting educators be required to have at least a baccalaureate degree in order to practice?
4. Which term is better: "parent educator" or "parenting educator?" Why?
5. What implicit and explicit rules were part of your family system when you were growing up? Over time were they stable or did they change?
6. Will you, or did you, keep these same rules for your children?
7. What is an example of a behavior that you modeled after a parent(s)?
8. Which theories related to a child's development seem the most useful?
9. What are some examples of bidirectional influences of parents and children?

ACTIVITIES

1. Investigate the availability of parenting education programs in your community. In what settings are they held (health care, community education, Extension)?
2. From the descriptions of the parenting programs, can you tell on which child development theory they are based (behaviorism, attachment, social learning, etc.)?
3. Scan the Internet or media for emerging issues of concern to parents (e.g., teen sleep, bullying, substance abuse, sexting). What are some ways in which parents can best respond?
4. Identify three ways that the overindulgence of children can be harmful to families and society.

International Perspectives
on Family Life Education

≡ Need for Global Awareness

We live in a complex world where understanding other individuals and cultures is critical. Global awareness is no longer a luxury, but a necessity as we extend our focus to families unlike our own. The need for students to become culturally competent and prepared to work with diverse populations is becoming increasingly important, particularly in the family science field. By incorporating cross-cultural awareness and sensitivity into our classrooms, we can enhance the understanding, appreciation, and acceptance of diverse families and cultures. This increased awareness can both enrich our own lives and contribute to the wellbeing of individuals and families worldwide.

More than ever, global issues are influencing the lives of families due to advances in communication, technology, science, and transportation. Globalization is the process of the world becoming increasingly connected through trade, ideas, and other aspects of culture along with the transmission of values; economic fragility or stability; and at times cooperation, unrest, or intervention. Information, goods, and services produced in one country are easily available to others in various parts of the world. The clothes we wear, the foods we eat, the music we enjoy, the art we view, the technology we employ, and the natural resources we use are all a result of this global process. Consequently, individuals and families around the world are becoming more connected to each other. The trends of globalization and the expanding interrelationships among nations and their peoples have resulted in global diversification, as well as a growing interdependence of the world's population racially, ethnically, culturally, and economically. Globalization has not only reduced distance and time, but has also linked countries at opposite ends of the Earth resulting in the complex transition of many advanced countries into multi-ethnic and multicultural societies (Dini, 2000; Foner, 2005).

The increasing globalization and technological development of our world will continue at a rapid pace resulting in anxiety, tension, and conflict for those cultures rooted in more traditional, agrarian, and patriarchal value systems. While Americans have a positive view of globalization overall, for many years globalization was perceived as "Americanization," so Americans had few adjustments to make within this paradigm. However, now globalization has taken a "Global-as-Asian" perspective that involves a two-way street for people, trade, influence, and ideas (Tay, 2010; World Public Opinion, n.d.). Currently Americans believe that the skills needed to work in a globalized world need to be taught in schools and that international content should be in state standards to make students "world ready" (Tay, 2010). In contrast, some countries ruled by fundamentalist religious leaders report frustration in the dress and actions of teenagers wearing rebellious fashions in public, as seen on popular Western television programs beamed down from satellites. As people are exposed to the more gender-equal and individualistic values of Western cultures, societal conflicts are erupting (Francoeur & Noonan, 2004a).

Although the functions and structures of families vary by culture, families are still the most important resource in each society. They provide the buffer and protection to keep children and other members safe. However, some families are vulnerable when dealing with health care, economics, environment, and social influences. At times, they cannot manage alone and government steps in to create policies and programs that could affect family structure, education, and financial well-being. While many professionals can help families, family life educators incorporate a preventative and educational approach to individual and family issues. They provide the skills and knowledge to enrich individual and family life.

An international perspective is needed when we teach about families. Many U.S. students attending American universities have an *ethno-centric* view of culture and may judge other cultures by the values and standards of their own culture. Therefore, it is important to provide an alternative perspective. We want to encourage an *ethno-relative* approach where cultures are understood relative to one another and characteristics are regarded as differences with no perception of being good or bad. Whether teaching about family relations, parenting, or marriage education, cultural differences and implications can enhance learning within our own society, as well as learning about others. We need to create a climate within family science classrooms that fosters thinking not only about family content, but also multicultural understanding. While some family science programs have specific courses in cultural diversity, cultural learning can also be infused into a variety of courses and topics in order to provide and enhance an international perspective to the study of families.

Global Issues of Concern to Families

> "The family is the natural and fundamental group unit of society and is entitled to protection by the society and the state."
> —Article 16(3) of the Universal Declaration of Human Rights
> (United Nations, 1948)

To better understand the context underlying the development of family life education programs internationally, an awareness of issues of concern to families is critical. These issues can vary from country to country. Some countries are facing the devastating effects of HIV/AIDS and other infectious diseases that kill far more people than man-made or natural disasters (Shah, 2011). Health concerns provide multiple stressors to families. Various countries have family planning and pregnancy as primary issues and are working to provide education regarding pregnancy prevention, prenatal care, and parenting. In other countries marriage education predominates with legislation to assist couples with premarital education, whereas some countries are focusing on helping couples with their relationships as they make the transition to parenthood. A number of communities are facing the devastation of war, terrorism, and economic instability that influences individuals and families as they deal with the physical and emotional pain of both the actual events, and the accompanying fear. Even several years after the current global financial crisis began, the world economy is still struggling to recover because countries are inextricably tied to each other's monetary well-being. Global unemployment rates remain high resulting in a synchronized economic downturn that affects both developed and developing countries (UNDESA, 2013b). While there are a variety of issues confronting individuals and families in various countries and regions of the world, from a global perspective there are some major trends that impact families (UNDP, 2003).

Rise of Migration

The number of countries concerned and involved in human mobility is steadily rising. None of the 196 sovereign states is beyond the reach of migration, being either countries of origin, transit, or destination for migrants, or often all three simultaneously. Whereas some migration is internal, the rising number of people crossing borders is the most reliable indicator of the intensity of globalization. As a result, the traditional boundaries between languages, cultures, ethnic groups, and nations are eroding. In 2010, first generation immigrants accounted for nearly 3% of the world's population, or more than 215 million international migrants, which is a three-fold increase since 1960 (UNDP, 2011). If all international migrants lived in the same place, it would be the world's fifth largest country (UNDESA, 2010). The annual number of migrants is estimated to be between 5 and 10 million people. Demographers not only project an increase in the world population to 9.3 billion by 2050, but also an increasing number of international migrants (405 million) and internal migrants (740 million) (IOM, 2010; UNDP, 2009). This migration is likely to transform the effects of environmental change, global-political and economic dynamics, technological revolutions, and social networks. A small percentage of migrants are refugees fleeing armed conflict, natural disaster, famine, or persecution because crises can displace a large number of persons in a short period of time (UNFPA, 2008). However, generally those who migrate are often highly educated and qualified persons so their departure results in a 'brain drain" from the home economy. Some prefer to be "circular" rather than permanent migrants, and thus eventually return home to family and friends. About half the migrants are women, most of reproductive age, who either migrated as spouses or family members or moved independently from their families to work abroad as primary breadwinners. Because opportunities for legal migration are limited, many women have resorted to unusual forms of migration involving smuggling and trafficking. As a result women are prone to experience gender-specific forms of abuse and exploitation (IOM, 2010; UNDESA, 2010).

While international migration can be seen as facilitating global interdependence and unity, it also brings widening demographic, economic, political, and ecological disparities that greatly influence families (Brubaker, 2001). Therefore, viewing families from a global context is not only important to increase our understanding of those beyond our borders, but also to gain insights about those who have recently immigrated to new countries. Because international travel and migration are bringing people of the world together, migration is emerging as one of the major issues of our times. The mobility of families is also a concern, because family members no longer live in close proximity. When family members move, they often become disconnected from the unifying features of their extended families. While some families maintain communication through the Internet and cell phones, quality time still may be lost. There may be circumstances due to geography, time, and finances that prevent families from returning home for important family occasions. Thus, family members may not be present for significant family transitions, times of joy and sorrow, or opportunities to resolve family issues and disagreements. Because of these challenges, younger generations of migrant families may also not have opportunities to interact and bond with their relatives as they did when living in their countries of origin.

Changes in Family Structure

In the past, many cultural groups assumed that couples would get married, stay married, have children, and deal with two sets of kin. However, in many societies this is changing. Increasing rates of cohabitation, divorce, mobility, migration, and aging have altered family structure, as well as the notion of intergenerational relationships. Other developments, such as the use of contraception and decreased childbearing, increasing numbers of singles and single parents, women joining the labor force, postponement of marriage, and improved education of women have resulted in smaller families and decreased potential for family caregivers (Annie E. Casey Foundation, 2013c; NIH, 2011; Steck, 2009). These changes are linked with other broader cultural transitions, such as the rise of individualism, secularism, and growth of the welfare state. Thus, some traditional values within a culture have been altered regarding childbearing and the expected ages at which family traditions, such as marriage and childbirth, commonly occur (Mills, 2014; UN, 2013). Moreover, poor economic conditions in some countries resulted in greater maternal and child mortality. Not only have the composition and structure of families changed in many countries, but also migrants who carried with them the idea of family structure based on their home countries often find that changes in culture and context evolve into further alterations to their families and feelings of uncertainty (UNDP, 2003).

Demographic Aging

The current rate of population aging is unprecedented, pervasive, and enduring, with increases in the proportions of older persons (60 years or older) being accompanied by declines in the proportions of the young (under age 15) (UNDESA, 2002). The aging of the world population will be even more rapid in the twenty-first century than in the past. The population over the age of 60 is projected to double worldwide in the next half century. However, the pace of change is quite varied and countries are at very different stages in this process. Those countries that started this process later will have less time to adjust. Because of decreasing fertility, we will not return to the young populations of our ancestors. The aging of the population will affect every man, woman, and child and will have a direct bearing on intergenerational and intragenerational relationships. Aging will not only influence the economics of countries, but also health and health care, family composition, living arrangements, housing, and migration. The world median age is currently 28.4, but by 2050 it is expected to be 38 years of age, with the most rapidly aging group being those over 80, which is expected to increase by five times (People & the Planet, 2008; World by Map, 2010).

HIV/AIDS Pandemic

A global summary of the AIDS epidemic indicated more than 70 million people have been infected with the HIV virus. While adult HIV rates have decreased in certain countries due to changes in behavior, progress is uneven (UNAIDS, 2012). About 35 million people have died of AIDS-related causes globally, while 34 million are living with HIV including 3.3 million children (Henry J. Kaiser Family Foundation, 2012; UNAIDS, 2012; WHO, 2013a). In 2011, more than 8 million people with HIV had access to antiretroviral therapy, however 7 million people who are eligible for treatment are not receiving it, including 72% of children living with HIV (UNAIDS, 2012). HIV/AIDS is the leading cause of death worldwide and the number one cause in Africa, where most new victims are women. These women are infected by their husbands who have both a "home wife" and one or more traveling wives as companions when they are away at work. Women are often ignorant about the ways HIV can be spread and are prevented by cultural norms from insisting on prevention methods when they have sexual relations with their husbands. Gender inequality makes it more difficult for African women to negotiate condom use. Moreover, sexual violence can increase the widespread risk of HIV transmission. There is also increasing prevalence of HIV in women in Asia, including large epidemics in China and India, due to women's low economic and social position and poor health status. In Asia, injection drug use in conjunction with sexual relations influences the HIV epidemic. As in Africa, gender inequalities and the cultural rules governing sexual relations for men and women are central to this health issue. Because of the increased number of people with HIV receiving treatment in resource-poor countries, deaths have declined and the epidemic has stabilized. Nevertheless, there are still more than 7,000 new infections per day (about 2.5 million in 2011) (UNAIDS, 2012). HIV not only affects the health of individuals, but also families, communities, and the economic development of countries (Henry J. Kaiser Foundation, 2012).

Armed Conflicts and Turbulence

While trouble spots exist in many parts of the world, when they erupt, suffering and hardship customarily follow. As a result of these conflicts, there are mass violations of human rights, including unlawful killings, torture, forced displacement, and starvation (Amnesty International, n.d.). While some conflicts have been ongoing for several years, others are of shorter duration with long-lasting effects. The "Arab Spring" began as protests of civil resistance involving demonstrations and rallies that "spilled over" into other countries through the effective use of social media. These conflicts resulted in consequences for the countries, economies, soldiers, and families. In addition to the deaths of soldiers and civilians, there are visible wounds and amputations, and also invisible trauma, such as brain injuries, post-traumatic stress disorder, and health issues, which can last a lifetime. Moreover, absence of individuals due to these conflicts and their subsequent reintegration into families can influence the ongoing development of couple and family relationships. Because of their global impact, wars, conflicts, and terrorism are no longer isolated to one or a few countries, but affect us all.

Multiple Meanings of "Family"

What Is a Family?

We live in a world of different meanings and contrasting perspectives of family life, so we cannot impose an arbitrary definition of what constitutes a family. Government entities, employers, religions, and individual family members and family groups may view families differently (Adams & Trost, 2005). They may perceive the meaning of "family" as family of origin, family of procreation (biological family), or family of commitment or affiliation. Socially-constructed families (family of commitment or affiliation) have been created to serve the nurturance and acceptance needs of the individual, which could have been influenced by abuse, rejection, or death within their family of origin. Depending on one's culture, family can be perceived as a nuclear family or extended family with multiple generations. Moreover, in some cultures the deceased are still considered as exerting a strong presence in the family. Family can also be defined legally as to who can be married or adopted by law, whereas some perceive taking in a child or nonfamily member as an act of love without the need of legal documentation. Thus, if we impose a single definition of family upon others, we may be sending a message that their family values and structures are not legitimate.

While there is no consensus as to what constitutes a family, particularly across cultures, it could be meaningful to view the family as a bonded unit of interacting and interdependent individuals who have some common goals, resources, and values, and may share living space for at least part of their life cycle (Darling, 2005). This non-exclusionary definition of the family embraces differing family forms, sizes, ages, and role patterns, whether we are discussing same-sex marriages and families, children who divorce their parents, or families who socially open their boundaries to a non-relative. Such a paradigm facilitates viewing the family as a collection of interdependent, yet independent, individuals whose group entity differs from characteristics of its individual members. When the family is viewed as an interacting group of individuals who are emotionally, physically, and socially interdependent, the focus shifts from the attributes of the group or the individual to the relationships among the family members. In the complex world in which we live, a flexible perspective of families is essential to facilitate the bonds that may have eroded through death, divorce, family separation, or circumstance (Darling, 2005). Recent natural disasters, wars, and terrorist activities have brought attention to the loss of family members and the need to adapt boundaries to incorporate those in need of familial support.

Using Theory to Understand International Families

There are multiple theories from various disciplines that can be used to understand international family structures and functions by providing reasonable explanations of individual and family behaviors. Although no single theory is intended to explain everything in the universe, scientific theory utilizes a certain set of concepts to explain a particular set of phenomena. Because we are affected by our childhood, familial, gendered, and socialization experiences along with our cultural beliefs, the integration of multiple theories is warranted. For example, exchange theory can be incorporated to understand the rewards and costs of living in particular location versus migrating to another country (White & Klein, 2008). Moreover, immigrants to various new cultures may experience differing levels of adaptation due to the stressors in their lives, availability of resources for coping, and perception of these events. Thus, understanding family stress theory and the ABC-X model as it applies to the normative and nonnormative stressors of immigrant families can provide insight into family adaptability, boundary ambiguity, and resilience (Boss, 2002; Weber, 2011). While families can be analyzed from numerous theoretical frameworks, a few can be highlighted to illustrate how theory can be applied to facilitate greater understanding of international families (see Chapter 8 for further details).

Family systems

Viewing the family as a system provides an important paradigm when analyzing human behavior globally (White & Klein, 2008). Cross-cultural understanding of intergenerational communications within families, physical and psychological boundaries, feedback in coupled relationships, and parent-child communications can provide insight into interpreting the complex relationships between individuals and their families. Theoretical insights and clarifications can evolve from discussions of boundaries, distance regulation, cohesion, and adaptability in various cultures. What types of cultural boundaries exist for persons of varying ethnic, age, or gender backgrounds? What kinds of expectations for family togetherness and adaptability exist for different ethnic and religious groups? For example, cohesion and enmeshment can have different meanings in cultures that value familism vs. individuality. A discussion of family stories, rituals, and rules can also provide understanding and meaning about differing cultural groups.

Developmental theory

Incorporating a developmental framework, for both individuals and families, can be helpful when trying to understand families across cultures within a perspective of change (White & Klein, 2008). Whereas change is ever present, gradual, and a part of individual aging, families and society are changing at an even faster rate. Along with media influences, alternate lifestyles, and advances in technology and biotechnology, family life has also evolved. Cultural assumptions and beliefs about family life change over time, as do its transitions of getting married, having children, becoming older, and dying. People in diverse cultures develop differently based on the values, economics, norms, and demographics in their cultures, so communicating with individuals from other cultures at varying points in their development can expand insights about family life.

Family ecosystems framework

When studying international families, there are not only many different family customs, but also the social contexts for those customs. Some customs, which may seem different to Westerners, are widow inheritance in Kenya, "adultery hoots" in Ghana, *hijra* in India, living apart together (LAT) in Germany and Sweden, transgendered *kaneeths* in Bahrain, *kathoey* in Thailand, temporary marriage (*mut'a*) in

Iran, hymen reconstruction in South Korea and Greek Cyprus, "try everything" (*faxendotudo*) advice given to Brazilian boys and girls, and the subordinate roles of women in many cultures (Francoeur, 2004).

In order to add an environmental context to international family life education, the family ecosystems approach can be quite useful (Bubolz et al., 1979; Bubolz & Sontag, 1993; Darling, 1987; Darling & Howard, 2009; Darling & Turkki, 2009). With individual, family, and world issues becoming increasingly complicated, a framework is needed to guide our thinking. The reciprocal interactions between environmental influences and families differentiate each country's issues and the preferred mode to ameliorate their concerns. There is increasing awareness that human beings are interdependent creatures and not independent organisms. This is not only true in our relationships with each other, but also with the total environment in which we live. Worldwide population growth, contamination of the environment, depletion of energy resources, war, and terrorism have made us aware of our interdependence with each other and with the environment. This holistic view of individuals and groups in their association with the physical, biological, and social conditions and events around them provides a frame of reference that has come to be generally known as "human or family ecology."

A core value in an ecosystems framework is survival, not just of humans, but the other living species as well. This also includes the survival and well-being of the nonliving environment, which is critical for sustaining all life. Most family life educators dealing with international family life education would resonate with the perspective of Bubolz and Sontag (1993), who proposed that the grounding of family ecology theory in values places an important responsibility on scholars and practitioners. We must attend to special problems of groups and subcultures that lack power, self-determination, and access to resources and who experience discrimination and prejudice. These can include racial and ethnic minorities, the handicapped, women, the poor, and the elderly. Attention must be given not only to the "haves," but also to the "have nots." The scope of family ecology must be international and address needs of people in developing nations, as well as the less privileged in more developed areas of the world. Because human betterment and the quality of the environment are interdependent, the value base of family ecology is grounded in this interdependence.

The major concepts of the family ecosystem involve the *organism* (individual or family) as it *interacts* with its multifaceted *environments*, i.e., natural, human-behavioral, and human-constructed environments (see Chapter 8 for further details). By applying the ecosystems framework, students can examine global issues of family concern and their impact on individuals and family members. This approach can provide an ethno-relative approach to understanding cultural perspectives of families, public policies, and environmental conditions.

What Is Family Life Education—International Perspectives

Various countries beyond the U.S. have developed extensive programs in family life education (e.g., Singapore); passed new legislation to support family life education (e.g., Taiwan); proposed marriage/couples/parent education (e.g., Norway); focused on issues of concern to families, such as AIDS and HIV (e.g., China,

India, and South Africa); and developed academic programs related to family life education (e.g., Taiwan and Canada). However, information and communication about the progress of these initiatives worldwide are varied and inconsistent. From an international perspective, family life education exits, but its definition, meaning, goals, and methods can be quite diverse. This is due, in part, to the breadth of the field and the different disciplines it encompasses, especially in the international arena. In fact, a recent Google search for "International Family Life Education" resulted in about 678,000,000 entries. While all these entries may not be applicable to specific programs, family concerns in various countries are resulting in organized programs to assist those in need.

Although there is little consensus regarding the definition of family life education within Western culture, generally it is perceived to be any effort to strengthen family life through education or support (see Chapter 1 for further details). Family life education can include anything from teaching about relationships in schools to providing premarital education, or dealing with the developmental issues of aging. Knowledge about human development, interpersonal relations, and family life is not innate; thus, there is a societal need to transmit knowledge about family living intergenerationally. While some of this learning is done informally, the complexities of society mandate that new methods be created to assist individuals preparing for family life and its responsibilities. The objective of all family life education is to enrich and improve the quality of life for individuals and families. While family life education does not impose some arbitrary definition of what constitutes a family, it does emphasize processes that help people develop into healthy adults, work together in close relationships, and bring out the best in others (Cassidy, 2003; Darling, 1987; National Council on Family Relations, 2003).

To understand the impact of culture when providing family life education, it might be helpful to learn about the experiences and insights of an American-born family life educator who has resided part-time in Japan (Southwick, personal communication, January 14, 2006; Southwick, 2011a, 2011b). For over 25 years Edward Southwick has been periodically providing counseling and self-improvement lessons for individuals, couples, groups, and communities through community-based, non-formal education programs in Japan. While he has ultimately been effective in helping people, developing a successful family life education business in Japan has been difficult, largely because of Japanese culture. According to Southwick, who has a lens of both an "insider" and "outsider" in viewing families and family life education:

- Family is not highly valued in Japan, especially in the business community as evidenced by the lack of time off provided for childbirth and parenting. Fathers rarely get to see their children in sporting events and frequently have to spend their after-work hours socializing with coworkers. Many are required to work in another city or country for periods of a year or longer without their families.

- The Japanese are very private people who keep their problems to themselves and consider receiving counseling or any assistance as a sign of weakness. Lack of communication is also an issue. In Japan, a saying similar to "silence is golden" has been mistakenly applied to almost every aspect of family communications, as well as relationships with friends and business.

- Framing of services as "lessons in self-improvement" is important to successfully promote and conduct family life education in Japan. Japanese families would not participate in family counseling or attend a parenting class for fear of being perceived as inadequate. However, if the same information was packaged as "self-improvement," it was acceptable. Therefore, family life education courses were marketed as instruction for "happiness and life success coaching," with attendees receiving a certificate upon completion. The premise was that those educated in this program would go on to provide guidance and training to others, thereby making it less stigmatizing to participate. However, those who attended the programs seldom went on to use the information professionally to help others. Rather, they found the information to be useful within their own families. Thus, promoting family life education courses in this way was well received.

Southwick's experience in providing family life education in Japan is helpful in revealing the role of culture in implementing family life education programs. Family life education has to develop in context of the ecosystem. It is important for educators to understand elements within the culture in which they will be teaching in order to offer guidance in a satisfactory form. To reduce the stigma of needing family assistance, marketing family life education through the media and television can make family life education courses more acceptable to potential students. It can also encourage government and business leaders to develop more family-friendly policies and certificate-based courses to assist families with their problems, while avoiding embarrassment.

Evolving Status of Family Life Education Internationally

There are numerous programs dealing with some aspect of family life education worldwide. However, we have little comparative data regarding the status of family life education in other countries. Conducting research internationally has several challenges involving communication, coordination, and interpretation. Nevertheless, it is important to get data from other countries and develop a global network of colleagues to assist each other with issues of professional and social concern.

Quantitative Examination of International Family Life Education

An exploratory *quantitative* study was conducted to determine the status of family life education internationally by examining the involvement, interest, and available course work offered in family life education worldwide (Darling & Turkki, 2009). While there can be limitations to interpretation based on the sample, questions, and data collection procedures, it is important to examine some worldwide family issues of public concern and how they relate to family life education.

The participants in this study consisted of international members (non U.S.) of four international organizations dealing with family issues through the coordination and support of the National Council on Family Relations (NCFR) and International Federation for Home Economics (IFHE). NCFR is an international multidisciplinary professional organization linking family research with family education, practice, and policy formation. IFHE is an international non-governmental organization concerned with home economics and consumer studies. Both have consultative status with the United Nations (Darling & Turkki, 2009).

After examining several United Nations documents to determine worldwide issues, a survey was developed with the assistance of international colleagues. Since professionals in various countries can have diverse definitions and perceptions of "family" and "family life education," pertinent definitions were included in the survey as they applied to family life education, marriage education, and parent education. In addition, some categories of questions included family issues of public concern, general level of legislation/regulation regarding family issues, and needs for professional training and family programs. While the survey was in English, many family professionals speak English as a second language to facilitate professional communication and collaboration. The final sample consisted of 277 respondents from five continents and 50 countries (Darling & Turkki, 2009).

Respondents were asked whether or not they were family life educators, marriage educators, and/or parent educators. Each question provided an operational definition of these three types of educators in order to provide a consistent perspective across cultures. Involvement in family life education was reported by 43.7% of the respondents, whereas 22.6% were involved in parent education and 10.7% considered themselves marriage educators. Interest in becoming a family life educator was expressed by 67.8% of the respondents with 25.9% indicating they were "very interested." When asked in a Likert-type question (1 = no interest to 5 = great interest) about public interest in their countries regarding legislation for family life, marriage, and parent education, there was more interest for parent education (mean = 3.65) followed by family life education (mean = 3.38) and marriage education (mean = 2.84). The developing international interest in family life education is obvious. While the contexts of these data were not apparent, the example of having to disguise family life education in Japan indicates that the perception of the name and what it means can be a problem when interpreting cross-cultural data.

Due to the increasing international interest in NCFR's Certified Family Life Educator credential, the respondents were asked to indicate the level of university-level course offerings in their country that were applicable to the 10 FLE content areas. The responses, which were ranked by their means, resulted from a Likert-type scale ranging from 1 = no coursework to 5 = considerable coursework.

Family Life Education Content Areas	Mean
Human Growth and Development across the Lifespan	3.78
Families and Individuals in Societal Contexts	3.74
Internal Dynamics of Families	3.52
Interpersonal Relationships	3.41
Family Law and Public Policy	3.25
Human Sexuality	3.23
Professional Ethics and Practice	3.16
Family Resource Management	3.15
Parent Education and Guidance	2.94
Family Life Education Methodology	2.77

The totals of the mean scores of involvement in each of these content areas by continent are shown in a stacked graph in Figure 12.1 on the following page. This graph is organized from the bottom upward by rank order, with the most prominent area being *Human Growth and Development* on the bottom and *Family Life Methodology* on the top. As gratifying as it is to see that so many continents and countries have coursework applicable to family life education, the need for family life education methodology is readily apparent.

These professionals noted that various family issues were of public concern to the people in their countries. Public concern for 30 issues related to family well-being was noted by a Likert-type scale of 1 = no interest to 5 = great interest. The five greatest issues of concern were drug and alcohol abuse, aging, family violence, adolescent health, and unemployment, whereas the issue of least concern was cohabitation, which was preceded by family structure and homelessness (see Table 12.1). Some of these issues, such as aging and HIV/AIDS, are related to previously reported global concerns, but a few are worth some special attention.

Drug and alcohol abuse

Worldwide data indicate that 15.3 million persons have problems with drug use. Injection drug use is reported in 148 countries with 120 countries indicating HIV infection among this population (WHO, 2013b). About 5% of the world's adult population is estimated to have used an illicit drug at least once in 2010 with problem users numbering about 27 million people (UNODC, 2012). Although global use has remained relatively stable in the last five years, it has been increasing in several developing countries. The use of psychoactive substances causes significant health and social problems for those who use them, as well as their families and communities. In addition, drug trafficking, which has global dimensions, also affects individuals, families, and countries (UNODC, 2012).

The harmful use of alcohol and other controlled substances is grow-

Table 12.1   Level of Interest in Family Issues of Public Concern

Public Issue	Mean*
Drug and Alcohol Abuse	3.88
Aging	3.82
Family Violence	3.70
Adolescent Health	3.66
Unemployment	3.64
Caregiving	3.53
Gender Equality	3.45
Health Insurance	3.41
HIV/AIDS	3.40
Divorce	3.40
Adolescent Pregnancy	3.38
Cultural Diversity	3.33
Parenting Issues	3.33
Maternal Health Care	3.26
Poverty	3.25
Universal Primary Education	3.25
Contraception	3.22
Family Well-Being	3.21
Legislative Support of Families	3.03
Family Planning	3.01
Therapy and Counseling	2.96
Marital Stability	2.94
Reduction of Child Mortality	2.88
Employer Support of Families	2.86
Fatherhood	2.85
Infertility	2.85
Adoption	2.85
Homelessness	2.80
Family Structure	2.76
Cohabitation	2.46

*Range: 1 = no interest to 5 = great interest

Figure 12.1   Level of Course Offerings in CFLE Content Areas by Continent

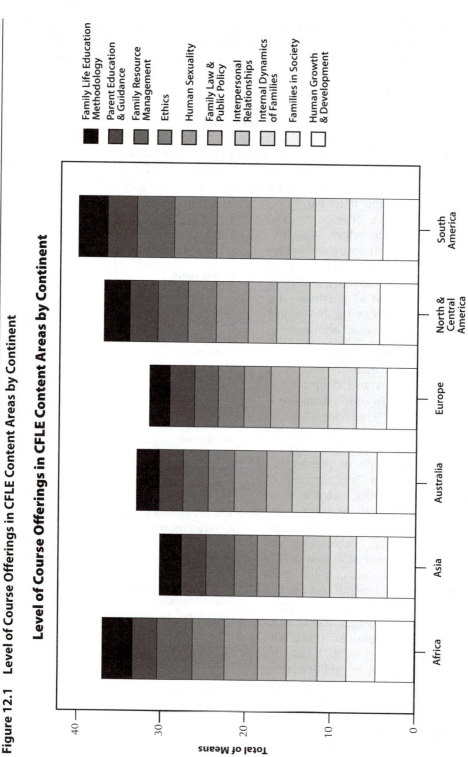

Darling, C., & Turkki, K. (2009). Global family concerns and the role of family life education: An Ecosystemic analysis. *Family Relations 58*, 14–27.

ing rapidly and contributing significantly to the global burden of disease taking a major toll on both individuals and families. There are 76.3 million persons diagnosed with alcohol-use disorders and about 2.5 million deaths each year with risk factors associated with many serious social and developmental issues, violence, child neglect, abuse, and workplace absenteeism (WHO, 2013b). Other risk factors include physical health associated with cardiovascular diseases; various cancers; and infectious diseases such as HIV/AIDS, tuberculosis, and sexually transmitted infections (STIs) (WHO, 2011). It also affects the well-being and health of people around the drinker, such as family members and those who suffer from injuries due to traffic accidents and violence caused by those who engaged in harmful drinking (WHO, 2013b). There is often a misconception that the problem with alcohol is due to dependence, but many public health problems arise from acute intoxication resulting from occasional high-risk drinking by normally light to moderate drinkers. Abuse of alcohol takes a disproportionate toll on the poor, who spend a greater percentage of their incomes on alcohol. When problems occur they also have less access to services, may lose their jobs, and bring difficulties to their families. Experience has shown that the most effective way of reducing consumption is by restricting availability in some manner (Sharman, 2005).

Domestic violence

Domestic violence is a serious worldwide problem and epidemic. A study on domestic abuse of 24,000 women from rural and urban areas in ten countries revealed that intimate partner violence is the most common form of violence in women's lives and surpasses assaults by strangers or acquaintances (WHO, 2005). While statistics vary, a significantly greater proportion of women than men are victims of intimate partner violence (IPV). Globally, almost one-third of women have experienced sexual and/or physical, emotional, or other kinds of violence during their lives (Advocates for Human Rights, 2013; Garcia-Moreno & Pallitto, 2013). In addition, approximately 38% of women who are murdered are killed by their intimate partner, along with 42% who have experienced injuries due to IPV. Domestic violence is known to affect women's sexual and reproductive health, as well as increase the risk of receiving a sexually transmitted infection (STI). They are 16% more likely to have a low-birth weight baby and twice as likely to have experienced an abortion or depression (Garcia-Moreno & Pallitto, 2013). Although perceived as a time when women should be protected, between 4% and 12% of pregnant women were beaten during pregnancy. Of these women, 90% had been abused by the father of their unborn child, and at least 20% of them had never told anyone about the abuse prior to being interviewed (WHO, 2005). The social and economic costs of family violence are considerable. The losses are not just financial, but involve the diminished productivity of individuals who are unable to function fully, have lost their psychic identity, or have died. Women often suffer isolation, an inability to work, a lack of participation in regular activities, and a reduced capacity to care for themselves and their children (WHO, 2012). Family violence is a human rights issue deeply rooted in cultural and religious gender bias and often supported by patriarchal societies.

Adolescent health

Adolescent health is a concern in both developed and developing countries, but the problems of youth are often ignored (Patton, 2012). Today's 1.8 billion adolescents are more often exposed to harmful alcohol consumption, STIs, and other risks than in the past. They also face other new challenges such as mental health problems and involvement in social media (*The Lancet*, 2012). Nearly two-thirds of premature deaths and one-third of adult health issues are associated with conditions or behaviors that began in adolescence. These issues include tobacco use, lack of physical activity, unprotected sex, or exposure to violence, which is the leading cause of death among young people, especially males. While adolescence is a period of exploration and experimentation, young people often lack the knowledge and ability to avoid some of the risks that confront them. Sexuality is a major challenge for healthy adolescent development with adolescents facing problems of early pregnancy, HIV infections, and STIs, which often go undetected. Moreover, unwanted pregnancies often result in poor prenatal and antenatal care, or are resolved by unskilled practitioners who perform unsafe illegal abortions. Tobacco use is another serious health issue for adolescents who are often enticed to smoke by adult smokers or advertising. Very few adolescent smokers actually stop smoking as adults; however, young people who do not use tobacco before age 20 are unlikely to start smoking as adults. In developing countries, many youth enter adolescence undernourished, making them vulnerable to disease and early death. In developed countries, obesity and being overweight can have serious health consequences. It is critical to raise attention to these issues by identifying effective ways to promote health gains through prevention and intervention among young people (Patton, 2012; WHO, 2013c).

A study of international colleagues indicated that family professionals who perceived public concern for family issues believed that the well-being of families was related to the availability of family life education (FLE) courses along with public and legislative interest in FLE. They also valued increased attention to family issues in the workplace. However, public concern for families was inversely related to assistance from a network of international colleagues. This could be due to apprehension about "outside" cultural influences on "inside" behaviors. These findings suggest the emerging importance of public consciousness about family matters and family life education in various countries of the world, as well as the need for local family professionals to resolve issues of concern. It is hoped that this public interest will further a global understanding and education of professionals and students about families (Darling & Turkki, 2009).

Qualitative Examination of International Family Life Education

While quantitative data provide important background information about international family life education, *qualitative* comments can provide a rich contribution to the perceived status and issues of family life education in various countries. Non-U.S. members of the National Council on Family Relations were contacted about the current status of family life education in their countries, with some of these members recommending other family colleagues in their countries. Colleagues (n = 141) in 6 continents and 38 countries were asked to give their general perceptions and insights about FLE in their countries, along with some generic questions that could stimulate their thinking. The responses were from 48 family colleagues representing 6 continents and 29 different countries (see the Preface for an acknowledgment of countries from which responses were received). The topics suggested for their input included (1) the existence of structured programs in the public schools or higher education that focus on studying families; (2) availability of community FLE in the public or private sector; (3) public interest in attending FLE programs; (4) promotion of FLE by agencies and policy makers; (5) critical issues facing individuals and families and educational efforts to assist them; and (6) the development of FLE programs in their countries. If family education exits in their countries, is it just beginning, making progress, or doing well? After analyzing the data, some of the resulting themes were related to perceptions, participation in FLE, and governmental and cultural influences on FLE.

Perceptions

When examining statements from international colleagues, many noted that their comments were "personal opinions" or "uninformed opinions." Others provided qualifying statements such as, "from my point of view," "that I know of," or "as far as I know." These were their impressions or based on the perspective of the agency or faith-based setting in which they worked. Thus, the following comments should be viewed from this context.

International participation in family life education or family education

Family life education is perceived as occurring in differing degrees in various countries, along with a need to certify family life educators. Various programs exist in primary and secondary schools, as well as higher education, but family programs vary by length of time and their inclusion within other curricula. Other nonformal FLE programs are available with varying levels of interest in participation.

Existence.   A primary issue examined was whether or not family life education (FLE) or family education (as it is called in some countries) exists in countries beyond the U.S. and to what degree. There was a range of responses from *FLE not existing* (e.g., Brazil, Guatemala, Ireland, Israel, Japan, Malaysia, Pakistan, Turkey) to *being in its infancy* or *scarcely existing* (e.g., Portugal, Saudi Arabia, Sweden) and *just beginning, developing, or existing but insufficient* (e.g., Germany, Japan, Trinidad and Tobago, United Arab Emirates). *Progress is being made* in some countries (e.g., Canada) and FLE is *doing well, developing rapidly, making good progress* (e.g., China, Ghana, Singapore, Taiwan), or *relatively well established* (e.g., Australia). (Note: Some respondents from Japan had the perception that there was no FLE, whereas others indicated that it was just beginning. However, in Japanese there is no word for "family life education," which may account for some of this confusion.) Whereas a need for FLE was indicated for Nigeria, there are few resources and data on the status of families and FLE, which is problematic because data are necessary as documentation to plan, implement, and/or coordinate new and on-going programs.

Certification and certificates in family life education.   There was some international interest in certifying family life educators. Canada has a Certified Canadian Family Educator (CCFE) program. Moreover, Taiwan has approximately 1,300 certified family educators. Students take 10 courses (5 required and 5 elective courses) and if they get a satisfactory grade or take an exam, they become certified by the government. As a result, the number of Taiwanese family life educators is increasing faster than expected. Whereas Switzerland is in the process of developing a certificate for parenting educators, the government in Singapore hopes to increase the number of family life educators by enhancing training programs and providing certificates in Family Life Education. While South Korea has tried to develop a FLE certificate program, there is a perception that it lacks credibility because of its low number of hours for structured training (only 40 hours for this credential). While there is no program at the university level in Guatemala, there is a structured three-year program at the high school level that allows students to obtain a specialized degree as a "home educator" by the time they graduate from high school. (Note: As clarified in Chapter 2, there is a difference between a certificate and certification. *Certificate* programs are offered by a professional agency, association, commercial enterprise, or university in response to the completion of a defined training program. It is a terminal award meaning that there is no ongoing requirement for continuing education or additional learning. *Certification* is a voluntary process by which a professional agency or association grants recognition to an individual who has met certain predetermined qualifications or standards specified by that agency, often demonstrated through an exam or portfolio review [e.g., CFLE, CFCS]. Certification is an ongoing credential that requires demonstration of continuing education in order to be maintained.)

Family life education programs. To differing degrees and for varying age levels, programs in family life education or family education exist in primary and secondary school systems and in university settings. Some countries also have culturally relevant nonformal programs on topics that pertain to their countries, although attendance varies depending on the country and topic.

Secondary school programs in family life education. Some FLE is taught in secondary schools, but it is mostly part of home economics programs. In Japan, both male and female students must take home economics in which studying families is part of the curriculum. This occurs in elementary school (5th to 6th grade), junior high school (7th to 9th grade), and senior high school (10th to 12th grade). However, it all depends on the "teacher's perceptions of the importance of studying families, since teachers trained in food and nutrition and clothing may find it difficult to teach about families and family life." In Ghana it is part of "home science" programs, while in Ireland it is in "social, personal, and health education" classes and in "social or moral education" in the United Kingdom. Family studies is also required in Guatemala at the middle school level. FLE exists in Portugal, as all public schools have to offer courses on sexuality in the secondary schools, while in Serbia there are educational programs about families in schools. Before the widespread initiation of formal schooling in Nigeria, young people were educated informally to prepare them for adult life. However, with the onset of rural to urban migration, young people became more involved in risky sexual behaviors. Thus in 2002, a Family Life and HIV Education (FLHE) curriculum was established for primary, secondary, and tertiary levels of education.

University programs in family life education.   University programs vary in name and focus. Some universities have no programs that deal with families (e.g., Brazil, Guatemala, Japan). Although there are only a few programs that offer majors in family studies and FLE (six universities in Taiwan, four masters programs in Hong Kong with two in marriage and family therapy), many programs infuse family studies content into their courses or programs in social science; counseling; sociology; social work; anthropology; psychology; personal, social, and humanities education; or women's studies (e.g., China, Hong Kong, Italy, Germany, Malaysia, Portugal, Taiwan, Turkey). These programs can also be found in Departments of Family and Early Childhood Education (e.g., China) or Andragogy (adult education) (e.g., Serbia).

Other family life education programs.   Many countries have nonformal programs, such as centers to promote programming related to family life education that was either developed by the government or NGOs (non-governmental organizations). Examples include the *Korean Institute for Healthy Families* with 152 branches throughout South Korea, the *Well-Baby* program in Israel, and the visiting program for families with infants younger than four years in Japan. Whereas the United Kingdom has a *OnePlusOne Program*, which is focused on strengthening relations—predominantly for couples, Ireland has a *Family Support Agency* that makes grants available to voluntary organizations to provide services, such as marriage and relationship counseling, marriage preparation courses, and child counseling in relation to parental separation, as well as bereavement counseling and support due to the death of a family member. Parenting courses in Ireland also exist in their *ParentsPlusProgrammes*. The term "family life education" does not exist in Brazil; rather it is called "socio-educative work," which is developed for families in welfare programs and intended to help families to surpass vulnerabilities linked to their living conditions. In Australia, *National Fertility Services* is part of the *Family Life Services Program* of the Catholic Church. They offer sexuality education and personal development, health, and physical education. There are also monthly community newsletters in Japan along with some FLE programs in city community centers, but these programs are not perceived as "holistic, theoretical, or practical." Educational programs in Nigeria are offered to individuals and families to improve family life. Many of these programs are within the private sector through international and local NGOs and designed to complement the work of the government in common areas of focus especially poverty alleviation, economic empowerment of low-income families, and sexual health (HIV/AIDS prevention). Media campaigns in Nigeria have been employed to raise awareness of HIV/AIDS and change risky behaviors. Artists, athletes, and other media figures have been become spokespersons for these campaigns. In addition, due to the recent spike in ownership of cell phones and the need to increase public awareness about HIV/AIDS, text messages with information about HIV/AIDS were sent to 9 million people.

Attendance of family life education programs.   Participation in nonformal family education programs is mixed. In Switzerland it is difficult to get parents to attend programs, but their geography could be a factor. There is also a reluctance to attend family education programs in Scotland, the United Kingdom, and Malaysia. Whereas some programs in Nigeria have significant interest (e.g., economic empowerment, health and nutrition), others have little citizen interest because they conflict with cultural or religious beliefs. For example, programs targeted at human sexuality (in a country with significant HIV/AIDS problems) have often been perceived as inappropriate by some citizens due to misconstrued beliefs that they lead to promiscuity. In Australia people are generally not interested except for the marital preparation courses, which are required by the church. In Canada, while there is a lot of citizen interest in family programs, psychologists often teach them, which inflates the cost. Thus, as long as it is accessible to the public, not too academic, and a reasonable cost, Canadians are interested. In Portugal, attendance is negatively affected by the long workdays of both men and women and their need of materials at a basic education level. In comparison, citizens of Pakistan are interested in attending family programs and in Jamaica there is a desire for more programs, especially after attending one. The educational programs offered by the *Family Education Centers* in Taiwan are quite popular, but while they are considered important, only some people will attend. Programs would reach more interested persons if they were well-structured and promoted as preventive in nature, because most of the time the programs are advertised to target families in crisis and that limits the audience attracted to them (Guatemala).

Generally females show more interest than males in FLE programs (e.g., Ghana, Taiwan), but there are also some specific programs for women, such as *Women and Development and Family Welfare, Reproductive Health and Childbirth* (e.g., Ghana, Japan, Netherlands, Nigeria, South Korea, Turkey), and *Legal Literacy for Women* (Ghana). Males are not only more reluctant than women to participate in family life education programs, but also may not allow their wives to attend any kind of training (Guatemala). The willingness to attend varies on family structure, education level, socioeconomic status, and gender (Guatemala). Women are exposed to family education through magazines, television talk shows, and websites (e.g., China, Germany, Hong Kong, Malaysia). There are also some programs being targeted toward males and fathers (e.g., Ireland, Japan, South Korea). South Korea has a particular focus on males by looking at their roles according to the child's developmental age, with a father's participation in parenting being quite important. They have course content for males in early marriage including paternal roles in understanding pregnant women and prospective parent education. The main content of courses for males in midlife includes problem solving between adolescents and fathers, problem solving with wives, understanding the changes that occur during midlife, preparation for aging, and father education with courses for aging males on problem solving with adult children, family life, and financial management after retirement (South Korea).

In some places there is interest in marital education, but people perceive it as remedial and are afraid of the stigma attached to attending this type of family program (e.g., China, Hong Kong, Malaysia, Japan). Parent-child relations and parenting education are easier for people to attend, but there is still a stigma attached to marriage programs. Similar to the U.S., one participant indicated that "people do not want to tell others what is happening in their house." Stigmatization was also perceived as an issue with same-sex couples/families, especially in Italy where they are invisible to providers of family services.

Governmental and cultural influences in family life education

Family life education programming, which is influenced by legislation and various governmental policies, is closely tied to the cultural context of the country. Countries in the same region/continent may have similar or different political, environmental, and cultural issues as indicated below:

- In Taiwan, the *Family Education Act* was passed in 2003 so that all schools have to include at least 4 hours of family life education activities each year. They also established family education centers for each city/county in Taiwan. All levels of government should proactively encourage teacher-training institutions to list family education-related courses as required or common courses. The law was enacted to further national knowledge and capabilities in respect of family life; the advancement of national physical and mental well-being; the fostering of happy families; and the establishment of a harmonious society. Family education should be conducted under the principles of diversity, flexibility, and lifelong learning depending on the needs of the target population. The Ministry of Education proclaimed 2013 as the "Family Education Year."

- In China, the *Chinese Women's Federation*, a government agency that focuses on the welfare of women and children, sponsors the *Chinese Association of Family Education*. The association has a website called *China Parent Education* that promotes parenting and parent education of children of all the ages from infancy to high school. It offers to a vast number of Chinese families and professionals research findings, news, parenting tips, blogs with experts, parenting classes, and jobs in family life education.

- In Singapore, the *Ministry of Social and Family Development* adopted a holistic approach to families by enacting legislation, formulating policies, providing services, and encouraging the development of programs for families. They formed the *Family Education and Promotion Division* in 2012 to strengthen family education and promotion efforts. This will enable a wide range of programs to target individuals and families at key stages including singles, "soon-to-weds," married couples, and parents. In 2013, the government launched *FamilyMatters!*, which aims to provide Singaporeans with easy access to family life education and resources at every life stage by providing $40 million over three years along with plans to double the outreach from approximately 1 million Singaporeans in 2012 to 2 million in 2015. The key components of *FamilyMatters!* are *FamilyMatters@School, FamilyMatters@Work, FamilyMatters@Community, FamilyMatters@Business*, and *Building Capability for Family Matters*.

- In South Korea, the content of FLE is restricted by law and includes preparation for marriage, parent education, education on family ethics, and education on the realization of the family's value of home life.

- In the United Arab Emirates (UAE), two universities that had family science programs were terminated in about 2005. The reasons were unclear, but it is believed that the ministry perceived these university programs were educating women to stay at home and be mothers. The UAE has some funding for weddings and dowries for citizens who need assistance, because weddings have become so expensive. With this support it is expected that the couple will receive a limited amount of premarital education. However, few trainers have received formal education in marriage and family, so these programs can be taught quite traditionally with gender biases.

- In Turkey, the *Ministry of Family and Social Policies,* as well as municipalities and the *Ministry of Education*, provide family education to families, couples, and individuals on issues such as family communication and pre-marriage education.

- In Germany, an increase in teaching about families came with legal changes in 2000 prohibiting any violence in parenting—physical punishment or psychological violence. To provide additional initiatives, the government began campaigns and educational programs offering parenting advice. There is high interest in attending these programs due to parents' considerable insecurity about how to best raise their children. There has been a shift in parenting attitudes and practices since the late 1960s with a change in parenting goals to autonomy and a decline in goals favoring obedience. Since then, issues of control in parenting have become a major topic along with the publication of many books on parenting.

- In Ireland, the government's *Family Support Agency* provides for a variety of services to assist families around the country, including 107 *Family Resource Centres* and counseling services for those experiencing marriage and relationship difficulties or bereavement.

- In the Netherlands, there is a statutory duty to provide prenatal education, as well as support for parenting and growing up. There should be opportunities for every child. Parents are responsible for ensuring their children grow up healthy and safe. If a child's development is in serious risk, the government must intervene in good time.

- In Switzerland, there is a new law financing parenting education and its coordination.

- In Scotland, there is a "bedroom tax" resulting in fewer housing benefits for those with an unused bedroom in their home. This works against helping poor families.

- In Nigeria, public policies have been created to promote Family Life and HIV Education (FLHE) programs at federal and state levels through the support of the FLHE curriculum. However, policy makers have been criticized for not doing enough to promote FLE programs to meet the diverse needs of the population.

- Responses from some countries indicate there is little governmental support for families (e.g., Portugal, Serbia, Sweden).

Cultural issues and challenges across countries were mostly similar. A frequently mentioned topic from multiple countries concerned issues of violence and abuse—violence prevention, domestic violence, violence against women, parenting violence, family violence, intimate partner violence, and cultural violence (e.g., Brazil, China, Germany, Ghana, Guatemala, Israel, Japan, Nigeria, Pakistan, Turkey), as well as child abuse (e.g., Brazil, Japan, Nigeria, Pakistan); elderly abuse (Brazil, Japan); and abuse of persons with disabilities (e.g., Brazil). School violence such as "mobbing" (bullying) was also noted in Switzerland. Other challenging issues for families that were reported included STIs and HIV/AIDS, sexuality, divorce, parenting (also single and teen parenting), developmental disabilities, sexual and reproductive health, gender inequality and gender mainstreaming, men's and women's roles, work-family balance, teen pregnancy, substance abuse, sexual promiscuity, child labor and child prostitution, poverty and parental unemployment, diversity of family forms, migrant families, delay of marriage, caregiving to elderly and persons with disabilities, increase in single households, polygamy, marital infidelity, and empowering orphans and widows. In addition to the above issues that were commonly noted for many countries, some specific cultural issues are highlighted below and loosely organized by region:

- Growth of *fly-in/fly-out employment* in the mining industry in which workers fly to remote locations to work for 10 to 15 days before returning home for 3 to 5 days. The ongoing absence of one partner has a significant cumulative impact for marital and parental relationships. (Australia)
- *Barrel children* are left with relatives by parents who work overseas with children receiving things from abroad on a regular basis. (Trinidad and Tobago)
- In Trinidad and Tobago weakening of the family structure is seen as the root cause of societal problems leading to a high crime rate, drug trade, alcoholism, and sexual promiscuity.
- Linguistic barriers to being employed and basic literacy in bilingual Quebec affect employment and family financial well-being. (Canada)
- Families in Singapore are generally healthy, emphasize strong family ties, and cherish family values. However, Singaporeans are facing challenges as more people are remaining single, while those who marry are doing so later compared to a decade ago. The median age at first marriage rose from 28.7 to 30.1 years for males and 26.0 to 27.8 years for females. The divorce rate has also increased from 6.4 in 2001 to 7.2 per 1000 married female residents in 2011.
- Chinese culture highly values the role of parents in their children's development. If a child does not behave, it is the parents' fault. Parents of only one child have more resources to provide for their child's living and education.
- *Parasite singles* beyond their late twenties return to live with their parents in order to enjoy a carefree and comfortable life. (Japan)
- *Karoshi* is death from overwork due to heart attacks and strokes resulting from stress. This occurs in young men in their prime years that die suddenly with no signs of previous illness. (Japan)
- *Hikikimori* means pulling inward and seeking extreme isolation, in which persons, often adolescents or young adults, do not go to school or work, refuse contact with people other than family members, and stay home for more than 6 months. This occurs in about 320,000 households. *Futoko* means students who opt out and refuse to attend school. (Japan)

- FLE colleagues in Japan have translated into Japanese the second edition of *Family Life Education: Working with Families across the Life Span* (Powell & Cassidy, 2007) along with the PowerPoint slides of the parable about family life education (see Chapter 1) developed by NCFR's CFLE Advisory Board.

- Malaysian government has made attempts to deal with family issues, but their efforts have been confined to the Muslim population.

- Family issues include refugees and post traumatic stress disorder (PTSD), families with developmental crises, socially and culturally deprived families, and families of marginalized groups due to the after-effects of violence during civil war. (Serbia)

- Italy has a familistic culture with women's employment rates being the lowest in western countries. It remains difficult for women to enter and remain in the labor market because gender discrimination is based on the widely held cultural assumption that looking after the family is exclusively a woman's job, along with a serious lack of state support and services for the care of young children and the elderly.

- Sweden, which is a country where many couples have cohabited for quite some time, has compulsory programs in all schools regarding sexuality and living together.

- The cultural environment of families in the United Arab Emirates is complex because in their rapid progress to join the modern world there has been amazing growth in infrastructure, commerce, tourism, and formal education. However, almost all UAE projects have relied heavily on international expertise, thus UAE nationals make up less than 15% of the total population.

- Issues related to poverty are prominent in some countries and related to single parents (e.g., Trinidad and Tobago) and survival (e.g., Ghana, Guatemala). In 2011, 53.7% of families in Guatemala were at the national poverty line. Poverty brings a lot of issues. However, most of the government's programs are focused on "giving families fish" rather than "teaching them how to fish," thus perpetuating the cycle of poverty and its accompanying ills (Guatemala).

- Despite its vast resources, Nigeria ranks among the most unequal countries in the world. While the Nigerian economy is growing, the proportion of Nigerians living in poverty is increasing every year with devastating impacts on families, including lack of access to basic and social needs such as food, shelter, clothing, schools, and health care.

- Nigeria is the most populous country in Africa (122.5 million people) and ranks third in the world with people living with HIV/AIDS (about 3.6% of the population). Although the first two cases of HIV/AIDS were identified in 1985, prevention, treatment, and care did not become a primary concern until 1999. This is now a public health problem of enormous magnitude impacting the lives of individuals and families. Moreover, since the advent of democracy in 1999, other social ills have evolved, such as child abuse, child marriage, and criminal activities, resulting in cultural and ethnic violence.

- Nigeria is a multilingual, multiethnic, and multireligious society with three different legal systems operating simultaneously—civil, customary, and Islamic. Therefore, the degree to which citizens are interested in participating in programs to improve family life often depends on the extent to which program activities and goals align with the beliefs and practices of select groups, as well as the public trust.

The perceptions of international family professionals highlight the standing of family life education in various countries and the progress that is being made. Formal and nonformal programs in FLE are offered within different settings, curricula, and lengths of time, along with varying preparation of teachers. Schools, governments, and family professionals are addressing family issues to some degree, but those countries that have governmental support via legislation, policies, and funding seem to be making more progress with family education programs in all kinds of settings.

Within certain geographical areas (continents as categorized by the United Nations), there are some similarities and differences. For example, in Asia there are some similarities in family education in Japan, China, and South Korea pertaining to being in the beginning stages of development of FLE, while Singapore and Taiwan have made considerable progress in legislation, governmental policies, and family education programming. Although Hong Kong is a part of China, there were notable differences. Hong Kong has masters programs in family education and intervention, as well as marriage and family therapy. A study by the Hong Kong government found that in 2010, 652 family education programs were held which drew 80,000 participants. In China, professionals in childhood education, women's studies, social work, and psychology provide family education. Chinese society emphasizes child education, especially academic education, with family studies being infused into various academic programs. Some Chinese psychology programs are building their graduate programs in marriage and family therapy. Whereas Middle Eastern countries are considered part of Asia, they are dissimilar to countries such as China, Japan, South Korea, and Taiwan with respect to family education, as family studies courses, faculty, and programs are few in number and based on individual faculty interest (e.g., Pakistan, Turkey).

While no one solution or program can meet all the needs of people in these countries, our awareness of the issues and challenges they face, along with their efforts to ameliorate family concerns are important for our understanding of the status of family well-being and family life education internationally. By understanding world families and international efforts in family life education, family professionals can promote multicultural understanding both at home and abroad.

Educational Methods to Enhance Cross-Cultural Awareness

Opportunities for Current Professionals

Preparation of family professionals to work with culturally diverse populations and increase their global awareness is becoming increasingly important. Current professionals can get involved in international conferences, meet with groups of international families within their own communities or universities, or become involved in international travel. While there are various exchange programs for students and professionals, the Fulbright Scholar Program is quite exceptional for providing cross-cultural understanding. As a Fulbright Scholar, one has an opportunity to be a cultural ambassador for the United States, while having a large array of experiences from which cross-cultural learning can be acquired. There are a number of Fulbright programs for both students and professionals, although the more familiar one provides travel and living allowances for U.S. Scholars to teach or conduct research abroad (www.cies.org). One should not be discouraged if you cannot find "family life educator" in the list of academic disciplines for potential exchange programs. Family life educators are welcomed in various other disciplines and professions, such as education, family and consumer sciences, or the social sciences. Whereas human development and family science departments are prominent in the U.S., the study of family is located within various other programs depending on the country of interest.

Opportunities for Future Professionals

Travel programs: Cross-cultural study courses

Future family professionals have various opportunities to get involved in cross-cultural study courses to learn about international families (Hamon & Fernsler, 2002). These programs provide experiential opportunities to help students develop an appreciation for families and cultures that are different from their own. Rather than merely visit a country, students become immersed in the culture and have sustained contact with families in the host culture that can involve home stays, ethnographies, and/or service projects as a part of their course work. Students can participate in activities of daily living, such as eating meals with the family, spending time with children, or becoming involved in family-related events. Students take an active part in these cross-cultural experiences by reading required books, writing papers, and sharing in planning their participation in field trips. In addition, students take part in organized "scavenger hunts" in the community by learning local facts and attending lectures or presentations on family-related topics. Being in a different environment can be a life-changing experience when confronting living standards different from one's own, realizing the importance of language in understanding others, being aware of looking different, facing one's own ethnocentricity, and observing similarities and differences in family life. Cross-cultural courses related to families provide excellent opportunities for exposing students to some of the content areas for NCFR's Certified Family Life Educator Program (see Appendix A), such as families in society, internal dynamics of families, family resource management, parent education and guidance, interpersonal relationships, and human sexuality.

Classroom activities: Brief reports

Since cross-cultural travel experiences are not always feasible for some students, various classroom experiences can be created to integrate cross-cultural learning into the classroom. These vary in complexity and depth of exposure. Individually or in small groups students can investigate a country by using international references on families (Adams & Trost, 2005; Francoeur & Noonan, 2004b). Through sharing with class members how families function in other countries and how culture has influenced the attitudes and behaviors of the people in that country, students become aware of the differences in families and family issues in diverse cultures.

Classroom activities: Electronic portfolios

Classroom projects can be expanded by having students create electronic portfolios on various countries (Subramaiam, 2006). Students incorporate technology and research to prepare an in-depth examination of a country and its families. They can examine the geography; lifestyles; political and economic systems; culture of families; economic data; financial management; and information on housing, health, and consumption patterns. As a group they prepare an electronic portfolio by creating a PowerPoint presentation using charts, tables, clip art, and video clips, along with developing a website. Several Internet sources are provided, such as the *International Database, Population Reference Bureau, Demography and Population Studies, United Nations Population Fund, United Nations Educational, Scientific, and Cultural Organization,* and *Fact Monster.* Students are not only able to enhance their research skills on the Internet, but also have a meaningful in-depth learning experience about families in other cultures.

Classroom activities: Circular role-play

In order to better understand and enhance a cross-cultural perspective in family science courses, a circular role-play teaching method can be implemented using any topic of interest, such as marital interaction, sibling relationships, or parent-child communication. By varying the focus, this activity can facilitate the infusion of cultural learning into a variety of courses and topics. While a family life educator can utilize any teaching method in different cultures for the purpose of comparison and cross-cultural sharing, Darling and Howard (2006) described a circular role-play technique, applying it to parent-youth communication about sexuality within three different cultural contexts—Finland, Costa Rica, and the U.S. In this experience, students were asked to depict the roles of a parent and then an adolescent daughter by listening to a scenario and then thinking through how they might react or what they might say as the parent and adolescent in that situation. The following steps were involved in this activity.

- Students were asked to bring a paper and pencil and join others in a small circle.
- A paragraph was read to the class about a potential dilemma for parent-youth communication regarding sexuality.
- Respondents were asked to write what they would say as a *parent* in this situation.
- The response was passed to the person on the right who, as a *teenager,* responded to the parental statement.
- The response of the teenager was passed back to the person role-playing his/her *parent* for a response to the adolescent statement.
- The second response of the parent was passed to the *teenager* on the right, who again responded to this parent.

Thus, each individual simultaneously played the roles of a parent and adolescent in two different hypothetical family scenarios. The parent and adolescent characters each wrote two comments due to time limitations, although this exchange could occur several more times.

After the exchange of statements between pairs of students, the parent-youth communication patterns were discussed from the perspective of the culture in which the activity was being conducted. Reactions from other cultures to the same scenario were then shared with the students, who were amazed at the differences in responses. While this teaching method could be used with any topic, the statements from students in these three cultures can be shared with students to illustrate cross-cultural differences in parent-youth interactions related to sexuality (Darling & Howard, 2006). This learning experience, along with the discussion of the results from other cultures, stimulated cross-cultural learning and understanding about the purposes and processes underlying family behaviors. By looking at cultural evidence from three countries, this teaching activity facilitated the exploration of the richness and diversity of parent-youth communication concerning sexuality issues from a cross-cultural perspective. Considering variations from others' experiences facilitates putting our own culture's parenting and sexual understandings in perspective.

Future Directions for International Family Life Education

What does the future hold? Globalization and struggles with interdependence will continue along with inherent issues in family adaptations to the stress of migration and acculturation. While there are several challenges that our students will need to face, there is also hope as evidenced by some family life education initiatives.

Worldwide Health Issues and Accessibility of Affordable Health Care

This is not just the obvious issue of HIV/AIDS, but other infectious diseases. What can we do to protect persons from the current and future pandemics? Family life educators need to work collaboratively with health professionals to provide relevant educational materials and determine what types of educational programs can provide the knowledge to assist families with these problems.

Population Growth, Decline, and Mobility

While the world's population is multiplying, some countries will experience a decline in inhabitants due to mobility. Migration will continue to be a major topic in the twenty-first century and will pose certain challenges in the future. What steps should family life educators take to help immigrants, who find themselves in a very different world from the one they left, with new traditions, attitudes, behaviors, and values? How can families manage their resources in crowded environments with a shortage of natural resources for sustenance?

Equality of Rights

In some countries, such as Nigeria and Pakistan, young women who have been raped and then courageously named their assailants have triggered international protests when they were tried and convicted of fornication and sentenced to death by stoning. Meanwhile other countries, such as China, still have one-child-per-family policies, forced abortions, female infanticide, and abandoned babies. Whereas some of these government policies are being relaxed, they still exist within the culture (Fisher, 2013; Francoeur & Noonan, 2004a). What can family life educators do to promote equal legal rights for all regardless of their age, gender, race, ethnicity, religion, or sexual orientation?

Gender Equity

Women are perceived to be a huge untapped economic resource and are taking more of a public stance for gender equality. Moreover, women are surpassing males in educational achievement and aspiration. Patriarchy will not disappear overnight, but there is a shift toward equality (Francoeur & Noonan, 2004a). Gender issues are evident when considering health, family structure, and violence. However, increasing the status of women does not necessarily decrease family violence, since often an increase in violence occurs when men feel threatened by a loss of power. Therefore, educators need to redesign curricula, texts, media presentations, and other activities to promote gender equality as part of cultural change.

Public Policies for Family Well-Being

There is an increasing need to incorporate a family lens when creating public policy. While progress is slow, family life educators should take notice of the passage of a "Family Education Law" in Taiwan on January 7, 2003. The Ministry of Education sought a legal means for promoting family education and the integration of work from all levels of governments, non-governmental organizations, and educational organizations to actively empower people of all ages to have a better family life. This legislation was to promote preventative education by improving family education knowledge, strengthening psychological and physical development, and improving family and social harmony. They define family education as all kinds of education activities for furthering family relations and functioning including parent education, filial education, sexuality education, marriage education, ethical education, education about family resources and management, and other family education matters. This legislation makes Taiwan the first country in the world that has passed a national bill regarding family life education, effectively rewriting world history regarding FLE (N. Huang, 2003; W. Huang, 2005).

Families have a profound impact on their members. However, when they cannot provide for the healthy nurturance of members, the effects reverberate across their lives and are ultimately felt by society (Public Education Committee on Family, 2001). As a result, there is a need for family life education aimed at strengthening family ties and relationships and preventing some of these problems. As the interest in family life education expands, we will also have to work on creating a variety of approaches that can be used by multiple countries, professions, and individuals.

As a call to action, data from the study to examine the international status of family life education indicated the level of interest in various professional issues concerned with the delivery of family life education (Darling & Turkki, 2009).

Ranging in desired emphasis from 1 = low emphasis to 5 = high emphasis, the top three professional issues with the greatest interest were increased attention to family issues in the workplace, increased research on issues critical to families, and increased assistance with family policy issues (see Table 12.2). Creatively targeting the workplace means that access to family life education is more readily available to all. In addition, the need for research-based curricula is also evident along with developing policies to aid families and family support services. The two lowest ranking issues dealt with increased international assistance and connections to colleagues. In other words, there is a higher priority on in-country assistance and progress compared to help from outsiders who may not understand the culture. Thus, multicultural understanding is paramount.

Table 12.2   Level of Interest in Professional Issues

Professional Issue	Mean*
Increased attention to family issues in the workplace	4.05
Increased research on issues critical to families	4.04
Increased assistance with family policy issues	3.79
Increased family programs—Planning and implementing FLE programs	3.63
Increased training opportunities for family professionals	3.60
Strengthening existing family life education programs	3.57
Connection with international network of family colleagues for advice	3.47
Increased assistance from colleagues in other countries	3.18

* Range: 1 = low level of emphasis to 5 = high level of emphasis

One way to gain multicultural understanding of families worldwide and the issues and changes they encounter is to pay attention to the 10-year anniversaries of International Year of the Family. The UN General Assembly proclaimed 1994 as the International Year of the Family (IYF) with its theme of "Family Resources and Responsibilities in a Changing World" (UNDESA, 1994). They proposed that the family constitutes the basic unit of society and therefore warrants special attention. This event was followed by the 10th anniversary of IYF in 2004, which was designed to highlight the role of families and increase awareness of family issues among governments and the private sector, as well as stimulate efforts to respond to family problems and improve collaboration among national and international non-governmental organizations (UNDP, 2003). Some suggestions from international colleagues (who reported on activities from their country's celebration of the 10th Anniversary of the International Year of the Family) included the following:

- Meetings with families and students from other cultures, with an opportunity to hear their concerns
- Academic symposia on various topics such as wellness of families, childcare and work, worldwide gender equality, national health insurance, family violence, parenting, HIV/AIDS and the teenage population, and the impact of war on family life

- Media presentations on family issues and family programs
- National Family Day
- International Family Strengths Conference
- Development of fact sheets on family issues
- Provision of new support services for international families
- Cross-cultural entertainment presentations

The 20th anniversary of IYF in 2014 focuses on exploring family-oriented policies and strategies aimed at managing family poverty, ensuring work-family balance, and advancing social integration and intergenerational solidarity.

With increasing numbers of educators and students who are teaching, studying, or doing research abroad, there is a definite need for developing innovative methods and materials that are culturally sensitive to people living in other countries. One cannot use family life education methods that work in the U.S. and assume that they are universal. The following are some suggestions for working with other cultures.

- Examine how different cultures perceive and value marriage, family, gender, aging, children, and parenting, as well as the roles of education, government, and religion. This knowledge can be gained from talking to individuals, families, and colleagues; attending seminars and classes; reading cross-cultural literature; conducting cross-cultural research; and studying public policies from other countries. We need to understand what is taught to whom and the differences in cultural perceptions of family structure, composition, and life stages.

- Understand personal assumptions, values, and biases regarding cultural diversity, in general, and specifically to the cultural group to be taught. Then assist family life education students to further understand their beliefs about culture. Using Bennett's "Model of Cultural Competency" can facilitate development of cultural sensitivity by moving from ethno-centrism to ethno-relativism (Bennett, 1993).

- Use current culturally-relevant research to support the content of the program. If you have not personally conducted such research, make contact with researchers in a country of interest. By incorporating research, you can display an understanding of the circumstances of the people in this country and a willingness to connect with relevant student issues.

- Incorporate applicable theory into your class content. Theory helps students of all ages to understand the knowledge, attitudes, and behaviors being integrated into the course. However, some theories that are quite usable in Western culture may not work in other cultures, or may have to be altered for different circumstances. For example, using developmental theory in some cultures may be difficult because different developmental transitions or milestones may vary in timing, definition, and importance. Using attachment theory may also have cultural implications.

- Build rapport with students by learning some phrases in their native language. Students appreciate attempts to speak their language and thereby embrace their culture.

- Be aware that some verbal and nonverbal communications may have different meanings in various cultures. Touch, hand gestures, or eye contact that might be acceptable in one country could be offensive in another. Therefore, sensitize students to various gestures and body language that can cause distress and misunderstandings when traveling abroad, interacting with international students, or teaching individuals and families in a cultural context beyond your own (Axtell, 1998).

- Use culturally-appropriate metaphors that relate to the country of interest. If using sports examples to communicate a concept, use soccer, rugby, cricket, or cycling rather than baseball or football depending on the popularity of a sport in that country.

- Attempt to understand the family boundaries, rituals, cohesion, and adaptability of cultures and apply metaphors to assist with learning abstract concepts. One example relates to Asians, who appreciate metaphors when discussing love, anxiety, and boundary issues. Therefore, a teacher could use Post-it notes and tell them that "healthy love is like Post-it notes—a little sticky, but not too sticky" (Huang, 2005, p. 171).

- Be sensitive to cultural norms since some content could put students at increased risk. In Asian countries women can be emotionally or physically harmed when they "speak their minds" (Huang, 2005). Awareness of multiple contexts in a culture is important. While some members of a culture may follow the traditional practices and views of a culture, others are more modern in their approaches. Thus, integrating theory and research may vary depending on the target audience in the country of interest.

- Experience the world around you and the differences that exist. Rather than traveling abroad, talk with people who are from a different culture. Engage in a meaningful conversation and find out something about them and how they see the world.

- Be patient. Finding simple answers to complex problems can take time. Americans do not always endure delays in progress, but cross-cultural rapport building and learning require tolerance and persistence without appearing frustrated.

In order for students to have a place in the evolving international importance of family education as a profession, it is essential to develop an exchange of ideas and practices regarding the content and direction of global approaches to family life education. We need to be internationally aware of the needs and concerns families experience and the environmental contexts of their ecosystems. If students cannot be engaged to think globally, they will fail to connect with the context in which families live. Including research, learning experiences and textbooks from the U.S. is not a viable approach when teaching in other cultures. Culturally-relative and sensitive methods and materials need to be incorporated for both classroom use and for professional development to assist teachers, leaders, and administrators in their work with families. It is important to both help individual families and sensitize public opinion on family-related issues. Since we are dealing with complex issues, we will need complex solutions to provide a preventative approach to assisting families. Thus, it will take a multinational, multicultural, and multidiscipline network of family professionals working together to enhance family well-being worldwide.

SUMMARY

This chapter examined the need for awareness and understanding of global issues of concern to families including migration, changes in family structure, aging, HIV/AIDS, and armed conflicts and turbulence. Family has different meanings and definitions in each culture, but using theory helps us to understand families and their interactions with multifaceted environments. Whereas family life education is evolving worldwide as demonstrated in quantitative and qualitative research studies, we share many of the same family issues that are still unresolved. Since family life educators and students often partake in international educational experiences, it is important to be cognizant of various cultures and use educational methods that will be sensitive and effective with others. While the teaching methods may vary, the global concerns that affect families, affect us all no matter where we live.

QUESTIONS AND ISSUES FOR DISCUSSION

1. What have you learned about children and families from foreign travels and visitors from other countries? What insights did you receive about your own culture?

2. In what country beyond the U.S. would you like to live? How would your life be different in regard to various changes in family life, school, gender, dating, extracurricular activities, or employment?

3. What are some cultural traditions in which you and your family participate either from U.S. culture or another cultural group? What traditions might you take with you into the next generation?

4. What are the biggest challenges facing our planet?

5. How can you enjoy a good quality life without causing problems for future generations?

ACTIVITIES

1. Using the ecosystems approach or any other theory mentioned in this chapter or text, analyze a global issue applying one or more theories.

2. Experience a cultural environment unlike the one with which you are familiar. This could be a cultural celebration, restaurant with specialized cultural foods, or religious setting. How does it feel to be different in this setting? What feelings might you have if you were to become a permanent or semi-permanent resident within this culture? What did you learn about this culture?

WEB RESOURCES

Confederation of Family Organizations in the European Union (COFACE)
www.coface-eu.org

COFACE links family organizations across Europe to discuss and work on issues such as balancing work and family life, children's well-being, solidarity between generations, migrant families, disabled and dependent persons, gender equality, education, parenting, health issues, and consumer affairs.

European Society for Family Relations (ESFR)
www.esfr.org

ESFR is an interdisciplinary scientific association for European research on families and family relations. Its purpose is to serve as a network, support and link family research, and exchange results. While ESFR was established as a federation of family researchers and family research institutes within Europe, it also welcomes researchers and institutes outside of Europe as affiliates.

National Council on Family Relations (NCFR)
www.ncfr.org

The National Council on Family Relations is a professional association for the multidisciplinary understanding of families. NCFR provides an educational forum for family researchers, educators, and practitioners from around the world to share in the development and dissemination of knowledge about families and family relationships, establish professional standards, and work to promote family well-being. NCFR is a nonpartisan, nonprofit, and international professional organization that links family research with policy formation and practice.

International Federation for Home Economics (IFHE)
www.ifhe.org

The International Federation for Home Economics is the only worldwide organization concerned with Home Economics and Consumer Studies and serves as a platform for international exchange within the field of Home Economics. IFHE provides opportunities for global networking among professionals, promotes the recognition of Home Economics in the everyday lives of individuals and families, promotes continuing education in Home Economics, and provides opportunities through practice, research and professional sharing that lead to improving the quality of everyday life for individuals, families, and households worldwide. IFHE is an International Non-Governmental Organization (INGO), having consultative status with the United Nations (ECOSOC, FAO, UNESCO, UNICEF) and with the Council of Europe.

The Family Life Education Framework

This framework expands on definitions of family life education by specifying major content for broad, lifespan family life education programs. It reflects current conceptual development and empirical knowledge in each content area, and gives attention to relevant knowledge, attitudes, and skills. The framework is not intended as curriculum, but as a guide for program development, delivery, and assessment. It is assumed that practitioners would select the most appropriate organization of concepts and kinds of methodologies in order to meet the needs of their specific audiences. Communication, decision-making, and problem-solving have not been treated as separate concepts but should be incorporated into each content area.

Areas Addressed in FLE Programs for Stages of Childhood, Adolescence, Adulthood and Later Adulthood

Families and Individuals in Societal Contexts

Internal Dynamics of Families

Human Growth & Development across the Lifespan

Human Sexuality

Interpersonal Relationships

Family Resource Management

Parent Education and Guidance

Family Law and Public Policy

Professional Ethics and Practice

Family Life Education Methodology

FAMILIES AND INDIVIDUALS IN SOCIETAL CONTEXTS
Childhood
- Describe jobs, employment, housing, transportation and the family
- Comprehend reciprocal influences on the family (economical, political, technological, environmental)
- Develop programs that support individuals and families
- Understand the importance of families, neighborhood, and the community
- Encourage families, schools, and other support organizations to work together
- Recognize and appreciate differing spiritual beliefs and practices
- Develop skills to negotiate risk and opportunity in external environments
- Understand individuals' and families' relationship to media and technology

Adolescence
- Examine families and the workplace
- Comprehend reciprocal influences on the family (economical, political, technological, environmental)
- Support education as preparation for the future
- Promote education throughout the lifespan
- Encourage individual and family responsibility in the community
- Recognize and appreciate the influence of religion and spirituality on families
- Support families with special needs and problems
- Understand the role of family in society
- Access supportive networks (family, peers, religious institutions, community)
- Negotiate risk and opportunity
- Foster resiliency
- Understand individuals' and families' relationship to media and technology

Adulthood
- Support family participation in the education of children
- Utilize the education system
- Recognize and appreciate the influence of religion and spirituality on families
- Use supportive networks (family, peers, religious institutions, community)
- Understand and obtain community support services
- Promote life-long learning
- Understand population issues and resource allocation
- Comprehend reciprocal influences on the family (economical, political, technological, environmental)
- Address economic fluctuations and their impact on families
- Understand the interrelationship of families, work, and society
- Encourage individual and family responsibility in the community

- Understand the role of family in society
- Foster resiliency
- Understand individuals' and families' relationship to media and technology

Later Adulthood
- Promote life-long learning
- Support the educational system
- Recognize and appreciate the influence of religion and spirituality on families
- Promote healthy development throughout the lifespan
- Encourage relationships with adult children, extended family, and peers
- Understand and obtain community support services
- Comprehend reciprocal influences on the family (economical, political, technological, environmental)
- Address economic fluctuations and their impact on aging families
- Knowledge of population issues and resource allocation (health care, transportation, housing)
- Address social issues (age discrimination, elder abuse prevention, caregiving)
- Understand the role of family in society
- Understand individuals' and families' relationship to media and technology

INTERNAL DYNAMICS OF FAMILIES

Childhood
- Recognize the individuality and importance of all family members
- Learn how to get along in the family (e.g., problem-solving)
- Express feelings in families
- Develop awareness of personal family history
- Appreciate family similarities and differences
- Realize the impact of internal and external change on families
- Understand the responsibilities, rights, interdependence of family members
- Increase awareness of family rules
- Distinguish families as sources of protection, guidance, affection, and support
- Recognize families as possible sources of anger and violence
- Acknowledge the presence and nature of family problems

Adolescence
- Navigate the transition to adulthood
- Increase awareness of changes in family composition (birth, marriage, divorce, illness, death)
- Manage and express feelings in families
- Cope with internal change and stress in the family
- Describe the interaction of friends and family

- Exhibit communication in families
- Identify interaction between family members
- Clarify different needs and expectations of family members
- Understand the responsibilities, rights, interdependence of family members
- Determine family rules (overt and covert)
- Increase awareness of intergenerational relationships
- Observe the influence of family background
- Take note of family history, traditions, and celebrations
- Distinguish families as sources of protection, guidance, affection, and support
- Recognize families as possible sources of anger and violence
- Clarify family differences (membership, economic level, role performance, values)

Adulthood
- Clarify individual development in the family
- Define individual and family roles
- Take note of intimate relationships in the family
- Identify sources of stress and coping with stress
- Distinguish lifestyle choices
- Adapt to changing needs and expectations of family members
- Negotiate intergenerational dynamics throughout the lifespan
- Understand the responsibilities, rights, and interdependence of family members
- Learn to navigate family transitions (birth, marriage, remarriage, divorce, illness, death)
- Consider value of family history, traditions, and celebrations
- Comprehend factors affecting marital and family relationships
- Give and receive affection
- Be aware of power and authority in the family
- Understand the effects of family on self-concepts of its members
- Distinguish families as sources of protection, guidance, affection, and support
- Clarify family differences (membership, economic level, role performance, values)
- Recognize families as possible sources of anger and violence
- Increase awareness of varying influences on family interaction patterns (ethnic, racial, gender, social, cultural)
- Determine family rules (overt and covert)

Later Adulthood
- Clarify individual development in the family
- Define individual and changing family roles

- Adapt to changing needs and expectations of family members
- Navigate family transitions (marriage, divorce, remarriage, illness, retirement, death)
- Understand the responsibilities, rights, interdependence of family members and productivity
- Nurture intimate relationships in the family
- Understand the effects of family on self-concepts of its members
- Comprehend factors affecting marital and family relationships
- Give and receive affection
- Be aware of the changes in power and authority in the family
- Identify sources of stress and coping with stress, diseases, and disabilities
- Determine family rules (overt and covert)
- Distinguish families as sources of protection, guidance, affection, and support
- Distinguish lifestyle choices and changes (retirement planning, retirement)
- Consider the value of family history, traditions, and celebrations
- Negotiate intergenerational dynamics throughout the lifespan
- Increase awareness of varying influences on family interaction patterns (ethnic, racial, gender, social, cultural)
- Recognize families as possible sources of anger and violence
- Clarify family differences (membership, economic level, role performance, values)

HUMAN GROWTH & DEVELOPMENT ACROSS THE LIFESPAN
Childhood
- Understand physical, cognitive, affective, moral, personality, social, and sexual development
- Take responsibility for keeping healthy (nutrition, personal health, exercise, sleep)
- Recognize the uniqueness of each person
- Identify similarities and differences in individual development
- Appreciate people with special needs
- Clarify perceptions about older people (adolescents, adults, elderly)
- Identify social and environmental conditions affecting growth and development

Adolescence
- Accept individual differences in development
- Take responsibility for personal health (nutrition, personal health, exercise, sleep)
- Understand the effects of chemical substances on physical health and development

- Comprehend and differentiate between types of development (physical, cognitive, affective, moral, personality, social, sexual)
- Distinguish the interaction among types of development
- Recognize patterns of development over the lifespan—conception to death
- Evaluate stereotypes and realities about adulthood and aging
- Describe developmental disabilities
- Identify social and environmental conditions affecting growth and development

Adulthood

- Understand the transition to adulthood
- Recognize factors influencing individual differences in development
- Comprehend and differentiate between types of development (physical, cognitive, affective, moral, personality, social, sexual)
- Distinguish the interaction among types of development
- Take responsibility for personal and family health
- Promote development in self and others
- Recognize patterns of development over the lifespan—conception to death
- Evaluate myths and realities of adulthood and aging
- Adjust to developmental disabilities
- Identify social and environmental conditions affecting growth and development

Later Adulthood

- Recognize factors influencing individual differences in development
- Comprehend and differentiate between types of development (physical, cognitive, affective, moral, personality, social, sexual)
- Distinguish the interaction among types of development
- Adjust to developmental disabilities
- Recognize patterns of development over the lifespan—conception to death
- Adapt to and cope with physical changes in later adulthood
- Take responsibility for personal health and safety
- Adjust to grief and loss
- Evaluate myths and realities of aging
- Identify social and environmental conditions affecting growth and development

HUMAN SEXUALITY

Childhood

- Respond to children's curiosity about their bodies
- Label physical and sexual development
- Clarify body privacy and protection against sexual abuse
- Conceptualize similarities and differences in individual sexual development
- Define aspects of human reproduction (prenatal development, birth, puberty)

- Expand the child's perceptions about sexuality
- Become aware of social and environmental conditions affecting sexuality

Adolescence

- Label physical and sexual development (sexual identity, sexual orientation etc.)
- Explain interaction among types of development
- Clarify body privacy and protection against sexual abuse
- Communicate about sexuality (personal values and beliefs, shared decision-making)
- Teach characteristics of healthy and ethical sexual relationships
- Understand the choices, consequences, and responsibility of sexual behavior
- Explain the transmission and prevention of sexually transmitted diseases and infections
- Describe human reproduction and conception
- Affirm the normality of sexual feelings and sexual responses
- Expand knowledge of interpersonal dynamics of intimacy
- Identify stereotypes and realities about human sexuality
- Increase awareness of varying family and societal beliefs, myths, and realities about sexuality

Adulthood

- Demonstrate responsible sexual behavior (choices, consequences, shared decision-making)
- Affirm normality of sexual feelings and sexual responses
- Communicate about sexuality (personal values and beliefs, shared decision-making)
- Observe characteristics of healthy and ethical sexual relationships
- Knowledge of interpersonal dynamics of sexual intimacy
- Explain the transmission and prevention of sexually transmitted diseases and infections
- Comprehend reproductive health (contraception, infertility, and genetics)
- Prevent sexual abuse
- Increase awareness of varying family and societal beliefs, myths, and realities about sexuality

Later Adulthood

- Understand human sexual response and aging
- Affirm normality of sexual feelings and sexual responses
- Clarify body privacy and prevention of sexual abuse
- Communicate about sexuality (personal values, beliefs, shared decision-making)
- Observe characteristics of healthy and ethical sexual relationships

- Value sexuality education in later adulthood
- Define sexual expression and intimacy
- Explain the transmission and prevention of sexually transmitted diseases and infections
- Develop appreciation of sexual needs in adult living situations
- Increase awareness of varying family and societal beliefs, myths, and realities about sexuality

INTERPERSONAL RELATIONSHIPS
Childhood
- Respect for self, others, and property
- Share feelings constructively
- Express emotions
- Develop, maintain, and end relationships appropriately
- Build self-esteem and self-confidence
- Identify and enhance personal strengths
- Communicate with others
- Share friends, possessions, and time
- Act with consideration for self and others
- Develop problem-solving and conflict management skills
- Accurately assess how one's words and behaviors affect others
- Appreciate diverse individuals, cultures, and communities

Adolescence
- Respect for self, others, and property
- Change and develop one's thoughts, attitudes, and values
- Deal with success and failure
- Accept responsibility for one's actions
- Assess and develop personal abilities and talents
- Communicate information, thoughts, and feelings
- Manage and express emotions
- Initiate, maintain, and end friendships
- Build self-esteem and self-confidence
- Assess compatibility in interpersonal relationships
- Act with consideration for self and others
- Understand the basis for choosing a family lifestyle (values, heritage, religious beliefs)
- Understand the needs and motivations involved in dating
- Recognize factors that influence mate selection (social, cultural, personal)

- Understand the dimensions of love and commitment
- Explore the responsibilities of marriage
- Discover where one fits in relation to others (the "me" among the "we")
- Appreciate diverse individuals, cultures, and communities

Adulthood

- Establish personal autonomy
- Build self-esteem and self-confidence
- Achieve constructive personal changes
- Communicate effectively
- Manage and express emotions
- Develop, maintain, and end relationships
- Exercise initiative in relationships
- Recognize factors associated with quality relationships
- Take responsibility and make commitments in relationships
- Evaluate choices and alternatives in relationships
- Act in accordance with personal beliefs with consideration for others' best interest
- Understand the effects of self-perceptions on relationships
- Recognize influences on roles and relationships (ethnic, racial, gender, social, cultural)
- Understand types of intimate relationships
- Create and maintain a family of one's own
- Be aware of changes in intimate relationships over time
- Manage and cope with crises
- Find meaning and purpose in relationship to others
- Appreciate diverse individuals, cultures, and communities

Later Adulthood

- Build self-esteem and self-confidence
- Understand the effects of self-perceptions on relationships
- Exercise initiative in relationships
- Continue intimate relationships
- Recognize factors associated with quality relationships
- Take responsibility and make commitments in relationships
- Evaluate choices and alternatives in relationships
- Act in accordance with personal beliefs with consideration for others' best interest
- Be aware of changes in intimate relationships over time
- Maintain relationships with one's own family

- Communicate effectively
- Manage and express emotions
- Recognize influences on roles and relationships (ethnic, racial, gender, social, cultural)
- Manage and cope with crises
- Share interpersonal wisdom and experiences with future generations
- Cope with stress
- Appreciate diverse individuals, cultures, and communities

FAMILY RESOURCE MANAGEMENT
Childhood

- Take care of possessions
- Help with family tasks
- Learn about time and schedules
- Learn to choose (develop decision-making skills)
- Understand how to earn, spend, and save money
- Develop awareness of space and privacy
- Develop talents and abilities
- Select options for food, clothing, and play
- Use, save and manage human and non-human resources
- Describe the influences on consumer decisions (personal values, costs, media, peers)

Adolescence

- Allocate time for work, school, and leisure
- Negotiate privacy and independence
- Select resources to meet personal needs (food, clothing, recreation)
- Use personal resources
- Understand how to earn, spend, and save money
- Participate in personal and family decision-making
- Take responsibility for decisions
- Develop leisure interests
- Clarify values as basis for choices
- Choose long- and short-term goals
- Explore career choices
- Assessment of and changes in personal and family resources
- Describe the influences on consumer decisions (personal values, costs, media, peers)

Adulthood
- Expend human energy
- Develop personal resources
- Develop personal resources through career choices
- Clarify values as basis for choices
- Develop leisure interests
- Recognize the varying needs of family members for privacy and independence
- Use resources to meet basic needs of family (food, clothing, shelter)
- Classify differing views about uses of family resources
- Establish long- and short-term goals
- Develop a financial plan
- Practice resource consumption and conservation (material and non-material)
- Balance family and work roles
- Describe the influences on consumer decisions (personal values, costs, media, peers)
- Plan for retirement and long-term care

Later Adulthood
- Clarify values as basis for choices
- Establish a plan for the distribution of resources and management if incompetent (will, living will, and advance health care directives)
- Use personal resources
- Expand leisure interests
- Balance life patterns of retirees with work roles of children
- Recognize the varying needs of family members for privacy and independence
- Practice resource consumption and conservation (material and non-material)
- Use resources to meet basic needs of family (food, clothing, shelter)
- Classify differing views about uses of family resources
- Establish long- and short-term goals (e.g., long-term care)
- Manage financial resources in retirement
- Describe the influences on consumer decisions (personal values, costs, media, peers)

PARENT EDUCATION AND GUIDANCE
Childhood
- Know the responsibilities of parents and caregivers
- Identify the rewards and demands of parenthood
- Develop awareness of varied parenting situations (single parenting, co-parenting, step-parenting, adoption, GLBT, parents who live away from children)
- Compare differing parenting styles and behaviors

- Meet children's needs at different stages of development
- Foster appropriate play and interaction with infants and young children
- Express caring and compassion
- Promote developmentally and individually appropriate guidance strategies for young children
- Cultivate caregiving skills
- Demonstrate safety, health, and the feeding of children
- Teach responsibilities of children in parent-child relationships
- Encourage communications with parents
- Teach problem-solving and conflict resolution
- Identify sources of help for parenting (family, neighborhood, community)
- Note problems of family violence, abuse, neglect
- Help parents cope with the stresses of parenting

Adolescence
- Teach responsibilities of parents and caregivers
- Identify the rewards and demands of parenthood
- Develop awareness of varied parenting situations (single parenting, co-parenting, step-parenting, adoption, GLBT, parents who live away from children)
- Understand marital, parenting, and children/youth roles in the family
- Comprehend factors to consider in deciding if and when to become a parent
- Compare differing parenting styles and behaviors
- Develop awareness of influences on parenting (ethnic, racial, gender, social, cultural, community)
- Observe and meet children's needs at different stages of development
- Respond to individual differences in children
- Promote developmentally and individually appropriate activities for children
- Foster appropriate play and interaction with infants and young children
- Express caring and compassion to children
- Promote developmentally and individually appropriate guidance strategies
- Guide and supervise access with media and technology
- Demonstrate safety, health, and nutrition for children
- Teach life skills of (self-sufficiency, safety, decision-making)
- Teach responsibilities of adolescents in parent-child relationships
- Encourage communications with parents
- Teach decision-making, problem-solving, and conflict resolution in the family
- Identify sources of help for parenting (family, neighborhood, community)
- Note problems of family violence, abuse, neglect

Adulthood
- Encourage care of self and adult relationships
- Recognize and build family and individual strengths for parenting
- Identify rewards and demands of parenthood
- Stress intentional parenting (goals, values, and traditions)
- Comprehend factors to consider in deciding if and when to become a parent
- Recognize changing parent-child relationships over the lifespan
- Observe and meet individual needs of children and adolescents at different stages of development
- Prepare for birth and parenthood
- Change parental responsibilities as children become independent
- Support youth in transition to adulthood
- Develop awareness of varied parenting situations (single parenting, co-parenting, step-parenting, adoption, GLBT, parents who live away from children)
- Understand marital, parenting, and children/youth roles in the family
- Compare differing parenting styles and behaviors
- Recognize importance of communications regarding child-rearing practices and decisions between parents, grandparents, and other caregivers
- Develop awareness of influences on parenting (ethnic, racial, gender, social, cultural, community)
- Provide and monitor a safe and healthy environment for children and youth
- Express care and compassion
- Promote developmentally and individually appropriate guidance strategies
- Guide and supervise access with media and technology
- Teach life skills to children and adolescents (self-sufficiency, safety, decision-making, problem-solving, and conflict resolution)
- Promote developmentally and individually appropriate activities for children
- Foster appropriate play and interaction with infants and young children
- Create learning environments and involvement in education of children and adolescents
- Encourage parent-child communications
- Receive and give support for parenting
- Identify sources of help for parenting (family, neighborhood, community)
- Prevent and respond to family violence, abuse, and neglect

Later Adulthood
- Encourage care of self and adult relationships
- Recognize and build family and individual strengths for grandparenting
- Value the importance of family stories and traditions

- Develop awareness of changing parent-child roles and relationships in later life
- Negotiate adult relationships with adult
- Identify demands and rewards of grandparenthood, including the possibility of rearing and caring for grandchildren
- Knowledge of intergenerational and diverse households (strengths, roles and challenges)
- Adapt to the complexities of varied parenting situations (blended families, single parenting, step-parenting, care-taking of disabled children, return of adult children to the household, parents and grandparents who live away from children, GLBT families)
- Express care and compassion to grandchildren and their parents
- Encourage grandparent-grandchild communication
- Stress the importance of communications between parents and grandparents regarding parenting styles, parenting decisions, and values
- Evaluate the role of media and technology in family relationships
- Receive and give support for parenting and grandparenting
- Identify sources of help for parenting (family, neighborhood, community)
- Teach decision-making, problem-solving, and conflict resolution in the family
- Note problems of family violence, elder abuse, and neglect

FAMILY LAW AND PUBLIC POLICY
Childhood
- Understand and respect the law
- Develop, evaluate, and implement laws and policies affecting families
- Formulate children's legal rights
- Advocate for resources that support the development of parent education
- Develop, evaluate, and implement public policy as it affects families with children (taxes, civil rights, social security, economic support laws, regulations)

Adolescence
- Respect the civil rights of all people
- Understand legal definitions and laws affecting families
- Comprehend individual and family legal protection, rights, and responsibilities
- Evaluate and comprehend laws relating to marriage, divorce, family support, child custody, child protection and rights, and family planning
- Describe family conflict and legal protection of and for family members
- Define the interaction of families and the justice system
- Understand families with incarcerated adolescents
- Identify the impact of laws and policies on families
- Develop, evaluate, and implement public policy as it affects families with children (taxes, civil rights, social security, economic support laws, regulations)

Adulthood
- Transmit values regarding education, justice, and the law
- Understand and influence laws and policies
- Evaluate and comprehend laws relating to marriage, divorce, family support, child custody, child protection and rights, and family planning
- Describe family conflict and legal protection of and for family members
- Develop, evaluate, and implement public policy as it affects families with children (taxes, civil rights, social security, economic support laws, regulations)

Later Adulthood
- Transmit values regarding education, justice, and the law
- Understand and influence laws and policies
- Protect the civil rights of all people
- Evaluate and comprehend laws relating to marriage, divorce, family support, protection and rights of vulnerable individuals, property, wills, estate planning, and living wills
- Describe family conflict and legal protection of and for family members
- Develop, evaluate, and implement public policy as it affects families with children (taxes, civil rights, social security, economic support laws, regulations)

PROFESSIONAL ETHICS AND PRACTICE
Childhood
- Take responsibility for actions
- Understand consequences of actions for self and others
- Honor spiritual ideas and beliefs
- Respect persons who are different
- Gain new rights and responsibilities with age
- Understand that rights are for all persons

Adolescence
- Develop a personal code of ethics
- Explore personal spirituality
- Connect personal autonomy and social responsibility
- Become aware of the interrelationship of rights and responsibilities
- Understand ethical principles as one kind of value
- Become aware of ethical implications of social and technological change
- Understand ethical dilemmas and conflicts

Adulthood
- Establish an ethical philosophy of life
- Act in accordance with personal beliefs with consideration for others
- Continue growth in spirituality

- Balance personal autonomy and social responsibility
- Become aware of the interrelationship of rights and responsibilities
- Understand ethical principles as one kind of value
- Use ethical values as a guide to human social conduct
- Assist others in the formation of ethical concepts and behavior
- Become aware of ethical implications of social and technological change

Later Adulthood

- Balance personal autonomy and social responsibility
- Continue growth in spirituality
- Act in accordance with personal beliefs with consideration for others
- Become aware of the interrelationship of rights and responsibilities
- Understand ethical principles as one kind of value
- Use ethical values as a guide to human social conduct
- Review quality of life and end of life issues
- Develop awareness for protection from exploitation
- Consider ethical implications of social and technological change
- Share life's wisdom and ethical experiences with future generations

From *The Family Life Education Framework* edited by David J. Bredehoft, Ph.D., CFLE and Michael J. Walcheski, Ph.D., CFLE of Concordia University, St. Paul, MN ©NCFR 2011.

This framework was originally developed by the National Council on Family Relations' Standards and Certification Committee (1984), building upon the earlier work of the Texas Council on Family Relations (1977). It was further revised and edited in 1997 by David J. Bredehoft, Ph.D., CFLE, Chair of Social and Behavioral Sciences, Concordia University, St. Paul, MN.

This current version was edited by David J. Bredehoft, Ph.D., CFLE, and Michael J. Walcheski, Ph.D., CFLE, Dean of the Graduate School, both of Concordia University, St. Paul, MN.

Special thanks to members of the original committee and members of the 1995–96 and 2010 Focus Groups for their input. Reprinted with permission.

Family Life Education Content Areas
Content and Practice Guidelines

These guidelines represent the content from the *University and College Curriculum Guidelines* and the knowledge, skills, and abilities included within the examination for the Certified Family Life Educator (CFLE) designation. These content areas include theory, research, and practice within the field of family life education. Examples of some of these core theories/frameworks/perspectives include family systems, ecosystems, individual and family development, exchange, symbolic interaction, conflict, feminist, and stress.

The FLE content areas are illustrated in the Family Life Education (FLE) Framework (Bredehoft & Walcheski, 2011), which outlines all ten content areas specific to four age groups: childhood, adolescence, adulthood, and older adulthood. The four age groups demonstrate the principle that FLE is relevant to individuals and families across the lifespan. The fact that FLE is inclusive of all audiences is represented by the words *Value*; *Diverse Cultures, Communities, and Individuals*; and *Justice*, that are woven throughout the framework. Finally, FLE has a foundation in systems thinking (both family systems and larger ecosystems) and this systems approach is represented by the words "within the context of the family system" and "reciprocal interactions between family and ecosystem" that also are woven throughout the framework.

There are two parts to each of the following 10 content areas. The first is "Content" which gives an overview of the subject matter in this area from the *University and College Curriculum Guidelines*. The second component includes "Practice" which relates to the tasks expected of an entry-level CFLE. *This "practice" segment is the basis of questions in the CFLE exam.*

NCFR (2009b).

I FAMILIES AND INDIVIDUALS IN SOCIETAL CONTEXTS

Content: An understanding of families and their relationships to other institutions, such as the educational, governmental, religious, and occupational institutions in society.

> e.g., Research and theories related to: Structures and Functions; Cultural Variations (family heritage, social class, geography, ethnicity, race and religion); Dating, Courtship, Marital Choice; Kinship; Cross-Cultural and Minority (understanding of lifestyles of minority families and the lifestyles of families in various societies around the world); Changing Gender Roles (role expectations and behaviors of courtship partners, marital partners, parents and children, siblings, and extended kin); Demographic Trends; Historical Issues; Work/leisure and Family Relationships; Societal Relations (reciprocal influence of the major social institutions and families, i.e., governmental, religious, educational, and economic).

Practice—A CFLE is prepared to:

a. Identify the characteristics, diversity, and impact of local, national, and global social systems

b. Identify factors (e.g., media, marketing, technology, economics, social movements, natural disasters, war) influencing individuals and families from both contemporary and historical perspectives

c. Identify factors that influence the relationship between work and family life

d. Identify social and cultural influences affecting dating, courtship, partner/marital choice and relationships, family composition, and family life

e. Recognize the reciprocal interaction between individuals, families, and various social systems (e.g., health, legal, educational, religious/spiritual)

f. Assess the impact of demographics (e.g., class, race, ethnicity, generation, gender) on contemporary families

II INTERNAL DYNAMICS OF FAMILIES

Content: An understanding of family strengths and weaknesses and how family members' relate to each other.

> e.g., Research and theories related to: Internal Social Processes (including cooperation and conflict); Communication (patterns and problems in husband-wife relationships and in parent-child relationships, including stress and conflict management); Conflict Management; Decision-making and Goal-setting; Normal Family Stresses (transition periods in the family life cycle, three-generation households, caring for the elderly, and dual careers); Family Stress and Crises (divorce, remarriage, death, economic uncertainty and hardship, violence, substance abuse); Special needs in families (including adoptive, foster, migrant, low income, military, and blended families as well as those with disabled members).

Practice—A CFLE is prepared to:
  a. Recognize and define healthy and unhealthy characteristics pertaining to:
      1. Family relationships
      2. Family development
  b. Analyze family functioning using various theoretical perspectives
  c. Assess family dynamics from a systems perspective
  d. Evaluate family dynamics in response to normative and non-normative stressors
  e. Evaluate family dynamics in response to crises
  f. Facilitate and strengthen communication processes, conflict-management, and problem-solving skills
  g. Develop, recognize, and reinforce strategies that help families function effectively

III HUMAN GROWTH AND DEVELOPMENT ACROSS THE LIFESPAN

Content: An understanding of the developmental changes (both typical and atypical) of individuals in families across the lifespan. Based on knowledge of physical, emotional, cognitive, social, moral, and personality aspects.

  e.g., Research and theories related to: Prenatal; Infancy; Early and Middle Childhood; Adolescence; Adulthood; Aging.

Practice—A CFLE is prepared to:
  a. Identify developmental stages, transitions, tasks, and challenges throughout the lifespan
  b. Recognize reciprocal influences
      1. Individual development on families
      2. Family development on individuals
  c. Recognize the impact of individual health and wellness on families
  d. Assist individuals and families in effective developmental transitions
  e. Apply appropriate practices based on theories of human growth and development to individuals and families

IV HUMAN SEXUALITY

Content: An understanding of the physiological, psychological, and social aspects of sexual development across the lifespan, so as to achieve healthy sexual adjustment.

  e.g., Research and theories related to: Reproductive Physiology; Biological Determinants; Emotional and Psychological Aspects of Sexual Involvement; Sexual Behaviors; Sexual Values and Decision-Making; Family Planning; Physiological and Psychological Aspects of Sexual Response; Influence of Sexual Involvement on Interpersonal Relationships.

Practice—A CFLE is prepared to:

a. Recognize the biological aspects of human sexuality

1. Sexual functioning

2. Reproductive health

3. Family planning

4. Sexually transmitted infections (STIs)

b. Recognize the psycho-social aspects of human sexuality

1. Characteristics of healthy and ethical sexual relationships

2. Interpersonal dynamics of sexual intimacy

3. Risk factors (e.g., substance abuse, social pressures, media)

c. Address human sexuality from a value-respectful position

V INTERPERSONAL RELATIONSHIPS

Content: An understanding of the development and maintenance of interpersonal relationships.

> e.g., Research and theories related to: Self and Others; Communication Skills (listening, empathy, self-disclosure, decision making, problem-solving, and conflict resolution); Intimacy, Love, Romance; Relating to Others with Respect, Sincerity, and Responsibility.

Practice—A CFLE is prepared to:

a. Recognize the impact of personality and communication styles

b. Recognize the developmental stages of relationships

c. Analyze interpersonal relationships using various theoretical perspectives

d. Develop and implement relationship enhancement and enrichment strategies

e. Develop and implement effective communication, problem solving, and conflict management strategies

f. Communicate aspects of relationships within the context of their developmental stages

VI FAMILY RESOURCE MANAGEMENT

Content: An understanding of the decisions individuals and families make about developing and allocating resources including time, money, material assets, energy, friends, neighbors, and space, to meet their goals.

> e.g., Research and theories related to: Goal Setting and Decision-Making; Development and Allocation of Resources; Social Environment Influences; Life Cycle and Family Structure Influences; Consumer Issues and Decisions.

Practice—A CFLE is prepared to:

a. Identify personal, familial, professional, and community resources available to families

b. Recognize the reciprocal relationship between individual/family/community choices and resources

c. Apply value-clarification strategies to decision-making

d. Apply goal-setting strategies and evaluate their outcomes

e. Apply decision-making strategies

f. Apply organizational and time management strategies

g. Apply basic financial management tools and principles

h. Inform individuals and families of consumer rights, responsibilities, and choices of action/advocacy

i. Apply stress management strategies

VII PARENTING EDUCATION AND GUIDANCE

Content: An understanding of how parents teach, guide and influence children and adolescents as well as the changing nature, dynamics and needs of the parent child relationship across the lifespan.

e.g., Research and theories related to: Parenting Rights and Responsibilities; Parenting Practices/Processes; Parent/Child Relationships; Variation in Parenting Solutions; Changing Parenting Roles across the Life Cycle.

Practice—A CFLE is prepared to:

a. Promote healthy parenting from a systems perspective

b. Promote healthy parenting from a child's and parents' developmental perspective

c. Apply strategies based on the child's age/stage of development to promote effective developmental outcomes

d. Identify different parenting styles and their associated psychological, social, and behavioral outcomes

e. Promote various parenting models, principles, and strategies

f. Evaluate the effectiveness and appropriateness of various parenting strategies

g. Recognize various parenting roles (e.g., father/mother, grandparents, other caregivers) and their impact on and contributionto individuals and families

h. Recognize parenting issues within various family structures (e.g., single, blended, same-sex)

i. Recognize the impact of societal trends on parenting (e.g., technology, substance abuse, media)

j. Recognize the influence of cultural differences and diversity

k. Identify strategies to advocate for children in various settings (e.g., schools, legal system, and health care

l. Recognize the various pathways to parenting and their associated issues and challenges, (e.g., assisted reproduction, adoption, childbirth, blending)

VIII FAMILY LAW AND PUBLIC POLICY

Content: An understanding of legal issues, policies, and laws influencing the well-being of families.

e.g., Family and the Law (relating to marriage, divorce, family support, child custody, child protection and rights, and family planning); Family and Social Services; Family and Education; Family and the Economy; Family and Religion; Policy and the Family (public policy as it affects the family, including tax, civil rights, social security, economic support laws, and regulations.)

Practice—A CFLE is prepared to:

    a. Identify current law, public policy, and initiatives that regulate and influence professional conduct and services

    b. Identify current laws, public policies, and initiatives that affect families

    c. Inform families, communities, and policy makers about public policies, initiatives, and legislation that affect families at local, state, and national levels

IX PROFESSIONAL ETHICS AND PRACTICE

Content: An understanding of the character and quality of human social conduct, and the ability to critically examine ethical questions and issues as they relate to professional practice.

    e.g., Research and theories related to: Formation of Social Attitudes and Values; Recognizing and Respecting the Diversity of Values and the Complexity of Value Choice in a Pluralistic Society; Examining Value Systems and Ideologies systematically and objectively; Social Consequences of Value Choices; Recognizing the Ethical Implications of Social and Technological Changes; Ethics of Professional Practice.

Practice—A CFLE is prepared to:

    a. Demonstrate professional attitudes, values, behaviors, and responsibilities to clients, colleagues, and the broader community, that are reflective of ethical standards and practice

    b. Evaluate, differentiate, and apply diverse approaches to ethical issues and dilemmas

    c. Identify and apply appropriate strategies to deal with conflicting values

    d. Demonstrate respect for diverse cultural values and ethical standards

X FAMILY LIFE EDUCATION METHODOLOGY

Content: An understanding of the general philosophy and broad principles of family life education in conjunction with the ability to plan, implement, and evaluate such educational programs.

    e.g., Research and theories related to: Planning and Implementing; Evaluation (materials, student progress, and program effectiveness); Education Techniques; Sensitivity to Others (to enhance educational effectiveness); Sensitivity to Community Concerns and Values (understanding of the public relations process).

Practice—A CFLE is prepared to:

    a. Employ a variety of current educational strategies

    b. Employ techniques to promote application of information in the learner's environment

   c. Create learning environments that are respectful of individual vulnerabilities, needs, and learning styles

   d. Demonstrate sensitivity to diversity and community needs, concerns, and interests

   e. Develop culturally-competent educational materials and learning experiences

   f. Identify appropriate sources for evidence-based information

   g. Develop educational experiences

      1. Needs assessment

      2. Goals and objectives

      3. Content development

      4. Implementation

      5. Evaluation/outcome measures

   h. Promote and market educational programs

   i. Implement adult education principles into work with families and parents

   j. Establish and maintain appropriate personal and professional boundaries

REFERENCES

Bredehoft, D. J., & Cassidy, D. (Eds.). (1995). *Family life education curriculum guidelines* (2nd ed.). Minneapolis: National Council on Family Relations.

Bredehoft, D. J. (Ed.). (1997). *Life span family life education.* (2nd ed.) [Poster]. Minneapolis: National Council on Family Relations.

National Council on Family Relations. (2007). Certified Family Life Educator (CFLE) exam content outline. In Bredehoft, D. J. & Walcheski, M. J. (Eds.), *Family life education: Integrating theory and practice* (2nd ed., pp. 261–263).

Career Opportunities in Family Sciences

Setting	Employment Opportunities
Business, Consumer, and Family Resources Services	Employee Assistance Specialist Corporate Childcare Administrator Family Financial Counseling and Planning Consumer Protection Agencies Family Resource Management Food Assistance Programs Child and Family Poverty Research Research on Work and Families Family Business Consultant
Community-Based Social Services	Youth Development Programs Adoption Agencies Foster Care Programs Teen Pregnancy Counselor Family Preservation Worker Welfare Assistance for Low-Income Families Vocational Rehabilitation and Job Training Adult Day Care Providers Gerontology Programs
Early Childhood Education	Childcare Centers Head Start Programs Preschools Montessori Schools Child Development Consultant
Education	Public School Teaching in Family and Consumer Sciences (Certification) Cooperative Extension University Teaching and Research in Family Science Departments Family Life Education Sexuality Education Programs in Parish and Community Settings Parent Educators Family Peace and Justice Education Children's Museum Education Marriage and Family Enrichment Facilitators High School Guidance Counselor

(continued)

Setting	Employment Opportunities
Faith-Based Organizations	Clergy Family Mentor Family Life Educator Parent Educator Youth Worker
Family Intervention	Individual and Family Therapy Case Manager for Family Treatment Plans Crisis and Hotline Services Court-Mandated Parent Education Programs Divorce Mediation Abuse Protection Services Sexual Violence Drug and Alcohol Prevention Counselors Residential Treatment Programs Victim/Witness Support Services
Government and Public Policy	Family Policy Analyst Advocate/Lobbyist on Behalf of Children, Women, and Family Well-Being Cooperative Extension Specialist Military Family Support Services Departments of Child and Family Services Juvenile Justice
Health Care and Family Wellness	Public Health Programs and Services Hospital Family Support Professionals Nutrition Education and Counseling Prenatal and Maternity Services Holistic Health Centers Long-Term Care Administrator Hospice Programs
International Education and Development	International Family Policy Analyst Peace Corps and NGO Leadership Global Family Planning Programs Community and Sustainable Development International Human Rights Advocacy Immigration and Migrant Families Services
Research	Grant Proposal Writing Academic and Government-Related Research in Family Science Content Areas Population Studies and Demographic Research Community-Based Research for Non-Profit Family Agencies Program Evaluation and Assessment
Writing and Communication	Curriculum and Resource Development Public Service Radio and TV Programming Newspaper and Magazine Journalism on Social Issues Affecting Children and Families

Careers in Family Science. (2009). Minneapolis: National Council on Family Relations.

Program Evaluation
The Five-Tiered Approach

Level/Title	Purposes of Evaluation	Audiences	Tasks	Kinds of Data to Collect/Analyze
Tier One—Needs Assessment	1. To determine the size and nature of a public problem 2. To determine unmet need for services in a community 3. To propose program and policy options to meet needs 4. To set a data baseline from which later progress can be measured 5. To broaden the base of support for a proposed program	1. Policymakers 2. Funders 3. Community stakeholders	1. Review existing community, county, and state data 2. Determine additional data needed to describe problem and potential service users 3. Conduct "environmental scan" of available resources 4. Identify resource gaps and unmet needs 5. Set goals and objectives for intervention 6. Recommend one program model for range of options	1. Extant data on target population; services currently available 2. Interviews with community leaders 3. Interviews or survey data from prospective participants 4. Information about similar programs in other locations
Tier Two—Monitoring and Accountability	1. To monitor program performance 2. To meet demands for accountability 3. To build a constituency 4. To aid in program planning and decision-making 5. To provide a groundwork for later evaluation activities	1. Program staff and administrators 2. Policymakers 3. Funders 4. Community stakeholders 5. Media	1. Determine needs and capacities for data collection and management 2. Develop clear and consistent procedures for collecting essential data elements 3. Gather and analyze data to describe program along dimensions of clients, services, staff, and costs	1. MIS (management information system) data; collected at program, county, and/or state level 2. Case material; obtained through record reviews, program contact forms, etc.
Tier Three—Quality Review and Program Clarification	1. To develop a more detailed picture of the program as it is being implemented 2. To assess the quality and consistency of the intervention 3. To provide information to staff for program improvement	1. Program staff and administrators 2. Policymakers 3. Community stakeholders	1. Review monitoring data 2. Expand on program description using information about participants' views 3. Compare program with standards and expectations 4. Examine participants' perceptions about effects of program 5. Clarify program goals and design	1. MIS monitoring data 2. Case material 3. Other qualitative and quantitative data on program operations, customer satisfaction, and perceived effects; obtained using questionnaires, interviews, observations, and focus groups

Level/Title	Purposes of Evaluation	Audiences	Tasks	Kinds of Data to Collect/Analyze
Tier Four— Achieving Outcomes	1. To determine changes, if any, have occurred among beneficiaries 2. To attribute changes to the program 3. To provide information to staff for program improvement	1. Program staff and administrators 2. Policymakers 3. Community stakeholders 4. Funders 5. Other programs	1. Choose short-term objectives to be examined 2. Choose appropriate research design, given constraints and capacities 3. Determine measurable indicators of success for outcome objectives 4. Collect and analyze information about effects on beneficiaries	1. Client-specific data; obtained using questionnaires, interviews, goal attainment scaling, observations, and functional indicators 2. Client and community social indicators 3. MIS data
Tier Five— Establishing Impact	1. To contribute to knowledge development in the field 2. To produce evidence of differential effectiveness of treatments 3. To identify models worthy of replication	1. Academic and research communities 2. Policymakers 3. Funders 4. General public	1. Decide on impact objectives based on results of Tier Four evaluation efforts 2. Choose appropriately rigorous research design and comparison group 3. Identify techniques and tools to measure effects in treatment and comparison groups 4. Analyze information to identify program impacts	1. Client-specific data; obtained using questionnaires, interviews, goal attainment scaling, observations, and functional indicators 2. Client and community social indicators 3. MIS data 4. Comparable data for control group.

Source: Jacobs, F. H., & Kapuscik, J. L. (with Williams, P. H., & Kates, E.) (2000). *Making it count: Evaluating family preservation services.* Medford, MA: Family Preservation Evaluation Project, Eliot-Pearson Department of Child Development, Tufts University.

References

ABC News. (2007, October 7). *Helicopter parents hover over kids' lives*. Retrieved from www.abcnews.go.com/GMA/AmericanFamily/story?id=3699441&page=1

ABC News. (2009). *"Helicopter moms": Hurting or helping your kids?* Retrieved from www.abcnews.go.com/2020/Parenting/story?id=8418453

Adams, B. N. (2004). Families and family study in international perspective. *Journal of Marriage and Family, 66*(5), 1076–1088.

Adams, B., & Trost, J. (2005). *Handbook of world families*. Thousand Oaks, CA: Sage.

Adams, P. (2006). Exploring social constructivism: Theories and practicalities. *Education, 34*(3), 243–257.

Adler, S. (2003). Asian american families. In J. Ponzetti, Jr. (Ed.), *International encyclopedia of marriage and family* (pp. 82–91). New York: Macmillan Reference.

Adler-Baeder, F. (2001). *Smart steps for adults and children in stepfamilies*. Lincoln, NE: Stepfamily Association of America, and Watertown, NY: Cornell Cooperative Extension of Jefferson County.

Adler-Baeder, F. (2002). Understanding stepfamilies: Family life education for community professionals. *Journal of Extension, 40*(6). Retrieved from www.joe.org/joe/2002december/iw2.php

Adler-Baeder, F., & Higginbotham, B. (2004). Implications for remarriage and stepfamily formation for marriage education. *Family Relations, 53*, 448–458.

Adler-Baeder, F., Kerpelman, J., Schramm, D., Higginbotham, B., & Paulk, A. (2007). The impact of relationship education on adolescents of diverse backgrounds. *Family Relations 56*, 291–303.

Adler-Baeder, F., Robertson, A., & Schramm, D. (2010). Community programs serving couples in stepfamilies: A qualitative study of format, content, and service delivery. *Journal of Extension 48*(5). Retrieved from www.joe.org/joe/2010october/rb1.php

Administration for Children and Families (ACF). (2005). *Healthy marriage matters*. Washington DC: Author.

Advocates for Human Rights. (2013). Prevalence of domestic violence. Retrieved from www.stopvaw.org/prevalence_of_domestic_violence

Advocates for Youth. (2001). Sexuality education programs: Definitions and point-by-point comparisons. *Transitions, 12*(3), 4. Retrieved from www.advocatesforyouth.org/storage/advfy/documents/transitions1203.pdf

Ahmed, R., (2005). Egyptian families. In J. Roopnarine & U. Gielen (Eds.), *Families in global perspective* (pp. 151–168). Boston: Pearson.

363

Ainsworth, M. (1973). The development of infant-mother attachment. In B. Caldwell & H. Ricciuti (Eds.), *Review of child development research* (Vol. 3, pp. 1–94). Chicago: University of Chicago Press.

Ainsworth, M., & Bowlby, J. (1991). An ethological approach to personality development. *American Psychologist, 46,* 331–341.

Alford, S. (2008). *Science and success (2nd ed.): Sex education and other programs that work to prevent teen pregnancy, HIV & sexually transmitted infections.* Washington, DC: Advocates for Youth.

Allemand, M., Steiger, A., & Hill, P. (2013). Stability of personality traits in adulthood: Mechanisms and implications. *The Journal of Gerontopsychology and Geriatric Psychiatry, 26*(1), 3–13.

Allen, W., & Blaisure, K. (2009). Family life educators and the development of cultural competency. In D. Bredehoft & M. Walcheski (Eds.), *Family life education integrating theory and practice* (2nd ed.). Minneapolis, MN: National Council on Family Relations.

Alliance for Children & Families. (n.d.). *A century of service.* Retrieved from www.alliance1.org/centennial/century-service-contents

Alliance for Work Life Progress (AWLP). (2005). The categories of work-life effectiveness. Retrieved from www.awlp.org/pub/work-life_categories.pdf

Amato, P. (2000). The consequences of divorce for adults and children. *Journal of Marriage and the Family, 62,* 1269–1287.

Amato, P. (2010). Research on divorce: Continuing trends and new developments. *Journal of Marriage and Family, 72*(3), 650–666.

Amato, P. (2011a). Marital quality in African American marriages. Retrieved from www.healthymarriageinfo.org/resource-detail/index.aspx?rid=3929

Amato, P. (2011b). Divorce among African Americans. Retrieved from www.healthymarriageinfo.org/resource-detail/index.aspx?rid=3929

Amato, P., & Cheadle, J. (2005). The long reach of divorce: Divorce and child well-being across three generations. *Journal of Marriage and Family, 67,* 191–206.

Amato, P., & Hays, L. (2014). "Alone together": Marriages and "living apart together" relationships. In A. Abela & J. Walter (Eds.), *Contemporary issues in family studies: Global perspectives on partnerships, parenting and support in a changing world.* Malden, MA: John Wiley & Sons.

Amato, P., Booth, A., Johnson, D.,& Rogers, S. (2007). *Alone together: How marriage in America is changing.* Cambridge, MA: Harvard University.

Amato, P., Kane, J., & James, S. (2011). Reconsidering the "good divorce." *Family Relations, 60,* 511–524.

American Association of University Women (AAUW). (2011). *Crossing the line: Sexual harassment at school.* Washington DC: Author.

Amnesty International. (n.d.). *Armed conflict.* Retrieved from www.amnesty.org/en/armed-conflict

Anderson, J., & Doherty, W. (2005). Democratic community initiatives: The case of over-scheduled children. *Family Relations, 54*(5), 654–665.

Anderson, L., & Krathwohl, D. (2001). *A taxonomy for learning, teaching, and assessing: A revision of Bloom's taxonomy of educational objectives.* Boston: Allyn & Bacon.

Andrews, M., Bubolz, M., & Paolucci, B. (1981). An ecological approach to study of the family. *Marriage and Family Review, 3*(1–2), 22–49.

Annie E. Casey Foundation. (2008). *Children of incarcerated parents fact sheet.* Baltimore, MD: Author. Retrieved from www.211.idaho.gov/pdf/COIP_Factsheet.pdf

Annie E. Casey Foundation. (2013a). *2013 Kids count data book.* Baltimore, MD: Author. Retrieved from www.kidscount.org

Annie E. Casey Foundation. (2013b). *Data book. State trends in child well-being*. Baltimore, MD: Author. Retrieved from www.datacenter.kidscount.org/files/2013KIDSCOUNTDataBook.pdf

Annie E. Casey Foundation. (2013c). *World family map*. Retrieved from www.childtrends.org/Files/Child_Trends-2013_01_15_FR_WorldFamilyMap.pdf

Arcus, M. E., Schvaneveldt, J. D., & Moss, J. J. (1993). The nature of family life education. In M. E. Arcus, J. D. Schvaneveldt, & J. J. Moss (Eds.), *Handbook of family life education: Foundations of family life education* (Vol. 1, pp. 1–25). Newbury Park, CA: Sage.

Arcus, M. E, & Thomas, J. (1993). The nature and practice of family life education. In M. E. Arcus, J. D. Schvaneveldt, & J. J. Moss (Eds.), *Handbook of family life education: Foundations of family life education* (Vol. 2, pp. 1–32). Newbury Park, CA: Sage.

Arcus, M.E. (1995). Advances in family life education: Past, present, and future. *Family Relations, 44*, 336–343.

Arditti, J. (2008). Parental imprisonment and family visitation: A brief overview and recommendations for family friendly practice. In T. LaLiberte & E. Snyder (Eds.), *CW360: A comprehensive look at prevalent child welfare issue: Children of incarcerated parents* (pp. 16, 32). St. Paul: University of Minnesota. Retrieved from www.cehd.umn.edu/ssw/cascw/attributes/PDF/publications/CW360_2008.pdf

Arnett, J. (2000). Emerging adulthood: A theory of development from the late teens through the twenties. *American Psychologist, 55*, 469–480.

Arnett, J. (2004). *Emerging adulthood: The winding road from the late teens through the twenties*. New York: Oxford University Press.

Arnett, J. (2007). Emerging adulthood: What is it and what is it good for? *Child Development Perspectives, 1*, 68–73.

Asay, S., Younes, M., & Moore, T. (2006). Transformation in higher education: The impact of international study tours on college students. In R. Hamon (Ed.), *International family studies: Developing curricula and teaching tools* (pp. 85–99). Binghamton, NY: Haworth Press.

ASPE—Office of the Assistant Secretary for Planning and Evaluation. Office of Human Services Policy. (2013). Key implementation considerations for executing evidence-based programs: Project overview. Washington, DC: U.S. Department of Health and Human Services. Retrieved from www.aspe.hhs.gov/hsp/13/keyissuesforchildrenyouth/keyimplementation/rb_keyimplement.pdf

Averting HIV and Aids (AVERT). (n.d.). Abstinence and sex education. Retrieved from www.avert.org/abstinence.htm

Axtell, R. (1998). *Gestures: The do's and taboos of body language around the world*. New York: John Wiley & Sons, Inc.

Bahr, K. (1990). Student responses to genogram and family chronology. *Family Relations, 39*, 243–249.

Baldwin, K. E. (1949). *The AHEA saga*. Washington, DC: American Home Economics Association.

Ballard, S., & Morris, L. (2003). The family life education needs of midlife and older adults. *Family Relations, 52*, 129–136.

Ballard, S. M. &, Taylor, A. C. (2012a). A framework for best practices in family life education. *Certified Family Life Educator Network, 24*(4), 12–13.

Ballard, S., & Taylor, A. (2012b). *Family life education with diverse populations*. Thousand Oaks, CA: Sage.

Bandura, A. (1977). *Social learning theory*. New York: General Learning Press.

Bandura, A. (1986). *Social foundations of thought and action*. Englewood Cliffs, NJ: Prentice-Hall.

Bandura, A. (1999). Social cognitive theory: An agentic perspective. *Asian Journal of Social Psychology, 2*, 21–41.

Barnes, C., Stanley, S., & Markman, H. (2004). Christian PREP: The prevention and relationship enhancement program. *Marriage & Family: A Christian Journal, 7*, 63–76.

Barnes, P., Adams, P., & Powell-Griner, E. (2010). Health characteristics of the American Indian or Alaska Native adult population: United States, 2004–2008. National Health Statistics Reports, no 20. Hyattsville, MD; National Center for Health Statistics. Retrieved from www.cdc.gov/nchs/data/nhsr/nhsr020.pdf

Barnes, S. (2001). Stressors and strengths: A theoretical and practical examination of nuclear, single-parent, and augmented African American families. *Families in Society: The Journal of Contemporary Human Services, 82*, 449–460.

Baugh, E., & Coughlin, D. (2012). Family life education with black families. In S. Ballard & A. Taylor (Eds.), *Family life education with diverse populations* (pp. 235–254). Thousand Oaks, CA: Sage.

Baumrind, D. (1991). The influence of parenting style on adolescent competence and substance abuse. *Journal of Early Adolescence, 11*(1), 56–95.

Baumrind, D., & Black, A. E. (1967). Socialization practices associated with dimensions of competence in preschool boys and girls. *Child Development, 38*(2), 291–327.

Bean, R., Perry, B., & Bedell, T. (2001). Developing culturally competent marriage and family therapists: Guidelines for working with Hispanic families. *Journal of Marital and Family Therapy, 27*, 43–54.

Bedi, R. (2012, February 27). Indian dowry deaths on rise. *The Telegraph.* Retrieved from www.telegraph.co.uk/news/worldnews/asia/india/9108642/Indian-dowry-deaths-on-the-rise.html

Beecher, C. E. (1858). *A treatise on domestic* economy (3rd ed.). New York: Harper & Brothers.

Bennett, M. (1993). Toward ethnorelativism: A developmental model of intercultural sensitivity. In R. M. Paige (Ed.), *Education for the intercultural experiences* (pp. 21–71). Yarmouth, ME: Intercultural Press.

Berman, L. (n.d.). The brain is the biggest sex organ. Retrieved from www.drlauraberman.com/sexual-health/sex-and-brain/brain-biggest-sex-organ#/slide-1

Bernier, J. (1990). Parental adjustment to a disabled child: A family-systems perspective. *Families in Society: The Journal of Contemporary Human Services, 10*, 589–596.

Biblarz, T., & Savci, E. (2010). Lesbian, gay, bisexual, and transgender families. *Journal of Marriage and Family, 72*, 480–497.

BigFoot, D. (2008). Cultural adaptations of evidence-based practices in American Indian and Alaska native populations. In C. Newman, C. Liberton, K. Kutash, & R. Friedman (Eds.), *A system of care for children's mental health* (pp. 69–72). Tampa: University of South Florida, Louis de la Parte Florida Mental Health Institute.

BigFoot, D., Willmon-Haque, S., & Braden, J. (2008). *Trauma exposure in American Indian/Alaska native children.* Oklahoma City, OK: Indian Country Child Trauma Center. Retrieved from www.icctc.org/Resources/Trauma_AIs_Children_Factsheet2.pdf

Billings, D. (2004). Primary colors personality text. Retrieved from www.dawnbillings.com/main/personalityHow

Bloom B. (1956). *Taxonomy of educational objectives, handbook I: The cognitive domain.* New York: Longman.

Blumenfeld, S. (2012). How to eradicate illiteracy in America. *The New American.* Retrieved from www.thenewamerican.com/reviews/opinion/item/13752-how-to-eradicate-illiteracy-in-americ

Bodenmann, G., & Shantinath, S. (2004). The couples coping enhancement training (SSET): A new approach to prevention of marital distress based upon stress and coping. *Family Relations, 53*, 477–484.

Bodenmann, G., Ledermann, T., & Bradbury, T. N. (2007). Stress, sex, and satisfaction in marriage. *Personal Relationships, 14*, 551–569.

Bond, J., Galinsky, E., & Hill, E. (2004). *When work works: Flexibility: A critical ingredient in creating an effective workplace.* New York: Families and Work Institute.

Boog, J. (2012). *Illiteracy in America: Infographic.* Retrieved from www.mediabistro.com/galleycat/illiteracy-in-america-infographic_b51032

Bookwala, J. (2005). The role of marital quality in physical health during the mature years. *Journal of Aging and Health, 17,* 85–104.

Bornstein, M. H. (Ed.). (2002). *Handbook of parenting, Vol. 1: Children and parenting* (2nd ed.). Mahwah, NJ: Lawrence Erlbaum.

Boss, P. (1999). *Ambiguous loss: Learning to live with unresolved grief.* Cambridge, MA: Harvard University Press.

Boss, P. (2002). *Family stress management: A contextual approach* (2nd ed.). Thousand Oaks, CA: Sage.

Bouchet, S. (2008). Children and families with incarcerated parents. Baltimore, MD: Annie E. Casey Foundation. Retrieved from www.f2f.ca.gov/res/pdf/ChildrenAndFamilies.pdf

Bouchet, S., Torres, L., & Hyra, A. (2013). Understanding Hispanic diversity: A "one size" approach to service delivery may not fit all. Office of Planning, Research, and Evaluation, Administration of Children and Families. Retrieved from www.acf.hhs.gov/sites/default/files/opre/hmmi_hispanic.pdf

Bowlby, J. (1969). *Attachment and loss: Vol. 1. Attachment.* New York: Basic Books.

Bowlby, J. (1988). *A secure base: Parent-child attachment and healthy human development.* New York: Basic Books.

Bowman, S., Rennekamp, D., & Wolfe, J. (2012). Findings from the National Forum on Professional Development Systems for Parenting Education. Hallie. E. Ford Center White Paper. Retrieved from www.npen.org/wp-content/uploads/2012/06/2011-Findings-from-the-National-Forum-on-Professional-Development-Systems-for-Parenting-Education.pdf

Boyd, L., Hibbard, C., & Knapp, D. (2001). *Market analysis of family life, parenting, and marriage education for the National Council on Family Relations.* Alexandria, VA: Human Resources Research Organization.

Boyle, C., Boulet, S., Schieve, L., Cohen, R., Blumberg, S., Yeargin-Allsopp, M., Visser, S., & Kogan, M. (2011). Trends in the prevalence of developmental disabilities in U.S. children, 1997–2008. *Pediatrics,* doi: 10.1542/peds.2010–2989.

Braithwaite, S., Delevi, R., & Fincham, F. (2010). Romantic relationships and the physical and mental health of college students. *Personal Relationships, 17,* 1–12.

Bramlett, M., & Mosher, W. (2002). *Cohabitation, marriage, divorce, and remarriage in the United States* (Series 22, No 2). Retrieved from www.cdc.gov/nchs/data/series/sr_23/sr23_022.pdf

Bray, J., & Kelly, J. (1998). *Stepfamilies: Love, marriage, and parenting in the first decade.* New York: Broadway.

Brazelton, T. B., & Cramer, B. (1990). *The earliest relationship.* Reading, MA: Addison-Wesley.

Bredehoft, D., & Walcheski, M. (Eds.). (2009). *Family life education: Integrating theory and practice* (2nd ed.). Minneapolis, MN: National Council on Family Relations.

Bredehoft, D., Mennicke, S., Porter, A., & Clarke, J. (1998). Perceptions attributed by adults to parental overindulgence during childhood. *Journal of Family and Consumer Sciences Education, 16,* 3–17.

Bredehoft, D. J., & Walcheski, M. J. (Eds.). (2011). The family life education framework poster and PowerPoint. Minneapolis, MN: National Council on Family Relations.

Brick, P., & Lundquist, J. (2003). *New expectations: Sexuality education for mid and later life.* New York: SIECUS.

Brick, P., & Taverner, B. (2001). *Positive images: Teaching abstinence, contraception, and sexual health.* Morristown, NJ: Planned Parenthood of Greater Northern New Jersey, Inc.

Brick, P., Davis, N., Fischel, M., Lupo, T., MacVicar, A., & Marshall, J. (1989). *Bodies, birth, and babies: Sexuality education in early childhood programs*. Hackensack, NJ: Planned Parenthood of Bergen County.

Brickman, P., Rabinowitz, V., Karuza, J., Jr., Coates, D., Cohn, E., & Kidder, L. (1982). Models of helping and coping. *American Psychologist, 37*, 368–384.

Bridgeman, R. P. (1930). Ten years' progress in parent education. *Annals of the American Academy of Political and Social Science, 151*, 32–45.

Brim, O. (1959). *Education for child rearing*. New York: Russell Sage Foundation.

Bristor, M. (2010). *Individuals and family systems in their environments*. Dubuque, IA: Kendall Hunt.

Brock, G. (1993). Ethical guidelines for the practice of family life education. *Family Relations, 42*(2), 124–127.

Brock, G. W., Oertwein, M., & Coufal, J. D. (1993). Parent education theory, research, and practice. In M. E. Arcus, J. D. Schvaneveldt, & J. J. Moss (Eds.), *Handbook of family life education* (Vol. 2, p. 88). Newbury Park, CA: Sage.

Bromwich, R. (1981). *Working with parents and infants*. Baltimore, MD: University Park Press.

Bronfenbrenner, U. (1979). *The ecology of human development*. Cambridge, MA: Harvard University Press.

Bronfenbrenner, U. (2005). *Making human beings human: Bioecological perspectives on human development*. Thousand Oaks, CA: Sage.

Brooks, J. (2011). *The process of parenting* (6th ed.). New York: McGraw-Hill.

Brotherson, S., & Duncan, W. (2004). Rebinding the ties that bind: Government efforts to preserve and promote marriage. *Family Relations, 53*, 459–468.

Brown, S., & Taverner, B. (2001). *Streetwise to sex-wise: Sexuality education for high-risk youth*. Morristown, NJ: Planned Parenthood of Greater Northern New Jersey, Inc.

Brubaker, R. (2001). International migration: A challenge for humanity. *International Migration Review, 25*, 946–957.

Bruess, C., & Greenberg, J. (2009). *Sexuality education: Theory and practice*. Sudbury, MA: Jones and Bartlett Publishers.

Bubolz, M., & Sontag, S. (1993). Human ecology theory. In P. Boss, W. Doherty, R. LaRossa, W. Schumm, & S. Steinmetz (Eds.), *Sourcebook of family theories and methods: A contextual approach* (pp. 419–448). New York: Plenum Press.

Bubolz, M., Eicher, J., & Sontag, S. (1979). The human ecosystem: A model. *Journal of Home Economics, 71*, 28–30.

Bureau of Justice Statistics. (2010). Terms and conditions. Retrieved from www.bjs.gov/index.cfm?ty=tda

Burgess, E. W. (1926). The family as a unit of interacting personalities. *The Family, 7*, 3–9.

Buston, K., Wight, D., Hart, G., & Scott, S. (2002). Implementation of a teacher-delivered sex education programme: Obstacles and facilitating factors. *Health Education Research, 17*, 59–72.

Byrne, A., & Carr, D. (2005). Caught in the cultural lag: The stigma of singlehood. *Psychological Inquiry: An International Journal for the Advancement of Psychological Theory, 16*(2–3), 84–91.

Calasanti, T., & Keicolt, K. (2007). Diversity among late-life couples. *Generations: Journal of the American Society on Aging, 31*, 10–17.

Campbell, D., & Palm, G. F. (2004). *Group parent education: Promoting parent learning and support*. Thousand Oaks, CA: Sage.

Cancian, M., & Reed, D. (2009). Family structure, childbearing, and parental employment: Implications for the level and trend in poverty. *Focus, 26*, 21–26.

Carnegie Mellon University (CMU). (n.d.). What are the benefits of group work? Eberly Center: Teaching Excellence and Educational Innovation. Retrieved from www.cmu.edu/teaching/designteach/design/instructionalstrategies/groupprojects/benefits.html

Carroll, E., Smith, C., & Behnke, A. (2012). Family life education with military families. In S. Ballard & A. Taylor (Eds.), *Family life education with diverse populations* (pp. 91–115). Thousand Oaks, CA: Sage.

Carroll, J., & Doherty, W. (2003). Evaluating the ineffectiveness of premarital prevention programs: A meta-analytic review of outcome research. *Family Relations, 52,* 105–118.

Carter, N. (1996). *See how we grow: A report on the status of parenting education in the U.S.* Philadelphia, PA: Pew Charitable Trusts.

Cassidy, D. (2003). The growing of a profession: Challenges in family life education. In D. Bredehoft & M. Walcheski (Eds.), *Family life education: Integrating theory and practice* (pp. 44–55). Minneapolis, MN: National Council on Family Relations.

Centers for Disease Control and Prevention (CDC). (2009). National Center on Birth Defects and Developmental Disabilities. Retrieved from www.cdc.gov/

Centers for Disease Control and Prevention. (2011). Youth risk behavior surveillance—United States, 2011. *MMWR, 61*(4), 1–168. Retrieved from www.cdc.gov/mmwr/pdf/ss/ss6104.pdf

Centers for Disease Control and Prevention (CDC). (2013). *Adverse childhood experiences (ACE) study.* Retrieved from www.cdc.gov/ace/index.htm

Chalmers, L., & Milan, A. (2005). Marital satisfaction during the retirement years. *Canadian Social Trends, 76,* 14–17.

Chamberlain, V., & Cummings, M. (2003). *Creative instructional methods for family & consumer sciences, nutrition & wellness.* Peoria, IL: Glencoe/McGraw-Hill.

Cherlin, A. (2010). Demographic trends in the United States: A review of research in the 2000s. *Journal of Marriage and Family 72*(3), 403–419.

Cherlin, A. (2009). The marriage-go-round: The state of marriage and the family in America today. New York: Alfred A Knopf.

Chibucos, T., Leite, R., & Weiss, D. (2005). *Readings in family theory.* Thousand Oaks, CA: Sage.

Clarke, J. (1998). *Who, me lead a group?* Seattle, WA: Parenting Press, Inc.

Clarke, J. I., Dawson, C., & Bredehoft, D. (2004). *How much is enough?* New York: Marlowe & Company.

Clauss, B. (2005). Syllabus objective guide. In M. Walcheski & N. Gonzalez (Eds.), *Teaching family life education: A syllabus collection* (pp. 7–8). Minneapolis, MN: National Council on Family Relations.

Coccia, C., Darling, C., Rehm, M., Cui, M., & Sathe, S. (2012). Adolescent health, stress, and life satisfaction: The paradox of indulgent parenting. *Stress and Health, 28,* 211–331.

Codrington, G. (2008). Detailed introduction to generational theory. *Tomorrowtoday.* Retrieved from www.tomorrowtoday.uk.com/articles/article001_intro_gens.htm

Cohen, J., Byers, E., Sears, H., & Weaver, A. (2004). Sexual health education: Attitudes, knowledge and comfort of teachers in New Brunswick Schools. *The Canadian Journal of Human Sexuality, 13,* 1–15.

Collins, C., Alagiri, P., & Summers, T. (2002). *Abstinence only vs comprehensive sex education: What are the arguments? What is the evidence?* Policy monograph. San Francisco: AIDS Research Institute. Retrieved from ari.ucsf.edu/science/reports/abstinence.pdf

Collins, W. A. (2003). More than myth: The developmental significance of romantic relationships during adolescence. *Journal of Research on Adolescence, 13*(1), 1–24.

Concordia Publishing House (n.d.). *Learning about sex complete set* (set of 11). St. Louis, MO: Author. Retrieved fromwww.cph.org/p-6917-learning-about-sex-complete-set-set-of-11.aspx

Connell. J., (2012). Parenting 2.0 summary report: Parents' use of technology and the Internet. Minneapolis: Minnesota Agricultural Experiment Station. Retrieved from www.cehd.umn.edu/fsos/projects/parent20/pdf/p20summaryreport-july2012.pdf

Cooke, B. (2011). National Parenting Education Network (NPEN): National effort to advance the field of parenting education. PowerPoint presentation at the National Forum on Professional Preparation Systems in Parenting Education. www.npen.org/profdev/forum/standards/nat-effort-ppt.pdf

Cooney, S. M., Huser, M., Small, S., & O'Connor, C. (2007). Evidence-based programs: An overview. *What works, Wisconsin—Research to practice series, 6*. Madison: University of Wisconsin-Madison/Extension. Retrieved from www.uwex.edu/ces/flp/families/whatworks_06.pdf

Coontz, S. (2005). Marriage, a history: From obedience to intimacy or how love conquered marriage. New York: Viking.

Costa, T., & McCrae, R. (2003) *Five factor model of personality.* Lutz, FL: Psychological Assessment Resources, Inc.

Coyne, J., Rohrbaugh, M., Shoham, V., Sonnega, J., Nicklas, J., & Cranford, J. (2001). Prognostic importance of marital quality for survival of congestive heart failure. *American Journal of Cardiology, 88*(5), 526–529.

D'Augelli, A. (2002). Mental health problems among lesbian, gay, and bisexual youth ages 14 to 21. *Clinical Child Psychology and Psychiatry, 7*(3), 433–456.

Dahl, G. (2010). Early teen marriage and future poverty. *Demography, 47*(3), 689–718.

Dail, P. (1984). Constructing a philosophy of family life education: Educating the educators. *Family Perspective, 18*(4), 145–149.

Daniels, H. (Ed.). (1996). *An introduction to Vygotsky.* London: Routledge.

Darity, W. (Ed.). (2008). Marriage. In *International encyclopedia of the social sciences.* Farmington Hills, MI: Gale, Cengage Learning.

Darling, C. (1987). Family life education. In M. Sussman & S. Steinmetz (Eds.), *Handbook of marriage and the family* (pp. 815–833). New York: Plenum Press.

Darling, C. A. (2005). Families in a diverse culture: Changes and challenges. *Journal of Family and Consumer Sciences, 97*, 8–13.

Darling, C., & Cassidy, D. (1998). Professional development of students: Understanding the process of becoming a Certified Family Life Educator. *Family Science Review, 11*, 106–118.

Darling, C., Fleming, M., & Cassidy, D. (2009). Professionalization of family life education: Defining the field. *Family Relations, 58*, 330–372.

Darling, C. A., & Howard, S. (2006). Cultural lessons in sexuality: Comparison of parent-child communication styles in three cultures. In R. Hamon (Ed.), *International family studies: Developing curricula and teaching tools* (pp. 41–98). Binghamton, NY: Haworth Press.

Darling, C. A., & Howard, S. (2009). Human sexuality. In D. Bredehoft & M. Walcheski (Eds.), *Family life education: Integrating theory and practice* (2nd ed., pp. 141–151). Minneapolis, MN: National Council on Family Relations.

Darling, C. A., & Mabe, A. (1989). Analyzing ethical issues in sexual relationships: An educative model. *Journal of Sex Education and Therapy, 15*, 234–246.

Darling, C., McWey, L., Howard, S., & Olmstead, S. (2007). College student stress: The influence of interpersonal relationships on sense of coherence. Stress *and Health, 23*, 215–219.

Darling, C., Senatore, N., & Strachan, J. (2012). Fathers of children with disabilities: Stress and life satisfaction. *Stress and Health, 28*, 269–278.

Darling, C. A., & Turkki, K. (2009). Global family concerns and the role of family life education: An ecosystemic analysis. *Family Relations, 58*, 14–27.

Deal, R. (2006). *The smart stepfamily: Seven steps to a happy family.* Bloomington, MN: Bethany House Publishers.

DeBord, K., Bower, D., Myers-Walls, J. A., Kirby, J. K., Goddard, H. W., Mulroy, M., & Ozretich, R. (2006). A professional guide for parenting educators: The National Extension Parenting Educator's framework. *Journal of Extension 44*(3). Retrieved from www.joe.org/joe/2006june/a8.php

DeLamater, J., & Hyde, J. (1998). Essentialism vs. social constructionism in the study of human sexuality. *Journal of Sex Research, 49*, 69–77.

Demick, J. (2002). Stages of parental development. In M. H. Bornstein (Ed.), *Handbook of parenting Vol. 3: Being and becoming a parent* (2nd ed.). Mahwah, NJ: Lawrence Erlbaum.

DeNavas-Walt, C., Proctor, B., & Smith, J. (2012). Income, poverty, and health insurance coverage in the United States: 2011. U.S. Department of Commerce, Economics and Statistics Administration. Retrieved from www.census.gov/prod/2012pubs/p60-243.pdf

Denzin, N., & Lincoln, Y. (2008). *Collecting and interpreting qualitative materials*. Thousand Oaks, CA: Sage.

DePanfilis, S. (2003). Child protective services: A guide for caseworkers. Washington, DC: Department of Health and Human Services. Retrieved from www.childwelfare.gov/pubs/usermanuals/cps/cps.pdf

DePaulo, B. (2006). *Singled out: How singles are stereotyped, stigmatized, and ignored and still live happily ever after*. New York: St. Martin's Press.

DePaulo, B., & Morris, W. (2013). The unrecognized stereotyping and discrimination against singles. *Personality & Social Psychology Bulletin, 39*, 237–249.

DeYoung, C., Quilty, L., & Peterson, J. (2007). Between facets and domains: 10 Aspects of the big five. *Journal of Personality and Social Psychology, 93*(5), 880–896.

Dib, C. (1988). Formal, nonformal, and informal education: Concepts/applicability. Cooperative Networks in Physics Education, Conference Proceedings, 173rd American Institute of Physics, New York: American Institute of Physics (pp. 300–315). Retrieved from www.techne-dib.com.br/downloads/6.pdf

Dickinson, H. E. (1950). The origin and development of the aims of family life education in American secondary schools. Unpublished doctoral dissertation. Nashville, TN: George Peabody College for Teachers.

Dillman, D., Smyth, J., & Christian, L. (2009). *Internet, mail, and mixed mode surveys: The tailored design method*. Hoboken, NJ: John Wiley & Sons.

Dini, L. (2000). An Italian statement on international migration. *Population and Development Review, 26*, 849–852.

Dion, M. (2005). Healthy marriage programs: Learning what works. *Future of children, 15*, 139–156.

Doherty, W. (2000). Intentional marriage: Your rituals will set you free. Presentation at Annual Smart Marriages Conference, Denver, Colorado. Retrieved from www.smartmarriages.com/intentionalmarriage.html

Doherty, W., & Anderson, J. (2004). Community marriage initiatives. *Family Relations, 53*, 425–432.

Doherty, W. J. (1995). Boundaries between parent and family education and family therapy: The levels of family involvement model. *Family Relations, 44*(4), 353–358.

Doss, B., Rhoades, G., Stanley, S., Markman, H., & Johnson, C. (2009). Differential use of premarital education in first and second marriages. *Journal of Family Psychology, 23*, 268–273.

Downing, C. (2008). Combining art studio and art history to engage today's students. In R. L. Badger (Ed.), *Ideas that work in college teaching*. Albany: State University of New York Press.

Doyle, J. (2006). Prevention and early intervention. Issue 1 Addendum. Retrieved from www.emqff.org/wp-content/uploads/Prevention-and-Early-Intervention-Issue-1-Addendum-03-07-06.pdf

Drucker, P. (1954). *The practice of management*. New York: Harper & Brothers.

Duncan, S., Holman, T., Yang, C. (2007). Factors associated with involvement in marriage preparation programs. *Family Relations, 56*, 270–278.

Duncan, S. F., & Goddard, H. W. (2011). *Family life education. Principles and practices for effective* outreach (2nd ed., pp. 15–19). Thousand Oaks, CA: Sage.

Duvall, E., & Miller, B. (1984). *Marriage and family development* (6th ed.). New York: Harper Row.

Duvall, E. M. (1950). *Family living*. New York: Macmillan.

Duvall, E. M., & Hill, R. (1945). *When you marry*. New York: Heath.

East, M. (1980). *Home economics: Past, present and future*. Boston: Allyn & Bacon.

Eberly Center. (n.d.). Grading and performance rubrics. Pittsburgh, PA: Carnegie Mellon University. Retrieved from www.cmu.edu/teaching/designteach/teach/rubrics.html

Eddy, J., & Poehlmann, J. (2010). *Children of incarcerated parents: A handbook for researchers and practitioners*. Washington, DC: Urban Institute Press.

Edin, K., & Kefalas, M. (2005). *Promises I can keep: Why poor women put motherhood before marriage*. Berkeley: University of California Press.

Ellenwood, S. (1998). *The art of loving well: A character education curriculum for today's teenagers*. Boston: Boston University Press.

Erikson, E. (1950, 1963). *Childhood and society*. New York: W.W. Norton.

Ertmer, P., & Newby, T. (1993). Behaviorism, cognitivism, and constructivism: Comparing critical features from a design perspective. *Performance Improvement Quarterly, 6*, 50–72.

Everson, R., Darling, C., & Herzog, J. (2013). Parenting stress among U.S. army spouses during combat-related deployments: The role of sense of coherence. *Child and Family Social Work, 18*(2), 168–178.

Fagan, J. (2009). Relationship quality and changes in depression symptoms among urban, married African Americans, Hispanics, and whites. *Family Relations 58*(3), 259–274.

Fairchild Bridal Group. (2002). American weddings: Fairchild bridal infobank American wedding study. Retrieved from www.sellthebride.com/documents/ americanweddingsurvey.pdf

Falicov, C. (2007). Working with transnational immigrants. Expanding meanings of family, community, and culture. *Family Process, 46*(2), 157–171.

Fawcett, E., Hawkins, A., Blanchard, V., & Carroll, J. (2010). Do premarital education programs really work? A meta-analytic study. *Family Relations, 59*(3), 232–239.

Federal Interagency Forum on Child and Family Statistics (FIFCFS). (2013). America's children: Key national indicators of well-being. Washington, DC: U.S. Government Printing Office. Retrieved from www.childstats.gov/pdf/ac2013/ac_13.pdf

Fein, D. (2009). Spending time together: Time use estimates for economically disadvantaged and nondisadvantaged married couples in the U.S. Office of Planning, Research, & Evaluation, Administration for Children and Families. Retrieved from www.mdrc.org/ sites/default/files/full_507.pdf

Fein, D., Burstein, N., Fein, G., & Lindberg, L. (2003). The determinants of marriage and cohabitation among disadvantaged Americans: Research findings and needs. Marriage and family formation data analysis project. Bethesda, MD: Abt Associates. Retrieved from www.acf.hhs.gov/sites/default/files/opre/determinants_findings_fin2_opt2.pdf

Felitti, V., Anda, R., Nordenberg, D., Williamson, D., Spitz, A., Edwards, V., Koss, M., & Marks, J. (1998). Relationship of childhood abuse and household dysfunction to many of the leading causes of death in adults: The adverse childhood experiences (ACE) study. *American Journal of Preventive Medicine, 14*(4), 245–258.

Fincham, F., & Beach, R. (2010). Marriage in the new millennium: A decade in review. *Journal of Marriage and Family, 72*, 630–649.

Fincham, F., Stanley, S., & Rhoades, G. (2011). Relationship education in emerging adulthood: Problems and prospects. In F. Fincham & M. Cui (Eds.), *Romantic relationships in emerging adulthood* (pp. 293–316). Cambridge, MA: Cambridge University Press.

FindLaw. (2013). State-by-state marriage "age of consent" laws. Retrieved from www.family.findlaw.com/marriage/state-by-state-marriage-age-of-consent-laws.html

Fink, L. (2005). A self-directed guide to designing courses for significant learning. Retrieved from www.deefinkandassociates.com/GuidetoCourseDesignAug05.pdf

Fisher, H. (2004). *Why we love: The nature and chemistry of romantic love.* New York: Henry Holt and Company.

Fisher, M. (2013, November 13). Why China's one-child policy still leads to forced abortions and always will. *The Washington Post.* Retrieved from http://www.washingtonpost.com/blogs/worldviews/wp/2013/11/15/why-chinas-one-child-policy-still-leads-to-forced-abortions-and-always-will/

Fisher, T. (2012). What sexual scientists know about gender differences and similarities in sexuality. Whitehall, PA: Society of Scientific Study of Sexuality. Retrieved from www.sexscience.org/PDFs/Gender%20Differences%20and%20Similarities%20in%20Sexuality%20Final.pdf

Fitzpatrick, J., Sharp, E., & Reifman, A. (2009). Midlife singles' willingness to date partners with heterogeneous characteristics. *Family Relations, 58*(1), 121–133.

Florida Statutes. (2011). Marriage fee reduction for completion of premarital preparation course. Retrieved from www.flsenate.gov/laws/Statutes/2011/741.0305

Foner, N. (2005). *In a new land: A comparative view of immigration.* New York: University Press.

Fong, T. (2008). *The contemporary Asian American experience: Beyond the model minority* (3rd ed.). Upper Saddle River, NJ: Prentice-Hall.

Fox News. (2013). Sheriff says FL 12-year-old committed suicide after being bullied online by over a dozen girls. Associated *Press.* Retrieved from www.foxnews.com/us/2013/09/13/sheriff-says-fla12-year-old-committed-suicide-after-being-bullied-online-by/

Francoeur, R. (2004). Foreword. In R. Francoeur & R. Noonan (Eds.), *The continuum complete international encyclopedia of sexuality* (pp. ix–x). London, England: Continuum International Publishing Group.

Francoeur, R., & Noonan, R. (2004a). Global trends: Some final impressions. In R. Francoeur & R. Noonan (Eds.), *The continuum complete international encyclopedia of sexuality* (pp. 1373–1375). London: Continuum International Publishing Group.

Francoeur, R., & Noonan, R. (Eds.). (2004b). *The continuum complete international encyclopedia of sexuality.* London: Continuum International Publishing Group.

Frank, L. K. (1962). The beginnings of child development and family life education in the twentieth century. *Merrill-Palmer Quarterly of Behavior and Development, 8,* 207–227.

Freeman, N. K. (1997). Using NAEYC's Code of Ethics: Mama and daddy taught me right from wrong. Isn't that enough? *Young Children, 52*(6), 64–67.

Friedman, E. (2009). Kids born to unwed moms hit record high. *ABC News.* Retrieved from www.abcnews.go.com/Health/WomensHealth/story?id=7575268&page=2#.UYbylIKC3u1

Fry. R. (2013). A rising share of young adults live in their parents' home. Washington, DC: Pew Research Center. Retrieved from www.pewsocialtrends.org/2013/08/01/a-rising-share-of-young-adults-live-in-their-parents-home/

Gagnon, J. (1990). The explicit and implicit use of the scripting perspective in sex research. *Annual Review of Sexual Research, 1,* 1–44.

Gagnon, J., & Simon, W. (1973). *Sexual conduct: The social origins of human sexuality.* Chicago: Aldine.

Galinsky, E., Aumann, K., & Bond, J. (2009). Times and changing: Gender and generation at work and at home. *Families and Work Institute.* Retrieved from www.familiesandwork.org/site/research/reports/Times_Are_Changing.pdf

Ganong, L., & Coleman, M. (2004). *Stepfamily relationships: Development, dynamics, and interventions.* New York: Kluwer Academic.

Ganong, L., Coleman, M., Feistman, R., Jamison, J., & Markham, M. (2012). Communication technology and post divorce coparenting. *Family Relations, 61,* 397–409.

Garcia-Moreno, C., & Pallitto, C. (2013). Global and regional estimates of violence against women: Prevalence and health effects of intimate partner violence and non-partner sexual violence. Geneva, Switzerland: World Health Organization. Retrieved from www.apps.who.int/iris/bitstream/10665/85239/1/9789241564625_eng.pdf

Gardener, H. (2006). *Multiple intelligences: New horizons.* New York: Basic Books.

Gardener, H. (2011). *Frames of the mind: The theory of multiple intelligences.* New York: Basic Books.

Gardiner, K., Fishman, M., Nikolov, P., Glosser, A., & Laud, S. (2002). State policies to promote marriage. Retrieved from www.aspe.hhs.gov/hsp/marriage02f

Gardner, S., & Howlett, L. (2000). Changing the focus of interventions: The need for primary prevention at the couple level. *Family Science Review, 13,* 96–111.

Gardner, S., Giese, K., & Parrott, S. (2004). Evaluation of the connections: Relationships and marriage curriculum. *Family Relations, 53,* 521–527.

Garofalo, R., Wolf, R., Kessel, S., Palfrey, J., & DuRant, R. (1998). The association between health risk behaviors and sexual orientation among a school-based sample of adolescents. *Pediatrics, 101*(5), 895–902.

Gates, G. (2013). LGBT parenting in the U.S. Los Angeles: The Williams Institute. Retrieved from www.williamsinstitute.law.ucla.edu/wp-content/uploads/LGBT-Parenting.pdf

Gay & Lesbian Advocates & Defenders (GLAD). (n.d.). Marriage—A history of change. Retrieved from www.outcast-films.com/res_marriage/historyofchange.PDF

Gelles, R., & Perlman, S. (2012). Estimated annual cost of child abuse and neglect in the United States. Chicago: Prevent Child Abuse America.

Gerbner, G. (2009). Cultivation theory. In E. Griffin (Ed.), *A first look at communication theory* (7th ed., pp. 353–354). New York: Frank Mortimer.

Gibbs, N. (2009). The growing backlash against overparenting. *Time.* Retrieved from http://web.uvic.ca/~gtreloar/Articles/Parenting/Helicoter%20Parents%20The%20Backlash%20Against%20Overparenting.pdf

Gibson, S. K. (2004). Social learning (cognitive) theory and implications for human resource development. *Advances in Developing Human Resources, 6,* 193–210.

Glaze, L., & Maruschak, L. (2008). Parents in prison and their minor children. *Bureau of Justice Statistics Special Report.* Washington, DC: U.S. Department of Justice. Retrieved from www.bjs.gov/content/pub/pdf/pptmc.pdf

Goddard, H. W., & Olsen, C. (2004). Cooperative extension initiatives in marriage and couples education. *Family Relations, 53,* 433–439.

Goldenberg, I., & Goldenberg, H. (2003). *Family therapy: An overview* (6th ed.) Pacific Grove, CA: Brooks/Cole.

Goldfarb, E. (2003). What teachers want, need, and deserve. *SIECUS Report, 31*(6), 18–19.

Gordon, L. (2000). *PAIRS for peers: Practical exercises enriching relationship skills,* Westin, FL: PAIRS Foundation.

Gore, A., & Gore, T. (2002). *Joined at the heart: The transformation of the American family.* New York: Henry Holt.

Gottman, J. M. (1994). *Why marriages succeed or fail and how you can make yours last.* New York: Simon & Schuster.

Gottman, J. M., & Silver, N. (1999). *The seven principles for making marriage work.* New York: Crown Publishers.

Gottman, J. S. (2007). Loving couples loving children. Seattle, WA: The Gottman Relationship Institute.

Gottman, J. M., Gottman, J. S., & DeClaire, J. (2006). *10 lessons to transform your marriage.* New York: Three Rivers Press.

Gray, J. (1992). *Men are from Mars, women are from Venus: A practical guide for improving communication and getting what you want in your relationships.* New York: Harper Collins.

Gross, P. (1993). *On family life education: For family life educators* (3rd ed.). Montreal, Quebec, Canada: Concordia University Centre for Human Relations and Community Studies.

Grzywacz, J. G., & Demerouti, E. (Eds.). (2013). *New frontiers in work and family research.* New York: Psychology Press.

Guerrero, L., Andersen, P., & Afifi, W. (2007). *Close encounters: Communication in relationships.* Thousand Oaks, CA: Sage.

Guttmacher Institute. (2013). State policies in brief: Sex and HIV education. New York: Author. Retrieved from www.guttmacher.org/statecenter/spibs/spib_SE.pdf

Hairston, J. (2002). Prisoners and families: Parenting issues during incarceration. *Paper presented at the U.S. Department of Health and Human Services prison to home conference.* Retrieved from www.urban.org/uploadedPDF/ACFBABE.pdf

Halford, W. K., Markman, H., & Stanley, S. (2008). Strengthening couples relationships with education: Social policy and public health awareness. *Journal of Family Psychology, 22*(3), 497–505.

Halford, W. K., Markman, H., Stanley, S., & Kline, G. (2003). Best practices in relationship education. *Journal of Marital and Family Therapy, 29,* 385–406.

Halford, W. K., Moore, E., Wilson, K., Farrugia, C., & Dyer, C. (2004). Benefits of flexible relationship education: An evaluation of the couple CARE program. *Family Relations, 53,* 469–476.

Halford, W. K., Nicholson, J., & Sanders, M. (2007). Couple communication in stepfamilies. *Family Process, 46,* 472–483.

Halford, W. K., O'Donnell, C., Lizzio, A., & Wilson, K. (2006). Do couples at high risk of relationship problems attend premarriage education? *Journal of Family Psychology, 30,* 160–163.

Hamilton-Mason, J., Hall, J., & Everett, J. (2009). And some of us are braver: Stress and coping among African American women. *Journal of Human Behavior in the Social Environment, 19*(5), 463–482.

Hammond, R., & Cheney, P. (2009). *Sociology of the family.* Online text retrieved from www.freebooks.uvu.edu/SOC1200/index.php/chapters.html

Hamon, R., & Fernsler, C. (2006) Using cross-cultural study courses to teach about international families. In R. Hamon (Ed.), *International family studies: Developing curricula and teaching tools* (pp. 347–364). Binghamton, NY: Haworth Press.

Hans, J. (Ed.). (2013). Degree programs in family science. Minneapolis, MN: National Council on Family Relations. Retrieved from www.ncfr.org/degree-programs

Harman, D., & Brim, O. (1980). *Learning to be parents: Principles, programs, and methods.* Beverly Hills, CA: Sage.

Harwood, H., Fountain, D., & Livermore, G. (1998). *The economic costs of alcohol & drug abuse in the U.S. 1992.* Rockville, MD: National Institute on Drug Abuse and National Institute on Alcohol Abuse and Alcoholism.

Harwood, R., Miller, S., & Vasta, R. (2008). Child psychology: Development in a changing society. Hoboken, NJ: John Wiley & Sons.

Hatry, H., van Houten, T., Plantz, M., & Greenway, M. T. (1996). *Measuring program outcomes: A practical approach.* Alexandria, VA: United Way of America.

Hawkins, A., & Ooms, T. (2010). *What works in marriage and relationship education? A review of lessons learned with a focus on low-income couples.* Littleton, CO: National Healthy Marriage Resource Center. Retrieved from www.archive.acf.hhs.gov/healthymarriage/pdf/whatworks_edae.pdf

Hawkins, A., Carroll, J., Doherty, W., & Willoughby, B. (2004). A comprehensive framework for marriage education. *Family Relations, 53,* 547–558.

Hawkins, A., Blanchard, V., Baldwin, S., & Fawcett, E. (2008). Does marriage and relationship education work? A meta-analytic study. *Journal of Consulting and Clinical Psychology, 76*(5), 723–734.

Heath, H., & Palm, G. (2006). Future challenges for parenting education and support. *Child Welfare, 85*(5), 885–895.

Heatherington, E. (2005). Divorce and the adjustment of children. *Pediatrics in Review, 26*(5), 165–169.

Hennon, C., Radina, M., & Wilson, S. (2013). Family life education: Issues and challenges in professional practice. In G. Peterson & K. Bush (Eds.), *Handbook of marriage and the family* (3rd ed., pp. 815–843). New York: Springer.

Henry J. Kaiser Family Foundation. (2012). *The global HIV/AIDS epidemic fact sheet.* Retrieved from www.kff.org/hivaids/upload/3030-17.pdf

Hildebrand, V., Phenice, L., Gray, M., & Hines, R. (2008). *Knowing and serving diverse families* (3rd ed.). Columbus, OH: Merrill.

Hildreth, G., & Sugawara, A. (1993). Ethnicity and diversity in family life education. In M. Arcus, J. Schvaneveldt, & J. Moss (Eds.), *Handbook of family life education: Foundations of family life education* (pp. 162–188). Newbury Park, CA: Sage.

Hill, M. (2008). Teachers sound off on benefits, disadvantages of teaching online courses. *Memphis Business Journal.* Retrieved from www.bizjournals.com/memphis/stories/2008/07/28/focus2.html?page=all

Hill, R. (1949). *Families under stress.* New York: Harper & Brothers.

Hines, S. (2006). Intimate transitions: Transgender practices of partnering and parenting. *Sociology, 40,* 353–371.

Hispanic Healthy Marriage Initiative (HHMI). (n.d.). Cultural adaptation and relationship dynamics. Retrieved from www.archive.acf.hhs.gov/healthymarriage/pdf/Cultural_Adaptation.pdf

Hofschneider, A. (2013, August). Bosses say "pick up the phone." *The Wall Street Journal.* Retrieved from http://online.wsj.com/news/articles/SB10001424127887323407104579036714155366866

Hogan, D. (2012). *Family consequences of children's disabilities.* New York: Russell Sage Foundation.

Holman, T., Busby, D., Doxey, C., Klein, D., & Loyer-Carlson, V. (1997). *RELATionship evaluation.* Provo, UT: The RELATE Institute.

Holmes, E. K., Galovan, A. M. Yoshida, K., & Hawkin, A. J. (2010). Meta-analysis of the effectiveness of resident fathering programs: Are family life educators interested in fathers? *Family Relations, 59*(3), 240–252.

Howard, R. (1981). *A social history of American sociology, 1865–1940.* Westport, CT: Greenwood.

Howe, G., Levy, M., & Caplan, R. (2004). Job loss and depressive symptoms in couples: Common stressors, stress transmission, or relationship disruption? *Journal of Family Psychology, 18,* 639–650.

Huang, N. (2003). *Family education law in Taiwan.* Paper presented at the annual meeting of the National Council on Family Relations, Vancouver, BC, Canada.

Huang, W. (2005). An Asian perspective on relationship and marriage education. *Family Process, 44*(2), 161–173.

Hughes, R., Bowers, J., Mitchell, E., Curtiss, S., & Ebata, A. (2012). Developing online family life prevention and education programs. *Family Relations, 61*(5), 711–727.

Hwang, S. (2012). Family life education with Asian immigrant families. In S. Ballard & A. Taylor (Eds.), *Family life education with diverse populations* (pp. 187–209). Thousand Oaks, CA: Sage.

Ingoldsby, B., Smith, S., & Miller, J. (2004). *Exploring family theories*. Los Angeles: Roxbury Publishing.

International Organization for Migration (IOM). (2010). World migration report, 2010: The future of migration, building capacities for change. Retrieved from www.publications.iom.int/bookstore/free/WMR2010_summary.pdf

Isabella, R. A., & Belsky, J. (1991). Interactional synchrony and the origins of infant-mother attachment: A replication study. *Child Development, 62*, 373–384.

Jacobs, F. H., & Kapuscik, J. L. (2000). *Making the count: Evaluating family preservation services*. Medford, MA: Family Preservation Evaluation Project, Tufts University.

Jarrett, R., Jefferson, S., & Kelly, J. (2010). Finding community in family: Neighborhood effects and African American kin networks. *Journal of Comparative Family Studies, 41*, 299–328.

Jayakody, R., Thornton, A., & Axinn, W. (2008). *International family change: Ideational perspectives*. New York: Lawrence Erlbaum.

Jayson, S. (2009). Family life, roles changing as couples seek balance. *USA Today*. Retrieved from http://usatoday30.usatoday.com/news/health/2009-04-18-families-conf_N.htm

Jelen, E. (2005). The family in Argentina: Modernity, economic crisis, and politics. In B. Adams & J. Trost (Eds.), *Handbook of world families* (pp. 391–413). Thousand Oaks, CA: Sage.

Jiang, C. (2013). Why Chinese couples are divorcing before buying a home. *Time, 181*(19). Retrieved from http://world.time.com/2013/04/29/why-chinese-couples-are-divorcing-before-buying-a-home/

Jones, S. T., Stranik, M., Hart, M. G., Wolf, J. R., & McClintic, S. (2013). A closer look at diverse roles of practitioners in parenting education: Peer educators, paraprofessionals and professionals. National Parenting Education Network (NPEN). Retrieved from www.npen.org

Juvenile Justice Evaluation Center. (2003). Evaluability assessment: Examining the readiness of a program for evaluation. Program evaluation briefing series, #6. Washington, DC: Author. Retrieved from http://www.jrsa.org/pubs/juv-justice/evaluability-assessment.pdf

Kacher, K. (2013, June). Work-life matters. *Minnesota Business Magazine*. Retrieved from http://minnesotabusiness.com/article/guest-column-work-life-matters

Kahn, K., Arino J., Hu W., Raposo P., Sears J., Calderon F., . . . Gardam, M. (2009). Spread of a novel Influenza A (H1N1) Virus via global airline transportation. *New England Journal of Medicine, 361*(2), 212–214.

Kamper, C. (2003). *Connections + PREP: Relationships & marriage interpersonal relationship program for secondary students: Instructor's manual*. Berkeley, CA: The Dibble Fund for Marriage Education.

Kamper, C. (2011). Connections: Relationships & marriage. The Dibble Institute. Retrieved from http://www.dibbleinstitute.org/connections-relationships-marriage/

Kapinus, C., & Johnson, M. (2003). The utility of family life cycle as a theoretical and empirical tool: Commitment and family life cycle state. *Journal of Family Issues, 24*, 155–184.

Karoly, L. A., Kilburn, M. R., Cannon, J. S., Bigelow, J. H., & Christina, R. (2005). *Many happy returns: Early childhood programs entail costs, but the paybacks could be substantial*. Santa Monica, CA: Rand Corporation. Retrieved from www.rand.org/publications/randreview/issues/fall2005/returns.html

Kelly, J. (2002). Psychological and legal interventions for parents and children in custody and access disputes: Current research and practice. *Virginia Journal of Social Policy and Law, 10*, 129–163.

Kelly, J., & Emery, R. (2003). Children's adjustment following divorce: Risk and resilience perspectives. *Family Relations, 32*, 252–262.

Kelly, T. (2004). Ireland. In R. Francoeur & R. Noonan (Eds.), *International encyclopedia of sexuality* (pp. 569–580). New York: Continuum.

Kemp, G., Segal, J., & Robinson, L. (2013). Guide to step-parenting & blended families. *Helpguide*. Retrieved from www.helpguide.org/mental/blended_families_stepfamilies.htm

Kempner, M. (2004). More than just say no: What some abstinence-only-until marriage curricula teach young people about gender. *SIECUS Report, 32*(3), 2–4.

Kennedy, S., & Bumpass, L. (2008). Cohabitation and children's living arrangements: New estimates from the United States. *Demographic Research, 19*, 1663–1692.

Kenny, L., & Sternberg, J. (2003). Abstinence-only-education in the courts. *SIECUS Report, 31*(6), 26–29.

Kim, I., Lau, A., & Chang, D. (2006). Family violence. In F. Leong, A. Inman, A. Ebreo, L. Yang, L. Kinoshita, & M. Fu (Eds.), *Handbook of Asian American psychology* (2nd ed., pp. 363–378). Thousand Oaks, CA: Sage.

King, V., & Scott, M. (2005). A comparison of cohabiting relationships among older and younger adults. *Journal of Marriage and Family, 67*(2), 271–285.

Kirby, D. (2007). Emerging answers: Research findings on programs to reduce teen pregnancy and sexually transmitted diseases. Washington, DC: National Campaign to Prevent Teen and Unplanned Pregnancy. Retrieved from http://www.urban.org/events/thursdayschild/upload/Sarah-Brown-Handout.pdf

Kizlik, B. (2012). Needs assessment information. *Adprima*. Retrieved from http://www.adprima.com/needs.htm

Kline, G., Stanley, S., Markman, H., Olmos-Gallo, P., St. Peters, M., Whitton, S., & Prado, L. (2004). Timing is everything: Pre-engagement cohabitation and increased risk for poor marital outcomes. *Journal of Family Psychology, 18*, 311–318.

Knapp, D., & Reynolds, D. (1996). Establishing credentialing policies and procedures. In A. Browning, A. Bugbee, & M. Mullins (Eds.), *Certification: A NOCA handbook* (pp. 191–214). Washington DC: National Organization for Competency Assurance.

The Knot. (2012). Results of largest wedding study of its kind. Retrieved from www.prnewswire.com/news-releases/theknotcom-and-weddingchannelcom-reveal-results-of-largest-wedding-study-of-its-kind-surveying-more-than-17500-brides-195856281.html

The Knot. (n.d.). Wedding money: What does the average wedding cost? Retrieved from http://wedding.theknot.com/wedding-planning/wedding-budget/qa/what-does-the-average-wedding-cost.aspx

Kolb, D. (1984). *Experiential learning: Experience as the source of learning and development.* Upper Saddle River, NJ: Prentice-Hall.

Koohang, A., Riley, L, Smith, T., & Schreurs, J. (2009). E-learning and constructivism: From theory to application. *Interdisciplinary Journal of E-Learning and Learning Objectives, 5*, 91–109.

Koropeckyj-Cox, T., Cain, C., & Coran, J. (2005). Small group learning and hypothetical families in a large introductory course. In D. Berke & S. Wisensale (Eds.), *Marriage & Family Review, 38*, 205–224.

Krane, D., Witeck, B., & Coombs, W. (2011). Surveying among gays & lesbians. *Harris Interactive*. Retrieved from www.harrisinteractive.com/vault/HI_CORP_PAPER_SurveyingGayLesbian.pdf

Krathwohl, D., Bloom, B., & Masia, B. (Eds.). (1973). *Taxonomy of educational objectives, the classification of educational goals. Handbook II: Affective domain*. New York: David McKay.

Kreider, R. (2005). Number, timing and duration of marriages and divorces: 2001. *Current Population Reports*, 70–97. Washington, DC: U.S. Census Bureau.

Kreider, R., & Ellis, R. (2011a). Living arrangements of children, 2009. *Current Population Reports*. Washington, DC: Government Printing Office. Retrieved from http://www.census.gov/prod/2011pubs/p70-126.pdf

Kreider, R., & Ellis, R. (2011). Number, timing, and duration of marriages and divorces: 2009. *Current Population Reports*, 70–125.Washington, DC: U.S. Census Bureau.

Krill, S. (2010). When one spouse returns from deployment: Tips for MRE practitioners working with military couples. National healthy marriage center. Retrieved from www.healthymarriageinfo.org/resource-detail/index.aspx?rid=3129

Krouse, A., & Howard, H. (2009). *Keeping the campfires going: Native women's activism in urban communities*. Lincoln: University of Nebraska Press.

Kuperberg, A. (2014). Age at coresidence, premarital cohabitation, and marriage dissolution: 1985–2009. *Journal of Marriage and Family, 76*, 352–369.

Kyler, S. J., Bumbarger, B. K., & Greenberg, M. T. (2005). *Technical assistance fact sheets: Evidence-based programs*. Pennsylvania State University Prevention Center for the Promotion of Human Development.

LaFromboise, T., Hoyt, D., Oliver, L., & Whitbeck, L. (2006). Family, community, and school influences on resilience among American Indian adolescents in the upper Midwest. *Journal of Community Psychology, 34*(2), 193–208.

Lake Placid Conference on Home Economics proceedings of the first, second, and third conferences. (1901). Geneva, NY: American Home Economics Association.

The Lancet. (2012). *Adolescent health*. Retrieved from http://www.thelancet.com/series/adolescent-health-2012

Larson, J. (2002). Consumer update: Marriage preparation. Washington, DC: American Association for Marriage and Family Therapy. Retrieved from www.aamft.org/imis15/Content/Consumer_Updates/Marriage_Preparation.aspx

Larson, J. (2003). *The great marriage tune-up book*. San Francisco: Jossey-Bass.

Larson, J. (2004a). Innovations in marriage education: Introduction and challenges. *Family Relations, 53*, 421–424.

Larson, J. (2004b). Premarital assessment questionnaires: Powerful tools for improving premarital counseling. *Marriage & Family: A Christian Journal, 7*, 17–28.

Laszloffy, T. (2002). Rethinking family development theory: Teaching with the systemic family development (SDF) model. *Family Relations, 51*, 206–214.

Ledermann, T., Bodenmann, G., Rudaz, M., & Bradbury, T. (2010). Stress, communication, and marital quality in couples. *Family Relations, 59*, 195–206.

Lenhart, A., Madden, M., Smith, A, Purcell, K., Zickuhr, K., & Rainie, L. (2011). Teens, kindness and cruelty on social network sites. Pew Internet & American Life Project. Retrieved from www.pewinternet.org/Reports/2011/Teens-and-social-media.aspx

Levin, I. (2004). Living apart together: A new family form. *Current Sociology, 52*(2), 223–240.

Lewis-Rowley, M., Brasher, R. E., Moss, J. J., Duncan, S. F., & Stiles, R. J. (1993). The evolution of education for family life. In M. E. Arcus, J. D. Schvaneveldt, & J. J. Moss (Eds.), *Handbook of family life education* (Vol. 1, pp. 26–50). Newbury Park, CA: Sage.

Lichter, D., & Qian, Z. (2008). Serial cohabitation and the marital life course. *Journal of Marriage and Family, 70*(4), 861–878.

Littell, J. H. (1986). *Building strong foundations: Evaluation strategies for family resource programs*. Chicago: Family Resource Coalition.

Lofquist, D., Lugaila, T., O'Connell, M., & Feliz, S. (2012). Households and Families: 2010. *U.S. Bureau of the Census*. Retrieved from www.census.gov/prod/cen2010/briefs/c2010br-14.pdf

Loper, A., Carlson, W., Levitt, E., & Scheffel, K. (2009). Parenting stress, alliance, child contact and adjustment of imprisoned mothers and fathers. *Journal of Offender Rehabilitation, 48*(6), 483–503.

Luo, S., & Klohnen, E. (2005). Assortative mating and marital quality in newlyweds: A couple-centered approach. *Journal of Personality and Social Psychology, 88*, 304–326.

Maccoby, E. (1980). *Social development: Psychological growth and the parent-child relationship.* New York: Harcourt Brace Jovanovich.

Mace, D. (1982). *Close companions: The marriage enrichment handbook.* New York: Continuum Publishing.

MacInnes, M. (2008). One's enough for now: Children, disability, and the subsequent childbearing of mothers. *Journal of Marriage and Family, 70*, 758–771.

Manning, W., & Cohen, J. (2012). Premarital cohabitation and marital dissolution: An examination of recent marriages. *Journal of Marriage and Family, 74*, 377–387.

Marano, H. E. (2008). *A nation of wimps.* New York: Random House.

Marketing Charts. (2007). Teen market to surpass $200 billion by 2011, despite population decline. The Teens Market in the U.S. Report. Retrieved from www.marketingcharts.com/wp/traditional/teen-market-to-surpass-200-billion-by-2011-despite-population-decline-817/

Markman, H., Stanley, S., & Blumberg, S. (2010). *Fighting for your marriage* (3rd ed.). San Francisco: Jossey-Bass.

Marquardt, E., Blankenhorn, D., Lerman, R., Malone-Colon, L., & Wilcox, W. (2012). The president's marriage agenda for the forgotten sixty percent. *The state of our unions.* Charlottesville, VA: National Marriage Project and Institute for American Values. Retrieved from www.stateofourunions.org/2012/SOOU2012.pdf

Maurer, L. (2012). Family life education with lesbian, gay, bisexual, and transgender families. In S. Ballard & A. Taylor (Eds.), *Family life education with diverse populations* (pp. 255–283). Thousand Oaks, CA: Sage.

Mbwana, K., Terzian, M., Moore, K. (2009). What works for parent involvement programs for children: Lessons from experimental evaluations of social interventions. Child trends fact sheet #2009–47. Washington, DC: Child Trends. Retrieved from http://www.childtrends.org/wp-content/uploads/2009/12/What-Works-for-Parent-Involvement-Programs-for-Adolescents-February-2010.pdf

McCawley, P. (2009). *Methods for conducting an educational needs assessment.* Moscow: University of Idaho Extension.

McDermott, D. (2011). What do parenting educators need to know and do? PowerPoint presentation at the National Forum on Professional Preparation Systems in Parenting Education. Retrieved from http://npen.org/profdev/forum/standards/parents-need-to-know.pdf

McGee, J. (n.d.). Teaching millennials. Retrieved from http://www.ame.pitt.edu/documents/McGee_Millennials.pdf

McGee, M. (2004). Talking with kids about pleasure. *Planned Parenthood Federation of America Educator's Update, 8*(4), 1–6.

McGregor, S., & Toronyi, K. (2009). A millennial recruitment and retention blueprint for home economics professional associations. *International Journal of Home Economics, 2*(2), 2–19.

McGroder, S., & Hyra, A. (2009). Developmental and economic effects of parenting programs for expectant parents and parents of preschool-age children. *Partnership for America's Economic Success.* Retrieved from http://www.readynation.org/docs/researchproject_mcgroder_200903_paper.pdf

McKeachie, W., & Svinicki, M. (2006). *McKeachie's teaching tips: Strategies, research, and theory for college and university teachers.* New York: Houghton Mifflin.

Merriam-Webster Dictionary. (n.d.). Definition of profession. Retrieved from http://www.merriam-webster.com/dictionary/profession

Mikulincer, M., & Shaver, P. (2012). Adult attachment orientations and relationship processes. *Journal of Family Theory & Review, 4*, 259–274.

Miller, J., & Seller, W. (1990). *Curriculum perspectives and practices.* New York: Longman.

Miller, P. M. (2011). Homeless families education networks: An examination of access and mobilization. *Educational Administration Quarterly, 47*, 543–581.

Miller, S., Miller, P., Wackman, E., & Nunnally, D. (n.d.). *Couple communication.* Retrieved from http://www.couplecommunication.com/index.html

Miller, T., & Hendrie, D. (2008). Substance abuse prevention dollars and cents: A cost-benefit analysis. U.S. Department of Health and Human Services. Rockville, MD: Center for Substance Abuse Prevention, Substance Abuse and Mental Health Services Administration.

Mills, M. (2014). Globalization and family life. In A. Abela & J. Walker (Eds.), *Contemporary issues in family studies: Global perspectives on partnerships, parenting and support in a changing world.* Malden, MA: John Wiley & Sons.

Min, P. (2006). *Asian Americans: Contemporary trends and issues.* Thousand Oaks, CA: Sage.

Minnesota Association for Family and Early Education (MNAFEE). (2011). Parent education core curriculum framework. A comprehensive guide to planning curriculum for parent education programs in the domains of parent development, parent-child relationships, early childhood development, family development, and culture and community. St. Paul, MN: Author. Retrieved from http://www.mnafee.org/index.asp?Type= B_BASIC&SEC={A2E3A088-D669-4806-911F-F92011A6BFED}

Minnesota Council on Family Relations (MCFR). (1997). *Ethical thinking and practice for parent and family educators.* Minneapolis, MN: Ethics Committee, Parent and Family Education Section.

Minnesota Council on Family Relations (MCFR). (2009). Ethical thinking and practice for parent and family life educators. In D. Bredehoft & M. Walcheski (Eds.), *Family life education: Integrating theory and practice* (pp. 233–239). Minneapolis, MN: National Council on Family Relations.

Modo, I. (2005). Nigerian families. In B. Adams & J. Trost (Eds.), *Handbook of world families* (pp. 25–46). Thousand Oaks, CA: Sage.

Montfort, S., & Brick, P. (1999). *Unequal partners: Teaching about power and consent in adult-teen relationships.* Morristown, NJ: Planned Parenthood of Greater Northern New Jersey, Inc.

Moore, T., & Asay, S. (2013). *Family resource management.* Thousand Oaks, CA: Sage.

Morin, R. (2008). America's four middle classes. Pew Research Center. Retrieved from http://www.pewsocialtrends.org/2008/07/29/americas-four-middle-classes/

Morrison, E., Price, M. (1974). *Values in sexuality: A new approach to sex education.* New York: Hart Publishing.

Mulroy, M. (2012). Family life education with prison inmates and their families. In S. Ballard & A. Taylor (Eds.), *Family life education with diverse populations* (pp. 41–59). Thousand Oaks, CA: Sage.

Mumola, C. (2000). Incarcerated parents and their children. *Bureau of Justice Statistics Special Report.* Retrieved from http://www.bjs.gov/content/pub/pdf/iptc.pdf

Myers-Walls, J. (1998). *What is your parent education approach?* Lafayette, IN: Purdue University Cooperative Extension Service.

Myers-Walls, J. (2012). Family life education with court-mandated parents with families. In S. Ballard & A. Taylor (Eds.), *Family life education with diverse populations* (pp. 61–90). Thousand Oaks, CA: Sage.

Myers-Walls, J. (n.d.). *Family life education materials: Quality assessment tool.* Lafayette, IN: Purdue Extension. Retrieved from http://www.extension.purdue.edu/purplewagon/FLEMat-QAT/FLEMat-QAT.htm

Myers-Walls, J., Ballard, S., Darling, C., & Myers-Bowman, K. (2011). Reconceptualizing the domains and boundaries of family life education. *Family Relations, 60,* 357–372.

Nakonezny, P., & Denton, W. (2008). Marital relationships: A social exchange theory perspective. *The American Journal of Family Therapy, 36,* 402–412.

Naser, R., & Visher, C. (2006). Family members' experiences with incarceration and reentry. *Western Criminology Review, 72*(2), 20–31.

National Adult Protective Services Association (NAPSA). (2005). Adult protective services core competencies. Retrieved from http://APSNetwork.org/Resources/docs/CoreCompetencies71005.ppt

National Center for Family & Marriage Research (NCFMR). (2010). Remarriage rate in the U.S. 2010. Retrieved from http://ncfmr.bgsu.edu/pdf/family_profiles/file114853.pdf

National Center for Transgender Equality (NCTE) & National Gay and Lesbian Taskforce (NGLT). (2009). *National transgender discrimination survey.* Retrieved from http://transequality.org/Resources/NCTE_prelim_survey_econ.pdf

National Commission on Family Life Education. (1968). Family life education programs: Principles, plans, procedures. A framework for family life educators. *The Family Coordinator, 17,* 211–214.

National Council on Family Relations (NCFR). (1984). *Standards and criteria for the certification of family life educators, college/university curriculum guidelines, and an overview of content in family life education: A framework for life span programs.* Minneapolis, MN: Author.

National Council on Family Relations (NCFR). (2003). *Assessing the future: Family life education.* NCFR Fact Sheet. Minneapolis, MN: Author.

National Council on Family Relations (NCFR). (2009a). *Family life educators code of ethics.* Retrieved from http://www.ncfr.org/sites/default/files/downloads/news/cfle_code__of_ethics_2012.pdf

National Council on Family Relations (NCFR). (2009b). *Family life education content areas: Content and practice guidelines. Minneapolis,* MN: Author. Retrieved from http://www.ncfr.org/sites/default/files/downloads/news/cfle_content_and_practice_guidelines_2014.pdf

National Council on Family Relations (NCFR). (2012). *Tools for ethical thinking and practice in family life education* (3rd ed.). Minneapolis, MN: Author.

National Council on Family Relations (NCFR). (2013). Standards and criteria. Certified family life educator program. Retrieved from http://www.ncfr.org/sites/default/files/downloads/news/standards_2013b.pdf

National Council on Family Relations (NCFR). (n.d.a). Family life education PowerPoint. Retrieved from http://www.ncfr.org/cfle-certification/what-family-life-education

National Council on Family Relations (NCFR). (n.d.b). Degree programs in family science Retrieved from http://www.ncfr.org/degree-programs

National Education Association (NEA). (2003). Guide to teaching online courses. Retrieved from http://www.nea.org/technology/images/onlineteachguide.pdf

National Healthy Marriage Resource Center (NHMRC). (2007). Become a marriage and relationship educator. Retrieved from http://www.healthymarriageinfo.org/educators/become-educator/index.aspx

National Healthy Marriage Resource Center (NHMRC). (2010). Covenant marriage: A fact sheet. Retrieved from www.healthymarriageinfo.org/download.aspx?id=329?

National Institute of Child Health and Human Development (NICHD). (2010). *Sudden infant death syndrome (SIDS): Healthy native babies.* Washington, DC: U.S. Government Printing Office.

National Institutes of Health (NIH). (2011). *Why population aging Metaurus global perspective.* Retrieved from http://www.nia.nih.gov/health/publication/why-population-aging-matters-global-perspective/trend-6-changing-family-structure

National Marriage Project & Institute for American Values (NMP & IAV). (2012). *The state of our unions: Marriage in America 2012.* University of Virginia and Center for Marriages and Families Institute. Retrieved from http://www.stateofourunions.org/2012/SOOU2012.pdf

National Parenting Education Network (NPEN). (2013). History of NPEN. Retrieved from www.npen.org

National Prevention Council. (2011). National Prevention Strategy, Washington, DC: U.S. Department of Health and Human Services, Office of the Surgeon General. Retrieved from http://www.surgeongeneral.gov/initiatives/prevention/strategy/report.pdf

National PTA. (n.d.). Today's PTA. Retrieved from http://www.pta.org/about/?&navItemNumber=503

National Stepfamily Resource Center (NSRC). (2013). Stepfamily FAQs. Retrieved from http://www.stepfamilies.info/faq.php

National Survey of Student Engagement (NSSE). (2006). Engaged learning: Fostering success for all students. Retrieved from http://nsse.iub.edu/NSSE_2006_Annual_Report/docs/NSSE_2006_Annual_Report.pdf

Neff, L., & Karney, B. (2004). How does context affect intimate relationships? Linking external stress and cognitive processes within marriage. *Personality and Social Psychology Bulletin, 30,* 134–148.

Neff, L., & Karney, B. (2007). Stress crossover in newlywed marriage: A longitudinal and dyadic perspective. *Journal of Marriage and Family, 69,* 594–607.

The New York Times. (2010). Raising successful children. Retrieved from http://www.nytimes.com/2012/08/05/opinion/sunday/raising-successful-children.html?pagewanted=all&_r=0

Newberger, C. M. (1980). The cognitive structure of parenthood: Designing a descriptive measure. *New Directions for Child Development: Clinical Developmental Research, 7,* 45–67.

Newman, B., & Newman, P. (2007). *Theories of human development.* Mahwah, NJ: Lawrence Erlbaum.

NICHD Early Child Care Research Network. (2003). Families matter—Even for kids in child care. *Developmental and Behavioral Pediatrics, 24*(1), 58–62.

Nielsen, A., Pinsof, W., Rampage, C., Solomon, A., & Goldstein, S. (2004). Marriage 101: An integrated academic and experiential undergraduate marriage education course. *Family Relations, 53,* 485–494.

Nilson, L. (2003). *Teaching at its best: A research-based resource for college instructors* (2nd ed.). Bolton, MA: Anker Publishing.

Nixon, E., Greene, S., & Hogan, D. (2012). Negotiating relationships in single-mother households: Perspectives of children and mothers. *Family Relations, 61,* 142–156.

Olsen, C. (1999). Stepping stones for stepfamilies. *The Forum for Family and Consumer Issues, 4*(3). Retrieved from http://ncsu.edu/ffci/publications/1999/v4-n3-1999-winter/showcase-usa.php

Olson, D. (2000). Circumplex model of marital and family systems. *Journal of Family Therapy, 22,* 147–167.

Olson, D., & DeFrain, J. (2006). *Marriages and families: Intimacy, diversity, and strengths.* New York: McGraw-Hill.

Olson, D., DeFrain, J., & Olson, A. (1999). *Building relationships: Developing skills for life.* Minneapolis, MN: Life Innovations.

Olson, D., Fournier, D., & Druckman, J. (1996). *PREPARE.* Minneapolis, MN: Life Innovations.

Olson, D., & Gorall, D. (2003). Circumplex model of marital and family systems. In F. Walsh (Ed.), *Normal family processes: Growing diversity and complexity* (3rd ed., pp. 514–548). New York: Guilford Press.

Olson, D., Larson, P., & Olson-Sigg, A. (2009). Couple checkup: Tuning up relationships. *Journal of Couple & Relationship Therapy, 8,* 129–142.

Olson, D., & Olson, A. (2000). *Empowering couples: Building on your strengths.* Minneapolis, MN: Life Innovations.

Olson, D., Olson-Sigg, A., & Larson, P. (2012). *The couple check-up.* Nashville, TN: Thomas Nelson.

Olson, D., Russell, C., & Sprenkle, D. (1989). *Circumplex model: Systemic assessment and treatment of families.* Binghamton, NY: Haworth Press.

Olson-Sigg, A. (2004). Premarital education programs for youth: Investing in prevention. *Marriage & Family: A Christian Journal, 7,* 123–129.

Ooms. T. (2002). Strengthening couples and marriage in low-income communities. In A. Hawkins, S. Wardle, & D. Coolidge (Eds.), *Revitalizing the institution of marriage for the twenty-first century: An agenda for strengthening marriage* (pp. 79–100). Westport, CT: Praeger.

Ooms, T., & Hawkins, A. (2012). Marriage and relationship education: A promising strategy for strengthening low-income, vulnerable families. *The state of our unions. Charlottesville,* VA: National Marriage Project and Institute for American Values.

Ooms, T., & Wilson, P. (2004). The challenges of offering relationship and marriage education to low-income populations. *Family Relations, 53,* 440–447.

Osborne, C. (2005). Marriage following the birth of a child among cohabiting and visiting parents. *Journal of Marriage and Family, 67,* 14–26.

Owen, J., Rhoades, G., Stanley, S., & Fincham, F. (2010). Hooking up: Relationship differences and psychological correlates. *Archives of Sexual Behavior, 39,* 553–563.

Paige, R. (2005). Sexual orientation, parents, & children: Proceedings of the American Psychological Association for 2004. *American Psychologist, 60*(5), 436–511.

Palm, G. (1998). Ethical thinking and practice for family professionals. *Views,* 14–17.

Palm, G. (2012). Professional ethics and practice in family life education. In *Tools for ethical thinking and practice in family life education* (pp. 1–9). Minneapolis, MN: National Council on Family Relations.

Pardini, D. (2008). Novel insights into long-standing theories of bidirectional parent-child influences: Introduction to the special section. *Journal of Abnormal Child Psychology, 36,* 627–631.

Parker, F. J. (1980). *Home economics: An introduction to a dynamic profession.* New York: Macmillan.

Parker, K. (2011). A portrait of stepfamilies. Pew *Research Center report.* Retrieved from http://www.pewsocialtrends.org/2011/01/13/a-portrait-of-stepfamilies/

Parker, K., & Wang, W. (2013). Modern parenthood. Roles of moms and dads converge as they balance work and family. Washington, DC: Pew Research Center. Retrieved from http://www.pewsocialtrends.org/files/2013/03/FINAL_modern_parenthood_03-2013.pdf

Patton, G., Coffey, C., Cappa, C., Currie, D., Riley, L., Gore, F., . . . Ferguson, J. (2012). Health of the world's adolescents: A synthesis of internationally comparable data. *The Lancet, 379,* 1665–1675. Retrieved from http://www.unicef.org/adolescence/files/Lancet-Adolescent-Data.pdf

Patton, M. Q. (1997). *Utilization-focused evaluation.* Thousand Oaks, CA: Sage.

Pearson, M. (2004). *LoveU2: Getting smarter about relationships.* Berkeley, CA: The Dibble Fund for Marriage Education.

Pearson, M., Stanley, S., & Kline, G. (2005). *Within my reach.* Greenwood Village, CO: PREP for Individual, Inc.

Pendergast, D. (2006). Sustaining the home economics profession in new times—A convergent moment. In A. Rauma, S. Pollanen, & P. Seitamaa-Hakkarainen (Eds.), *Human perspectives on sustainable future* (pp. 3–39). Joensuu, Finland: University of Joensuu.

Pendergast, D. (2009). Generational dynamics: Y it matters 2 u & me. *International Journal of Home Economics, 2*(2), 67–84.

Pendergast, D. (2010). Connecting with millennials: Using tag clouds to bring a folksonomy from key home economics documents. *Family & Consumer Sciences Research Journal, 38*(3), 289–302.

People & the Planet. (2008). The ageing world. Retrieved from http://www.peopleandplanet.net/?lid=25995&section=33&topic=26

Permenter, C. (2013). Telecommuting an attractive option for millennials. USA *Today.* Retrieved from http://www.usatodayeducate.com/staging/index.php/career/telecommuting-an-attractive-option-for-millennials

Perrote, D., & Feinman, S. (2012). Family life education with American Indian families. In S. Ballard & A. Taylor (Eds.), *Family life education with diverse populations* (pp. 141–164). Thousand Oaks, CA: Sage.

Peterson, B. (2004). *Cultural intelligence: A guide to working with people from other cultures.* Yarmouth, MA: Intercultural Press.

Peterson, G., Hennon, C., & Knox, T. (2010). Conceptualizing parental stress with family stress theory. In S. Price, C. Price, & P. McKenry (Eds.), *Families & change: Coping with stressful events and transitions* (pp. 25–49). Thousand Oaks, CA: Sage.

Pew Research Center. (2011). A portrait of stepfamilies. Retrieved from http://www.pewsocialtrends.org/2011/01/13/a-portrait-of-stepfamilies/

Pew Research Center. (2013a). A survey of LGBT Americans: Attitudes, experiences, and values in changing times. Retrieved from http://www.pewsocialtrends.org/2013/06/13/a-survey-of-lgbt-americans/9/

Pew Research Center. (2013b). Cell phone ownership hits 91% of adults. Retrieved from http://www.pewresearch.org/fact-tank/2013/06/06/cell-phone-ownership-hits-91-of-adults/

Pew Research Center. (April 2006–May 2013). Internet & American life project surveys. Retrieved from http://www.pewinternet.org/Static-Pages/Trend-Data-%28Adults%29.aspx

Phillips, J. (1981). *Piaget's theory: A primer.* San Francisco: Freeman.

Piaget, J. (1950). *The psychology of intelligence.* London: Routledge & Kegan Paul.

Piaget, J., & Inhelder, B. (1969). *The psychology of the child. New* York: Basic Books.

Pittenger, K., & Heimann, B. (1998). Barnga©, a game on cultural clashes. *Developments in Business Simulation and Experiential Learning, 25,* 253–254. Retrieved from http://sbaweb.wayne.edu/~absel/bkl/vol25/25ch.pdf

Pizzigati, K., Stuck, E., & Ness, M. (2002). *A child advocacy primer: Experience and advice from service providers, board leaders, land consumers.* Washington, DC: Child Welfare League of America Press.

Polson, M., & Piercy, F. (1993). The impact of training stress on married family therapy trainees and their families: A focus group study. *Journal of Family Psychotherapy, 4,* 69–92.

Popenoe, D., & Whitehead, B. D. (2003). *The state of our unions, 2003.* New Brunswick, NJ: National Marriage Project, Rutgers University.

Powell, L., & Cassidy, D. (2007). *Family life education: Working with families across the life span.* Long Grove, IL: Waveland Press.

Prensky, M. (2001). Digital natives, digital immigrants. *On the Horizon, 9*(5), 1–6.

Prensky, M. (2006). Listen to the natives. *Educational Leadership, 63*(4), 8–13.

Proulx, C., Helms, H., & Buehler, C. (2007). Martial quality and personal well-being: A meta-analysis. *Journal of Marriage and Family, 69,* 576–593.

Public Education Committee on Family. (2001). *Family matters: Report of the Public Education Committee on Family*. Singapore, Malaysia: Ministry for Community Development and Sports.

Quigley, E. (1974). *Introduction to home economics* (2nd ed.). New York: Macmillan.

Radley, M., & Randolph, K. (2009). Parenting sources: How do parents differ in their efforts to learn about parenting? *Family Relations, 58*, 536–548.

Rasmussen, W. D. (1989). *Taking the university to the people*. Ames, IA: University Press.

Raymond, M., Bogdanovich, L., Brahmi, D., Cardinal, L., Fager, G., Frattarelli, L., Hecker, G., Jarpe, E., Viera, A., Kantor, L., & Santelli, J. (2008). State refusal of federal funding for abstinence-only programs. *Sexuality Research and Social Policy, 5*(3), 44–55.

Reeves, R. V., & Howard, K. (2013). *The parenting gap*. Washington, DC: The Brookings Institution. Center on Children & Families. Retrieved from http://www.brookings.edu/research/papers/2013/09/09-parenting-gap-social-mobility-wellbeing-reeves

Roberts, B., & Mroczek, D. (2008). Personality trait change in adulthood. *Current Directions in Psychological Science, 19*(1), 31–35.

Roberts, B., Kuncel, N., Shiner, R., Caspi, A., & Goldberg, L. (2007). The power of personality: A comparative analysis of the predictive validity of personality traits, SES, and IQ. *Perspectives on Psychological Science, 2*(3), 31–35.

Roehl, A., Reddy, S., & Shannon, G. (2013). The flipped classroom: An opportunity to engage millennial students through active learning strategies. *Journal of Family & Consumer Sciences, 105*(2), 44–49.

Rohrbaugh, M., Shoham, V., & Coyne, J. (2006). Effect of marital quality on eight-year survival of patients with heart failure. *American Journal of Cardiology, 98*(8), 1069–1072.

Roopnarine, J., & Gielen, U. (2005). Families in global perspective: An introduction. In J. Roopnarine & U. Gielen (Eds.), *Families in global perspective* (pp. 3–13). Boston: Pearson.

Rosen, L. (2010). Welcome to the igeneration. *Psychology Today*. Retrieved from www.psychologytoday.com/blog/rewired-the-psychology-technology/201003/welcome-the-igeneration

Rosenbaum, J. (2009). Patient teenagers: A comparison of the sexual behavior of virginity pledgers and matched nonpledgers. *Pediatrics, 123*, 110–120.

Royse, D. (2001). *Teaching tips for college and university instructors: A practical guide*. Needham Heights, MA: Allyn & Bacon.

Ruey, S. (2010). A case study of constructivist instructional strategies for adult online learning. *British Journal of Educational Technology, 41*(5), 706–720.

Sassler, S. (2010). Partnering across the life course: Sex, relationships, and mate selection. *Journal of Marriage and Family, 72*, 557–575.

Schick, V., Herbenick, D., Reece, M., Sanders, S., Dodge, B., Middlestadt, S., & Fortenberry, J. (2010). Sexual behaviors, condom use, and sexual health of Americans over 50: Implications of sexual health promotion for aging adults. *The Journal of Sexual Medicine, 7*, 315–329.

Schlossman, S. L. (1976, August). Before home start: Notes toward a history of parent education in America, 1897–1929. *Harvard Educational Review, 46*(3), 436–467.

Schmitt, E., Hu, A., & Bachrach, P. (2008). Course evaluation and assessment: Examples of a learner-centered approach. *Gerontology and Geriatrics Education, 29*(3), 290–300.

Schmuck, R., & Schmuck, P. (2013). Group processes in the classroom. Retrieved from http://education.stateuniversity.com/pages/2022/Group-Processes-in-Classroom.html

Schultz, J. B. (1994). Family life education: Implications for home economics teachers' education. *Journal of Home Economics, 86*, 30–36.

Schvaneveldt, P., & Behnke, A. (2012). Family life education with Latino immigrant families. In S. Ballard & A. Taylor (Eds.), *Family life education with diverse populations* (pp. 165–186). Thousand Oaks, CA: Sage.

Schwartz, P. (1994). *Love between equals: How peer marriage really works*. New York: Free Press.

Schwartz, P. (2001). Peer marriage: What does it take to create a truly egalitarian relationship? In A. S. Skolnick & J. Skolnick (Eds.), *Families in transition* (pp. 182–189). Boston: Allyn & Bacon.

Schwartz, P. (2006). *Finding your perfect match*. New York: Penguin.

Seefeldt, K., & Smock., P. (2004). Marriage on the public policy agenda: What do policy makers need to know from research? *National Poverty Center*. Retrieved from http://www.npc.umich.edu/publications/workingpaper04/paper2/04-02.pdf

Serlin, R. (2005). The advantages and disadvantages of online courses. Retrieved from http://www.gened.arizona.edu/sites/default/files/AdvantagesDisadvantagesOnlineCourses.pdf

Sesame Street. (2013). Little children, big challenges: Incarceration. Retrieved from http://www.sesamestreet.org/parents/topicsandactivities/toolkits/incarceration

Sexuality Information and Education Council of the United States (SIECUS). (1998). *Filling the gaps: Hard to teach topics in sexuality education*. New York: Author.

Sexuality Information and Education Council of the United States (SIECUS). (2004). *Guidelines for comprehensive sexuality education: Kindergarten through 12th grade* (3rd ed.). New York: Author. Retrieved from http://www.siecus.org/_data/global/images/guidelines.pdf

Sexuality Information and Education Council of the United States (SIECUS). (2007). On our side: Public support for comprehensive sexuality education. Retrieved from http://www.siecus.org/_data/global/images/public_support.pdf

Sexuality Information and Education Council of the United States (SIECUS). (2008). Sex respect review. *Community Action Kit*. Retrieved from www.communityactionkit.org/index.cfm?fuseaction=page.viewpage&pageid=990

Sexuality Information and Education Council of the United States (SIECUS). (2009). *In their own words: What abstinence-only-until marriage programs say*. Washington, DC: SIECUS Public Policy Office. Retrieved from www.siecus.org/index.cfm?fuseaction=Page.ViewPage&PageID=1199

Sexuality Information and Education Council of the United States (SIECUS). (n.d. a). *Abstinence only until marriage programs*. Retrieved from http://www.siecus.org/index.cfm?fuseaction=Page.viewPage&pageId=523&parentID=477

Sexuality Information and Education Council of the United States (SIECUS). (n.d. b). *Comprehensive sexuality education*. Retrieved from http://www.siecus.org/index.cfm?fuseaction=page.viewPage&pageId=514&parentID=477

Sexuality Information and Education Council of the United States (SIECUS). (n.d. c). *Talk about sex: What is sexuality*. Retrieved from http://www.seriouslysexuality.com/index.cfm?fuseaction=Page.ViewPage&pageId=1071

Shah, A. (2011). Health issues. *Global issues: Social, political, economic and environmental issues that affect us all*. Retrieved from www.globalissues.org/issue/587/health-issues

Sharman, C. (2005). The problem with drinking. *Perspectives in Health: Magazine of the Pan American Health Organization*. Retrieved from www.paho.org/English/DD/PIN/Number21_article04.htm

Sheng, J. (2005). Chinese families. In B. Adams & J. Trost (Eds.), *Handbook of world families* (pp. 99–128). Thousand Oaks, CA: Sage.

Shlafer, R., Gerrity, E., Ruhland, E., & Wheeler, M. (2013). Children with incarcerated parents—Considering children's outcomes in the contexts of family experiences. *Children's mental health ereview*. St. Paul: University of Minnesota Extension, Children, Youth, and Family Consortium.

Shor, L., & Freire, P. (1986). *A pedagogy for liberation: Dialogues on transforming education*. South Hadley, MA: Bergin & Garvey.

Silliman, B., & Schumm, W. (2004). Adolescents' perceptions of marriage and premarital couples education. *Family Relations, 53*, 513–520.

Simon, R. (2002). Revisiting the relationships among gender, marital status, and mental health. *American Journal of Sociology, 107*, 1065–1096.

Simon, S., Howe, L., & Kirschenbaum, H. (1972). *Values clarification: A handbook of practical strategies for teachers and students.* New York: Hart Publishing.

Simon, W., & Gagnon, J. (1984). Sexual scripts. *Society, 22*, 53–60.

Simpson, E. (1972). *The classification of educational objectives in the psychomotor domain: The psychomotor domain* (Vol. 3). Washington, DC: Gryphon House.

Singh, J. (2005). The contemporary Indian family. In B. Adams & J. Trost (Eds.), *Handbook of world families* (pp. 129–166). Thousand Oaks, CA: Sage.

Skinner, B. (1953). *Science and human behavior.* New York: Macmillan.

Skinner, B. (1957). *Verbal behavior.* New York: Appleton-Century Crofts.

Skinner, B. (1974). *About behaviorism.* New York: Knopf.

Skogrand, L., Reck, K., Higginbotham, B., Adler-Baeder, F., & Dansie, L. (2010). Recruitment and retention for stepfamily education. *Journal of Couple & Relationship Therapy, 9*, 48–65.

Small, S., & Memmo, M. (2004). Contemporary models of youth development and problem prevention: Toward an integration of terms, concepts, and models. *Family Relations, 53*, 3–11.

Small, S. A., Cooney, S. M., & O'Connor, C. (2009). Evidence-informed program improvement: Using principles of effectiveness to enhance the quality and impact of family-based prevention programs. *Family Relations, 58*, 1–13.

Smith, A. (2013). Smart phone ownership 2013. *Pew Internet.* Retrieved from http://pewinternet.org/Reports/2013/Smartphone-Ownership-2013/Findings.aspx

Smith, C. A., Cudaback, D., Goddard, H. W., & Myers-Walls, J. (1994). *National extension parent education model.* Manhattan: Kansas Cooperative Extension Service.

Southwick, E. (2011a). *All about happiness.* Retrieved from www.allabouthappiness.com/about-edward.html

Southwick, E. (2011b). *Happiness and life success coaching with Edward Southwick, Jr.* Retrieved from www.youtube.com/watch?v=y-oOMQ86Jvk

Spigner-Littles, D., & Anderson, C. (2010). Constructivism: A paradigm for older learners. *Educational Gerontology, 25.* doi: 10.1080/036012799267828, pp. 203–209.

Spoth, R, Guyll, M., & Day, S. (2002). Universal family-focused interventions in alcohol-use disorder prevention: Cost-effectiveness and cost-benefit analyses of two interventions. *Journal of Studies on Alcohol and Drugs, 63*(2), 219–235.

Squires, N., & Smith, R. (2006). What is marriage education. Married for good. Retrieved from http://www.marriageeducation.ca/philosophy.html (Site discontinued)

Sroufe, A. L. (2002). From infant attachment to promotion of adolescent autonomy: Prospective, longitudinal data on the role of parents in development. In J. G. Borkowski, S. Landesman Ramey, & M. Bristol-Power (Eds.), *Parenting and the child's world* (pp. 187–202). Mahwah, NJ: Lawrence Erlbaum.

Stangler-Hall, K., & Hall, D. (2011). Abstinence-only education and teen pregnancy rates: Why we need comprehensive sex education in the U.S. *PLOS ONE 6*(10), e24658. doi:10.1371/journal.pone.0024658. Retrieved from http://www.plosone.org/article/info:doi/10.1371/journal.pone.0024658

Stanley, S. (2001). Making the case for premarital education. *Family Relations, 50*, 272–280.

Stanley, S. (2002). *What is it with men and commitment, anyway?* Keynote address to the 6th Annual Smart Marriages Conferences. Washington, DC.

Stanley, S., Allen, E., Markman, H., Saiz, C., Bloomstrom, G., Thomas, R., Schuum, W., & Bailer, A. (2005). Dissemination and evaluation of marriage education in the Army. *Family Process, 44*(2), 187–201.

Stanley, S., Amato, P., Johnson, C., & Markman, H. (2006). Premarital education, marital quality, and marital stability. Findings from a household survey. *Journal of Family Psychology, 20*(1), 117–126.

Stanley, S., Markman, H., & Jenkins, N. (2004). *Marriage education using PREP with low-income and diverse clients.* Denver, CO: PREP.

Stanley, S., Markman, H., Jenkins, N., & Blumberg, S. (2009). *PREP version 7.0b leaders manual.* Greenwood Village, CO: PREP Educational Products.

Stanley, S., Rhoades, G., & Markman, H. (2006). Sliding versus deciding: Inertia and the premarital cohabitation effect. *Family Relations, 55,* 499–509.

Stanley, S., Whitton, W., & Markman, H. (2004). Maybe I do: Interpersonal commitment levels and premarital or non-marital cohabitation. *Journal of Family Issues, 25,* 496–519.

State of Minnesota. (n.d.). Parent and family education teacher licensure requirements. Retrieved from https://www.revisor.mn.gov/rules/?id=8710.3100

Staton, J., & Ooms, T. (2012). "Something important is going on here!" Making connections between marriage relationship quality and health: Implications for research and health-care systems, programs and policies. Fairfax, VA: National Healthy Marriage Resource Center (NMHRC). Retrieved from http://www.healthymarriageinfo.org/resource-detail/index.aspx?rid=3984

Steck, P. (2009). Addressing changes in family structures. *International Social Security Administration (ISSA).* Retrieved from www.issa.int/content/download/75658/1435994/file/2TR-29.pdf

Steele, M. (2005). Teaching students with learning disabilities: Constructivism or behaviorism? *Current Issues in Education, 8*(10), 6–16.

Sternberg, R. (1986). A triangular theory of love. *Psychological Review, 93,* 119–135.

Stevenson, B., & Wolfers, J. (2013). Where do you stand in the global love ranking? Retrieved from http://www.bloomberg.com/news/2013-02-14/where-do-you-stand-in-the-global-love-ranking-.html

Stiffman, A., Brown, E., Freedenthal, S., House, L., Ostmann, E., & Yu, M. (2007). American Indian youth: Personal, familial, and environmental strengths. *Journal of Child and Family Studies, 16*(3), 331–336.

Stokes-Eley, S. (2007). Using Kolb's experiential learning cycle in chapter presentations. *Teacher Development, 13,* 26–29.

Strauss, W., & Howe, N. (1991). *Generations.* New York: Williams Morrow.

Subramaiam, A. (2006). Creating an electronic portfolio to integrate multiculturalism in teaching family economics. In R. Hamon (Ed.), *International family studies: Developing curricula and teaching tools* (pp. 487–414). Binghamton, NY: Haworth Press.

Substance Abuse and Mental Health Services Administration (SAMHSA). (2012). Non-researcher's guide to evidence-based program evaluation. *SAMHSA's NREPP.* Retrieved from www.nrepp.samhsa.gov/Courses/ProgramEvaluation/resources/NREPP_Evaluation_course.pdf

Tamminen, S. (2003). *Making sense of the Finns—A cross-cultural training program.* Helsinki, Finland: Cultrane Ky.

Taner, E. (2013a). FLE from womb to tomb—The wheels are moving forward. *Certified Family Life Educator Network, 24*(4), 18–19. Minneapolis, MN: National Council on Family Relations.

Taner, E. (2013b). The wheel is moving forward. *NCFR Network, 25*(3), 18–19.

Taverner, B., & Montfort, S. (2005). *Making sense of abstinence: Lessons for comprehensive sex education.* Morristown, NJ: Planned Parenthood of Greater Northern New Jersey, Inc.

Taverner, B. (2006). Tips for emerging sexology professionals: Networking and nurturing. *Contemporary Sexuality, 40*(2), 1–8.

Tay, S. (2010). America's call to globalization. *Forbes*. Retrieved from www.forbes.com/2010/09/22/asia-america-globalization-markets-economy-book-excerpt-simon-tay_2.html

Taylor, A. C., & Ballard, S. M. (2012). Preparing family life educators to work with diverse populations. In S. M. Ballard & A. C. Taylor (Eds.), *Family life education with diverse populations* (pp. 285–302). Los Angeles: Sage.

Taylor, C., & Taylor, G. (2003). *Designing dynamic stepfamilies: Bringing the pieces to peace.* Video series. Retrieved from designingdynamicstepfamilies.com

Taylor, P., Funk, C., & Clark, C. (2007). As marriage and parenthood drift apart, public is concerned about social impact. *Pew Research Center*. Retrieved from http://www.pewsocialtrends.org/files/2007/07/Pew-Marriage-report-6-28-for-web-display.pdf

Taylor, P., Funk, C., & Craighill, P. (2006). Are we happy yet? *Pew Research Center*. Retrieved from http://pewresearch.org/files/old-assets/social/pdf/AreWeHappyYet.pdf

Thiagarajan, S., & Thiagarajan, R. (2011). *BARNGA*. Boston: Intercultural Press.

Thomas, J., & Arcus, M. E. (1992). Family life education: An analysis of the concept. *Family Relations, 41*, 3–8.

Thomas, R. (1996). Reflective dialogue parent education design. Focus on parent development. *Family Relations, 45*(2), 189–200.

Thomas, R., & Footrakoon, O. (1998). What curricular perspectives can tell us about parent education curricula. Retrieved from http://parenthood.library.wisc.edu/Thomas/Thomas.html

Tieffer, L. (2004). *Sex is not a natural act and other essays* (2nd ed.). Boulder, CO: Westview Press.

Timmerman, G. (2008). Teaching skills and personal characteristics of sex education teachers. *Teaching and Teacher Education, 25*, 500–506.

Tippett, D. (2003). The learners we teach. In V. Chamberlain & M. Cummings (Eds.), *Creative instructional methods for family & consumer sciences, nutrition & wellness* (pp. 17–29). Peoria, IL: Glencoe/McGraw-Hill.

The Today Show. (2013). Don't turn your child into a praise junkie! Retrieved from http://www.today.com/id/12648314/ns/today-parenting_and_family/t/dont-turn-your-child-praise-junkie/

Toossi, M. (2012). Labor force projections to 2020: A more slowly growing workforce. *Monthly Labor Review, 135*(1), 43–64.

Torstendahl, R., & Burrage, M. (1990). *The formation of professions: Knowledge, state and strategy*. London: Sage.

Trenholm, C., Devaney, B., Fortson, K., Quay, L., Wheeler, J., & Clark, M. (2007). Impacts of four title V, section 510 abstinence education programs. *Final report*. Princeton, NJ: Mathematica Policy Research Group.

Tschofen, C., & Mackness, J. (2012). Connectivism and dimensions of individual experience. *International Review of Research in Open and Distance Learning, 13*(1), 124–143. Retrieved from http://search.proquest.com/docview/1140135888?accountid=4840

Umberson, D., Williams, K., Powers, D., Liu, H., & Needham, B. (2006). You make me sick: marital quality and health over the life course. *Journal of Health and Social Behavior, 47*, 1–16.

United Nations (UN). (1948). Universal Declaration of Human Rights—Article 16(3). Retrieved from http://www.un.org/en/documents/udhr/

United Nations (UN). (2008). Divorces and crude divorce rates by urban/rural residence: 2004–2008. Demographic yearbook, 2008. Retrieved from http://unstats.un.org/unsd/demographic/products/dyb/dyb2008/Table25.pdf

United Nations (UN). (2013). Global issues: Family. Retrieved from http://www.un.org/en/globalissues/family/index.shtml

United Nations (UN). (n.d.). Ending violence against women and girls. Retrieved from http://www.un.org/en/globalissues/briefingpapers/endviol/index.shtml

UN Department of Economic and Social Affairs (UNDESA). (1994). The international year of the family (IYF) 1994. Retrieved from http://social.un.org/index/Family/InternationalObservances/InternationalYearoftheFamily.aspx

UN Department of Economic and Social Affairs (UNDESA). (2002). World population ageing: 1950–2050. Retrieved from http://www.un.org/esa/population/publications/worldageing19502050/

UN Department of Economic and Social Affairs (UNDESA). (2010). International migrant stock: The 2008 revision. Retrieved from http://esa.un.org/migration/

UN Department of Economic and Social Affairs (UNDESA). (2013a). Twentieth anniversary of the international year of the family, 2014. Retrieved from http://social.un.org/index/Family/InternationalObservances/TwentiethAnniversaryofIYF2014.aspx

UN Department of Economic and Social Affairs (UNDESA). (2013b). World economic situation and prospects. Retrieved from http://www.un.org/en/development/desa/policy/wesp/index.shtml

UN Development Programme (UNDP). (2003). *Major trends affecting families: A background document.* New York: United Nations.

UN Development Programme (UNDP). (2011). *Sustainability and equity: A better future for all.* New York: United Nations.

UN Office on Drugs and Crime (UNODC). (2012). World drug report. Retrieved from http://www.unodc.org/documents/data-and-analysis/WDR2012/WDR_2012_web_small.pdf

UN Population Fund (UNFPA). (2008). Linking population, poverty, and development—Migration: A world on the move. Retrieved from http://www.unfpa.org/pds/migration.html

UN Statistics Division (UNSD). (2008). Minimum legal age for marriage without consent. Retrieved from http://data.un.org/Data.aspx?d=GenderStat&f=inID:19

UNAIDS. (2012). Global fact sheet: World AIDS Day 2012. Retrieved from http://www.unaids.org/en/media/unaids/contentassets/documents/epidemiology/2012/gr2012/20121120_FactSheet_Global_en.pdf

University of Minnesota. (1991). Family education/parent education licensure. St. Paul, MN: Department of Work, Family and Community Education.

U.S. Bureau of the Census. (2006). *Statistical abstract of the United States* (122nd ed). Washington, DC: U.S. Government Printing Office.

U.S. Bureau of Labor Statistics (BLS). (2013). 2012–2013 *Occupational outlook handbook.* United States Department of Labor. Retrieved from http://www.bls.gov/ooh/

U.S. Census Bureau. (2012a). One-parent unmarried family groups with own children. Current population survey, 2012 annual social and economic supplement. Retrieved from www.census.gov/hhes/families/data/cps2012.html

U.S. Census Bureau. (2012b). Profile America facts for features. Retrieved from www.census.gov/newsroom/releases/archives/facts_for_features_special_editions/cb12-ff18.html

U.S. Census Bureau. (2012c). U.S. Census Bureau projections show a slower growing, older, more diverse nation a half century from now. Retrieved from www.census.gov/newsroom/releases/archives/population/cb12-243.html

U.S. Census Bureau. (2013). Asians fastest-growing race or ethnic group in 2012. Retrieved from www.census.gov/newsroom/releases/archives/population/cb13-112.html

U.S. Census Bureau News. (2012). Profile America facts for features: Unmarried and single Americans Week September 15–21, 2013. Retrieved from www.census.gov/newsroom/releases/archives/facts_for_features_special_editions/cb13-ff21.html

U.S. Department of Agriculture, National Institute of Food and Agriculture (USDA, NIFA). (n.d.). History of extension. Retrieved from http://www.csrees.usda.gov/qlinks/extension.html#yesterday

U.S. Department of Defense. (2009). Plans for the department of defense for the support of military family readiness. Retrieved from www.militaryonesource.mil/12038/MOS/Reports/FY2009_Report_MilitaryFamilyReadinessPrograms.pdf

U.S. Department of Housing and Urban Development, Office of Community Planning and Development. (2010). The annual homeless assessment report to Congress. Retrieved from www.hudhre.info/documents/2010HomelessAssessmentReport.pdf

USA Today. (2012). Self-sufficiency elusive to young adults of hovering parenting. Retrieved from http://usatoday30.usatoday.com/money/jobcenter/workplace/bruzzese/story/2012-08-26/helicopter-parents-hurt-generation-of-workers/57292900/1

USA Today. (2013a). One in ten high school seniors are extreme binge drinkers. Retrieved from http://www.usatoday.com/story/news/nation/2013/09/16/extreme-binge-drinking-seniors/2809739/

USA Today. (2013b). Overdoses attributed to club drug "Molly" increase. Retrieved from http://www.usatoday.com/story/news/nation/2013/09/25/club-drug-molly-abuse-increases/2868811/

Veldorale-Griffin, A., Coccia, C., Darling, C., Rehm, M., & Sathe, S. (2013). The role of parental indulgence and economic stress in life satisfaction: Differential perceptions of parents and adolescents. *Journal of Family Social Work, 16,* 205–224.

Vespa, J., Lewis, J., & Kreider, R. (2013). America's families and living arrangements: 2012. Current population reports (pp. 20–270). Washington, DC: U.S. Census Bureau. Retrieved from http://www.census.gov/prod/2013pubs/p20-570.pdf

Vogt, S. (n.d.). What makes marriage work: Common values. Retrieved from http://www.foryourmarriage.org/everymarriage/what-makes-marriage-work/common-values/

Vygotsky, L. (1978). *Mind in society: The development of higher psychological processes.* Cambridge, MA: Harvard University Press.

W. K. Kellogg Foundation. (2004). Using logic models to bring together planning, evaluation, and action. *Logic model development guide.* Battle Creek, MI: Author. Retrieved from http://www.wkkf.org/knowledge-center/resources/2006/02/wk-kellogg-foundation-logic-model-development-guide.aspx

Wages, S., & Darling C. (2004). Evaluation of a marriage preparation program using mentor couples. *Marriage & Family: A Christian Journal, 7,* 103–121.

Waite, L., & Gallagher, M. (2000). *The case for marriage: Why married people are happier, healthier, and better off financially.* New York: Doubleday.

Walters, A., & Hayes, D. (2007). Teaching about sexuality. *American Journal of Sexuality Education, 2*(2), 27–49.

Walters, J., & Jewson, R. (1988). *The National Council on Family Relations: A fifty-year history, 1938–1987.* Minneapolis, MN: National Council on Family Relations.

Wandersman, L. P. (1987). New directions for parent education. In S. L. Kagan & E. F. Zigler (Eds.), *America's family support programs.* New Haven, CT: Yale University Press.

Warren, J. (2008). One in 100: Behind bars in America in 2008. *Pew Center on States.* Retrieved from http://www.colorado.gov/ccjjdir/Resources/Resources/Ref/PEW_OneIn100.pdf

Wartella, E., Rideout, V., Lauricella, A. R., & Connell, S. L. (2013). *Parenting in the age of digital technology: A national survey.* Report of the Center on Media and Human Development, School of Communication, Northwestern University.

Watkins, R., Meirs, M., & Visson, Y. (2012). *A guide to assessing needs: Essential tools for collecting information, making decisions, and activity development.* Washington, DC: The World Bank. Retrieved from http://www.needsassessment.org/

Watson, J. (1925) *Behaviorism*. New York: W.W. Norton.

Waxman, H. (2004). *The content of federally funded abstinence-only education programs*. Washington, DC: U.S. House of Representatives Committee on Government Reform.

Weahkee, R. (2010, June). Message from the director, division of behavioral health. *Indian Health Service Headquarters Division of Behavioral Health Newsletter*, 1–12.

Weber, J. G. (2011). *Individual and family stress and crisis*. Thousand Oaks, CA: Sage.

Webster-Stratton, C., & Reid, M. J. (2003). The incredible years parent, teacher, and child training series: A multifaceted teaching approach for young children with conduct problems. In A. Kazdin & J. Weiss (Eds.), *Evidenced-based psychotherapies for children and adolescents* (pp. 224–240). New York: Guilford Press.

Weigley, E. (1976). The professionalization of home economics. *Home Economics Research Journal, 4*(4), 253–259.

Weiss, E., & Lee, G. (2009). Parenting education is economic development. Partnership for America's economic success. Retrieved from http://www.readynation.org/uploads/20090708_PAESParentingBriefFinal.pdf

Weiss, H. B., & Jacobs, F. H. (1988). *Evaluating family programs*. New York: Aldine de Gruyter.

Weston, M. (1994). How to fox-trot while your partners tango: Joys and challenges of step-family life. National Stepfamily Resource Center. Retrieved from http://www.stepfamilies.info/articles/joys-and-challenges-of-stepfamily-life.php

Whitchurch, G. (2005). Walking the walk: Teaching systems theory by doing theory. In V. Bengston, A. Acock, K. Allen, P. Dilworth-Anderson, & D. Klein (Eds.), *Sourcebook of family theory & research* (pp. 573–574). Thousand Oaks, CA: Sage.

White, J., & Klein, D. (2008). *Family theories*. Thousand Oaks, CA: Sage.

Wilcox, B. (2010). When marriage disappears: The retreat from marriage in middle America. *The state of our unions 2010*. Charlottesville, VA: National Marriage Project and Institute for American Values.

Williams, L. (2004). The meaning of marriage: Two churches, one marriage. Retrieved from http://www.sandiego.edu/interchurch/index.html

Williams, L., & McBain, H. (2006). Integrating gender on multiple levels. A conceptual model for teaching gender issues in family therapy. *Journal of Marital and Family Therapy, 32*(3), 385–397.

Wood, D., Bruner, J., & Ross, G. (1976). The role of tutoring in problem solving. *Journal of Child Psychology and Child Psychiatry, 17*, 89–100.

Wood, M. (2003). Experiential learning for undergraduates: A simulation about functional change and aging. *Geriatrics & Geriatrics Education, 23*(3), 37–38.

Wood, R., Avellar, S., & Goesling, B. (2008). Pathways to adulthood and marriage: Attitudes, expectations, and relationship patterns. U.S. Department of Health and Human Services. Retrieved from http://aspe.hhs.gov/hsp/08/pathways2adulthood/index.shtml

World by Map. (2010). Median age of the world. Retrieved from http://world.bymap.org/MedianAge.html

World Health Organization (WHO). (2005). WHO multi-country study on women's health and domestic violence against women. Retrieved from http://www.who.int/gender/violence/who_multicountry_study/en/

World Health Organization (WHO). (2010). Global health observatory: HIIV/AIDS. Retrieved from http://www.who.int/gho/hiv/en/index.html

World Health Organization (WHO). (2011). Global status report on alcohol and health. Retrieved from http://www.who.int/substance_abuse/publications/global_alcohol_report/msbgsruprofiles.pdf

World Health Organization (WHO). (2012). Intimate partner and sexual violence against women. Retrieved from http://www.who.int/mediacentre/factsheets/fs239/en/

World Health Organization (WHO). (2013a). Management of substance abuse. Retrieved from http://www.who.int/substance_abuse/facts/alcohol/en/index.html

World Health Organization (WHO). (2013b). Young people health risks and solutions. http://www.who.int/mediacentre/factsheets/fs345/en/index.html

World Public Opinion. (n.d.). Globalization. Retrieved from http://www.americans-world.org/digest/global_issues/globalization/culture.cfm

Youcha, G. (1995). *Minding the children: Childcare in America from colonial times to the present.* New York: Scribner.

ZERO TO THREE. (2011). Using evidence-based programs to support children and families experiencing homelessness. An Initiative of Conrad N Hilton Foundation in partnership with the National Center on Family Homelessness, National Alliance to End Homelessness, and ZERO TO THREE. National Center for Infants, Toddlers and Families. Retrieved from http://www.zerotothree.org/about-us/funded-projects/strengthening-at-risk-and-homeless-young-mothers-and-families/strength_ebp122111.pdf

Zickuhr, K. (2011). Generations and their gadgets. *Pew Internet.* Retrieved from http://pewinternet.org/Infographics/2011/Generations-and-gadgets.aspx

Zinn, M., Eitzen, D., & Wells, B. (2011). *Diversity in families.* Boston: Allyn & Bacon.

Index